Becoming a

Foodservice Professional

YEAR 2

National Restaurant Association
EDUCATIONAL FOUNDATION

ACKNOWLEDGMENTS

The production of this book would not have been possible without the expertise of our many advisors and manuscript reviewers. The National Restaurant Association Educational Foundation is pleased to thank the following professionals for their time and efforts during the development of this curriculum:

GINI LA FLEUR	La Fleur and Associates, South Holland, IL
KAREN REINHARD	Woodstock High School, Woodstock, IL
NANCY STEWART	Stewart and Associates, Laguna Niguel, CA

The ProStart program was developed with a gift from the American Express Foundation.

DISCLAIMER

The information presented in this book has been compiled from sources and documents believed to be reliable and represents the best professional judgment of the National Restaurant Association Educational Foundation. However, the accuracy of the information presented is not guaranteed, nor is any responsibility assumed or implied by the National Restaurant Association Educational Foundation for any damage or loss from inaccuracies or omissions.

Inventory Code: PSST2

ISBN Number: 1-58280-002-2

October 1998

10 9 8 7 6 5 4 3 2 1

Dedicated to

Virginia La Fleur,

whose spirit lives on in our hearts and in the pages of this book.

Thanks, Gini
1949-1997

Dear Students:

WELCOME TO THE RESTAURANT INDUSTRY!

Your experience with the National Restaurant Association's ProStart program will, I hope, be the beginning of a long and happy love affair with the industry. I speak from experience. Restaurants are one of the most dynamic industries in the U.S. today—a shining example of entrepreneurial spirit and the American Dream, an industry that's a fast track to success, a place where every single day in this country employees become owners.

The restaurant industry offers literally millions of opportunities for nurturing and developing your talents and emerging a leader. A chance to use your creativity in developing your menu...financial savvy in controlling your profits and losses...marketing ideas for reaching your customers...management skills to lead a team to accomplish an objective...and the scientific know-how that goes into preparing and serving food safely. The restaurant industry is a place to learn, grow, and develop—and now you're a part of it.

What's more, restaurants are here to stay. With nearly half of the dollars Americans spend on food today now being spent on food away from home, the restaurant industry has a huge impact on our national economy. Whether it's a quick-service restaurant, a family operation or a multimillion-dollar company providing on-site foodservice at schools or hospitals, the restaurant industry is the place to realize your dreams.

SO WORK HARD, TAKE ADVANTAGE OF EVERY OPPORTUNITY TO LEARN—AND I WISH YOU THE BEST IN PURSUING YOUR DREAMS.

Sincerely,

Herman Cain
Chief Executive Officer and President
National Restaurant Association

Table of Contents

YEAR 2

INTRODUCTION: PREPARING FOR A SUCCESSFUL CAREER

Unit 3 292

Unit 4 410

INTRODUCTION

Preparing For A Successful Career

Dave Thomas

Founder and Senior Chairman of the Board
Wendy's

I never knew my birth parents. Rex and Auleva Thomas, a couple from Kalamazoo, Michigan, adopted me when I was six weeks old. Auleva died when I was five, and my early years included numerous moves from state to state as my father sought work. These frequent moves were challenging. I felt like I had no roots or sense of belonging. Always the new kid on the block, I sought refuge in work. One of the things I enjoyed most during my childhood was going to restaurants to eat. I'd see families eating together and enjoying the friendly atmosphere. I decided at an early age that I was going to have my own restaurant with great food that families would visit again and again.

I started working at age 12, delivering groceries in Knoxville, Tennessee, but I was fired after a misunderstanding with my boss about my vacation. My second job was as a soda jerk at Walgreen's, but I was fired again when my boss found out I wasn't 16. While applying for my next job, still 12 years-old, I landed a job at the counter at the Regas Restaurant in Knoxville. I worked hard, putting in 12-hour shifts, constantly afraid I'd lose yet another job.

The Regas brothers treated me like one of their family, providing me with encouragement and a caring mentorship that has had a positive and lasting effect. By the time I was 15, I'd moved again and was working full-time at The Hobby House Restaurant in Ft. Wayne, Indiana. As my family prepared for another move, I decided to stay in town and took a room at the local YMCA. Then I made the biggest mistake of my life: I dropped out of high school to work full-time. I thought I could learn more about the restaurant business with a hands-on education than I could learn in school.

When I was 18, I joined the Army, eventually becoming one of the youngest soldiers to manage an enlisted men's club. After my service, I returned to The Hobby House, where I met my future wife, Lorraine, a waitress, whom I married in 1954.

In 1956, my boss, Phil Clauss, and I opened a barbecue restaurant called The Ranch House. There, I met the man who became one of the greatest influences in my life—Colonel Harlan Sanders, founder of Kentucky Fried Chicken. Clauss bought a KFC franchise from the Colonel, and, all of a sudden, I was in the chicken business. In 1962, Clauss offered me a chance to turn around four failing KFC carryouts he owned in Columbus, Ohio. If I could turn the carry-outs around and pay off a big debt, Clauss would give me 45 percent of the business. Although daunting, this was the kind of challenge I liked.

After a lot of hard work, the restaurants began to prosper, and I added four more restaurants. I'm grateful and lucky to say, I was a millionaire at age 35. I opened the first Wendy's Old Fashioned Hamburgers restaurant on November 15, 1969, in Columbus. I named the restaurant after my 8-year-old daughter, Melinda Lou, nicknamed "Wendy" by her older brother and sisters. The first Wendy's menu included fresh, made-to-order hamburgers, chili, french fries, soft drinks, and a Frosty Dairy Dessert. The decor was homey, with bentwood chairs and tiffany-style lamps. I planned to open several restaurants around Columbus, giving my children a place to work during the summers. Wendy's grew and prospered.

In 1973, I began franchising the Wendy's concept, pioneering the idea of selling franchises for entire cities and parts of states, rather than single units. Wendy's grew rapidly, with more than 1,000 restaurants opening in its first 100 months. That rapid growth continues: Wendy's and its franchisees now operate more than 4,800 restaurants in the U.S. and 34 countries.

In early 1989, I agreed to appear in Wendy's commercials as the company spokesman. I guess because of those commercials, most people recognize me now. In 1990, I became a national spokesman for the White House initiative on adoption, called "Adoption Works For Everyone." Since then, I've been a national adoption advocate, working to raise awareness for the tens of thousands of children who need permanent homes and loving families.

While dropping out of school was my biggest mistake, it led to one of my proudest accomplishments. In 1993, 45 years after leaving school, I earned my GED certificate and received my high school diploma from Coconut Creek High School in Ft. Lauderdale, Florida. I was voted Most Likely to Succeed by the graduating class, and attended the prom with my wife Lorraine, where we were named Prom King and Queen.

I think the hospitality industry is one of the most exciting fields to work in. We need young people who are creative and innovative, and ready to meet the challenges of a business that's always on the move. With a good education and work experience (and if you're lucky, a good mentor), you can go as far as your dreams take you.

From my early days as a soda jerk and short order cook, to becoming an entrepreneur and TV spokesman, I've been recognized for my work in the restaurant industry and for children. I've received lots of restaurant industry honors and Entrepreneur and Man of the Year awards. The adoption community has honored me with a variety of awards, and I've attended special receptions at the White House in recognition for my work for adoption. I've also testified before Congress in support of tax credits for adoptive parents.

On the rare occasions when I'm not in the studio making commercials or traveling the country for interviews or speeches, you might find me on the golf course, perfecting my game.

There are a million opportunities in our industry. If you're willing to work hard and have a burning desire to succeed, you will succeed. That's what makes the difference. That's the true recipe for success.

Intro.I

SECTION i.1

Working in the Hospitality Industry

AFTER STUDYING SECTION i.1, YOU SHOULD BE ABLE TO:

- State in your own words the importance of service to success in the hospitality industry.
- List the elements of excellent service and give examples.
- State the difference between school and workplace environments.
- Develop a list of workplace guidelines.
- Identify and give examples of positive work attitudes.

This is an exciting time to begin a career in the hospitality industry. More new restaurants are opening each year, and many restaurant chains are ranked among the nation's top corporations. Many jobs and opportunities exist in the foodservice industry for people who possess the right combination of interests, skills, education, and training. Job opportunities in this industry are varied and unique.

People choose careers in the hospitality industry for a variety of reasons.

"No matter what segment of the industry you choose," agrees Rosalyn Mallet, FMP*, a vice president of franchise development, "you can be sure that hospitality is an industry where, if you're willing to work hard and network, you can do almost anything."

An FMP is a Foodservice Management Professional certification earned through educational experience in the industry.

"There is no bigger thrill than talking to happy customers who let you know all your hard work and creativity has paid off," says Darlene Tegtmeier, an assistant bar manager/bartender in a fine-dining restaurant.

Attracted to the fast pace of the foodservice industry, Steven Hartenstein, General Manager of a fine-dining restaurant, says he does "everything from A to Z. I'm responsible for purchasing and receiving food supplies, and managing the finances of the restaurant. I enjoy all of the daily challenges, and the fact that every day is different from the last."

A unique element of the foodservice industry is that the customer and the manufacturer of the product are in direct contact. Food is prepared and served, then purchased directly by customers, who are the guests that you serve.

When you work in the foodservice industry you have daily contact with guests and often receive immediate feedback about the quality of food and service. So the quality must be right the first time!

More than anything else, people who work in food service must love to serve others. They must also enjoy working with food, be efficient, flexible, able to work cooperatively, and remain calm under pressure in a fast-paced environment.

A Commitment to Service

Before you begin a career in the hospitality industry, it's important to understand what service is all about. Working in a service industry means that it's your job to serve people directly. People who work in a service industry don't spend much of their time in an office by themselves (as accountants, advertising copywriters, and clerks do), and they don't make things that are to be sold to the public in stores (those are manufacturing industries, and people who work in them produce shoes, computer parts, or cars, for example). Service professionals include police officers, restaurant and hotel workers, nurses, retail salespeople, teachers, theater ticket-takers, lawyers, landscapers, and nutritionists.

People who serve the public are people with a special commitment to others as well as the skills and knowledge to perform their jobs. People who work in the hospitality or foodservice industry must enjoy serving others, because service is the most important element of their jobs.

Serving customers means making them feel like they're special guests in your home. Good service comes from a natural desire to serve, but it can be improved through training, effort, stamina, and commitment. Serving people all day is not always easy. Think about the last time you were at a restaurant or in your school cafeteria or at a ball park. Did you notice how busy the servers were? Were there customers who were rude to them or were demanding? To be successful in the hospitality industry, you have to be able to give people what they want, and make them feel they are getting good value for their money. Pleasing others will make you feel good about your job as well as help you earn money.

Think About It

The more you know about yourself, the easier it will be to make choices about your career. Following are some suggestions to help you choose a career that will be right for you.

- **What are some of your favorite classes, activities, and interests? Why do you enjoy them?**
- **What special skills, talents, and abilities do you possess?**
- **What ideas, values, goals, and causes are important to you?**
- **Remember, many people change careers during their lifetime. Never be afraid to investigate an opportunity that sounds more interesting and challenging than what you are doing.**

Service with a Smile

In any foodservice operation, customers must be served pleasantly, correctly, and in a timely manner. Customers expect the people who serve them to be pleasant, helpful, and friendly. What does this mean for you? The following are some tips for anyone working in food service or hospitality.

Exhibits i.1 and i.2
Knowing how to serve people is the key to success in the hospitality industry.

- Always greet customers. Smile and look people in the eye when you speak to them.
- Fulfill guests' requests pleasantly, without appearing irritated or annoyed.
- Always say "thank you."
- Cooperate with coworkers who request food, equipment, or help in better serving customers.

From the moment you are hired for a job you can begin planning for your first day of work. Employers do not expect you to know all the procedures and responsibilities of your new position immediately. However, you can become familiar with the guidelines for professionalism and business courtesy, so that on your first day on the job you will know what is expected.

Welcome to the "Real World"

The world of work is very different from the world of school that you've been living in. Sure, you may not get a grade based on how well you do a job, but your performance at work will determine whether or not you get a raise or promotion. Employers will be watching closely to see if you are the kind of employee they want to give additional responsibilities (and money) to.

Another difference between the classroom and the "real world" is that if your performance or attitude is poor, an employer can terminate (fire) you. If this happens, you will need to find another job, but it will be difficult without a good reference from your last employer.

When you enter the world of work, even as a part-time employee, you are expected to follow guidelines of professional, adult behavior. These guidelines help all employees work well together and contribute to the success of the organization. Qualities that employers expect to find in successful employees are really a matter of common sense.

Exhibit i.3
Employers will expect you to follow their workplace guidelines.

Workplace Guidelines

Attendance—Always call if you are going to be out sick or arriving late. Your managers expect you to be available and on time—they count on you to be there as promised.

Teamwork—Teamwork is vital to any foodservice operation. Employees must be willing to do their assigned work and sometimes more if necessary. Cooperation with coworkers is a must for getting the job done.

Promptness—When someone tells you to do something, do it right away.

Positive Attitude—Having a positive attitude means being enthusiastic about your work and your coworkers. A positive attitude increases your self-confidence, helping you deal with challenges as well as the daily routine.

Dependability—Dependability is important in any career. It means that you will meet your job commitments effectively and on time.

Ask questions—If you don't know or don't understand something, ask. Your employer or supervisor will be more than happy to answer your questions or direct you to the person who can.

Fairness and honesty—It is important to be fair and honest with your employer. No one has to give you a job. A job is an agreement between you and your employer to perform a day's work for a day's pay.

Exhibit i.4
Teamwork is one of the most important guidelines you'll need to practice every day.

Intro.2

SECTION i.2

Career Opportunities in Food Service

AFTER STUDYING SECTION i.2, YOU SHOULD BE ABLE TO:

- Give examples of career opportunities in the foodservice industry.
- Make a list of qualities of successful foodservice employees.

It's never too early to begin thinking about your career. A **career** is a profession or work in a particular field, such as food service, that you choose for yourself. Even though you're in school, you can still be thinking about how your interest in food, for example, experimenting with recipes, preparing meals, or organizing parties, could someday lead to a career in food service.

For organizational purposes, jobs in the foodservice industry are divided into two categories: front-of-the-house and back-of-the-house. **Front-of-the-house** employees serve guests directly. Front-of-

KEY TERMS

- Back-of-the-house
- Career
- Career ladder
- Entry-level job
- Entrepreneur (ON-trah-prah-NOOR)
- Foodservice management
- Front-of-the-house

the-house positions include managers, assistant managers, hosts/hostesses, cashiers, bar staff, wait staff, and buspersons.

Exhibit i.5
Cooks and chefs are considered back-of-the-house employees because they don't usually have direct customer contact.

Back-of-the-house employees work outside the public space. Back-of-the-house positions include chefs, line cooks, pastry chefs, dishwashers, bookkeepers, storeroom clerks, purchasers, dietitians, and menu planners. While these employees don't ordinarily serve guests directly, they are service professionals because they serve the people who serve the guests. They are said to serve their "internal customers," which includes the servers and other front-of-the-house employees.

Entry-level Jobs

Whether your interest is in a job in the front- or the back-of-the-house, you can expect to begin your career in an entry-level position. An **entry-level job** is one that requires little or no previous experience. Such jobs are an important starting point in your career. Entry-level jobs usually lead to other positions with more responsibility. The foodservice industry has many entry-level positions to offer, and the industry as a whole is expected to generate more new jobs than any other service industry during the next decade.

Entry-level jobs in the foodservice industry include busperson, assistant cook, server, and dishwasher. It is easy to see why these jobs are important to the foodservice operation. Each role is key to the success of the operation as a whole. The operation can only be as good as its team.

Following are brief descriptions of the responsibilities you can expect in some popular entry-level jobs in food service.

Busperson—The work that a busperson does makes an impression on customers as soon as they are seated. Seeing that their table is set properly and then having the table cleared quickly allows guests to relax and enjoy themselves, knowing that their needs are being taken care of. Guests will often ask buspersons for water, condiments, fresh silverware, and other extras. A quick and polite response to such requests further enhances a guest's enjoyment.

Dishwasher—Clean, sparkling, sanitary tableware is essential to an enjoyable meal and it is the responsibility of the dishwashers to see that this function is fulfilled. Although the dishwashers work in the back-of-the-house, their work is very visible in the front-of-the-house, helping determine the guests' overall impression of the operation. The dishwasher also keeps an eye on service areas, making certain that supplies do not run out.

Host/hostess or entrance employee—The very first impression of an operation that guests receive is from the host/hostess or employee who meets them at the entrance. If that impression is a friendly, hospitable, and gracious one, guests will feel relaxed and ready to enjoy themselves. In addition to greeting customers, hosts assist guests with coats or other things they wish to check; take reservations; seat customers; ask whether departing customers enjoyed their meals; thank customers for their visit; and answer customers' questions about hours of the operation, types of credit cards accepted, and what menu items are available.

Server—Whether in a full-service or quick-service operation, servers spend more time with the guests than any other employee. The server's attitude and performance has a tremendous impact on the guest's enjoyment of the dining experience. In a full-service operation servers greet customers; take their order; serve the order; check on customers' needs after serving the meal; and continue to provide service until customers have left the table.

Exhibit i.6
Service with a smile brings customers back again and again.

Counter servers in a quick-service operation usually have only brief contact with each customer. This means that servers have only a few moments to make a good first impression. Counter servers greet customers; take their order; accept payment; and thank customers for their patronage.

Assistant cooks help the more experienced cooks and chefs prepare and cook guests' orders. Often assistant cooks prep meals—which means to portion out food, precook it, or get it ready ahead of time—so everything is ready to assemble when guests order it.

A Selection of Foodservice Careers

Already you can see that jobs in food service can be varied and unique. Higher level jobs include planning menus, developing recipes, managing a foodservice operation, writing about food, developing marketing and advertising strategies, teaching others about food and nutrition, and supplying food to restaurants.

Following are some careers in the foodservice industry.

Foodservice management is the running of a foodservice operation. It includes the coordination of people, resources, products, and facilities related to the design, preparation, and presentation of food outside the home.

Restaurant manager—Managers are responsible for both front-of-the-house and back-of-the-house operations. They are responsible for service; staff training; maintaining the restaurant and its property; keeping food safe; keeping guests and employees safe; marketing and promoting the operation; ensuring profits; keeping costs down; purchasing and storing food; and supervising employees. In short, the manager oversees everything that happens in the foodservice operation.

Assistant managers—Assistant managers are responsible for helping the manager oversee all aspects of operations. Assistant manager is the usual training position for future managers.

Exhibit i.7
Managers are responsible for overseeing all aspects of the operation.

Executive chef—The executive chef oversees the entire kitchen, from supervising all kitchen employees, to purchasing food supplies and making decisions about menu items. Chefs and executive chefs must be trained and educated in the culinary arts and are certified by a professional organization.

Chefs and cooks—An assistant executive chef is responsible for the kitchen team in the executive chef's absence and also lends his or her cooking expertise to overall food preparation. Other chef positions include pantry cook, who is responsible for cold food trays and buffet arrangements; roast cook, who prepares all meat, poultry, and fish; sauce and stock cook, who prepares all sauces and stocks; vegetable cook, who prepares all vegetables and soups; and pastry chef, who prepares all desserts and specialty baked goods. These positions are typically found only in fine-dining restaurants.

Home economists have degrees in food and nutrition and are employed by schools, county or regional health services, and government agencies where they educate consumers about food preparation and healthy food choices.

Exhibits i.8 and i.9
Strong writing skills are important in foodservice marketing.

Communication writers—People with strong communication skills are needed to write books, magazine articles, and brochures, providing consumers with information about food and related matters. Writers may also contribute their talents to the development of training and instructional materials for both restaurants and foodservice companies.

Food stylists arrange food attractively for photographs to be included in magazines and brochures, and to be used by government agencies, associations, and food producers and distributors.

Food service marketers are active in sales, management, and distribution of food products and services. An enormous variety of food items and products must be marketed and sold to foodservice operators.

Research and development—Opportunities in research and development involve the development and testing of new products in test kitchens and laboratories. The government, food producers, universities, and manufacturers of kitchen appliances all need people with these interests and skills.

Food science—Food scientists study the composition of foods. They develop new food products as well as new ways to process and package them. In addition, they test foods for quality, purity, and safety to ensure that they meet government standards.

Dietitians—Dietitians are trained in the principles of food and nutrition. They help people make wise food choices and help develop special diets when needed. Dietitians typically work in universities, restaurants, schools, hospitals, and institutional cafeterias developing nutritious menus.

Food production and food processing—Careers in this area include everything from farming, to running a food processing facility, to distributing food products to restaurants. The production of food and delivering it to consumers requires a large network of dedicated people.

Accounting—Accountants in the foodservice industry are knowledgeable about trends in the industry, give financial advice, and handle payroll and financial procedures.

Exhibit i.10
Accounting requires a good understanding of mathematics.

Entrepreneur—Entrepreneurs (ON-trah-prah-NOOR) own and run their own businesses. Successful entrepreneurs must dedicate themselves to their business, be well-organized, committed to working long hours, and have a general knowledge of business practices. Entrepreneurs are generally risk-takers who work well without supervision.

Trainers are teachers who conduct training sessions for groups of employees or managers. Typically, trainers work for large foodservice companies that own many units. Training managers are responsible for ensuring that all employees and managers receive the right kind of training for their job.

Grocery store and deli managers are increasingly finding that their jobs are like those of restaurant managers. Many stores sell foods that are ready to eat, so managers and employees must know how to prepare food, understand and apply food safety standards, and promote what they have to their customers. This area of the industry is growing rapidly, and many employees and managers will be needed in years to come to supply this demand.

What Brings Success?

If you have had a part-time or summer job, you might already know the kind of work you enjoy doing. You also know that working helps you develop such essential skills as responsibility, self-confidence, and decision making, while you earn a paycheck. If you haven't had a job yet, don't worry. You've already made the most important first step toward a good career by taking classes in school that will help build your skills.

People advance in their careers by mastering the skills needed for their jobs and by showing that they are qualified to take on new responsibilities. Training and experience are important, but employers are also looking for certain skills that you can develop while you are still in school. Training and additional education can help motivated individuals

Exhibit i.11
Sample career ladder.

move higher up the career ladder. A **career ladder** is a series of jobs through which a person can advance to further their career, as shown in Exhibit i.11.

The ability to communicate effectively is one of the top skills that employers look for. Communication skills include writing, speaking, reading, and listening. Speaking to coworkers and customers; writing reports; reading company guidelines; and listening to supervisors, customers, and coworkers are essential in any job.

How can you develop good listening skills?

- **Avoid the tendency to finish another person's sentence—in your mind or aloud.**
- **Focus immediately on the first few words the other person is saying.**
- **Stay focused on what the person is saying.**
- **Repeat the message—put what the person is saying in your own words.**
- **Ask questions if you don't understand something.**
- **Remain calm if someone says something that you strongly disagree with; react to the message, not the messenger.**
- **Concentrate on key ideas and phrases.**
- **Read between the lines. Often it's not what someone says but how the person says it.**
- **Spend more than 50 percent of your time listening. Become a better listener than talker.**

Computer skills are also valuable in the foodservice industry. Most jobs today require some knowledge of computers. For example, in many restaurants servers place orders on computers; cashiers and counter servers in quick-service operations use computerized cash registers. Math skills are also essential, even though computers may be used. For example, if a customer tells a server to keep 15 percent of the payment as a tip, the server needs to know how to calculate that percentage.

Critical thinking and problem solving are also important skills to develop. Employers value employees who can think of fresh solutions to problems.

Maintaining a positive attitude is a key attribute of any employee. Employers, customers, and coworkers value a person who is enthusiastic and optimistic. Another related quality is the ability to work as part of a team. Employees, especially in food service, must be team players, doing their share of the work load—and more if that's what it takes to get the job done.

Willingness to learn new technology and new ways of doing things is important to career success. Employees who advance are the ones who are willing to learn new skills and techniques and not think that the way they know is the only way to do something.

Exhibit i.12
Computer skills are important in the hospitality industry.

How can you develop these skills now?

- Make a commitment to put forth your best effort, both in your studies and in your favorite school activities.
- Be active in school clubs and activities that interest you.
- Volunteer your time in the community—help out in your local library, hospital, nursing home, or pet shelter.
- Take some time to read and learn on your own.
- If you can use a computer in school, the library, or your home, become familiar with basic computer functions and software programs, including word processing, the Internet, and CD-Roms.

Take advantage of every opportunity to improve your learning and work habits while you're still in school and working part time. The more you practice these habits now, the farther you will be able to advance in your career.

Intro.3

SECTION i.3

Starting Your Career in Food Service

AFTER STUDYING SECTION i.3, YOU SHOULD BE ABLE TO:

- Outline a plan for an effective job search.
- Given a list of effective cover letter elements, write a cover letter.
- Demonstrate networking skills.

KEY TERMS

- Cover letter
- Networking

Now that you've focused on your interests and career goals, it's time to consider the continuing education you will need to achieve those goals. Most careers in the foodservice industry require at least a high school diploma or the equivalent. Admission to a college or trade school also requires a high school diploma. No matter what careers interest you, completing high school and continuing your education are the first steps to a successful future.

Although not all foodservice careers require a college education, today many do. For instance, to become a professional chef, dietitian, nutritionist, food stylist or scientist, marketer, home economist, or accountant, you will most likely need to complete additional classes and training.

Choosing a College or Trade School

You will need to consider the following questions when you decide which college or trade school to attend.

Does the school have a program in your chosen field that fits your needs? Do they offer the certification, associate's degree, or bachelor's degree in which you are interested? What is the reputation of the program? If class times or schedules conflict with your other priorities, find out if the school offers evening classes or correspondence classes through video, satellite, or Internet broadcasts.

What are the entrance requirements or fees for applying? Several schools place just as much emphasis on motivation and interest in succeeding as they do on grades and test scores.

Where is the school? Can you live at home or must you live on campus? Will you need your own car? If the school's main location is not convenient for you, remember that many colleges offer classes in several locations. If you are interested in visiting campuses, colleges offer tours for prospective students and their families.

How much does it cost? What kind of financial aid is available? Are scholarships available for which you would qualify? Many colleges have private and federally funded financial aid programs, including grants, loans, scholarships, and work-study programs. Be sure to ask about them.

What is the success rate of the graduates of the school? Does the school assist former students in their job search? Several schools actually have their own placement offices that help link graduates directly with employment opportunities.

What other activities are available at the school? What kinds of clubs and organizations are available for you to explore your interests and develop skills? Participation in college organizations can also contribute to an impressive résumé.

To find the answers to these questions, begin with your high school guidance office or local library. Don't be afraid to make some phone calls. You can also find college application and financial aid information, as well as phone numbers, on the Internet.

The Job Search

Do you have a part-time job? The skills you used to find that job are the same skills you will need to advance your professional career. If you learn how to find a job now, you'll have a head start when you're ready to work full time. Finding and keeping a job will help you develop both personal and career skills.

Job hunting can be exciting and fun. The job market is the ideal place to tell others about your abilities, talents, and dreams. As the average age of people in today's workplace grows older, younger people have even more opportunities before them.

People find jobs in a wide variety of ways. Some employers recruit graduates from a particular high school, and many recruit from colleges and universities. Others print employment ads in local newspapers. Other sources include school placement offices, employment agencies, community agencies, local Yellow Pages, and web pages on the Internet.

Job ads in newspapers are listed alphabetically by job title or job category. For example, if you're looking for a position as a busperson, there may be an ad under "B" for busperson, or there may be an ad under "R" for restaurant. Most ads will specify how you are to apply for the job—in person, by mail, or by phone. Sometimes foodservice operations state a designated time for prospective employees to apply in person. Others will request that you send a cover letter with a résumé or that you phone them directly.

Give it a try!

Try it: get a classified section of your local newspaper and find the restaurant job listings. How many different headings can you find? How much do the jobs pay? How does one apply? What are the hours?

What Is a Cover Letter?

When you send your résumé to a potential employer, you should send a cover letter along with it. A **cover letter** is a brief letter in which you introduce yourself to the employer. The letter highlights your strengths and confirms your interest in the position being offered. In a cover letter, you can explain your qualifications with a more personal touch.

Keep your cover letter brief, to the point, and straightforward. It should be typewritten, using correct grammar and punctuation. Make sure the company name, address, and person's name are all correct. If you use a computer, remember to use the spellcheck function. Always read letters carefully before you send them. Remember, first impressions are critical, and many employers who see a sloppy cover letter will get the feeling that your work might be sloppy too.

Following are tips for writing a cover letter:

Attention. Grab your reader's attention in the first paragraph to make sure the person keeps on reading. State why you're writing the letter.

Interest. Hold the reader's interest by telling how you got their name or found out about the company or the job.

Ms. Louise Brown
Manager
Blue Parakeet Café
82 South Pleasant Street
Funtown, USA 50094

July 28, 2002

Dear Ms. Brown:

I would like to schedule an appointment to meet with you regarding a position as part-time server.

Your advertisement in the *Anytown Daily News* for servers at the Blue Parakeet Café offers a great opportunity for me to begin my career in foodservice. I'm a junior at Anytown High School where I'm currently enrolled in a new program that includes food preparation classes as well as business management courses.

For your review, I'm enclosing a copy of my résumé that shows my qualifications. I:

- Am hard-working, dependable, and honest
- Have a pleasant disposition and outgoing personality
- Enjoy being with people
- Have an excellent memory for names and faces

I am sure that once you've had a chance to look over my résumé and meet with me, you'll agree that my enthusiasm and willingness to learn will make me an ideal server at the Blue Parakeet Café. You can reach me after 3:00 p.m. at 123-456-7890. I look forward to hearing from you at your earliest convenience. Thank you for your consideration.

Sincerely,

Rose J. Hernandez

Rose J. Hernandez
2340 East 83rd Street
Anytown, USA 85467

Exhibit i.13
Here is an example of a good cover letter.

Desire. Tell the reader what you want to do for their company. List your qualifications and the reasons why you want the job.

Action. End your letter by saying that you look forward to meeting them in an interview.

Always keep a copy of your cover letter and the ad to which you responded. This will help you follow up your request for an interview with a phone call. A follow-up phone call proves that you're serious about wanting the job.

Here is an example of a follow-up phone call.

1. Call the manager and introduce yourself. Be friendly, yet businesslike.

   "Good afternoon, Ms. Brown. My name is Rose Hernandez. How are you today?"

2. State the purpose for your call.

   "Ms. Brown, I'm calling to follow up on the letter and résumé I sent you last week responding to your ad for servers. I wanted to be sure that you received it."

3. Ask for the interview.

   "Would it be possible for us to meet and discuss a part-time server position? Do you suppose you might have time Thursday or Friday afternoon this week?"

4. Stay calm, truthful, and expect the unexpected.

   "I guess I'm a little nervous because I've never called a manager before about a job. You were about to call me for an interview? That's great!"

5. Politely end the conversation and confirm the interview date and time.

   "Thanks so much, Ms. Brown. I look forward to meeting you at 3:30 on Thursday afternoon."

How Networking Works

An important tool for your job search is networking. **Networking** means contacting people who can give you information about job openings. For example, your teachers may know of job openings; your friends who are working may provide job leads; your parents, relatives, or neighbors may also know of employment opportunities. The more people who know about your job search, the better your chances of finding a position.

The following is an example of networking:

Say you have a friend whose sister is a server at a local family restaurant. You could call that server, identify yourself as a friend of her brother, and ask her if she knows of any openings.

The conversation might sound like this:

> *"Hi, Kyana. This is Aaron. You don't know me, but I'm a friend of your brother's from school. Bryan said you're working at the Blue Parakeet Café these days, and you said it's pretty decent over there. I need a favor and I was wondering if you could help. I'm looking for a job as a busperson or a kitchen helper. Do you know if the manager is hiring anyone? Or could you give me the manager's name so I could call myself?"*

If the person knows of an opening, ask for a recommendation. For example:

> *"So, Kyana, when I call Mr. Ramirez (the manager), would you mind if I said that you recommended that I give him a call?"*

Be sure to thank the person, and if you have an interview, call the person to let him or her know how you did. For example:

> *"Hi, Kyana. It's me, Aaron. Guess what?! I just wanted to let you know we're going to be working together Tuesday and Thursday nights. Mr. Ramirez hired me for that kitchen helper spot—and he said I could help out with that little league baseball party Saturday afternoon for some extra cash. Very cool—thanks for your help!"*

Intro.4

SECTION i.4

Preparing Your Portfolio and Résumé

AFTER STUDYING SECTION i.4, YOU SHOULD BE ABLE TO:

- Compile the best examples of your work into a portfolio.
- Write a résumé that lists your skills and competencies.

KEY TERMS

- **Portfolio**
- **References**
- **Résumé (RE-zoo-may)**

Just as you need the proper kitchen tools for food preparation, you need the appropriate tools for your job search. These tools are your portfolio and résumé. Creating your portfolio and résumé will make you feel more confident and they will present a clear picture of your interests, abilities, and talents to a prospective employer.

A Winning Portfolio

A **portfolio** is a collection of samples that showcase your interests, talents, contributions, and studies. A portfolio displays your finest efforts and is a good self-marketing tool to show potential employers. Exhibit i.14 provides a list of things a portfolio may include.

Portfolios should be complete, neat, and well-organized. Include a cover page that gives your full name, address, phone number; your career objectives; and a brief description of the contents. Select

Exhibit i.14
Portfolios can include a variety of items.

- A list and samples of your skills and abilities (such as the list of competencies you will be learning at your worksites)
- Samples of your work (for example, if you decorated a cake that you're especially proud of, take a picture of it and include it as a sample; or describe how you decorated it or what inspired you)
- Examples of problems you solved (at school, in your community, with your friends)
- Examples demonstrating your teamwork
- Examples that show your leadership and responsibility
- Important experiences and what you learned from them
- Certificates of recognition and reward (the certificate you will receive upon successful completion of this program and your high school diploma are two examples)
- Newsletters or announcements (with your name or group highlighted)
- Essays, reports, and papers that you're proud of (and those with high grades or positive teacher remarks)
- Letters of thanks
- Your résumé
- Audio or video tapes that display your abilities
- Test scores
- Original recipes that you created
- Letters of recommendation from past employers or groups you have worked with. (These can be from the sponsors of a charity walk-a-thon in which you participated, or a school event, for example.)

samples that clearly highlight your best talents. Each sample should be accompanied by a brief explanation of why it is important. Type information whenever possible. Include clean photocopies of letters and other important documents or certificates.

Your portfolio is best displayed in a three-ring binder or folder. It's a good idea to use three-ring, clear plastic sheets to hold your samples. Your portfolio should be about ten pages in length and easy to carry to interviews. A portfolio that is sloppy, too long, or too big does not make a good impression.

Start collecting materials for your portfolio now, while you're still in school. Creating a complete and accurate portfolio is an ongoing process. Think about what would impress you if you were a potential employer. Ask friends and family for advice.

An Effective Résumé

A key ingredient in your portfolio is your résumé. A **résumé** (RE-zoo-may) is a written summary of your experience, skills, and achievements that relate to the job you're seeking. A résumé is not your life story; rather, it is like a sales brochure that tells an employer why you are the best person to hire for the job. When looking at your résumé, ask yourself, "If I were the employer, would I hire this person?"

Your résumé should be short—no more than one page—and contain only the most important information. Include relevant work experience on your résumé. If you do not have any work experience, concentrate on the activities that show your skills and abilities and how they relate to the job for which you are applying. Following is a sample résumé format.

Name (first name first)

Home street address

City, State, Zip code

Phone number where you can be reached

Objective:

What job are you seeking?

Qualifications:

What are your skills/capabilities?

Experience:

How have you demonstrated these skills/capabilities in the past? List all jobs here, beginning with the most recent.

Education:

Name of your high school; your status (junior, senior); the courses you are taking

References available on request.

References are people who aren't related to you but who know you well and can provide information about you—your character, work ability, or academic standing. Some people to consider as references are teachers, previous employers, church leaders, and neighbors. It is considerate to ask these people first before you use them as job references. Be sure to have their full names, addresses, and phone numbers with you when you apply so you can give this information to the potential employer.

Notice how this student emphasized his current job. The other work experience is important as well. As you gain more work experience, you can eliminate less important items. When you graduate from high school, you would state on the education line:

Education:
1998; Diploma, Your High School, Your Town, Your State

Courses:
Pre-Management and Foods Courses
ProStart certificate from the National Restaurant Association

Your résumé will change as you do, as you gain more experience, training, and education. Like your portfolio, developing a résumé is an ongoing process. No matter how much experience you have, your résumé should be an easy-to-read outline of your successes and achievements.

Harvard Lippman
1234 Main Street
Funtown, USA 12345
Phone: 123.456.7890

Objective: Server, part-time

Qualifications:
- Ability to use a computer
- Received high grades in food classes
- Know how to organize work
- Work well with others
- Would like to manage a restaurant

Work Experience:
1996-present, Busperson, First-Class Café, Funtown, USA
- Clear tables quickly and set correctly
- Refill water and other beverages during dinner service
- Assist servers in serving food, as needed
- Received certificate for annual "Smile Award"

Other Experience:
- Help serve food at high school café (sponsored by Foodservice Class)
- Organized annual junior class bake sale (sponsored by Foodservice Class)
- Developed new recipe for lowfat brownies sold at annual bake sale
- Used computer program to type recipes for class cookbook
- Volunteer kitchen worker at community Thanksgiving dinner

Education:
- Junior at Funtown High School
- Currently taking food and management classes in Foodservice school-to-career program

References available on request

Exhibit i.15
Here is how a résumé looks when it is completed.

Intro.5

SECTION i.5

Completing Application Forms

AFTER STUDYING SECTION i.5, YOU SHOULD BE ABLE TO:

- Read and complete a college application form.
- Read and complete a job application form.

KEY TERMS

- Application form
- College application
- Job application
- Trade school application

Whether you apply to a college, a trade school, or for a job, you will have to complete an application form. An **application form** asks basic personal information about you and your background.

College Applications

In addition to asking for your name and address, **college** or **trade school applications** require education information. The application may also require that you state the program or course of study you are applying for and ask you to complete a short essay. You will be asked to have your high school transcript sent to the college also. The admissions office at the school will look at your application and transcript to see the courses you took and your grade point average. This information helps determine whether or not you will be accepted into the program.

It is *not* illegal for college applications to ask about your race, national origin, or birth date. However, you may choose not to answer these questions. Schools do not use this information to decide who gets accepted. Rather, they use the information to gather statistics about their student population.

Job Applications

The **job application** is important because it gives general information and it reveals some insights about you to the employer. It shows how well you can follow instructions, your ability to read and write, as well as your employment history. Treat the application seriously and take time to fill it out carefully and completely. It is illegal for a job application to ask about marital status, height, weight, age, handicaps, race or national origin, religion, or political information. The job application form usually asks you to state your work experience and list references.

Completing a Job Application Form

When you are filling out the job application, be sure to write or print clearly. Use correct grammar and punctuation, and organize your thoughts before you write them on the form. If your responses on an application are unclear or messy you will not make a good impression on the interviewer.

If there is something on the form that you don't understand, leave the space blank or write *please see me* in the space. Write *n/a* if a question is *not applicable* (doesn't apply) to you. Later, you can ask the person who handed you the application to explain any questions you have, or you can discuss them with the interviewer.

When answering questions about money on the application, write *Open*. You first need to learn about the job before you can make any decisions about the salary. You will be asked to state how much money you earned on any previous jobs. Be honest; don't exaggerate.

Even if you have no work experience, you still have qualities and skills that are needed in the workplace. List any volunteer work, baby-sitting jobs, or school or church activities that show that you have had experience contributing your efforts to projects.

You will be asked to sign your name on the application form to state that you have

Let's Try it!

Stop at a local business that interests you and ask for a job application. Bring it to class and complete it. Ask classmates to review your application for spelling errors. Then turn it in to the employer. Follow up with the employer and see what happens!

answered all questions and given information that is true and accurate to the best of your knowledge. Being dishonest on a job application can be a reason for immediate termination (firing). Employers do check on your educational and work background, as well as contact your references.

All job applications are basically the same, so once you have completed one form, you will know what to expect on others. Exhibit i.16 lists some terms that will likely appear on the job application.

Exhibit i.16
Words commonly found on job application forms.

WORD	*MEANING*
Employment	Work; a job
Personal information	Facts about yourself
Social security number	Numbers assigned by the government to all people who apply; everyone with a job is required to have a social security number
Related	From the same family
Employment desired	The kind of job you want
Position	Job; area you want to work in
Salary desired	Wage or salary you will accept to do a job
Inquire	Ask
Education	School experience
Location	Where something is
Permanent address	The location of your permanent home
Date graduated	The day, month, and year you finished school; if you are still in school, you can write your expected graduation date
Activities	Things you do, especially for relaxation or fun
Former employers	People for whom you used to work
References	People who know you and will tell an employer about you
Business	The kind of work a person does
Years acquainted	How long you have known someone
Physical conditions	State of health or fitness
Injured	Hurt
Detail	A small item or piece of information
Emergency	An unexpected situation calling for fast action
Notify	To inform

Intro.6

SECTION i.6

The Job Interview

AFTER STUDYING SECTION i.6, YOU SHOULD BE ABLE TO:

- List the steps to an effective job interview.
- Explain the follow-up steps for a job interview.

KEY TERMS

- **Etiquette (EH-tah-kit)**
- **Job interview**

If an employer likes your cover letter and résumé, you may be asked for a job interview. At the **job interview,** you'll meet with the employer to discuss your qualifications for the job. This is your opportunity to "show your stuff" in person to a potential employer, and you want to do everything possible to make the interview a success.

This first impression to your potential employer will make the strongest statement about you. Make sure that you make your first impression a great one! Your résumé and cover letter will be remembered if the person interviewing you likes what he or she sees in the office. The following key points will help you make a great first impression.

Appearance—If you look neat and clean, you give the impression that your work will also be neat and clean. You don't have to wear expensive clothes to have a good appearance. Wear clothes that are clean and appropriate for the job for which you are interviewing. The key is to avoid wearing anything in excess.

Good personal hygiene is a must. The most important point to remember is that you will be working with food and people—preparing, serving, and removing food or greeting guests in a foodservice operation. In the foodservice industry, cleanliness and neatness are absolutely essential.

Just a note: *Employers expect you to be clean and neat in your appearance every day on the job, too.*

Positive attitude—If you smile and are enthusiastic, it suggests that you will do your work with that same attitude. Remember, the ability to smile and stay calm under pressure is necessary for a successful career in food service. Don't worry if you're a little nervous during your interview. Most interviewers will see that you are a person who takes a serious attitude toward work.

Good manners—Good manners are the basis for business **etiquette** (EH-tah-kit). Saying *please, thank you,* and *excuse me* all show good manners. If you are considerate and thoughtful, your behavior implies that you will also act that way around coworkers and customers—and excellent customer service is expected in the foodservice industry. The first rule of business etiquette is to arrive at the interview on time. Punctuality for the interview indicates that you will be punctual on the job.

Exhibit i.17
Proper etiquette will help you in several business and professional situations.

When you meet the person who will interview you, smile, extend your hand, and exchange a friendly greeting. Always call the interviewer *Mr.* or *Ms.* unless the person asks you to use his or her first name. Wait until the interviewer invites you to sit down, and then sit up straight in the chair—don't slouch or sprawl out. Avoid nervous fidgeting, such as playing with your hair, drumming your fingers, or tapping your pen. It's best to sit still, look alert, and pay attention to what the interviewer is saying. Practice effective listening skills (as discussed in Section i-2). If you bring someone with you to the interview, have that person wait outside.

It is a good idea to learn basic facts about the company before the interview. It shows you are serious about working for the company and are interested in the job. Also, the potential employer may ask you what you know about the company. Information you should know includes the company size and reputation, its key products and services, and names of its competitors. This information can be found in your school library/media center, your community library, and local chambers of commerce and business associations.

WHAT METERIALS DO YOU NEED TO BRING WITH YOU TO THE INTERVIEW?

What materials do you need to bring with you to the interview?

- *Portfolio, including your résumé*
- *Names, addresses, and phone numbers of three people you plan on using as references*
- *Birth certificate or valid passport; social security card; or proof that you are able to work in the United States*

If you're unsure about what work documents to bring, call the person who will be interviewing you. A potential employer will be impressed by your preparedness and attention to detail.

Some key business publications that are helpful for finding company information include *Fortune Magazine*, *The New York Times*, *The Wall Street Journal*, *Barron's*, *Forbes*, *Dun & Bradstreet* and the *Thomas Register*. Your community newspapers are also good sources for information about local businesses. There are also many computer on-line sources of information. Your school or community librarian can help you access these services.

INTERVIEW QUESTIONS AND ANSWERS

Most job interviews last about an hour, depending on the job level. Most interviewers try to help you relax and feel comfortable. Your potential employer will ask questions to get to know you better and to see if your talents would be a suitable match for the job available. The potential employer has a job position to fill and wants to hire someone capable of doing the job or learning it quickly. The interviewer also wants to know whether you will fit in with the foodservice team and the organization as a whole.

Think of the interview as a chance to visit a workplace, to learn more about an interesting job, and an opportunity to meet new people. It's important to make a good impression, but it's also important to be yourself. Practicing your interviewing skills with a friend is a good way to prepare yourself for the real interview. A friend, family member, or teacher can play the role of the employer and ask you sample interview questions. Give each question serious thought and come up with an answer that is honest and complete. Practicing before an interview will help you answer questions quickly and accurately during the actual interview.

While there are no correct or incorrect answers to interview questions, some responses are more appropriate than others. The first question the interviewer may ask is, *Why don't you tell me a little about yourself?* The appropriate response is to talk about your accomplishments, experience, and qualifications. Practice a three-minute statement that presents your capabilities. Here is an example:

Exhibit i.18
Interviews vary in length and formality. Be prepared for anything!

"My name is Ira Levin, and I'm looking for a job that will get me started in my professional foodservice career. Currently, I'm a junior at Funtown High School where I'm enrolled in a program that teaches both food preparation and business management skills. For the past two years, I've been a server in our school cafeteria, the Jazzy Café, where I also work as a kitchen helper—the chef has even used some of my original low-fat dessert recipes. I'm a good team player and I'm dependable. My grades are above average, and I really enjoy working with people. My goal is to be a restaurant manager some day. That's why I thought this position as a part-time server at the Blue Parakeet Café would be a great opportunity to move up the career ladder."

Now for practice, take a few minutes to write a "Tell me about yourself" statement on a separate sheet of paper.

"My name is ______________________. Currently, I'm a ______________________ at ______________________ high school where I'm enrolled in/studying courses in ______________________.

(Mention key skills/accomplishments/experiences/areas of strength here)
____
____
____
____
______________________.

That's why I thought this position as ______________________ at ______________________ would be a great opportunity for me."

Exhibit i.19
Here are some examples of personal characteristics that you could use to describe yourself during an interview.

accurate	enthusiastic	like people
able to remain calm under pressure	good attitude	responsible
communicate well	hard worker	sense of humor
dependable	know computer skills	tolerant
energetic	high standards	trustworthy
entertaining	leader	willing to learn and take instructions

Here are examples of typical interview questions you may be asked to answer on your job interview.

Why do you want to work for this company? Why do you want to be a __________ in this company?

Reply: Talk about why the job or the company interests you. Avoid any reference to money.

What contributions can you make to this company?

Reply: Talk about your qualifications and skills and how they will benefit the company.

How did you hear about us?

Reply: Through the newspaper, a friend, a relative, or a teacher.

The next three questions are relevant if you have previous work experience:

How many jobs have you had during the past three years?

Reply: State how many jobs you've had.

What exactly did you do on your last job/current job?

Reply: Talk about your responsibilities, duties, and achievements.

Why are you leaving your present job? Why did you leave your last job?

Reply: Be honest, but don't speak ill of your previous employer or job responsibilities. Appropriate responses depend on your situation. You could say that the previous/current job allowed you to work part time, and you're now ready to commit to full-time employment. You could also say that you are now ready to take on more responsibilities, but those opportunities were not available with your current/previous employer. Other reasons include layoffs, reduction in work hours, or the employer was not able to accommodate your school schedule.

If we hire you, how long do you think you would be able to work here?

Reply: If you're looking at a part-time job for one semester, say so. If you're looking for full-time permanent employment, say you hope to stay with the organization for a long time.

What are your favorite subjects in school? Why?

Reply: Name your favorite subjects and tell why.

What subject do you find most difficult?

Reply: Here is one example: *World history was my worst subject—it really bored me, and my grades showed it. But I knew a 'D' would hurt my overall grade average, so I found a senior to tutor me in exchange* *for typing her term papers. By the end of the semester, I was able to pull a 'B'.* The interviewer is trying to determine your ability to persevere under less than favorable circumstances. Everyone has difficulty learning things sometimes, but a person with ambition will find a workable solution. That's what the potential employer is looking for in a good employee.

Did you participate in any school activities? Why or why not?

Reply: Name the activities. Joining school activities shows that you're a sociable person. If you had to work after school and for this reason you were not able to join any activities, say so. Be sure your answer reflects that you do work well with others.

Do you plan to continue your education?

Reply: Continuing your education is not limited to college. It can include taking additional courses in food preparation, for example, or a willingness to participate in on-the-job training. Your answer should reflect that you want to gain as much knowledge and training as possible to advance in your foodservice career.

How many days of school or work did you miss during the last year?

Reply: While regular attendance and punctuality are extremely important in any workplace, foodservice operators in particular depend on employees who show up for work every day and on time. Someone who is absent for several days at school or work may not be dependable on the job. If you have been absent for many days at school or work, have a reasonable explanation prepared.

Other questions you may be asked include questions about salary, what motivates you to do a good job, and whether you have ever been fired from a job. For questions regarding salary on previous jobs, tell the truth. If the interviewer asks you what salary you are looking for in this job, be diplomatic. You should say that you have no set figure in mind, or ask the person what salary is usually offered to someone with your qualifications. If you've ever been fired from a job, don't panic. Reply that while you usually can work with everyone, this particular boss and you just weren't a good match, in spite of your efforts to work out the problems.

Before ending the interview, the potential employer will ask you if you have any questions. This is your chance to show that you have confidence in yourself and also want to be sure the job is a good match for your personal and professional goals.

Here are some questions you might consider asking the interviewer:

- Is this a new position or would I be replacing someone?
- Was the person who previously had this job promoted? (This is very important for a full-time job. The object is to discover whether the company is promoting employees or if there is a high rate of employees leaving the company because they are unhappy.)
- Could you please describe a typical work day for me?
- If you hired me, when would you expect me to start working?
- How long would it take for me to be trained for the job?
- When do you plan on filling the position? If the interviewer says a decision will be made within one or two weeks, ask if you may call to inquire about the decision.

Avoid asking questions about salary, vacation, bonuses, or holidays. Salary is a sensitive issue. Wait for the interviewer to bring up the subject. Ask the interviewer what the standard salary is for someone with your qualifications. It's a good idea to have a general idea of the salary range for the job before you go to the interview. You can find this information at your school or community library. While you should not be the one to begin the discussion, you should leave the interview knowing the overall salary range.

When the interview is ended, smile, shake the person's hand, and thank the interviewer for taking the time to explain the job to you. If you do want the job, this is the time to say so. For example, you might say, *This would be a great opportunity for me—I hope you give my qualifications serious consideration. I know I'd work well with your foodservice team.* Even if you know you don't want the job, it is important to observe business courtesy.

Follow Up After the Interview

A simple thank-you note can make you stand out from the crowd of job seekers. It's a good idea to write the thank-you note as soon as you arrive home. This proves to the employer that you really want the job.

The note should be short, confirm that you want the job, reinforce your qualifications, give a time you will follow up with a phone call, and offer to meet with the potential employer again to answer any additional questions. Ending the letter with a sentence that encourages the potential employer to call you is a good marketing idea. Most people read the beginning few sentences and the last sentence before reading the body of any letter. Here is a sample thank you letter.

Ms. Louise Brown
Manager
Blue Parakeet Café
82 South Pleasant Street
Funtown, USA 50094

August 3, 2002

Dear Ms. Brown:

Thank you for meeting with me on Thursday afternoon to explain the part-time server position at the Blue Parakeet Café. The responsibilities of the server position, along with the training and flexible hours, would give me a head start in my foodservice career. I definitely want to be a member of your team!

I'm confident that I can quickly learn the service techniques and become a productive member of your staff. My teachers have told me that I am a fast learner and I'm willing to attend your weekend training classes.

If I may, I'll call you next Thursday to see if you've made a decision and to answer any additional questions you may have. Please don't hesitate to call me at 123-456-7890 if you have any new questions in the meantime. Once again, thank you for considering me for the position.

Sincerely,
Rose J. Hernandez
Rose J. Hernandez
2340 East 83rd Street
Anytown, USA 85467

Exhibit i.20
Sample thank you note.

The follow-up phone call should be on the day you promised. Here is a sample follow-up phone call.

1. **Remind the person who you are.**

   "Good afternoon, Ms. Brown. This is Rose Hernandez. How are you today?"

2. **State the reason for your call—what position you applied for.**

   "Ms. Brown, I'm calling to follow up on our meeting last Thursday regarding the part-time server position. It sounded like the ideal job for me."

3. **Find out if the potential employer made a decision.**

   "I was wondering if you had made a decision yet."

4. **If you got the job, write down the answers to the following questions:**

   "When would you like me to start working and what time should I be there?"

   "What should I bring with me?"

   "Where should I go on my first day?"

   "Who should I see?"

   "I just need to coordinate my bus schedule—do you know how many hours I'll be working on my first day?"

5. **If the employer has not made a decision, don't panic.**

   "I understand. Could you please tell me if you're still considering me for the position?"

If you are a candidate:

"Are there any questions I can answer that will show you I'm really the server you're looking for?"

If there are no questions:

"Thanks again, Ms. Brown. I hope you'll call me if you do have any questions, and I look forward to hearing from you soon."

If you didn't get the job:

"Oh, I'm sorry to hear that. Thank you for taking the time to explain the position to me. I hope you'll think of me if you have other openings."

If you did not get the job, it is acceptable to ask the person for constructive feedback on your interviewing skills, or ask the interviewer what you could do to get more experience or training. Sometimes interviewers can refer you to other jobs that would be more suitable for your abilities. Don't be afraid to ask the person. Even if you didn't get the job, don't be too disappointed. Every interview is an opportunity to sharpen your communication skills and meet foodservice professionals. It also helps you find out your strengths and weaknesses and gives you the chance to do better next time.

Before, During, and After the Interview

Before the interview:

- *Know the route to the job. Take a preview trip to the interview site. Make sure you consider traffic.*
- *If you're taking public transportation, bring enough money.*
- *Know what materials to take with you.*
- *Review important interview questions and how you will respond.*
- *Practice aloud what you will say to the interviewer about yourself.*
- *Bring a pen that writes clearly and a clean notebook.*
- *Write down the name, address, and telephone number of the person you're meeting, and bring it with you.*
- *Give yourself enough time to get ready.*
- *Get a good night's sleep.*
- *Arrive at the interview 15 minutes before your appointment.*
- *If you are going to be late, call the interviewer.*
- *Good luck and relax!*

During the interview:

- *Smile, look interested, and pay attention.*
- *Sit with your back straight; lean back in the chair.*
- *Practice good listening skills.*
- *Never say unkind or bad things about your previous boss or coworkers.*
- *Be an interactive participant. Avoid answering questions too quickly—it looks like you're not giving the answers enough thought.*
- *Ask questions.*
- *Look confident (and you'll feel confident).*
- *Sell yourself! Explain how your skills and abilities make you the ideal person for the job.*

After the interview:

- *Write a brief thank-you note to the interviewer as soon as possible.*
- *Follow up with a phone call to the interviewer.*
- *Congratulate yourself on doing your best!*

Intro.7

SECTION i.7

Working on the Job

AFTER STUDYING SECTION i.7, YOU SHOULD BE ABLE TO:

- State your interpretation of a first day on the job.
- Outline the steps to resigning a job.

KEY TERMS

- **Employee manual**
- **Orientation**

Congratulations! You're about to go to your first day in your new job. What can you expect your first day to be like? Orientation and training will fill most of your first day. **Orientation** is the process that helps new employees learn about the procedures and policies of the operation and introduces them to their coworkers. Your employer wants to give you a positive impression of the operation, the management, and all other staff members. The purpose of orientation is to make you feel comfortable in your new job, to know what your responsibilities are, and to make you feel part of the team.

The type of orientation you receive depends on the size of the organization. If you're working in a large operation, you may see a video, hear lectures, and receive printed manuals. Smaller operations might give you a typed employee manual, an individual tour of the operation, and introduce you to coworkers.

Exhibit i.21
Orientaion is a process to help new employees learn about the organization and what is expected of them.

The type of training you receive depends on your job and the size of the organization. Some training may be accomplished by watching videos and reading workbooks, similar to your high school classroom experience. Other training may be hands-on, similar to working in a your classroom kitchen or cafeteria kitchen. The purpose of training is to be sure that you know how to do the job on your own. Remember to ask questions.

DURING ORIENTATION YOU CAN EXPECT TO LEARN:

- *The history of the foodservice operation.*
- *Key company goals that are important to your job.*
- *How the company is organized; who reports to whom.*

It shows that you are serious about doing a good job.

Your supervisor will give you whatever tools you need on your first day. These might include:

- **Name tag**
- **Locker or other personal space**
- **Uniform**
- **Office, cubicle, desk, or work area**
- **Telephone**
- **Employee manual (containing general information concerning employment)**
- **Training materials to help explain the work you will be doing**
- **First week's schedule**

An **employee manual** is a written booklet containing general information about employment, including company policies, rules and procedures, employee benefits, and other topics related to the company. It is similar to a high school student manual. When you receive the employee manual, you will be asked to sign a form stating that you have received it. Your signature means that you have read the information and agree to follow the rules and policies it contains. Exhibit i.22 lists some items a typical employee manual may contain.

Exhibit i.22
Contents of a typical employee manual.

Employment Policies
- Absence from work
- Schedule substitutions and trading work shifts
- Paid holidays
- Overtime
- Tips
- Pay periods
- Shift changes
- Time cards
- Performance appraisals
- Wage and salary reviews
- Work breaks

Rules and Procedures
- Dress Code
- Illegal activities (drinking alcohol, drugs)
- Grievances (complaints or problems at work)
- Disciplinary procedures
- Probationary policies
- Causes for dismissal
- Emergencies (injuries, fires, natural disasters, robberies)
- Safety rules
- Off-duty time at the operation
- Friends visiting the operation
- Personal telephone use

Employee Benefits
- Medical and dental insurance coverage
- Sick leave and disability
- Meals
- Pension, retirement, and/or death benefits
- Profit sharing
- Retirement

Other Topics That May Be Included
- Employee and locker areas
- History and mission of the organization
- How the company is organized (the chain of command)
- Job description
- Where to enter and leave the facility
- Smoking and nonsmoking areas
- Restrooms
- Breakage (accidents, broken dishes or equipment)
- Parking
- Training opportunities
- Employee assistance programs
- Job openings and postings

Moving On

There will probably be a time when you will leave your job because of a better opportunity, change in school schedule, or any number of reasons. It is standard business practice to give your current employer a two-week notice before you leave. You can inform your employer in person or you can write a letter of resignation.

Take care in writing a letter of resignation. You may include your reasons for leaving, but always be polite. Avoid any negative comments, and always thank your employer for giving you the opportunity to work for the company. As you learned from filling out a job application, prospective employers ask about your work record and request references from previous employers. If you show anger or negativity when you resign, you may be hurting yourself in the future.

A good guide to follow throughout your working career is always to leave on a positive note. If you keep your long-term goals in mind, you will be able to rise above any negative words and attitudes of others. You will have the patience and persistence to see your career vision to its ultimate goal. Possessing excellent skills and having good education and training are only part of the equation for a successful career in food service: commitment to service, a positive attitude, and perseverance are also needed to take you to the top!

Ms. Louise Brown
Manager
Blue Parakeet Café
82 South Pleasant Street
Funtown, USA 50094

March 10, 2003

Dear Ms. Brown:

As much as I have enjoyed working as a server at the Blue Parakeet Café, I must resign effective March 20, 2003.

I have been offered a position as assistant manager in a full-service restaurant in Anytown that will enable me to continue to pursue my long-term goals in food service. Working at the Blue Parakeet Café has been a wonderful training experience for me. I know I'll be more considerate of all servers in my new position!

Thank you personally for setting such a great example as a manager. I hope you'll visit me at the Anytown Grand Café at your earliest convenience.

Thank you again for giving me the opportunity to work at the Blue Parakeet Café.

Sincerely,

Rose J. Hernandez

Rose J. Hernandez
2340 East 83rd Street
Anytown, USA 85467

Exhibit i.23
An example of a resignation letter.

Flashback

INTRODUCTION

SECTION i.1: WORKING IN THE HOSPITALITY INDUSTRY

- The hospitality and foodservice industry is unique because it is the only type of business where the customer and the manufacturer of a product are in direct contact.
- People who work in hospitality and food service must be committed to service. They must be efficient, flexible, a team player, and able to remain calm under pressure in a fast-paced environment.
- Hospitality and foodservice professionals view customers as guests, try to make their dining experience enjoyable, and serve them nutritional, safe food.
- It is essential to treat everyone—customers, coworkers, and supervisors—with respect and consideration.
- Working in the hospitality and foodservice industry means serving people directly. Service professionals include hotel workers, nurses, sales people, lawyers, and landscapers, just to name a few.
- Good service requires first of all that you like people; then training, stamina, effort, and commitment also come into play. Hospitality professionals enjoy their jobs of helping people get what they want.
- Customers expect anyone who serves them to have a pleasant, helpful, and friendly manner.
- The world of work is *very different* from the school environment. When you enter the world of work, even as a part-time employee, you are expected to follow guidelines of professional, adult behavior.
- Attendance, team work, promptness, a positive attitude, dependability; asking questions when necessary; and fairness and honesty on the job are essential for your success in a foodservice profession.

SECTION i.2: CAREER OPPORTUNITIES IN FOOD SERVICE

- A **career** is a profession or work in a certain field that usually begins with an **entry-level job.**

- Whatever career you choose, you can expect to begin your career in an entry-level job, which is an important starting point in your work experience.
- Examples of entry-level jobs in the foodservice industry include busperson, kitchen helper, server, and dishwasher.
- Training and additional education are ways by which motivated individuals can move higher up the **career ladder.** A career ladder is a series of jobs through which a person can advance in a career.
- Even though you are still in school, you can start planning for a foodservice career that you will enjoy.
- Foodservice jobs range from serving food, preparing food, developing recipes, managing a foodservice operation, writing articles about food, developing marketing and advertising strategies, to teaching and educating others about food and nutrition.
- There are two categories of personnel necessary to run a foodservice establishment: front-of-the-house positions, which are involved with guest service, and back-of-the-house positions, which are those jobs in all areas outside the public space.
- **Front-of-the-house** foodservice professionals include restaurant manager and assistant manager.
- **Back-of-the-house** professionals include executive chef, assistant chef, and other specialized chef positions.
- Other career opportunities related to food service are varied. These include home economics; communication and writing; foodservice marketing; research and development; food science; dietetics; food production and food processing; accounting; training; grocery and deli managers; and **entrepreneurs.**
- A part-time or summer job helps you develop skills such as responsibility, self-confidence, and decision making; however, you can acquire other essential skills while you are still in school. These include communication skills—writing, speaking, reading, and effective listening; computer competency; and math skills.
- Critical thinking and problem solving are also important on the job. Employers value employees who can think of new solutions to problems.
- Other personal qualities viewed favorably by employees include a positive

attitude, team spirit, and a willingness to learn new technology and new ways of doing things.

SECTION i.3: STARTING YOUR CAREER IN FOOD SERVICE

- Preparing for a career means deciding where your interests lie, what your career goals are, and the type of continuing education you will need to be successful.
- No matter what careers interest you, completing high school and continuing your education are steps to a successful future.
- You must consider your own goals and individual requirements before deciding which college or trade school to attend.
- Your job search might very likely begin in the high school guidance office.
- Other useful sources for your job search include: employment ads in local newspapers; community college bulletin boards; vocational school placement office; state or regional job service offices; counseling services of community agencies; local telephone directories (yellow pages) to contact employers directly; and on-line computer services.
- It is customary to send a typed **cover letter** with a résumé to the potential employer.
- To ensure that your cover letter is read, keep the copy brief and stick to the point. Write in a straightforward manner, and use correct grammar and punctuation.
- A good cover letter should capture the reader's attention, interest, and desire, concluding with a call to action. Follow up all cover letters with a phone call to the potential employer.
- **Networking,** which means contacting people who can give you information about job openings, is an effective job hunting technique.

SECTION i.4: PREPARING YOUR PORTFOLIO AND RÉSUMÉ

- A **portfolio** is a collection of samples that highlight your interests, talents, contributions, and studies.
- Types of items included in a portfolio depend on you and the job you desire. Portfolio samples include lists of your skills and abilities; examples of problem-solving abilities, teamwork, leadership, and responsibility; certificates or awards; newspaper clippings; essays or reports; résumé; test scores; letters of recommendation; or other samples that present your achievements.

- Portfolios should be complete, neat, and well organized.
- A **résumé** is a written summary of your past experience, education, previous jobs, skills, and achievements related to the job you're seeking.
- Résumés and portfolios will change as you gain more experience, training, and education.
- **References** are those people who know you well and can provide information about your character, work ability, or academic standing.

SECTION i.5: COMPLETING APPLICATION FORMS

- **Application forms** ask basic personal information about the applicant's background.
- **College** or **trade school applications** require that you give your education background. The application may also require that you state the program or course of study you are interested in and ask you to complete a short essay.
- You will be asked to have your high school transcript sent to the college also.
- The **job application** form usually asks about your work experience and for references.
- Always check with people before you use them as job references.
- Use correct grammar and punctuation, and organize your thoughts before you write them on the form.
- Leave blank or indicate *n/a* on questions that you do not understand or that do not apply to you.
- Avoid giving salary amounts, except when asked how much money you earned on any previous jobs. Be honest.
- If you have no prior work experience, list any volunteer work or other activities that show you know what is expected at the workplace.
- Dishonesty on a job application can result in immediate termination of your employment. Employers check on educational and work background. They also contact references.

SECTION i.6: THE JOB INTERVIEW

- To create a good first impression at a **job interview,** remember three key points: present a well-groomed personal appearance, have a positive attitude, and use good manners, which are the basis for business **etiquette.**
- Check with the potential employer if you are unsure about what materials you should bring.

- Research basic information about the company before the interview, including the company size and reputation, key products and services, and names of competitors.
- The potential employer will ask questions to see if your talents would be a suitable match for the job available and how you would work with the existing foodservice team.
- There are no correct or incorrect answers to interview questions; however, some responses are more appropriate and impressive than others.
- To break the ice, the interviewer will ask you to talk about yourself. The appropriate response is to discuss your accomplishments, experience, and qualifications in a three-minute summary.
- Other interview questions will attempt to get your view of the company, how you could improve the organization, previous work experience, personal goals, education, work ethic and attitude, dependability, ability to handle pressure, and salary.
- Be prepared to ask questions about the position, advancement opportunities, description of an average work day, starting date, and training.
- Avoid asking questions about money, vacation, bonuses, or holidays. Allow the potential employer to initiate the discussion; however, you should not leave the interview without knowing the salary range.
- Follow up after the interview with a brief note to potential employers thanking them for their time, confirming that you want the job, reinforcing your qualifications, and giving a time when you will follow up with a phone call.
- During the follow-up phone call: remind the person who you are, state the reason for your call, and find out if the potential employer has made a decision.
- If the employer has not made a decision, offer to answer any further questions the interviewer may have about your qualifications.
- Every interview is an opportunity to sharpen your communication skills and meet foodservice professionals.

SECTION i.7: WORKING ON THE JOB

- While your employer won't expect you to learn all procedures your first day on the job, there are certain workplace guidelines that all employees should know.

- You can expect orientation and training the first day of your new job.
- **Orientation** is the process that helps new employees learn about the procedures and policies of the operation and introduces them to their coworkers.
- Training may be done through instruction, as you're used to in the classroom, by viewing videos accompanied by workbooks, or through hands-on training.
- One of the most important items is the **employee manual.**
- A typical employee manual contains information on employment policies; rules and procedures; employee benefits; and other topics, including company history, employee personal space, and job opportunities.
- When you leave a job, for whatever reason, standard business practice recommends you notify your current employer two weeks before you leave, either in writing or in person.
- Write a letter of resignation carefully; you may include your reasons for leaving, but always be polite.
- Avoid negative remarks, and always thank your employer for giving you the opportunity to work for the company.

Welcome back! This unit begins with a review of how the restaurant industry developed, explores cooking techniques for essential starches, and takes a look at opportunities in the lodging industry.

UNIT I

PROFILE

Carol Kizer

Chairperson, Hospitality Management Dept.
Columbus State Community College
Columbus, Ohio

I began working in college, first as part of the kitchen crew on campus, then later as the Women's Work Manager, where I scheduled students for all shifts in the kitchen, laundry room, housekeeping, student center, and library. Managing the students and gaining hands-on experience helped me realize that a foodservice management career was right for me.

I earned a Bachelor's degree in Foods/Nutrition and Institutional Management at the University of Iowa. My first real professional job was as a dietitian and assistant to the director of food service at the Children's Hospital in Columbus, Ohio. I supervised employees, prepared food for patients, catered hospital functions, and managed on-site restaurants.

I came to Columbus State Community College in 1965 to develop and direct one of the first associate degree programs in foodservice management in the country. The program has expanded over the past 30 years to include majors in foodservice/Restaurant Management, Chef Apprenticeship, Dietetic Technician, and Travel/Tourism/Hotel Management, as well as numerous certificate and continuing education programs to match industry needs.

Over the past 30 years, I have been able to work very closely with both the students and the industry. Coordinating student cooperative work experiences offers me the chance to stay in close contact with the industry and to monitor trends and assess how our students are being prepared. If students are going to be successful and truly understand this business, they need to be aware of changing trends, as well as the history behind this industry. What would cooking be today without the knowledge, skills, and innovations of people like Carême and Escoffier!

Not only has history affected how our industry has evolved, but past and current trends continually change the path of the food service. From improved technology, demands for "healthy" menu items, and even the increase in standards from regulatory agencies, such as OSHA and the FDA, the foodservice industry is always evolving. Education and training to prepare oneself to manage these issues is a priority.

To grow with this rapidly expanding industry, students need to understand how the industry has evolved, and how current and future trends will improve the industry as we know it today. We truly learn from past history every day, as we take the best from each situation and learn from our own mistakes.

CHAPTER 1

The History of Food Service

SECTION 1.1

Creating the Modern Restaurant

AFTER STUDYING SECTION 1.1, YOU SHOULD BE ABLE TO:

- Trace the history of the foodservice industry and explain its relationship to world history.
- List famous chefs from history and note their major accomplishments.

This is an exciting time to begin a career in food service. To understand how food service has evolved, we'll take a look at historical events that have affected how we do things today. In this chapter you will learn how the trading of foods, cultures, and traditions led to worldwide expansion of many unique and equally important cultures.

Ancient Greece and Rome

Imagine for a moment that you are a citizen of ancient Greece, visiting Athens for the Olympics. After watching the original games all day, you and your friends decide to go out to eat at a restaurant. Where did you get that idea? **Restaurants,** stores that sell prepared meals for on-site consumption, will not be invented for another 2,000 years!

KEY TERMS

- Café
- Epicurean (ep-ih-KUR-ee-an)
- Guilds
- Haute cuisine (hote kwee-ZEEN)
- Herbs
- Kitchen brigade system
- Pasteurization
- Restaurant
- Spices
- Toque (toek)

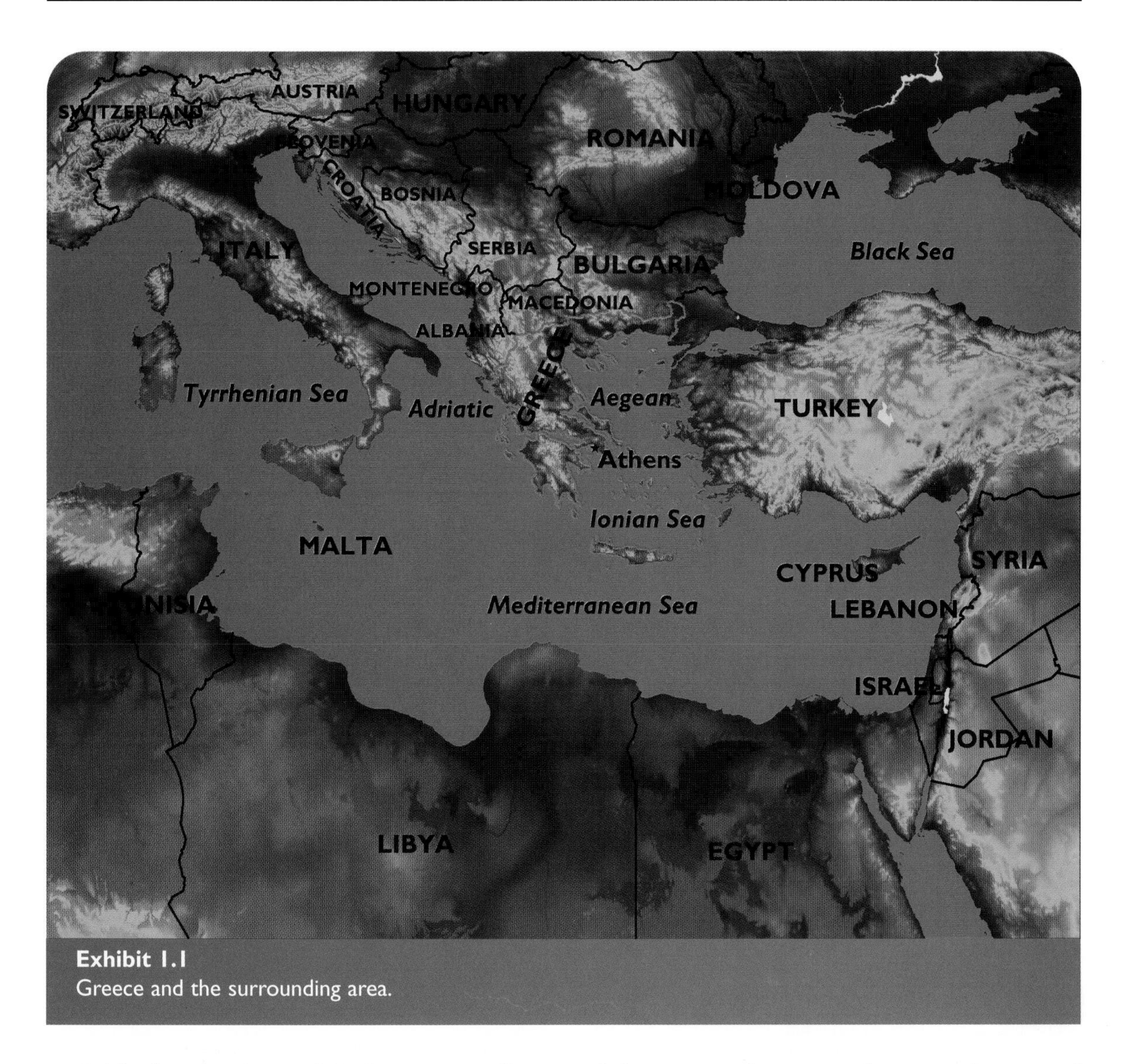

Exhibit 1.1
Greece and the surrounding area.

Did the ancient Greeks never dine out? Of course not. They enjoyed the social aspect of dining and often got together for banquets but they rarely dined out. They did have private clubs called *lesche* that offered food to its members and establishments called *phatnai*. These clubs catered to travelers, traders, and visiting diplomats. But instead of dining out, it is most likely that they brought standard fare like grapes, olives, bread made from barley, dried fish, cheese and wine with them to these clubs.

Exhibit 1.2
Grapes were among the standard fare for the ancient Romans.

In ancient Greece, meals were considered a time to nourish the soul as well as the body. They ate while reclining on couches and enjoyed music, poetry, and dancing to enhance the experience. The Greeks believed that pleasure was the purpose of life and that it was achieved through restraint and balance. A man named Epicurious was the leader of this movement. From his example, we now derive the term **Epicurean** (ep-ih-KUR-ee-an), a person with a refined taste for food and wine.

In 282 B.C. Rome conquered the lands surrounding the Mediterranean Sea that the Greeks had formerly occupied. Unlike the Greeks with their discriminating tastes, the Romans were just the opposite. While the ordinary citizens lived on a simple diet of barley, olive oil, pine nuts, and fish, the wealthy aristocrats held enormous banquets filled with exotic foods, such as humming bird tongues and camel's heels.

The main meal of the day was called *cenna,* or dinner. Often, more than 100 different kinds of fish were served accompanied by wild boar, venison, ostrich, ducks, and peacocks. Dining in public was considered undignified and only men in the lowest classes frequented early taverns.

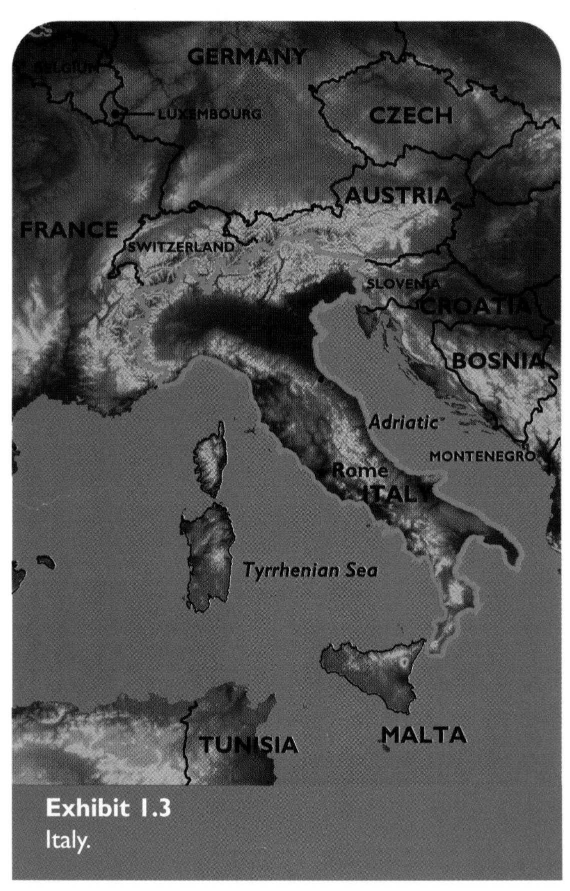

Exhibit 1.3
Italy.

Emperor Lucullus, a Roman general, had a great love for fancy and expensive banquets. Today, people all over the world still describe a fancy and elaborate dining experience as a "meal worthy of Lucullus."

Romans' desires for exotic foods and spices increased trade and stretched the Roman Empire further east and north. They invaded modern day France, Germany, and England as well as west into Spain and Portugal. With their power came increased wealth, which they lavishly spent on banquets for their friends and *cliens,* people of a lower social standing who depended on the aristocracy for financial aid in exchange for political support.

The high ranking politicians also believed that they owed their position in society to the peasant and slave classes and held enormous shows in the coliseum. Every year the newly appointed emperor tried to out-do the previous emperor's event. Chariot races, gladiator fights, and even flooding the floor of the coliseum to stage naval battles were common.

These extravagances eventually began to bankrupt the economy. One Roman in particular, Marcus Apicius, took great effort to obtain the most exotic foods possible for his feasts. He was so interested in cooking that he wrote one of the earliest known cookbooks, *De Re Coquinaria (On Cooking).* Recipes from this book are still used today. His exploits eventually cost him his life. When he realized that he would soon go broke, he poisoned himself rather than die from hunger.

The riches that Romans had accumulated soon interested the nomadic tribesmen in the north. These *barbarians,* the name applied to anyone who was not Roman, repeatedly attacked the Roman settlements in Gaul (the area now known as France).

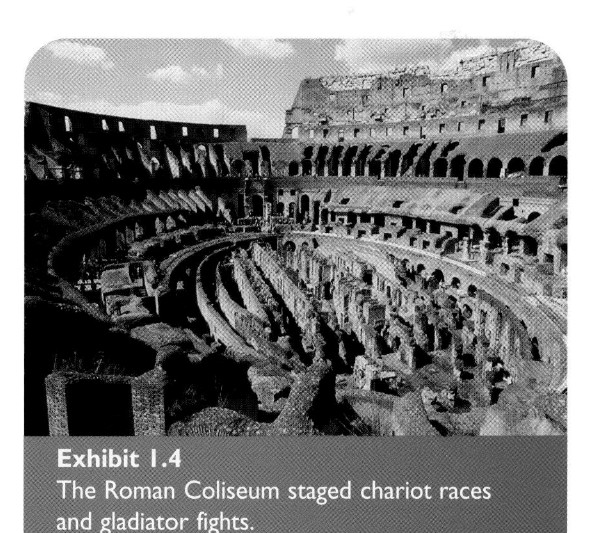

Exhibit 1.4
The Roman Coliseum staged chariot races and gladiator fights.

Due in large part to the declining economy, the Roman armies were unable to stop the Germanic tribes and in A.D. 475 they conquered Rome.

The Early Middle Ages (A.D. 475 - 1000)

The end of the Roman Empire was the beginning of a long, slow period of change in Europe. The conquering German tribes did not adopt Roman democracy. Instead, they returned to their homeland with the same hierarchical system they had followed for centuries. They established small kingdoms and continued to live in small tribes with one chieftain overseeing the entire clan.

What they did take back to Germany was Christianity. Their new faith led to two major changes in their way of life. First, it united Europe into one large church-state called Christendom and second, it ended their view that gods and spirits inhabited the forest. These ancient Nordic myths included the belief that trees were sacred and could not be cut down and that diverting river water for agriculture would displease the gods of the rivers. With this fear dispelled, they began to clear large tracts of land and moved from a nomadic people dependent on hunting and foraging for food to an *agrarian* (farming) society.

Clearing land and developing a farming system required a lot of manual labor. At the same time the small kingdoms were constantly attacking each other to increase their riches. The situation eventually evolved into *feudalism,* the exchange of working the fields and turning over some of the proceeds to the landowner in exchange for safety from invaders.

Life was hard and boring for the *serfs,* the people who worked the fields in a feudal society. They lived on bread made from wheat, peas that could be dried for consumption in the winter months, turnips and onions that could be stored year-round, and cabbage that they fermented into sauerkraut. Their diet was supplemented by meat from pigs that they either salted or smoked to preserve. Hunting was forbidden, since the wild game was owned by the lord of the manor.

The landowner, however, lived in relative comfort. When he wasn't under attack or out attacking someone else, large banquets were held almost every night. Unlike the banquets of the Greeks and Romans, a medieval dinner had only one purpose—to eat!

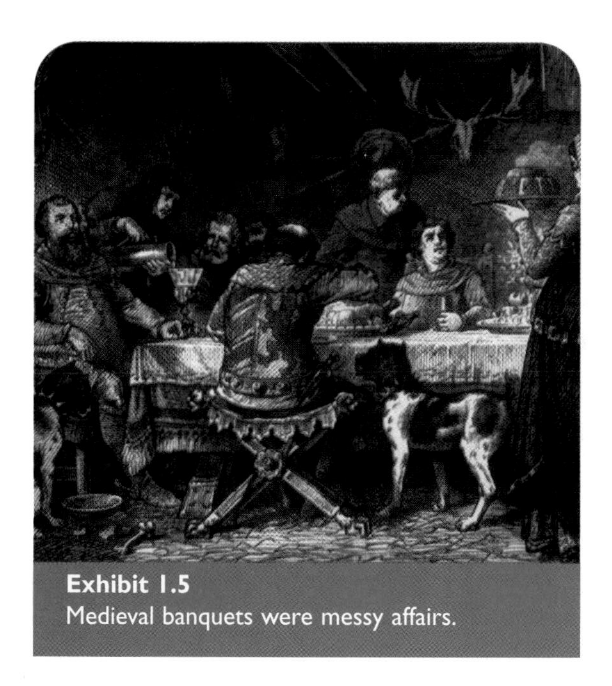

Exhibit 1.5
Medieval banquets were messy affairs.

All the food arrived at the table at the same time. People ate with their fingers and often pulled out knives to cut away huge chunks of meat. Instead of plates, large slices of stale bread called *trenchers* were used to absorb the drippings and were either eaten at the end of the meal or thrown to the dogs who scavenged for scraps of meat and bones that were thrown on the floor.

Travel in those times was extremely dangerous. Trade with the Far East and India was greatly reduced and came to a stop when the *Moors* invaded Spain in A.D. 800 and blocked the shipment of spices and fine goods from reaching Europe. For the next two-hundred years, Europe remained isolated from the rest of the world. It wasn't until A.D. 1095, when Pope Urban II called for the removal of the Moors from Spain and the Holy Lands, that Europeans looked beyond their borders.

The Renaissance (A.D.1400-1600)

The basic diet in the Middle Ages was bland and lacked variety. **Herbs,** aromatic plants used for seasoning, such as thyme, rosemary, and sage grew in the wild and were readily available. What the aristocracy craved, however, were **spices** (bark, roots, seeds, bulbs, or berries from an aromatic plant), used to flavor foods.

To show off their wealth, noblemen instructed their cooks to use large amounts of these spices in their foods. It wasn't long before merchants in Venice held a monopoly on the spice trade. Because of their location on the Adriatic Sea, they could easily obtain spices from India and sell them at very high prices to distributors headed north.

Venice prospered as a seaport, and bought and sold spices and other goods to buyers bound for other destinations.

The desire to break up the Venetian monopoly of the spice market led to the discovery of the New World, the

Americas. Recent technical advances in navigation and shipbuilding made it possible to travel further by sea. The Portuguese sailors were the first to sail around South Africa to India and established a new spice route. As you probably know, Christopher Columbus was looking for a shorter route to India when he discovered America.

This expansion into world travel changed the mindset of the artists and philosophers of that time. They embraced Epicurean lifestyles once again. While this new interest in all things Greek and Roman did not affect the majority of the population, it did much to create the food preparation system we now call **haute cuisine** (hote kwee-ZEEN), a highly skilled system of food preparation.

Exhibit 1.6
The port of Venice.

Today, sitting down to dinner brings to mind visions of plates, cups, silverware, and napkins. As we've already learned, the medieval meal was a messy affair. It wasn't until the *Renaissance,* with its new ideas of life and art and a return to an Epicurean lifestyle, that a higher style of eating began. The movement started in Italy and was carried into France by Catherine de Medici in 1533 when she married King Henry II of France. She brought her entire staff of cooks, their refined recipes for artichokes, spinach dishes, and ice cream to the French court. She also introduced the French to the fork. The use of silverware quickly caught on and soon people could be found carrying their own silverware with them whenever they dined out.

International trade greatly improved the European way of life. They were introduced to coffee from Africa. This new drink quickly became very popular and coffeehouses sprang up in all major cities. The first coffeehouse, or **café** opened in 1650 in Oxford, England. Unlike the dark and imposing taverns, pubs, and ale

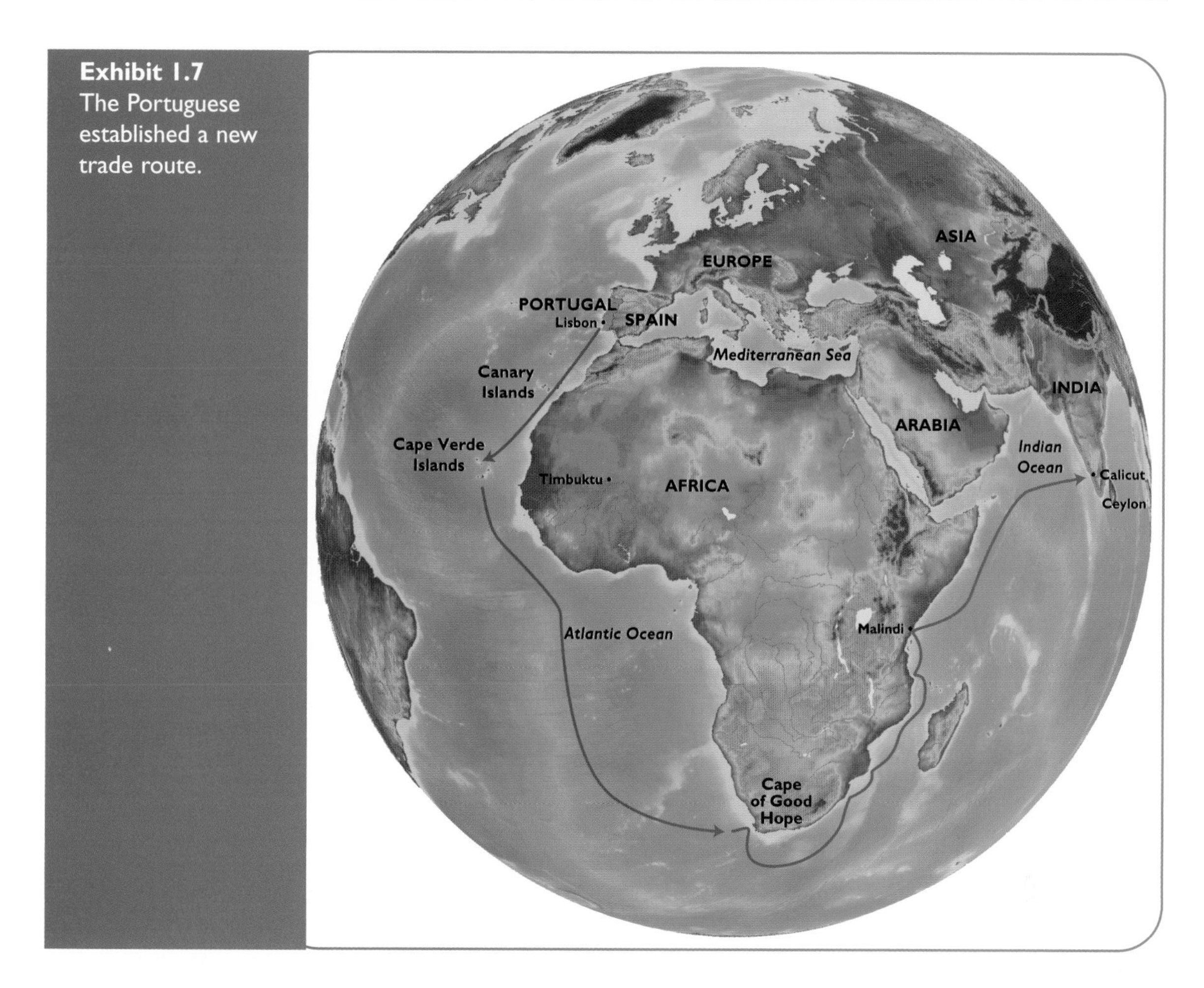

Exhibit 1.7
The Portuguese established a new trade route.

houses that catered only to men, the new coffeehouses were open, airy, and inviting. Smart bakers soon started offering pastries at these establishments. Women were welcome, and the coffee shop soon made it acceptable to eat in public.

Guilds—associations of people with similar interests or professions—were organized during the reign of Louis XIV in France (1643-1715), in an attempt to increase the state's control over the economy. Each guild controlled the production of its specialties and could prevent others from making and selling the same items. Two of these guilds were the *Chaine de Rotissieres (roasters)* and the *Chaine de Traiteurs (caterers)*. Cooking guilds established many of the professional standards and traditions that exist today.

To this day, dishes prepared with spinach are still called *florentine* (such as Eggs Florentine and Chicken Florentine) after Catherine's birthplace, Florence, Italy.

In 1765, a man named Boulanger began serving hot soups in his café that he called *restaurers* for their health restoring properties. He called his café a *restorante,* the origin of our modern word *restaurant.* His *restorante* became very popular. People enjoyed having a place to go to have a hot meal and good conversation with friends.

The foodservice guilds believed that he was moving in on their business and took their case to court. They argued that Mr. Boulanger's soups were under their domain and demanded that he stop immediately. They had a strong case, but the government was under even stronger pressure to alleviate the poverty that was causing social unrest in Paris. The French government had been helping pay for the price of bread in Paris, where the poverty was at its worst. They saw Mr. Boulanger's new business as a way to employ more people and allowed him to continue.

Despite the government's attempt to end the political unrest, the French Revolution erupted anyway. When the French Revolution was over, large numbers of cooks and other guild members found themselves unemployed, since their employers were either dead or banished from France. They followed Boulanger's example and began opening restaurants of their own. Noblemen who had survived opened restaurants in their homes. Within 30 years Paris had over 500 restaurants serving meals. Dining out on a large scale was born.

Exhibit 1.8
New coffeehouses were open, airy, and inviting.

The sign that someone was a member of a cooking guild was the pleated chef's hat called a toque (toek). The white toque was worn by apprentices, or chefs in training. A black toque became the mark of a master chef. Today, the Society of the Golden Toque in the United States is an organization of master chefs elected by their peers.

Industrial Revolution

While Europe was importing silver and spices, they were finding a large international market for their finished goods, in particular, cloth made from wool, silk, or linen. Turning raw wool into cloth is a slow process that requires a lot of different steps. In order to keep up with the demand, wool merchants developed a putting-out system of production that created *cottage industries.* Cottage industries were made up of families that worked together in the home to produce goods. These cottage industries put cash in the hands of farm laborers and eventually lead to the start of the Industrial Revolution.

Realizing that farmers sat idle most of the year, merchants persuaded farmers to work for them. Entire families were involved in producing goods, like wool for clothing.

Unfortunately, problems arose from these cottage industries. Cheating often occurred. For example, disputes over the weight of wool given to the family compared to the amount of finished goods was a constant complaint. Sometimes the families had trouble meeting their weekly quotas. After being paid, the men of the family often spent the weekend drinking in

Exhibit 1.9
After the French Revolution, cooks and other guild members found themselves unemployed.

taverns until the money ran out and then returned home too late to make the next week's quota.

Merchants soon decided to find a better way to control production and began to build factories near large towns where they could find employees. These early factories were operated by children from local orphanages, but when the English government outlawed this practice, merchants again turned to the farming family. Realizing the opportunity to earn a better living, entire families moved to the city to find work in these emerging factories.

Exhibit 1.10
Making cloth from wool became a cottage industry during the Industrial Revolution.

This mass migration put a heavy stress on cities. People needed to live close enough to the factory to walk to work, go home for lunch, and again for dinner. This packed the inexpensive areas of town with people. The sewage system was inadequate to handle the population and often backed up, filling the streets with filth. It was extremely unsanitary. The problem became so intolerable that cities such as Paris began to run horse and buggy transit buses to help employees move out of the overcrowded areas.

Since work in the factory was long, up to 12 hours a day, entertainment became a necessary way to escape the drudgery. Music houses and review shows that served ale soon flourished.

Science, Technology, and Food Service

While the Renaissance did not affect the poorest in society, it sparked the scientific revolution known now as the *Enlightenment* which changed the way

Exhibit 1.11
During the Industrial Revolution, people crowded into cities.

knowledge was obtained and accepted. The new scientific method relied on information from direct observation and mathematical logic, instead of previously accepted sources, such as ancient religious texts and traditions. This period of intellectual growth in the 18th century changed the way scientists looked at the world and affected the health of everyone.

One of the most important improvements in health from scientific research was the discovery of vitamins in 1919. Fruit, vegetables, and whole grain breads were considered poor man's food. The very wealthy dined exclusively on meat at all meals, varied only by sauces, cheeses, and wine. A large portion of the aristocracy suffered from *gout*—a painful inflammation in the feet and hands. Soon it was learned that iodine was needed to avoid this disease. To this day, iodine is added to certain food items, like salt, to prevent this disease.

As more people moved to the cities it became necessary to increase food production. Scientists met this challenge by inventing chemical fertilizers and pesticides that doubled food production. They also taught farmers how to rotate crops. Instead of leaving half or a third of the fields *fallow*—fields plowed but not seeded for a year to allow them to restore necessary nutrients—farmers learned that some plants, like peanuts and beans, could return much needed nitrogen—an essential element for all growth—to the soil.

During this advancement in science and the increased interest in food production, Louis Pasteur developed a process to make milk safe to drink called **pasteurization.** By heating milk to a certain temperature, the harmful bacteria were destroyed. Another scientist named Nicolas Appert discovered a way to can food to keep it fresh and safe to eat. The discovery of refrigeration kept food from spoiling quickly and also helped to feed larger numbers of people.

Carême and Escoffier

Today, the term *chef* is a mark of respect and distinction that describes a professional cook who has reached the position through hard work and dedication to quality. There are two men in history that helped advance the role of the chef, earning the level of respect and admiration it has today. These men were Carême and Escoffier.

In the late 18th century, dining in France was elevated to new heights. More and more restaurants were opening and serving a wide variety of people, from the very wealthy, to the very poor. A few of these restaurants focused on serving *grand cuisine,* or elaborate meals with many courses of intricately prepared food.

Exhibit 1.12
Louis Pasteur developed the process of pasteurization.

The art of grand cuisine was perfected by Marie-Antoine Carême, one of the world's most famous chefs. Carême was born just before the French Revolution into a large and very poor family, and at the age of ten was sent to make his way in the world.

He learned the basics of cooking in a small restaurant. Carême soon developed a reputation for excellence, and worked with the greatest chefs of the time.

Carême also perfected the recipe for many fine French sauces and dishes like *consommé* and *pièces mountées* (food that has been decoratively shaped). Many would agree that Carême's greatest claim to fame was training many famous chefs who became his followers and continued his tradition in many fine hotels and restaurants.

In 1898, a chef named Georges Auguste Escoffier, along with Cesar Ritz, opened London's Savoy Hotel. Georges Auguste Escoffier is credited with refining the grand cuisine of Carême into *classical cuisine.* Escoffier simplified the flavors, dishes, and garnishes of grand cuisine believing that fewer ingredients in a meal maintain balance and perfection. For example, he simplified Carême's system of classifying sauces into the five grand sauces that are still used today. You will learn more about sauces in *Chapter 10: Stocks, Soups, and Sauces.*

Exhibit 1.13
Marie-Antoine Carême perfected the art of grand cuisine.

Escoffier not only took great care in his food preparation, he also established exact rules of conduct and dress for his chefs. In the kitchen, Escoffier's staff always dressed neatly and worked quietly. He also organized and defined the role of workers in the professional kitchen. He was the first to use the **kitchen brigade system,** a system that assigns certain responsibilities to kitchen staff. For example, Escoffier introduced the *aboyuer,* or announcer, who takes orders from servers and calls out the orders to the various production areas in the kitchen. This system is still used today, and has been adapted to fit the modern restaurant.

As you can see, the development of the foodservice industry can be traced back for centuries. The growth of ancient civilizations, trade among nations, and improvements in science and technology all played a part in making food service the successful industry it is today. In Section 1.2 you will learn how some of the unique cuisines of the world developed.

FUN FOOD FACT

Marie-Antoine Carême was known as the "cook of kings and the king of cooks." He worked as a chef for the French statesman Tallyrand, Czar Alexander I of Russia, and the banking giant, Baron Rothschild.

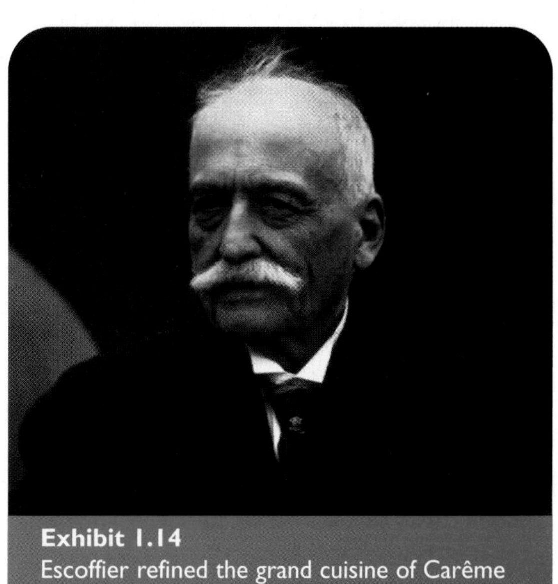

Exhibit 1.14
Escoffier refined the grand cuisine of Carême into classical cuisine.

Review Your Learning 1.1

1. Which Roman created one of the first cookbooks, *De Re Coquinaria (On Cooking)?*
   a. Marcus Apicius
   b. Emperor Lucullus
   c. King Henry II
   d. Catherine de Medici

2. What did the Ancient Greeks and Romans have in common?
   a. They all ate from trenchers
   b. They ate salted, or preserved, meat as their main staple
   c. They enjoyed feasting at large banquets
   d. They developed cooking guilds

3. What culinary advancement did Catherine de Medici bring to France?
   a. Grand cuisine
   b. Haute cuisine
   c. Classic cuisine
   d. Noveau cuisine

4. How did Boulanger affect the growth of the foodservice industry?
   a. He invented cooking guilds
   b. He developed the method of pasteurization
   c. He opened the first café
   d. He opened the first restaurant

5. Pasteurization is the process of:
   a. canning foods to keep them fresh and safe to eat.
   b. heating milk to remove harmful bacteria.
   c. boiling water to eliminate germs.
   d. cleaning cooking utensils to make sure they are safe and sanitary.

6. What were the significant contributions made to food service by Escoffier and Carême?

1.2

SECTION 1.2

Cuisines of the World

AFTER STUDYING SECTION 1.2, YOU SHOULD BE ABLE TO:

- Identify global cultures and traditions related to food.

Food has always been the center around which people have come together to share stories, enjoy each other's company, and celebrate wonderful occasions.

KEY TERMS

- Cajun
- Ché (kay)
- Chutney
- Clambake
- Creole (KREE-ole)
- Curry
- Roux (roo)
- Shish kebab
- Tao (dow)

In this section, we will explore other regions of the world and how they combine food, culture, and tradition. The regions of the world we will discuss are:

- Asia (China, Japan and India);
- the Middle East and Africa; and
- the Americas—including the Caribbean Islands, Latin America, and North America.

Asian Cuisine

Cooking in China

The Chinese were the first to control fire and apply it to the cooking of food. In China, foods have meaning beyond the nourishment they provide. Their cuisine is based on the *yin* and *yang* philosophy of the Tao (dow)—the belief that a single guiding principle orders the universe. Foods should not be forced to become something they are not, and should be kept in their most natural and pure state. They believe that every

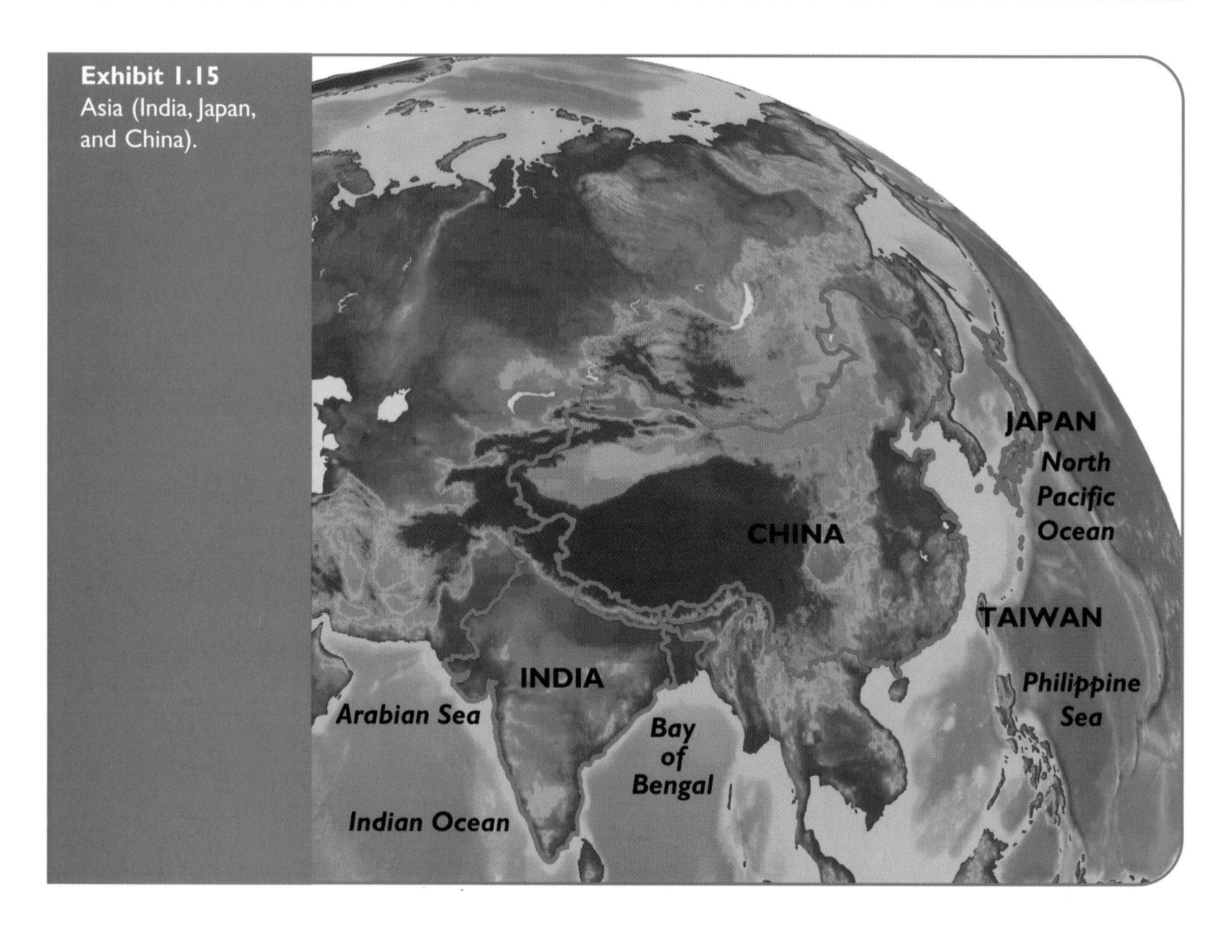

Exhibit 1.15
Asia (India, Japan, and China).

food has an inherent character ranging from hot to cold. For example, cooked soybeans are hot, vinegar is mild, and spinach is cold. The Chinese often say that they eat the symbol, not the nourishment.

A Chinese religious belief divides the world into five parts: earth, wood, fire, metal, and water. These correspond to the five flavors: sweet, sour, bitter, pungent, and salty. Each of these affect different parts of the body: stomach, liver, heart, lungs, and kidneys.

Another important principle is balance. Unlike a western meal with its division of meat, starch, and green vegetables, a Chinese recipe carefully combines *tan* (grains and

Exhibit 1.16
The five parts of the world and their corresponding flavors.

Part		Flavor
Earth	→	Sweet
Wood	→	Sour
Fire	→	Bitter
Metal	→	Pungent
Water	→	Salty

rice) with *ts'ai* (vegetables and meat). Think for a moment of Broccoli Beef or Sweet and Sour Pork—these classic dishes are good examples of combining tan and ts'ai.

In the 14th century a scholar named Chin a Ming wrote a treatise on the properties of various foods called *Yin Shih Hou Chih (the Essential Knowledge of Eating and Drinking)*. He listed the characteristics of 50 different grains, beans, and seeds; 87 vegetables; 63 fruits and nuts; and 33 flavorings such as vinegar, oils, and sauces. It is important to note the large variety of foods available to the Chinese at that time compared to the limited diet in Europe.

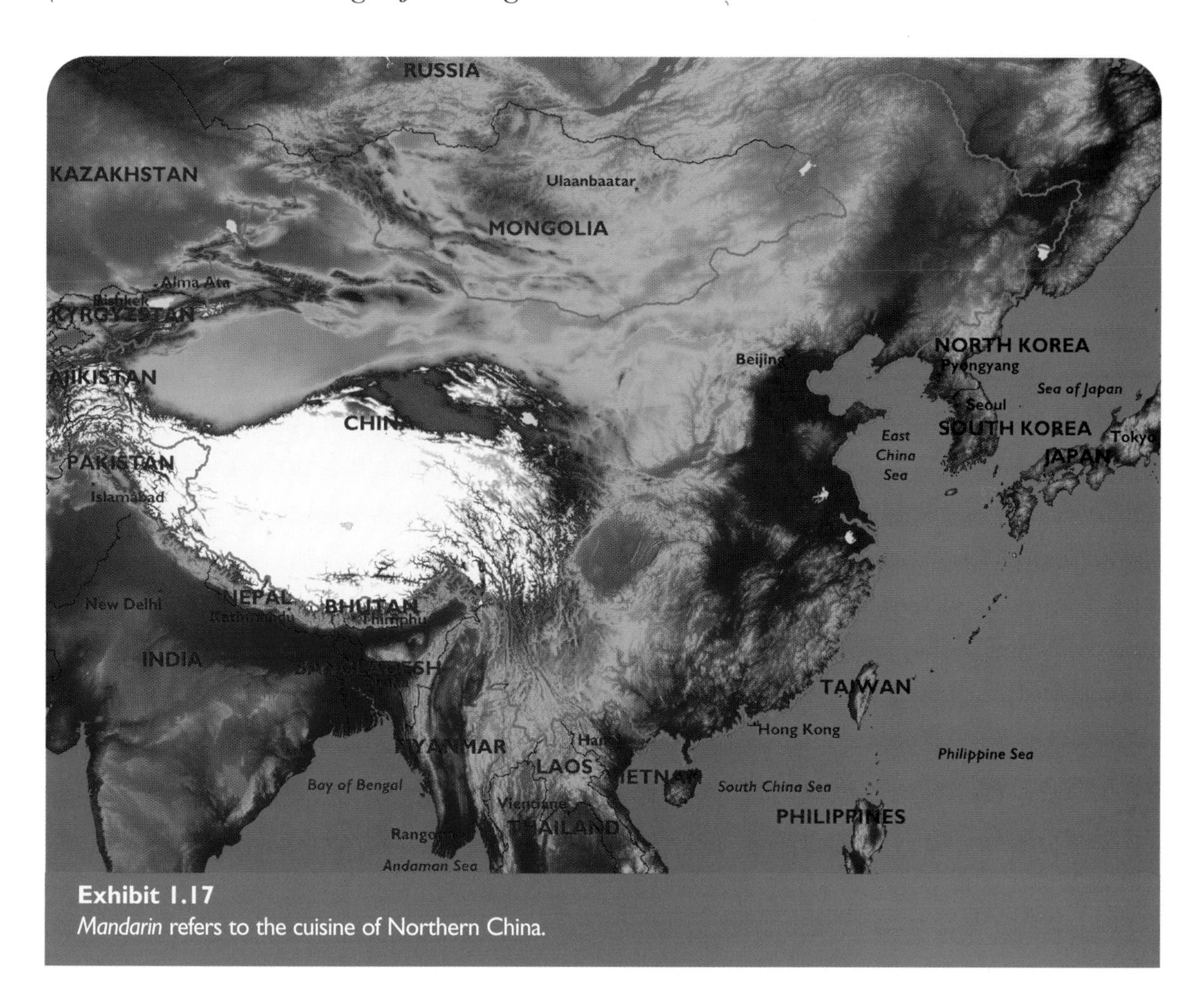

Exhibit 1.17
Mandarin refers to the cuisine of Northern China.

China has the largest population in the world. The country is vast with many different climates, from the cold mountains in the north, the coastal regions in the southeast and the desert step in the west. There are also a number of different languages and dialects as well as native cooking styles that have developed over the centuries. Three of these cuisines are especially important to us since they are the most well known in the United States.

Mandarin

Mandarin is the cuisine of the northern region of China. Mandarin cuisine refers to the elaborate and delicate specialties prepared for the elite members of the Imperial court in Peking. Typical flavors include soy bean paste, dark soy sauce, rice wine, and onions including garlic, leeks, scallions, and chives. Unlike other parts of China, wheat, not rice, is the standard starch. Foods such as dumplings, noodles, and steamed buns filled with pork or minced garlic and scallions are frequently found on the menu. This region is famous for *Bird's Nest Soup, Peking Duck,* and *Mu Shoo Pork.*

Szechwan-Hunan

The cuisine from the neighboring provinces of Szechwan and Hunan are best known for their hot, spicy foods. The introduction of hot chili peppers 150 years ago from South America greatly changed the cooking style of this region. Once again, balance is an important factor in the cuisine. A well-trained chef uses the hot spices to enhance the flavor of foods. As the heat fades away, the underlying five flavors practiced by the Tao should come forward.

Aside from chilis, cooks also use Szechwan pepper, garlic, scallions, five-spice powder (a blend of anise seed, Szechwan pepper, fennel seed, cloves, and cinnamon), mushrooms, ginger, and fennel. The primary meats are chicken and pork. Due to its distance from the sea, fish plays a very small part in their diet. Examples of this cuisine that you may be familiar with are *Kung Pao Chicken* (Hunan) and *Hot and Sour Soup* (Szechwan).

Canton

The city of Canton is situated on the Pearl river, 90 miles inland from the South China Sea. Because of this important location, it became an international trading center.

This cuisine was the first to be introduced to the United States. The Chinese men who immigrated to California during the gold rush and later to work on the

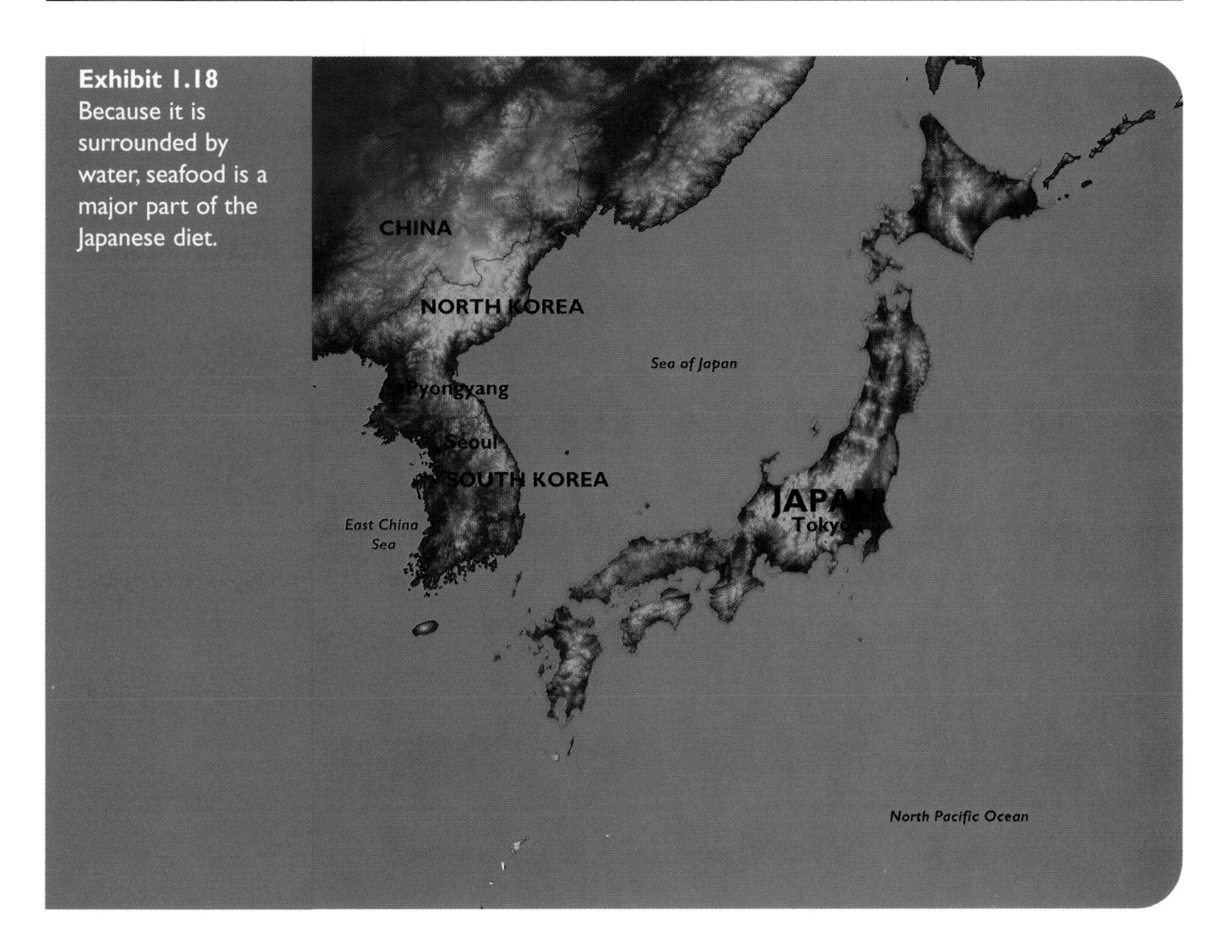

Exhibit 1.18
Because it is surrounded by water, seafood is a major part of the Japanese diet.

building of the trans-continental railroad brought with them their cooking techniques. Many of their native dishes remained the same, but in their attempts to attract Americans to their cuisine they invented Chop Suey and fortune cookies. The cuisine of this region strives for color harmony as well as a yin and yang balance. The most notable dishes are *Sweet and Sour Pork, Egg Foo Yung,* and *Lemon Chicken.*

Cooking in Japan

Japan's cuisine is highly stylized with more of an emphasis on artistic presentation rather than flavor. They use almost no spices or herbs and only a small amount of seasonings, such as soy sauce and vinegar.

Chinese traders introduced tea to the Japanese in the 13th century. It was first used by Buddhist monks to stay awake during long sessions of meditation. The practice of drinking tea spread and developed into an elaborate ceremony called *Cha-no-Yu*. In the 16th century a man named San Rikyu formalized the ceremony that is still followed today.

The ceremony takes place in a small detached building away from the house. To show cleanliness, guests must first wash their hands and rinse their mouths before entering. Once inside, the host serves small sweets and then prepares the tea. The leaves are first pulverized and then quickly stirred in hot water. The tea is usually thin and frothy with a mild flavor. Once the tea is consumed, the guests are free to inquire about the various tools used in the ceremony. They might also discuss the paintings, calligraphy, and floral arrangements displayed in the room. Afterward, the tea service is carried from the room and the ceremony is over.

The Japanese rely on fish as a major source of food. The rich variety from the waters that surround them have led to numerous techniques of preparation. There are three main ways to prepare Japanese food.

- *Tempura*—This method of breading and then deep frying was introduced by the Portuguese. The Japanese however made it their own by using a much more delicate batter.

Exhibit 1.19
A plate of sushi.

- *Sashimi* and *Sushi*—Sashimi is sliced raw fish. Sushi can be raw fish or eggs, fish roe, or shrimp and is served with cold rice flavored vinegar.
- *Yakimosno*—These are foods that are broiled and are best known by the names of Yakitori (marinated skewered chicken), Teriyaki (marinated meat or fish), Sinoyaleil (fish salted for 1–2 hours before broiling), and Tappan-Yaki (food cooked on a table-top grill).

They also enjoy soups, most of which are clear, and lightly seasoned. Thicker *miso* soups are flavored with fermented soybean paste.

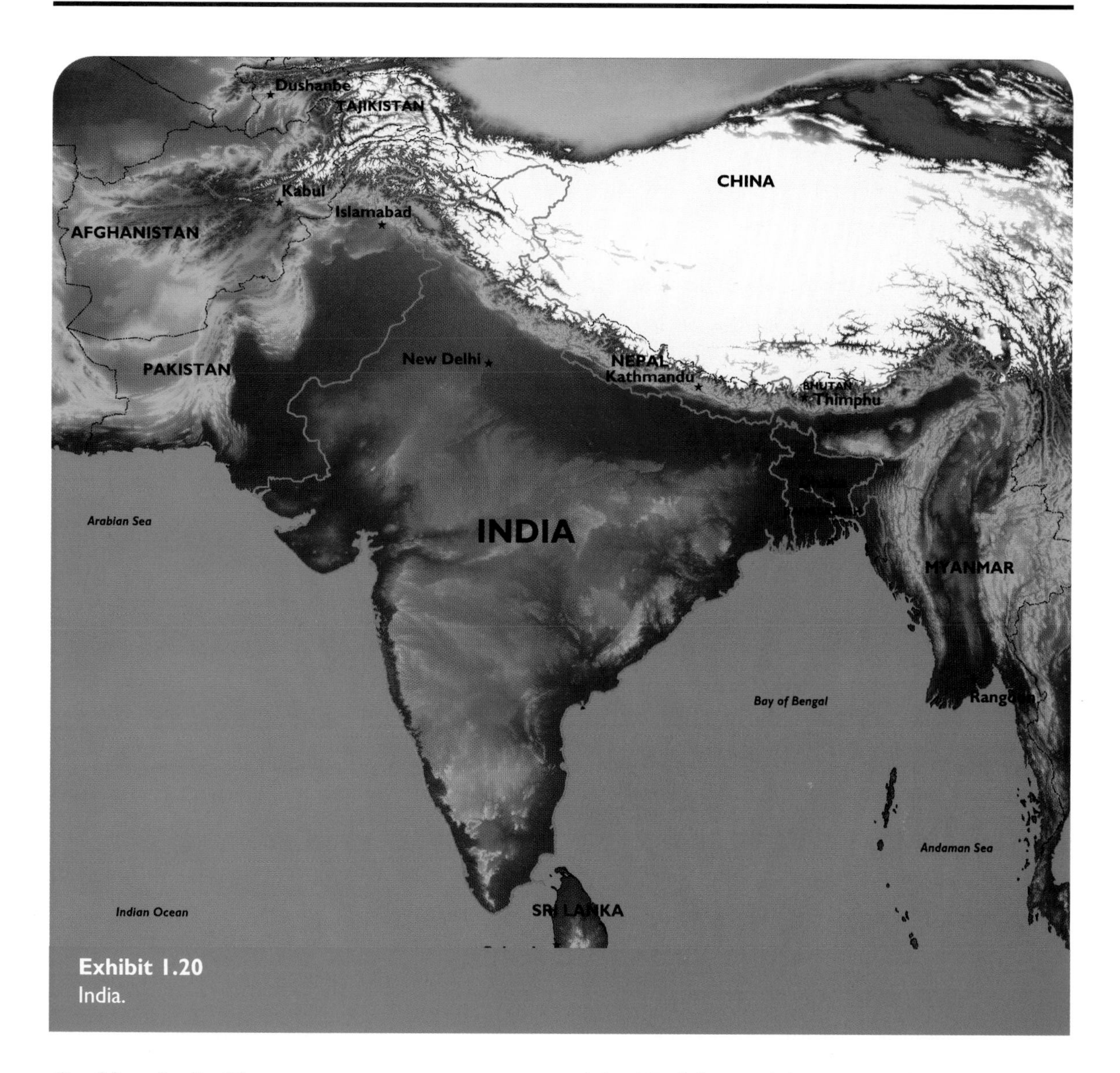

Exhibit 1.20
India.

Cooking in India

No other country's cuisine has been so heavily influenced by its religion than has India's cuisine. India's Hindus are almost all vegetarians. Their belief in the cleansing properties of cow's milk and **ché** (kay) (clarified butter) has turned the cow into a sacred animal. To this day, large cows can be seen roaming freely in the streets of major cities.

Another interesting fact about Hindus is their tolerance for other religions. Many

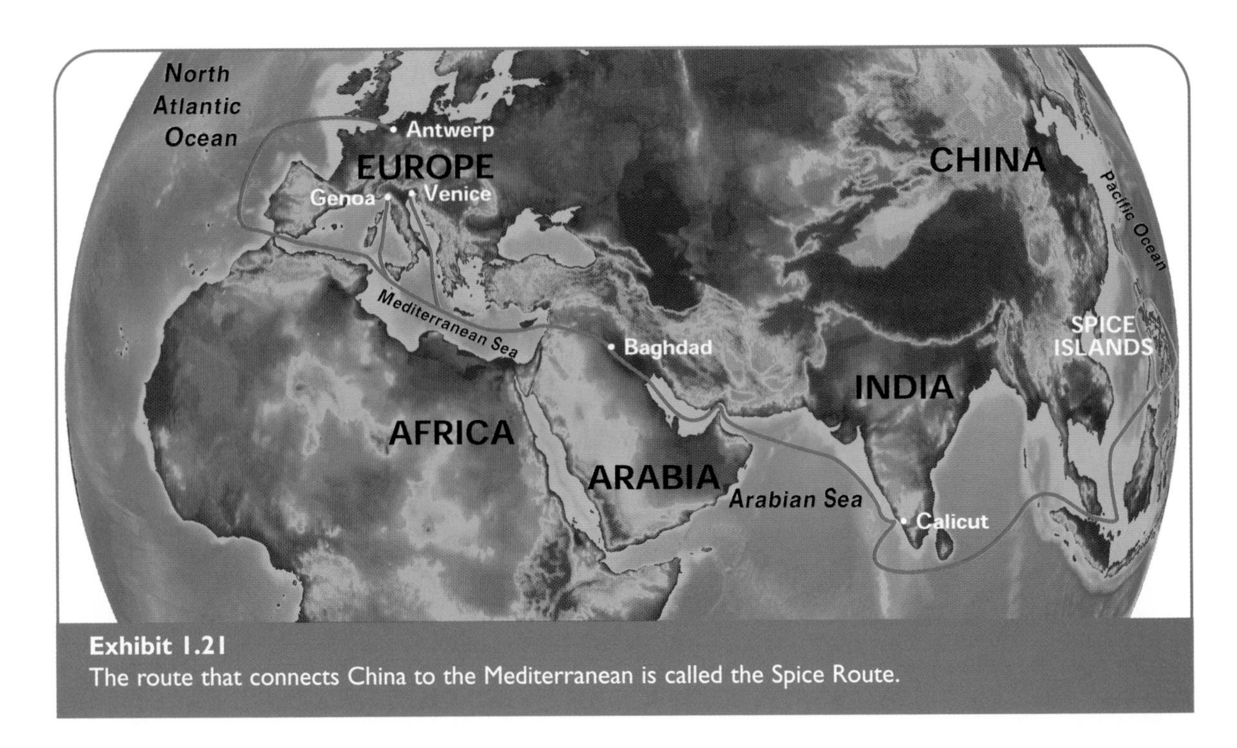

Exhibit 1.21
The route that connects China to the Mediterranean is called the Spice Route.

countries have occupied India in order to control the trade of their high quality rugs and spices. Because Hinduism incorporates all forms of worship without requiring followers to choose one idea over another, they have easily coexisted with these conquerors. This is especially evident in the north, where a large percentage of the population does eat meat, mostly mutton and beef.

How did this happen? India is the place where east meets west. Early Chinese traders traveled across the northern portion of the country to sell their goods to the ancient Greeks living along the Aegean Sea. Eventually, India joined this movement, offering their prize tapestries, rice, numerous exotic foods, and spices to people in China and Greece. This highway, that stretches from China to the Mediterranean, is known as the *Spice Route.* Numerous invaders have tried to control it. For a long time the Islamic people controlled the traffic and settled in the northern part of India to regulate trade. They brought with them their Muslim faith that allows them to eat meat. Today a large portion of the population is still Muslim.

The Indian cuisine exposes its diners to more flavor combinations than any other cooking style in the world. A typical kitchen has more than 30 spices to choose from. A quick glance at any traditional Indian recipe will show a long list of spices. Some combinations are standard and were packaged and sold by English merchants as **curry**, which is made of turmeric, coriander, cumin, red and black pepper, cinnamon, ginger, star anise, cloves, and nutmeg. Most people recognize curry for its bright orange color but in different parts of the country or in different dishes it may be green, yellow, orange, or even red-brown.

They use their mastery of spices to produce dishes that are either hot and sour, hot and nutty, sweet and hot, bitter and hot, bitter and sour, or sweet and salty. Sometimes, to achieve a desired combination, **chutney**—a relish made of fruits, spices, and herbs—is served on the side.

Exhibit 1.22
Fresh ginger is found in curry.

Traditionally, Indians eat with their hands. They use *naan,* a whole wheat flat bread, crisp on the outside and spongy inside, to scoop. The bread is baked on the inside walls of a *tandoor* oven (a clay oven) while cooking tandoori chicken, a succulent red chicken.

Rice is native to the southern area of India and has been introduced to countries throughout the world. Unlike the standard long grain rice that is now common in American households, Indians choose from over 2000 varieties, each with its own distinctive flavor, such as *Jasmine* and *Basmati.*

Africa and the Middle East

Cooking in the Middle East

The Middle Eastern nations of Turkey, Syria, Egypt, Saudi Arabia, Iran, Iraq, Kuwait, Israel, Jordan, and Lebanon sit at the eastern end of the Mediterranean Sea. Nestled between India and the Far East, Europe, and Africa, these nations for centuries have been the crossroads of international trade and exploration. While each nation has developed distinct cuisines, all of these nations share many common foods that form the basis of their cooking.

For centuries, the spice trade from the Far East and India to Europe and other parts of the world traveled through the Middle East. This brought new foods and spices to the land. For example, eggplant was first planted in the Middle East over 1,500 years ago and has been a major part of the Middle Eastern diet ever since. It is often served in stews, fried, or grilled. Spices like pepper, cinnamon, and cardamom were introduced to the Middle East, and along with flavorings native to the region like lemon, lime, garlic, mint, and dill, flavor many Middle Eastern dishes.

Just as in India, cattle are rarely eaten in Middle Eastern nations. The hot, dry climate is not suitable to raise cattle.

Exhibit 1.24
The Middle East has long been a crossroads of international trade and exploration.

Exhibit 1.23
Shish kebab is a common Middle Eastern dish.

Instead, sheep are raised and lamb is by far the most popular and commonly eaten meat in the Middle East. Lamb is often cubed and cooked on skewers with other vegetables called **shish kebab.**

Lamb is also often mixed with grains and yogurt, another Middle Eastern staple, and used as stuffing for all kinds of vegetables like peppers, tomatoes, and zucchini. They especially like to stuff grape leaves with minced lamb, rice, beans, and even yogurt. When grapes leaves are unavailable they use spinach or cabbage leaves.

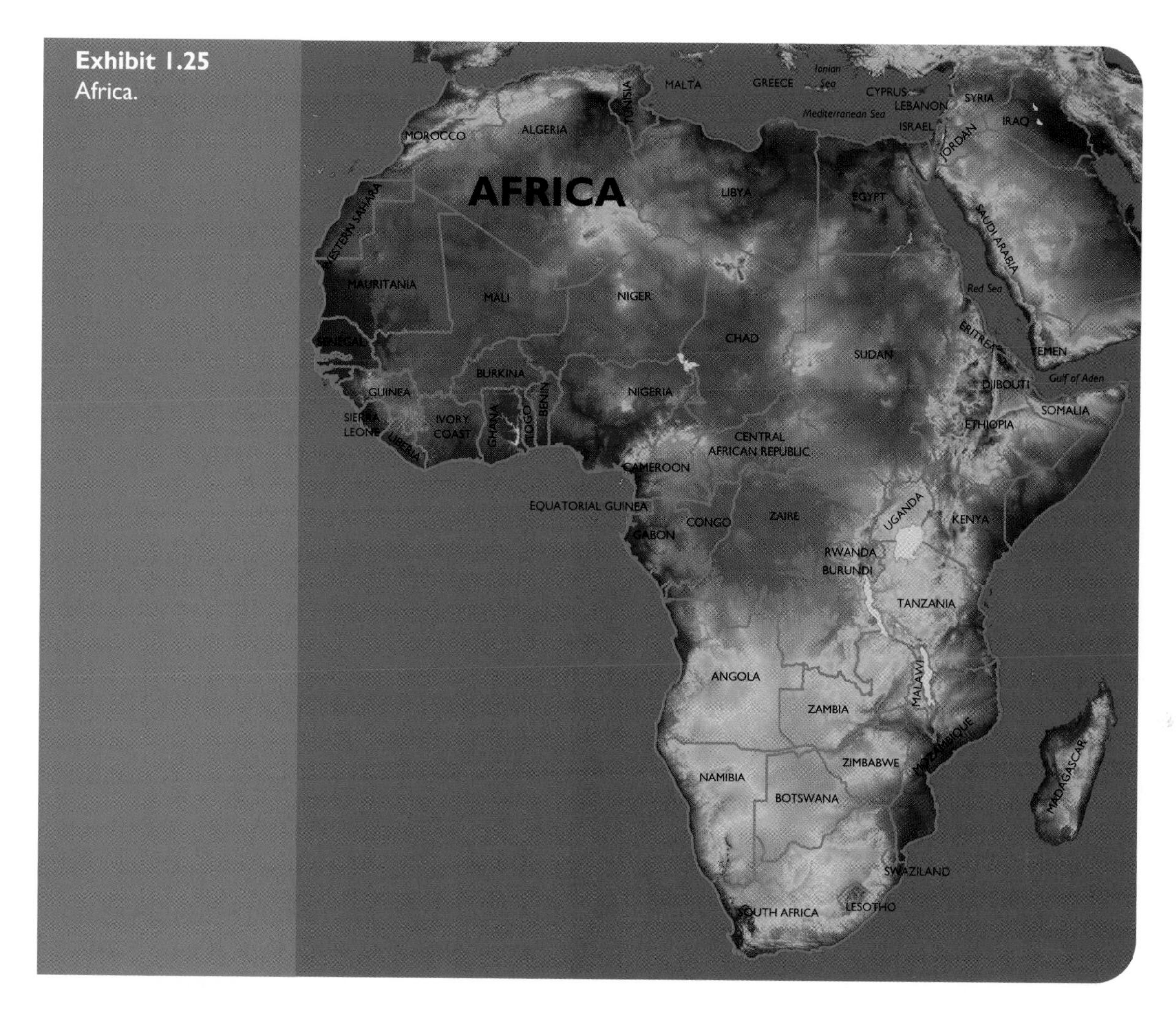

Exhibit 1.25
Africa.

Cooking in Africa

Africa is home to 800 languages, thousands of dialects, and many different cultures. Like all of the countries and regions we've learned about so far, African culture and cuisine have been influenced by hundreds of years of invasions, settlers, and trade with other countries.

The African landscape is extremely diverse, as it includes deserts, rainforests, lakes, mountains, and an immense and expansive coastline. Though Africa is a large continent, there are common foods that form the basis for African cuisine.

Throughout Africa, beans, lentils, barley, millet, wheat, peanuts, and yams are the

Exhibit 1.26
Bananas are grown in the rainforests of western Africa.

main food staples. Grains are made into breads, dumplings, and biscuits that are eaten at most meals, along with stews of vegetables, beans, and meat. For African countries that border the ocean, fresh fish and seafood are also a major part of the diet. Further inland, milk and dry curd cheeses are major sources of protein. The tropical rainforests and jungles of western Africa provide an abundance of exotic foods like coconut, bananas, plantains, and palm oil and palm nuts from the palm tree.

European settlers introduced a number of new foods to Africa. Portuguese explorers brought spices from India, like cloves, saffron, cinnamon, and pepper. From South America came chili peppers, tobacco, tomatoes, pineapple, corn, and sweet potatoes. Over the centuries, these foods have become an important part of African cuisine.

The Cuisines of the Americas

Caribbean Cooking

After the discovery of the New World, tales of unbelievable wealth soon traveled throughout Europe. Explorers quickly left for the Americas in search of these riches. They initially followed Christopher Columbus' route and settled on different islands in the Caribbean and influenced the local cuisine. On Martinique and Haiti the focus is French, while on Jamaica and Barbados, English foods and language are most common. The recipes of Puerto Rico and Cuba are Spanish in nature.

The tropical climate was perfect for agricultural development, and soon the production of native foods such as sugarcane, bananas, coconut, and mango trees began. Settlers also imported staples from home such as flour, olive oil, spices, pigs, chicken, and cattle.

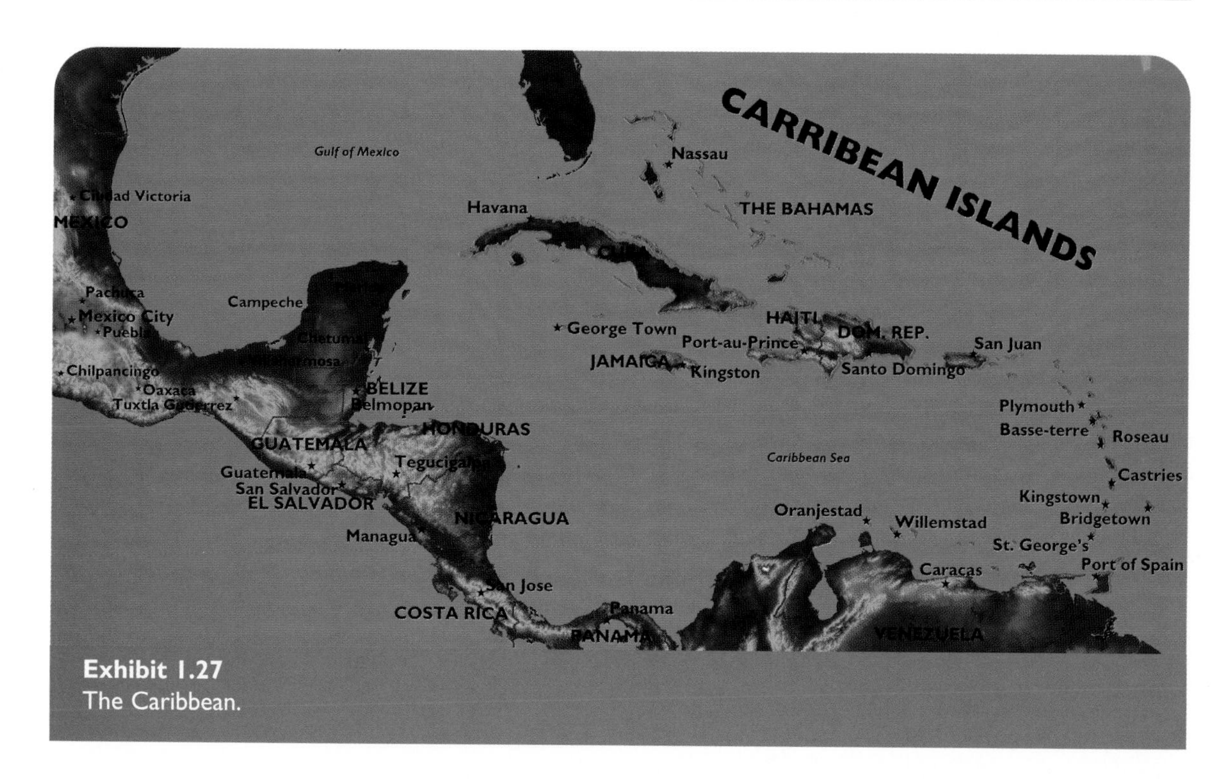

Exhibit 1.27
The Caribbean.

The real riches in the Caribbean are its shellfish, such as spiny lobster and conch. Allspice is indigenous to the islands and is a distinctive flavoring widely used in Caribbean cuisine. Today a visitor to the islands would sample such local specialties as *Conch Soup,* spicy Jamaican *Jerk* rubs (used for barbecues), *Shrimp and Papaya Salad,* or *Mango Pork.*

Latin and South American Cooking

When the Spanish conquerers first arrived in Latin America they found a highly developed civilization living in the mountainous region of Peru. While they never found the cities of gold they were after, they did find a number of foods that became important additions to European cuisine including peppers (both hot and mild), tomatoes, corn, beans, potatoes, squash, peanuts, avocados, and chocolate.

There were almost no domesticated animals in Latin America when the Spanish arrived. The *Aztecs* lived high up on steep mountains. The coastal areas along the Pacific are too dry and inhospitable to sustain life. In order to feed themselves they made terraces in the mountains to plant crops. This land did not offer enough space to raise animals for food. They ate no dairy

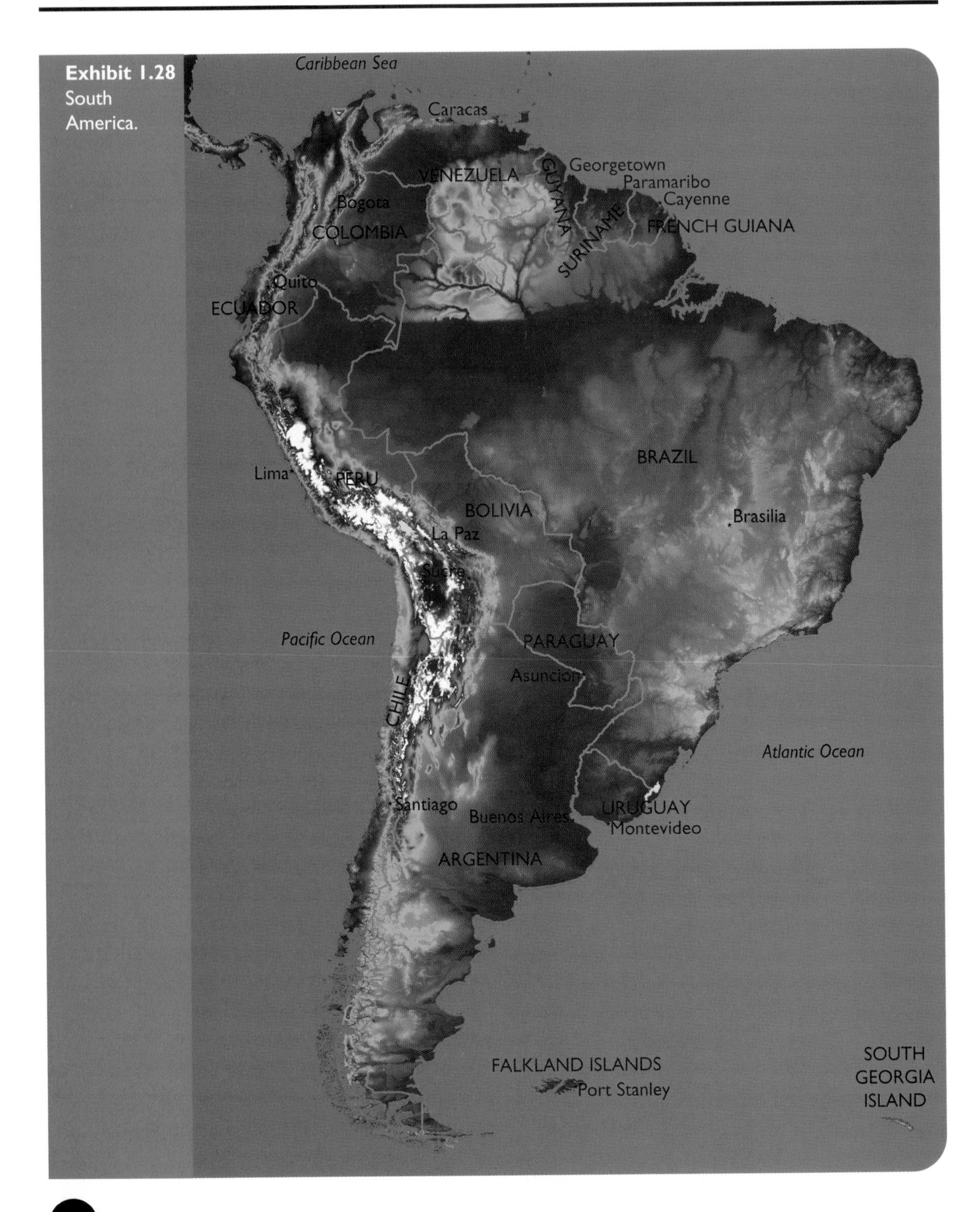

Exhibit 1.28 South America.

products and what little meat they had was mostly from guinea pigs. They raised llamas for their wool and as pack animals.

The Spanish added wheat, nuts, and meats like beef, lamb, and chicken to their diet. They also introduced pigs, which not only added a new source of protein to the Aztec, *Mayan,* and *Inca* Indians, but also a new cooking technique. They had never used animal fats before, and the Spanish showed them how to use fat to fry foods.

Exhibit 1.29
The ancient Aztecs terraced mountainsides to plant crops.

Latin American vegetarian cuisine is best known for its use of corn to make tacos, tostadas, and tortillas. *Salsa,* an uncooked sauce made from tomatoes, hot chilis, onions, and cilantro, is now a very popular food throughout the world. Over time the cooking techniques and styles of the old and new world have blended together. While variations do exist, it is this blend that we most often think of when we think of Latin American cooking.

North American Cooking

If you were asked to name a few Native American dishes how would you answer? Popcorn quickly comes to mind. *Succotash*—a stew made of corn and beans, and hominy (corn treated with lye, dried, and then reconstituted by slow cooking in water) are two other foods we have inherited. Not much else remains of the Native American dishes in our modern lives. Their diet relied heavily on wild game such as turkey, deer, and buffalo. While we still eat these foods, as well as other native foods like cranberries and tomatoes, we adapted these recipes to European ways of cooking.

People traveling from many countries came to North America. As you know from

Exhibit 1.30
North America.

previous history classes, the eastern coast was mostly English. The French settled in the Midwest and Canada, while the Spaniards occupied Florida, the Gulf Coast, California, and the Southwest. Later, Dutch immigrants settled Pennsyl- vania, while the Swedish settled in the upper midwest.

These separate and distinct groups brought with them their favorite foods and have given us a number of regional cuisines that we can call American. Let's examine their differences by region.

New England

This northeast corner of the United States has a bountiful supply of fish and seafood from the Atlantic, as well as cranberry bogs and wild blueberries on land. Syrup made from maple trees is a major source of sweetener for their cooking.

Native American Indians introduced the early settlers to the foods native to North America. These foods included corn, beans, peanuts, pumpkins, vanilla, red and green peppers, tomatoes, avocados—even tobacco. The Indians also taught the settlers how to cook these foods. For example, the **clambake,** a cooking method where fish and corn are cooked in a pit dug in wet sand, quickly became a popular way to cook both fish and vegetables. Clambakes are still done today, especially on the East Coast.

Exhibit 1.31
When European settlers first landed in New England, they were introduced to native foods like corn, beans, and pumpkins.

Other common New England dishes include:

- *Boston baked beans;*
- *Clam chowder;*
- *Maple syrup*; and *candy*.

Pennsylvania Dutch

The Europeans who settled the area known today as Pennsylvania were *Quakers, Amish,* and *Mennonites.* These hard-working people still live without many modern conveniences. Their meals are heavy and nutritious, based on the foods they made in the old country. Some of the most recognized are potpies and scrapple.

Southern Cooking

The majority of the land in the southern states was devoted to tobacco and cotton farming. Still, this didn't keep the plantation owners from eating well. Some of the foods you will still find on a visit to these states include:

- *hush puppies*—corn dumplings fried alongside catfish;
- *chitlins* (or *chitterlings*)—fried or boiled hog intestines; and
- *pecan pie*—pecans are native to the southern United States.

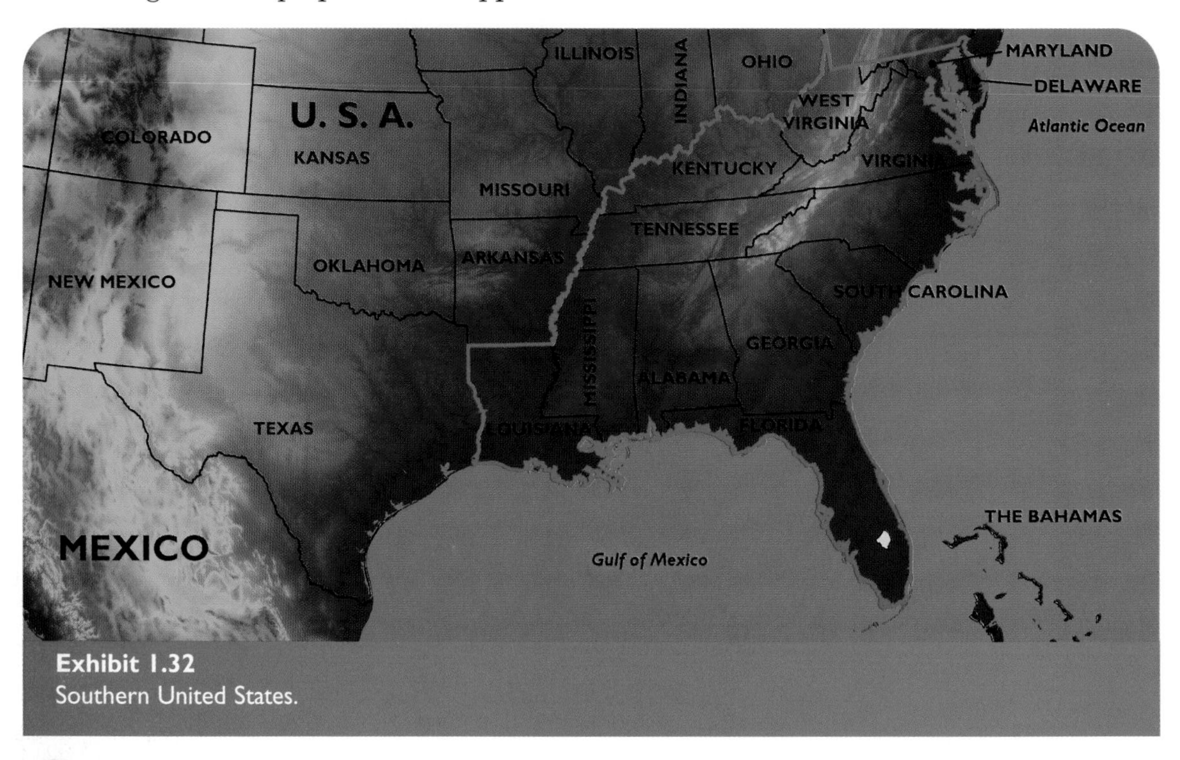

Exhibit 1.32
Southern United States.

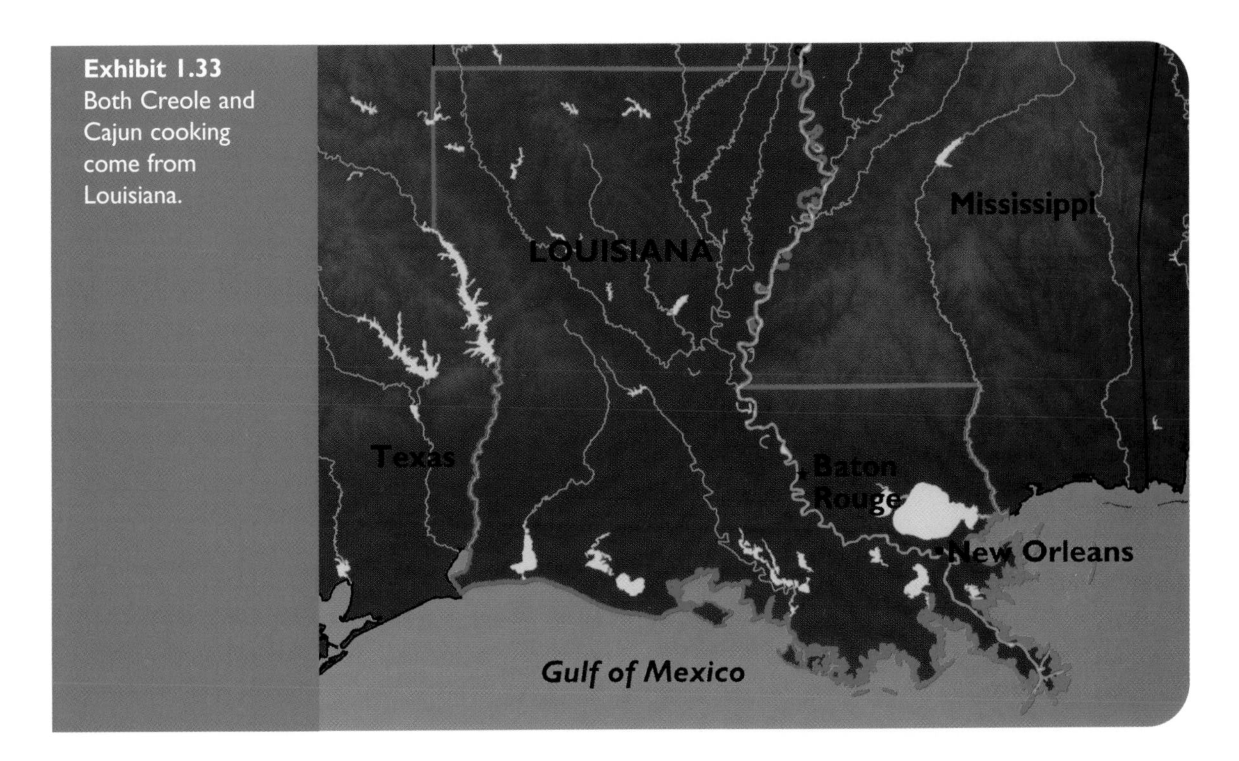

Exhibit 1.33
Both Creole and Cajun cooking come from Louisiana.

Creole and Cajun Cooking

New Orleans, Louisiana, is the home of these two styles of cooking. They are a blend of French, American Indian, African, and Spanish styles.

Creole (KREE-ole) developed in the city of New Orleans in the homes of the rich French and Spanish land-owners. These recipes often still carry the French names that inspired them. The people who developed this cooking style were French who originally settled in Nova Scotia. They were forced to relocate after England gained control of Canada, and moved to the Gulf Coast where the Spanish settlers accepted them.

Cajun-style cooking is from the swamps and bayous of southwestern Louisiana. Many Cajun dishes are based on a **roux** (roo)—a mixture of oil or butter and flour cooked for 20 to 30 minutes until it turns a rich brown color. Some of the foods that can be found in Cajun cooking are:

- *Jambalaya*—a spicy rice dish with chicken, andouille sausage, vegetables, herbs, and seasonings—much like Spanish paella

- *Andouille*—pork sausage with a strong, smoky, garlicky taste
- *Gumbo*—hearty soup thickened with brown roux containing okra, and filé, made from dried sassafrass leaves

Exhibit 1.34
Okra is an essential ingredient in gumbo.

Southwest

In Texas, where cattle is king, chili is a popular food. There are many debates and lots of recipes, but the one thing all Texans agree on is that chili is their specialty. Southwestern cuisine can be found in New Mexico and Arizona. It is a more refined form of Mexican cooking, often made using haute cuisine techniques.

The foods cultivated by the American Indians, along with culinary influences from Latin and South America, the Caribbean and Europe, are still very much a part of North American cuisine. Looking back over history, it is clear that the same is true for other parts of the world we have discussed in this section. Trade and exploration allowed people to share their native cuisines, cultures, and traditions with other countries.

In Sections 1.3 and 1.4, you will see how the foodservice industry has grown in the United States, and what the future of food service holds.

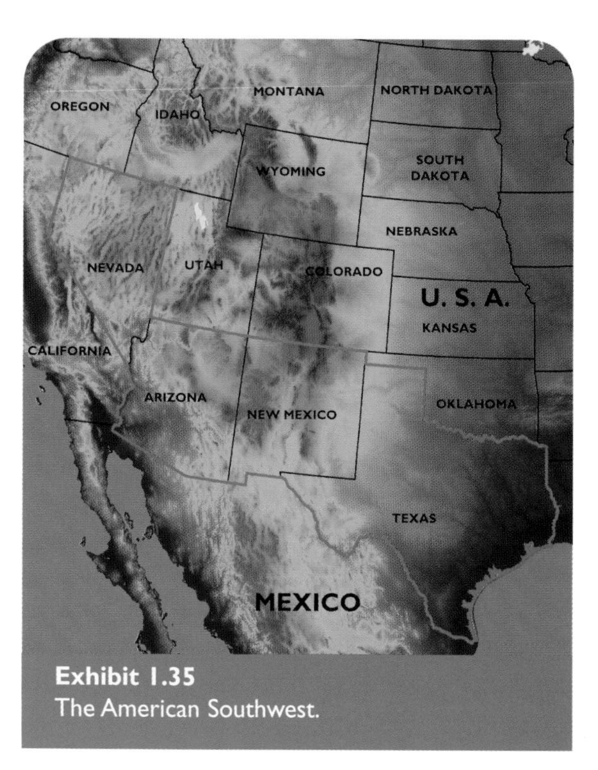

Exhibit 1.35
The American Southwest.

Review Your Learning 1.2

1. How does the Tao influence Chinese cooking?
   a. All foods are cooked together in one pot to combine their flavors.
   b. Foods should not be forced to become something they are not, and should be kept in their most natural and pure state.
   c. Foods should be flavored with many spices to enhance their unique flavors.
   d. All foods should be boiled before they are cooked to rid them of any impurities.

2. What culinary tradition was brought to Japan from China centuries ago?
   a. Tea drinking
   b. Growing grains, like barley and wheat, to make bread
   c. Steaming rice
   d. Using spices like curry, cumin, and coriander to enhance the flavor of their foods

3. What spice mixture is often used to flavor Indian cuisine?
   a. Ginger and garlic
   b. Cinnamon and nutmeg
   c. Turmeric and cumin
   d. Curry

4. Some staple foods of Middle Eastern cuisine are:
   a. beef, corn, and milk.
   b. lamb, yogurt, lentils, and eggplant.
   c. tropical fruits and fresh seafood.
   d. grains like barley, millet, and wheat.

5. Settlers from mostly what parts of the world influenced African cuisine?
   a. North and Latin America
   b. India and the Middle East
   c. Europe and South America
   d. The Far East

6. What foods are common in Caribbean and Latin American cuisine?

7. What foods and cooking techniques were brought to Latin America from other parts of the world?

SECTION 1.3

Food Service in the United States

AFTER STUDYING SECTION 1.3, YOU SHOULD BE ABLE TO:

- Outline the growth of food service throughout the history of the United States.
- List historical entrepreneurs who influenced food service in the United States.

KEY TERMS

- **Cafeteria**
- **Chain**
- **Diner**
- **Fast-food operation**

The first Europeans to settle in North America were city dwellers, poorly equipped for farming. Since North American winters are much colder and last longer than in Europe, the earliest settlers suffered severe losses. Without support from Native American Indians, many more would have died.

As more people immigrated to the New World to find their fortunes or to escape religious persecution, cities along the east coast grew. Boston and New York became major centers of trade. As early as 1634, an inn in Boston called Cole's offered food and lodging to travelers.

However, very few colonial Americans ever traveled or dined out. Once they settled down they rarely traveled more that 25 miles from their homes. However, some people did travel. When these travelers stayed at inns, they often slept together in the same large room and often shared a single bed. Not much care was given to the preparation of meals at these inns and if a traveler arrived after dinner had been served, he would have to go without.

When the Industrial Revolution began in the United States, more and more places were built for people to dine out. As in Europe, when factories opened, people flocked to the cities for jobs. The cities in the northeast, where most of the factories were located, grew quickly. By 1800 European-style coffee shops began to open. Oysters were plentiful and all-you-can-eat oyster houses could also be found.

The classic American diner also traces its roots to this time period. Factory workers who were unable to go home for lunch needed to be fed. To meet this need, cooks designed **diners,** horse drawn kitchens on wheels, and drove them to factory entrances to sell food. The practice caught on and soon there were a number of these traveling diners competing for business. To increase sales, some began adding chairs to allow their customers a place to sit down and enjoy their meal. By 1912, there were more than 50 of these roaming diners clogging the streets of Providence, Rhode Island. The city passed an ordinance that forced these diner carts off the streets after 10 a.m. To stay in business, some owners found permanent places to park their carts and are still serving food today.

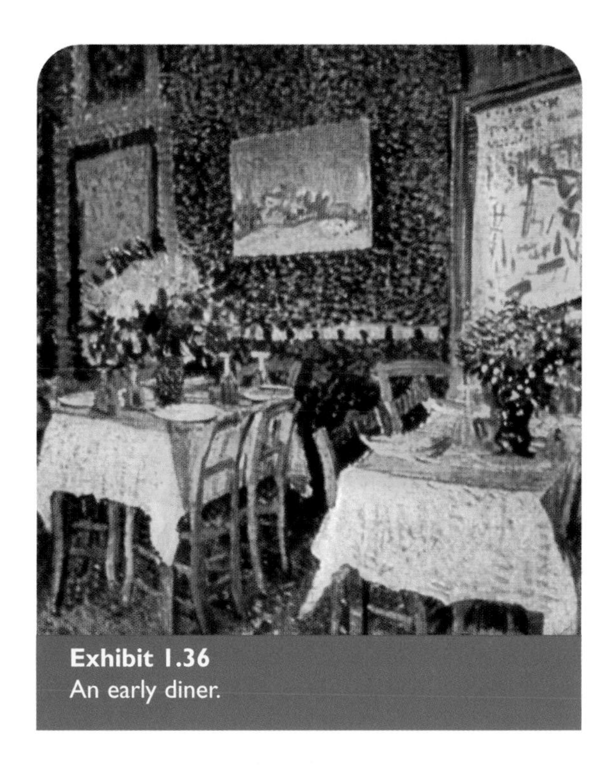

Exhibit 1.36
An early diner.

The Gilded Age 1850–1890

America's standard of living greatly improved during the 19th century, but the people who profited most were factory owners, oil barons, and other leaders of new industries.

The Enlightenment's concept of progress that was measured in scientific knowledge was adopted by America's industrial leaders. Progress was now defined by goods and profits. Workers were subjected to long hours at low wages while the profits for the owners continued to rise. These industrial leaders made a lot of money, and began showing off their fortunes. They built homes in fashionable locations in the cities, and summer houses that they might only visit for a few weeks during the year.

They had an idealized notion of European society and spent lavish amounts of money to copy it. They vacationed in Europe and returned with art, clothing, and antiques. Some went so far as to buy castles and ship them back brick by brick to their summer locations to be re-built there.

They hosted lavish parties to impress people with their wealth, serving enormous meals to huge numbers of guests. It was also fashionable to go out simply to show off recently purchased gowns from Paris. Every afternoon scores of expensively dressed women could be seen walking through Central Park in New York.

The desire for luxury dining also increased. When high society dined out, they wanted to do so in style. Ornate restaurants such as *Delmonico's* and the *Astor House* opened to meet this desire to be seen in elegant surroundings. Dinners of up to 18 courses were not uncommon.

A typical menu for a dinner party would begin with an appetizer such as oysters, followed by consommé, fish, sweetbreads, beefsteak, pâté de foie gras, puff pastry filled with creamed chicken, lamb chops, sherbet, salad, cheese, and a spectacular dessert. When Lorenzo Delmonico and his brothers opened other restaurants in Manhattan, they began what was the first restaurant **chain,** or group of restaurants owned by the same business organization.

In 1849, gold was discovered in California and people poured into the state

Exhibit 1.37
The wealthy Vanderbilts built their lavish home, the Breakers, in Newport, Rhode Island.

to claim their fortune. Some of these travelers hit the jackpot and with their newfound wealth wanted to enjoy the fine dining that they knew existed in New York. A number of fine restaurants quickly opened.

During William McKinley's presidency (1897-1901), McKinley presided over a 71-course meal. Entertaining in grand style was the only way to meet the accepted standards of high society. Multi-course dinners and elaborate decorations were the rule as each hostess tried to outdo the last.

Unfortunately, far more people struggled to stay afloat. With such a sudden growth of people coming into Northern California, meeting the demand to feed them was nearly impossible. As a result of this, the **cafeteria,** an assembly-line process of serving food quickly and cheaply without the need for servers, was invented.

The growing population in the western states increased the need to connect the country and the transcontinental railroad was built. Not only was commerce improved, but with a growing middle class, travel became a new luxury. In order to feed people as they took the week-long journey from New York to San Francisco, restaurants began to open up at railroad stations. One of the most famous was the *Harvey House,* which developed into one of the earliest nationwide chain restaurants. Unlike our modern chain restaurants such as *Denny's* or *The International House of Pancakes,* the Harvey Houses carefully developed menus to make sure that travelers never received two identical meals on their long trip.

Exhibit 1.38
The transcontinental railroad connected the east coast to the west coast.

The 20th Century

By the turn of the century (early 1900s) employment in the United States was at an all time high as more and more people went to work in new factories, stores, and office buildings. Because of this, people were eating out, especially for lunch. Restaurants opened that specialized in serving lunch, like *Child's, Schrafft's,* and *Savarin.* These were among the first lunch-time restaurants and coffee shops, a foodservice innovation which has continued to grow.

Exhibit 1.39
The first McDonald's restaurant.

In the 1930s there was an important advancement in the foodservice industry. The first *White Castle* restaurant was created, serving food that could be prepared and eaten quickly. This signified the birth of the **fast-food operation,** or quick-service restaurant.

After World War II, in the 1940s and 1950s, other quick-service restaurants were started. Restaurants like *Kentucky Fried Chicken* and *McDonald's* sprang up across the country and are still serving food today. The low prices at quick-service restaurants were affordable for Americans on-the-go. They could also be assured of quality, taste, and that the food was safe. The high volume of these fast-food restaurants offset the low prices, so profits could be quite high.

- **The Waldorf-Astoria in New York City became the model of hotel high-life. Since 1893, its management has sought to provide the height of elegance in dining and entertainment. One maître d' and celebrity of the hotel became known as Oscar of the Waldorf. He was responsible for many award winning recipes on the menu, including the famous Waldorf Salad.**
- **The Parker House, founded in 1855 by Harvey D. Parker, is one of Boston's most renowned eating establishments. It is also the birthplace of Parker House rolls (yeast rolls folded to look like small purses).**
- **George Crum, chef of New York's famous spa, Saratoga Springs, in the 1800s, created potato chips in response to a customer's demand for very thin french fries. He called them Saratoga Chips.**

Review Your Learning 1.3

1. Who began the first restaurant chain, and what was the name of the restaurant?

2. The gold rush brought lodgers and diners to what part of the United States?

3. How did the development of the railroad system in the United States cause the foodservice industry to grow?

4. Restaurants like White Castle, Kentucky Fried Chicken, and McDonald's are examples of what kind of restaurant?
   a. Full service
   b. Fast-food
   c. Cafeteria
   d. Fine dining

5. What happened in the early 1900s that helped the foodservice industry grow in the United States?
   a. More people were working and eating out for lunch, causing lunch-time restaurants to open, like Schrafft's, Savarin, and Child's.
   b. The art of fine dining was perfected, and multiple-course meals were common.
   c. Fast-food, or quick-service restaurants, opened up all over the country.
   d. Delmonico started the first restaurant chain.

1.4

SECTION 1.4

The Future of Food Service

AFTER STUDYING SECTION 1.4, YOU SHOULD BE ABLE TO:

- List current trends in society and explain how they influence the foodservice industry.
- Categorize and differentiate the segments of the foodservice industry.
- Investigate and draw conclusions on the impact of future economic, technological, and social changes in the foodservice industry.

KEY TERMS

- Aquaculture
- Commercial segment
- Customer service
- Genetic engineering
- Hospitality
- Hydroponic (hi-droh-PON-ick) farming
- Noncommercial segment
- Organic farming
- Trend

How many times a week do you eat out? Some foodservice analysts predict that in the near future, people will eat more than 50% of their meals outside the home. Currently, the foodservice industry is the fastest growing industry in the United States with more than 10.2 million employees. On a typical day, the restaurant industry is estimated to have sales in excess of $922 million!

Trends

Trends in food service reflect the changes in lifestyle and economic conditions that exist in our culture. A **trend** is a current style or preference. One enormous trend has been the increase in the number

Exhibit 1.40
Women are now a prominent part of the modern workforce.

of women in the workforce since the early 1960s.

More women are employed in the restaurant industry today than ever before. In fact, in 1996 the typical food-service industry employee was a single female under 30. Because women are now a prominent part of the modern workforce, they are making their own money and spending it as well. This trend has not only helped the restaurant industry expand over the years, but has contributed to the overall economy in the United States.

Another trend that has had a positive effect on the foodservice industry is the rising number of single adults that live in this country. More and more people are waiting to get married until their 30s and 40s. This segment of the population, both single men and women, tend to eat out more often than their married counterparts.

Other trends that influence the foodservice industry are the growing interest in nutrition and healthy living. Restaurants are responding by using low-fat cooking methods and healthier ingredients. Today, more than seven out of ten menus include lighter-fare, grilled entrées.

Exhibit 1.41
Grilling foods is just one of the ways to prepare lighter entrées.

Environmental concerns, increasing government controls, computer-assisted management functions, and the popularity of convenience foods are also trends that affect the growth of the foodservice industry. Advances in packaging, holding, and portioning foods are keeping costs down and preserving the quality of food.

Innovative farming methods have also contributed to the growth of food service by making more fresh foods available year-round. These include:

- **aquaculture**—the farm-raising of fish and seafood;
- **organic farming**—growing food without using chemicals or pesticides;
- **hydroponic** (hi-droh-PON-ick) **farming**— growing food in nutrient-enriched water rather than soil; and
- **genetic engineering**—improved meats and produce through genetic alteration.

One of the most important trends currently is the need to find more time in the day. The large number of parents working outside the home has reduced the amount of leisure time they have on a day-to-day basis. The foodservice industry is meeting this demand by offering:

- *Home meal replacements*—fully cooked and complete home-style dinners that can be bought at supermarkets;
- *Home delivery systems*—services that deliver restaurant menu items, sometimes from a variety of different restaurants; and
- *Cybershopping*—grocery orders placed over the Internet, selected by employees and delivered to your door.

Think About It…

Boston Market is one example of a restaurant that offers home meal replacement. Can you think of others?

Organization

The foodservice industry can be divided into two major parts:

- Commercial
- Noncommercial

The **commercial segment** prepares and serves food and beverages for a profit. The commercial segment of the foodservice industry includes restaurants and bars, supermarket delis, as well as operations that sell prepared food, like convenience stores, lodging facilities, and other recreational areas. The commercial segment makes up about 75% of the foodservice industry.

The **noncommercial segment** prepares and serves food as a supportive addition to the main function, or purpose, of the establishment. For example, a cafeteria at a local university supports the school's main purpose of educating students by serving them meals. The noncommercial segment (about 25% of the foodservice industry) includes businesses and industry, hospitals, nursing homes, schools (including colleges and universities), airlines, and the military.

Customer Service and Hospitality

At the beginning of the 20th century, most businesses in this country were manufacturing companies that sold goods. Over the past 30 years, the United States has changed to a service-oriented economy. More than half of our gross national product comes from selling a service to customers instead of a tangible product. The foodservice industry is considered a service industry. Certainly, food is for sale, but it is the pleasure and convenience that people pay for.

Exhibit 1.42
Good customer service is essential in all segments of the foodservice industry.

Think About It...

Why do you go out to eat? Not only for the food, but to relax, socialize and have a good time. The only way that can happen is if all foodservice employees give good customer service.

Customer service, making customers feel comfortable and satisfied with the choices they have made, should be the goal of every foodservice operation. Restaurants can spend time and money on advertising, promotions, and state-of-the-art equipment, but this is a waste if customers do not receive exceptional customer service from everyone in the operation. Customers who enjoy the food and service they receive are more likely to return. Repeat business is one of the best ways to ensure success.

In the foodservice industry, it is the responsibility of each and every manager and employee to ensure that guests are treated courteously, made to feel comfortable, and satisfied. This is known as **hospitality**, or being kind and respectful to those that visit your establishment. It is an ancient, respected tradition in many cultures. Hospitality, like customer service, is important for success in the foodservice industry. Making guests feel as if they are friends whom you're glad to see is a dignified and acquired skill.

Today, when a headwaiter or hostess greets guests as they come into the dining area to be seated, the same spirit of welcome and hospitality should be expressed. Good service and hospitality takes training, skill, effort, stamina, commitment, and—most importantly—a genuine love of working with people.

The Future of Foodservice

As we've discussed so far in this chapter, many factors have worked together over the centuries to influence and shape the foodservice industry. Thanks to the ancient Greeks and Romans, the French Revolution, the Industrial Revolution, and countless entrepreneurs and explorers, the foodservice industry has evolved into the $600 billion industry it is today.

What qualities will future managers and employees need to take the foodservice industry successfully into the 21st century? Here is what the National Restaurant Association's panel of foodservice analysts forecast.

- Managers in the foodservice industry of tomorrow will need strong communication and administration skills. They must diligently offer excellent customer service and hospitality—to both employees and customers.
- Managers will be directly involved in teaching, training, and motivating their employees and in handling all types of human resources issues. To do this, they will need:

  —strong team leadership; and

  —a culturally diverse staff.
- Future managers and employees will be dealing with consumers concerned with nutrition and healthy living. Because of this emphasis on diet and nutrition, managers will need a greater knowledge of recipe ingredients and nutritional content. Growing ethnic

diversity will also be an issue. To reach all cultures and ethnicities, menus will feature more ethnic and international cuisine.

- In addition, managers will play a greater role in supporting environmental issues that directly affect their operations, such as waste management and recycling.
- Managers in the 21st century will emphasize their own professional career development by taking classes to continue their training and becoming certified in such topics as safe food preparation and handling. Consequently, salaries will be closely linked to on-the-job performance.

Exhibit 1.43
The top 10 most likely developments for foodservice managers in the 21st century.

1. Managers will need greater computer proficiency.
2. They will supervise a more culturally diverse staff.
3. Service will provide the competitive edge in selecting a restaurant.
4. Managers will need better teaching and training skills.
5. They will need better skills for managing people.
6. They will need excellent interpersonal skills.
7. They will play a bigger role in waste management and recycling.
8. They will deal with a more educated customer regarding nutrition.
9. They will need to cater to the service demands of more diverse customers.
10. They will give front-of-the-house employees the authority and training they need to give better service.

Review Your Learning 1.4

1. The ______________________ segment of the foodservice industry accounts for nearly 75% of the industry.
   a. noncommercial
   b. quick-service
   c. commercial
   d. fine-dining

2. Providing what service to customers should be the goal of all foodservice operations?
   a. Excellent customer service
   b. Top of the line advertising and promotions
   c. State-of-the-art equipment
   d. Extravagant and expensive meals

3. What are some of the skills that foodservice managers will need in the 21st century?

4. What current trends are affecting the growth of the foodservice industry?

5. Explain the differences between *aquaculture, organic farming*, and *hydroponic farming*.

Flashback

CHAPTER 1

SECTION 1.1: CREATING THE MODERN RESTAURANT

- Ancient Greeks rarely dined out. But they did enjoy the social aspect of dining out, and often gathered together for banquets even though **restaurants,** stores that sell prepared meals for on-site consumption, were not invented for another 2000 years.
- *Lesches* were private clubs that offered food to its members and establishments called *phatnai.* These clubs catered to travelers, traders, and visiting diplomats.
- Meals were considered a time to nourish the soul as well as the body. The Greeks believed that pleasure was the purpose of life and that it was achieved through restraint and balance.
- Epicuriuos was the leader of this movement. Epicurean is a term used to describe a person with a refined taste for food and wine.
- In 282 B.C., Rome conquered the lands surrounding the Mediterranean Sea. Ordinary Roman citizens lived on a simple diet of barley, olive oil, pine nuts, and fish. Wealthy aristocrats held enormous banquets filled with exotic foods.
- Dining in public was considered undignified and only men in the lowest classes frequented early taverns.
- Romans' desires for exotic foods and spices increased trade and stretched the Roman Empire further east and north.
- Politicians believed they owed their position in society to the peasant and slave classes and held enormous shows in the coleseum, like chariot races and gladiator fights.
- Marcus Apicus took great effort to obtain the most exotic foods for his feasts. He wrote one of the first cookbooks, *De Re Coquinaria (On Cooking),* which is still used today.
- Germanic tribes soon conquered the Roman Empire. They did not adopt Roman democracy, but they did bring Christianity to Germany. This ended

the view that gods and spirits inhabit forests, which turned Europeans into a farming society.

- This need to develop land led to *feudalism,* the exchange of working the fields and turning over some of the proceeds to the landowner in exchange for safety from invaders.
- *Serfs,* who were forbidden to hunt, lived on bread made from wheat, peas that could be dried for consumption in the winter months, turnips and onions that could be stored year round, and cabbage that was fermented into sauerkraut.
- Landowners lived in comfort and held large banquets almost every night. They ate with their fingers and off of large slices of stale bread called *trenchers.*
- Travel to the Far East and India was greatly reduced when the *Moors* invaded Spain and blocked shipment of spices and fine goods from reaching Europe.
- The basic diet in the Middle Ages was bland and lacked variety. **Herbs** grew in the wild and were available, while the craved **spices** to flavor foods.
- This demand caused merchants in Venice to hold a monopoly on the spice trade because of their location on the Adriatic Sea. The desire to break up this monopoly led to the discovery of the New World, America by the Portugese, who were looking for a shorter route to India.
- During the Renaissance, Catherine de Medici introduced **haute cuisine,** or high food preparation to France, along with sweet new foods like ice cream, and vegetables like spinach. She also introduced the use of silverware.
- The first **café** opened in 1650 in Oxford, England, which served coffee brought from Africa. Soon, cafes were sprouting up all over Europe, making it acceptable to eat in public.
- **Guilds,** or associations of people with similar interests or professions, were formed to organize the growing number of merchants and craftsmen. Cooking guilds established many of the professional standards and traditions that exist today.
- In 1765, Boulanger began serving hot soups called *restaurers* in his café. He began calling his café a *restorante,* or restaurant. Within 30 years, Paris had

over 500 restaurants and dining out on a large scale was born.

- *Cottage industries* developed by wool merchants to create a putting-out system of production, soon led to the start of the Industrial Revolution, when merchants found a better way to control production by building factories.
- A mass migration soon brought farming families to cities so they could be close to the new factories. This caused many stresses on the city, which led to the development of horse and buggy transit buses to help employees move out of crowded areas.
- Entertainment became the only way to escape the drudgery of the long work day, so music houses and review shows that served ale soon flourished.
- The *Enlightenment* changed the way knowledge was obtained and accepted, and many advancements in science and technology were made.
- Vitamins were discovered, as were chemical fertilizers and pesticides that doubled food production. Louis Pasteur discovered the process of **pasteurization.** Another scientist, Nicolas Appert, discovered the process of canning foods to keep them fresh and safe to eat.
- Marie-Antoine Carême is one of the world's most famous chefs. He perfected *grand cuisine,* and recipes for many fine French sauces and dishes like *consommé* and *pièces* mountées.
- Georges Auguste Escoffier refined grand cuisine into *classical cuisine.* He created the **kitchen brigade system** and established the exact rules of conduct and dress for chefs that are still used today.

SECTION 1.2: CUISINES OF THE WORLD

- Chinese cooking has been greatly influenced by the **Tao,** or single guiding principle that orders the universe. The Chinese believe that food should not be forced to become something it is not, but should be kept in its most natural and pure state.
- Mandarin cuisine in the north is light and mild, and includes foods like scallions, leeks, and garlic.
- The western Chinese cuisine of the Szechwan and Hunan provinces is hot and spicy. Szechwan peppercorns and chili peppers are commonly used in this cuisine.

- The Cantonese cuisine strives for balance and color harmony. It was the first Chinese cuisine introduced to the United States.
- From China, the Japanese received the ancient custom of tea-drinking called *Cha-no-Yu.* The Japanese always use simple ingredients when cooking, like fresh seafood, vegetables, and rice.
- In early times, India was an important part of the trade route. Goods from other countries passed through India and were adopted, like spices from southern Asia and the Middle East. **Curry,** a blend of several native spices, is used to flavor the foods that make up the Indian diet, like breads, meat, rice, vegetables, and fish.
- While each nation in the Middle East has developed distinct cuisines, all of these nations share many common foods that form the basis of their cooking. Lamb, eggplant, and yogurt are staples of Middle Eastern cuisine. Spices from India were introduced to the Middle East, like cinnamon, pepper, and cardamom, and are still used today to flavor their staple foods and dishes.
- Beans, lentils, barley, millet, wheat, peanuts, and yams are the main food staples found all over Africa. European traders and explorers, mainly the Dutch, Portuguese, Spanish, French, and British, began colonizing, or settling in Africa during the 1500s. They brought foods like strawberries, asparagus, farm animals, and spices from India and the Far East.
- Caribbean cuisine consists mainly of their abundant natural resources. The warm climate allows an abundance of trees and plants to grow providing tropical foods like coconut, bananas, mangos, papayas, plantains, and sugar cane. The surrounding Atlantic Ocean and Caribbean Sea provide the Islands with fresh fish and seafood.
- The Ancient Aztec and Mayan Indians of Latin America were experts at cultivating food thousands of years before the Europeans landed there. Foods like corn, beans, tomatoes, potatoes, squash, peppers, bananas, avocados, and the cacao bean (used to make chocolate) are still staples in Latin American cuisine. Spanish settlers brought meats like beef, chicken, and lamb, along with wheat and nuts

to Latin America. Soon, these foods became a central part of the cuisine.

- When the first Europeans landed on what is now the East Coast in North America, they found the dense and wooded land difficult to grow the grains they brought with them. Fortunately, the Native American Indians introduced them to the foods from this new land. Corn, beans, peanuts, pumpkins, vanilla, red and green peppers, tomatoes, avocados, and even tobacco, grew in North America. These foods are still a part of our cuisines today.
- Regional American cuisine includes clambakes, clam chowder, and maple syrup from New England; hush puppies and chitlins from the South; jambalaya and gumbo from New Orleans; and chili from Texas.

SECTION 1.3: FOOD SERVICE IN THE UNITED STATES

- Many people from Europe immigrated to the United States in the 1600s to find their fortunes and escape religious persecution. Cities along the east coast, like Boston and New York, grew.
- As early as 1634, an inn in Boston called Cole's offered food and lodging to travelers.
- However, very few colonial Americans traveled or dined out. However, the introduction of the Industrial Revolution in America created more and more places for these new Americans to dine out.
- The classic American **diner** traces its roots back to this period, when traveling diners went to factories to feed hungry workers. Diners are still used today.
- America's standard of living greatly improved during the 19th century, but the people who profited the most were the factory owners, oil barons, and other leaders of new industries.
- Progress was defined by goods and profits. Industrial leaders made a lot of money, and built expensive homes, vacationed in Europe, and even brought back pieces of castles and antiques to recreate the European experience in the United States.
- This new wealthy class hosted lavish parties, serving enormous meals. The desire for luxury dining was increasing, and high society wanted to dine out in style.

- Ornate restaurants like the *Astor House* and *Delmonico's* opened to meet the demand for elegant dining. Lorenzo Delmonico, founder of *Delmonico's,* opened up other restaurants in Manhattan and began what was the first restaurant **chain,** or group of restaurants owned by the same business organization.
- The growth of the foodservice industry continued with the gold rush in California. In 1849, people poured into California to claim their fortune. With all of the people going to northern California, the **cafeteria,** an assembly-line process of serving food quickly and cheaply, was created to feed the growing population.
- The growing population in the west increased the need for the country to be connected.
- The transcontinental railroad was built, and soon, travel became a new luxury. People began to travel by train from New York to San Francisco, stopping at railroad stations along the way. Here, travelers found restaurants like the *Harvey House,* to feed these hungry travelers.
- By the 20th century, more and more people were working in factories, stores, and office buildings. Soon, restaurants opened to serve noontime lunch, like *Savarin, Child's,* and *Schrafft's.*
- In the 1930s, the **fast-food** segment of the foodservice industry began with the introduction of *White Castle.* Later, in the 1940s and 1950s, other fast-food restaurants opened, like *Kentucky Fried Chicken* and *McDonald's.*

SECTION 1.4: THE FUTURE OF FOOD SERVICE

- Trends in food service reflect the changes in lifestyle and economic conditions that exist in our culture.
- A **trend** is a current style or preference. Important trends, like the increase of women in the workforce, the rising number of single adults, and the growing interest in nutrition and healthy living have all contributed to the growth of the foodservice industry.
- Environmental concerns, increasing governmental controls, computer-assisted management functions, and the popularity of convenience foods are also trends that affect the foodservice industry.

- Innovative farming methods like **aquaculture, organic farming hydroponic farming,** and **genetic engineering** have also contributed to the continued expansion of food service.
- The foodservice industry has responded to these trends by offering *home meal replacements, home delivery systems,* and *cybershopping.*
- The foodservice industry is divided into two segments: commercial and noncommercial.
- The **commercial segment** makes up about 75% of the foodservice industry and included restaurants and bars, supermarket delis, and operations that sell prepared food.
- The **noncommercial segment** makes up around 25% of the industry and includes businesses and industry, hospitals, nursing homes, schools, airlines, and the military.
- Food service is a service-oriented industry. **Customer service,** making customers feel comfortable and satisfied with the choices they have made, should be the goal of every foodservice operation.
- Hospitality, like customer service, is essential to ensuring success in the foodservice industry.
- **Hospitality** is being kind and respectful to those that visit your foodservice operation. Giving good service and hospitality takes training, skill, and effort, but most importantly, a genuine love of working with people.
- The foodservice industry exists in an environment of constant economic and social change.
- The foodservice managers and employees of the 21st century will need specific qualities to succeed, like excellent communication and administration skills; strong team leadership; and a culturally diverse staff.
- Managers in the 21st century will play a greater role in environmental issues such as waste management and recycling, and will have a growing knowledge of recipe ingredients and nutritional content of the foods they serve.
- Greater emphasis will be placed on continued learning, as managers and employees in the foodservice industry in the 21st century take classes in topics such as safe food handling.

PROFILE

Sandra Duncan

Catering Sales Manager
Michael Jordan's Restaurant
Chicago, Illinois

I started out working as a flight attendant for American Airlines while completing my Bachelor of Arts degree in Marketing and Public Relations. I then decided that I wanted to work in the hospitality and restaurant industry, which would would allow me to use the customer service skills that I developed as a flight attendant, as well as my marketing and public relations education. I first worked as a concierge in the Ambassador West, a large hotel in Chicago. Soon after that, I got my job at Michael Jordan's as the Catering Sales Manager.

Every day is different. There are many small details that require my attention. A large part of my day is meeting with customers and ensuring that all their needs are met. My job does not end with the signing of a contract. I make sure that customers' experiences at Michael Jordan's exceed their expectations. At Michael Jordan's, we take pride in the food that we serve. We know people come for the atmosphere, and to be around Michael, but we want them to leave commenting on the excellent meal.

The food we serve is of the highest quality. Our menu is really diverse because it is important to offer variety to customers. Here at Michael Jordan's, we really consider such staples as potatoes and pasta to be the key to our successful menu. We find that most of our customers enjoy these foods, so we make sure to provide them in many unique and innovative ways. From salads and appetizers to the main entrée, pastas of all shapes and sizes and a multitude of potatoes can be found jazzing up the menu.

The more familiar I am with the menu, the easier my job will be because I can suggest our hottest sellers and best entrées to customers. They really appreciate my knowledge of the menu. No matter what career you choose, make sure you learn as much as possible about every part of the industry—it will make your job a lot of fun!

CHAPTER 2

Potatoes and Grains

2.1

SECTION 2.1

Selecting and Storing Potatoes, Grains, Legumes, and Pasta

AFTER STUDYING SECTION 2.1, YOU SHOULD BE ABLE TO:

- Outline methods to select, receive, and store potatoes and grains.
- Distinguish between various forms of wheat.

Potatoes

Potatoes are native to North and South America. They were first introduced in Europe in the 15th century by the Spanish explorer Francisco Pizarro, who sent them back to Spain. Spanish soldiers learned to cultivate the plants and cook the round root. Potatoes became a staple in many countries, particularly Ireland, as an inexpensive, nourishing, and easy-to-grow vegetable.

KEY TERMS

- Bran
- Durum wheat
- Endosperm
- Germ
- Grain
- Hull
- Legume (LEG-yoom)
- Milling process
- Semolina
- Solanine (SOLE-ah-neen)
- Stone ground
- Whole grain

When selecting potatoes, choose potatoes that are firm and relatively smooth. Any potatoes with dark spots, green areas, mold, or large cuts should not be eaten. Store potatoes in a cool, dry place at temperatures ranging from 55°F to 60°F (12.8°C to 15.6°C). The maximum storage period for russet and all-purpose potatoes is 30 days. New potatoes, a small, immature red potato, should be stored no longer than one week. All potatoes are best stored in ventilated containers.

Potatoes that are exposed to light may develop a greenish color. While the color is harmless, it means that the potato contains **solanine** (SOLE-ah-neen), a harmful, bitter-tasting substance. Potato sprouts can also contain solanine. Cut away and discard sprouts and any green portions before using potatoes. Always discard potatoes if you have any doubts about their freshness or safety.

Exhibit 2.1
Potatoes are inexpensive, nourishing, and easy to grow.

Wash potatoes thoroughly and cut away any green or damaged spots before use. These spots may contain a natural toxin, solanine, which can be harmful to your health.

GRAINS

Grains, which are grasses that grow edible seeds, along with meals and flours, are all essential for everyday cooking. Exhibit 2.2 describes various grains and their uses.

Whole grains are grains that have not been milled. In the **milling process,** the germ, bran, and hull of the grain are removed, or polished. The **hull** of a whole grain is the protective coating, or husk, that surrounds the grain. **Bran,** a great source of fiber and B vitamins, is the tough layer surrounding the endosperm. The **endosperm** is the largest part of the grain, and a major source of protein and carbohydrate. The smallest part of the whole grain is the **germ.** It is important because it provides a trace of fat and is rich in thiamin. See Exhibit 2.3 for the parts of a grain.

Exhibit 2.2
Grains, meals, flours, and other starches.

NAME	French/Italian Names	PURCHASE FORM	MAIN USES
Wheat	*Froment; frumento*		
Whole		Unrefined or minimally processed kernels	Side dish
Cracked		Coarsely crushed, minimally processed kernels	Side dish, hot cereal
Bulgur		Hulled, cracked hard or soft wheat: parboiled and dried	Side dish, salad, (tabbouleh)
Semolina	*Semoule; semolino/semola*	Polished wheat kernel (bran and germ removed), whole or ground	Pasta, flour, couscous (below)
Couscous	*Couscous; cuscusu*	Semolina pellets, often parcooked	Side dish(often served with stew of same name)
Farina	*Farine*	Polished, medium-grind wheat kernels	Breakfast cereal
Bran	*Son; crusca*	Separated outer covering of wheat kernel; flakes	Added to baked goods, prepared cereals, and other foods to increase dietary fiber
Germ		Separated embryo of wheat kernel; flakes	Added to baked goods and cereals to boost flavor and nutrition
Wheat Flour			
Whole	*Farine; farina*	Finely ground, whole kernels	Baked goods
All-purpose		Finely ground, polished kernels; usually enriched; may be bleached	Baked goods, thickener, other kitchen uses
Bread		Finely ground, polished hard wheat kernels; usually enriched; may be bleached	Bread dough
Cake		Very finely ground, polished soft wheat kernels; usually enriched and bleached	Cakes and other delicate baked goods
Pastry		Very finely ground, polished soft wheat kernels; usually enriched and bleached	Pastry and other delicate baked goods
Self-rising		Very finely ground, polished soft wheat kernels to which baking powder and salt have been added; usually enriched and bleached	Cakes and other baked goods not leavened with yeast
Rice	*Riz; riso*		
Brown		Hulled grains, bran intact; short, medium, or long grain; may be enriched	Side dish, other
White		Polished grains, usually enriched; long or short grain	Long grain: side dish. Short grain: pudding, risotto
Converted		Parcooked, polished grains, may be enriched	Side dishes, other
Basmati		Delicate, extra-long grain, polished	Side dish, including pilaf
Italian short-grain		Short grain, polished; types include Piedmontese and Arborio	Risotto
Wild	*Zizanie*	Long, dark-brown grain not related to regular rice	Side dish, stuffings, other

Exhibit 2.2 (CONTINUED)
Grains, meals, flour, and other starches.

Glutinous		Round, short grain, very starchy; black (unhulled) or white (polished)	Sushi, other Oriental dishes
Rice flour		Very finely ground polished rice	Thickener
Corn	*Maïs; granoturco*		
Hominy		Whole, hulled kernels; dry or canned	Side dish including succotash, in soup or stew
Grits		Cracked hominy	Side dish, hot cereal, baked goods
Meal	*Farine de maïs; farina gialla*	Medium-fine ground, hulled kernels; white or yellow	Baked goods, coating, polenta
Masa Harina		Corn processed with lime to remove hull, medium ground; dry, dough, raw, or cooked tortillas	Tortillas and other Mexican dishes.
Cornstarch	*Farine de maïs; farina finissima di granoturco (corn starch)*	Very finely ground, hulled kernels	Thickener, coating
Barley			
Pot or Scotch	*Orge mondes; orzo*	Coarse, whole kernels; ground (barley meal)	Side dish, hot cereal, soups, meal, baked goods
Pearl	*Orge perle; orzo*	Polished, whole kernels; ground (barley flour)	Side dish, hot cereal, soups, flour, baked goods
Buckwheat	*Blé noir/blé sarrasin; grano saraceno*	Whole, coarsely cracked (kasha) flour	Whole, side dish, flour, pancakes, baked goods
Millet	*Millet*	Whole, flour	Side dish, flat breads
Oats	*Avoine*	Rolled, cut (oatmeal, below)	Hot cereal, baked goods
Oatmeal		Ground coarse or fine	Filler in sausages, baked goods
Oat bran		Separated outer covering of grain, flakes	Added to cereals and baked goods for dietary fiber
Rye	*Seigle*	Cracked, flour	Cracked: side dish, flour, baked goods
Sorghum	*Sorgho; sorgo*	Whole, flour, syrup	Porridge, flat breads, beer; syrup and molasses
Other Starches			
Arrowroot		Fine, starchy powder made from a tropical root	Thickener
Filé (gumbo spice)		Fine, starchy powder made from sassafras leaves	Thickener, (especially in Creole dishes such as gumbo)

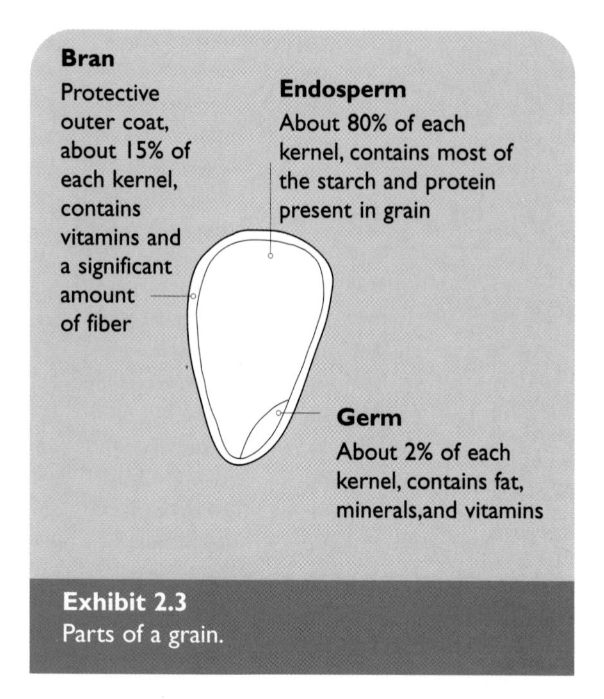

Exhibit 2.3
Parts of a grain.

Grains that are ground and broken down are called **stone ground.** In this process, the grains retain more of their nutrients because the germ, bran, and hull are left intact.

Some grains you may be familiar with are:

- *Wheat:* Classified as soft or hard, depending on the protein content.
- *All-purpose white flour:* Flour milled from low-protein wheat; good for making muffins and pancakes; not recommended for making bread.
- *Soft wheat:* Good for making cakes and pastries.
- *Hard wheat:* Good for making bread.
- **Durum wheat:** A type of hard wheat; good for making pasta.
- **Semolina:** Refined durum; good for making pasta.

Whole grains have a shorter shelf life than milled grains and should be purchased in quantities that can be used within three weeks. Grains should be carefully inspected when they are delivered. Check bags, boxes, and all containers to make sure they are intact, clean, and in no way below standard.

Store dry grains above floor level on shelves in a dry, ventilated, and accessible area. Whole grains should be stored in the freezer. Brown rice and wild rice should be refrigerated.

Legumes

Legumes (LEG-yooms) are seeds from pod-producing plants. They include *yellow split peas, Great Northern beans, kidney beans, pinto beans, lentils,* and *navy beans.* Dried legumes have many uses in cooking, from salads and appetizers, to main courses and desserts.

Legumes should be stored in cool, dry, well-ventilated areas, away from light and excessive heat. Always discard any beans

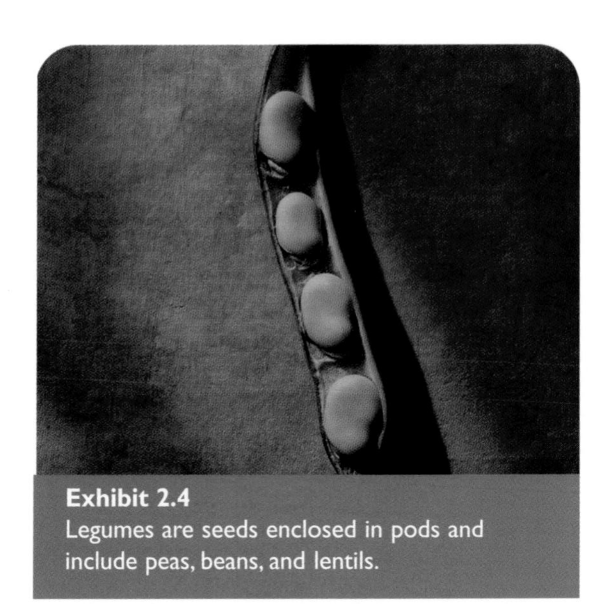

Exhibit 2.4
Legumes are seeds enclosed in pods and include peas, beans, and lentils.

or peas that appear moldy, damp, or wrinkled. For example, dried beans can be kept for one to two years; however, they are best when they are used within six months of purchase. Beans and peas are also available fresh, canned, or frozen.

Legumes are known as the "meat alternative" because of their high protein content. They contain more protein than any other vegetable group. However, they are more than just a meat substitute; they are also a great source for complex carbohydrates, B vitamins, and dietary fibers.

PASTA

Fast becoming a staple food item in America, pasta is one of the most versatile and convenient foods to prepare. Dried pasta and noodles are essential foods because they store well, cook quickly, and provide a base or accompaniment for many popular dishes. Colored and vegetable-flavored pastas can add color and nutrition to many entrées.

When receiving pasta, inspect all bags, boxes, and containers to make sure they are intact and clean. Store dry pastas in an area that is properly dry, ventilated, and accessible. All goods should be placed above floor level, on shelving or pallets. Be sure that dates of receipt are marked on packages and can be seen easily. In this way, it's easier to use the first in, first out (FIFO) method of inventory and stock rotation. Exhibit 2.6 describes various dried pasta and their uses.

Exhibit 2.5
Different shapes of pasta.

Exhibit 2.6
Dried pasta and noodles.

NAME (ITALIAN/ENGLISH)	DESCRIPTION (SHAPE,BASE FLOUR*)	MAJOR DISHES
Acini di pepe (peppercorns)	Tiny, pellet-shaped; wheat flour	Soups
Anelli (Rings)	Medium-small, ridged, tubular pasta cut in thin rings; wheat flour	Soups
Arrowroot Vermicelli	Very thin Chinese noodles; arrowroot starch dough enriched with egg yolks	Oriental dishes
Cannelloni (large pipes)	Large cylinders	Stuffed with cheese or meat, sauce, and baked
Capellini (hair)	Very fine, solid cylindrical; the finest is *capelli d' angelo* (angle's hair); wheat flour	With oil, butter, tomato, seafood, or other thin sauce; soup
Cavatappi (corkscrews)	Medium-thin, hollow, ridged pasta twisted into a spiral and cut into short lengths; wheat flour	With medium and hearty sauces
Cellophane noodles	Very thin, transparent noodles; in bunches or compressed bundles; mung bean starch	Oriental dishes: fried crisp for garnish or boiled for lo mein
Conchiglie (shells)	Large or medium, ridged shell shape; *conchigliette* are small shells; wheat flour	Filled with meat or cheese and baked; *conchigliette*: soups
Cresti di gallo (cocks' combs)	Ridged, hollow, elbow-shaped noodles with a ruffled crest along one edge; wheat flour	With hearty soups
Ditali (thimbles)	Narrow tubes cut in short lengths; *ditalini* are tiny thimbles; wheat flour	With medium-texture sauces; *ditalini:* soups
Egg flakes	Tiny, flat squares; wheat flour	Soups
Egg noodles	Usually ribbons in varying widths; may be cut long or short, packaged loose or in compressed bundles; may have spinach or other flavorings; wheat flour dough enriched with egg yolks	Buttered, casseroles, some sauces, puddings
Elbow macaroni	Narrow, curved tubes cut in short lengths; wheat flour	Macaroni, and cheese, casseroles,
Farfalle (butterflies)	Flat, rectangular noodles pinched in center to resemble butterfly or bow; may have crimped edges; *farfallini* are tiny butterflies	With medium or hearty sauces; baked
Fettuccine	Long, flat, ribbon-shaped, about 1/4 inch wide; wheat flour	With medium-heavy, rich sauces; (e.g., alfredo)
Fiochetti (bows)	Rectangles of flat pasta curled up and pinched slightly in the center to form bow shapes	With medium and hearty sauces
Fusilli (twists)	Long, spring-or corkscrew-shaped strands, thicker than spaghetti	With tomato and other medium-thick sauces
Lasagne	Large, flat noodles about 3 inches wide; usually with curly edges; wheat flour	Baked with sauce, cheese, meat, and vegetables
Linguine	Thin, slightly flattened, solid strands, about 1/8 inch wide; wheat flour	With oil, butter, marinara, or other thin sauces
Maccheroni (macaroni)	Thin, tubular pasta in various widths; may be long like spaghetti or cut into shorter lengths	With medium and hearty sauces

* Where base flour is listed as wheat, usually durum semolina is used. Wheat pastas may be made from other flours, including whole wheat and buckwheat, and they may be flavored with vegetable and/or herb purees.

Exhibit 2.6 (CONTINUED)
Dried pasta and noodles.

NAME (ITALIAN/ENGLISH)	DESCRIPTION (SHAPE,BASE FLOUR*)	MAJOR DISHES
Mafalde	Flat, curly-edged, about 3/4 inch wide; sometimes called lasagnette or malfadine; wheat flour	Sauced and baked
Manicotti (small muffs)	Thick, ridged tubes; may be cut straight or on an angle; wheat flour	Filled with meat or cheese and baked
Mostaccioli (small mustaches)	Medium-sized tubes with angle-cut ends; may be ridged; wheat flour	With hearty sauces
Orecchiette (ears)	Smooth, curved rounds of flat pasta; about 1/2 inch in diameter; wheat flour	With oil and vegetable sauces or any medium sauce; soups
Orzo (barley)	Tiny, grain-shaped; wheat flour	Soups
Pastina (tiny pasta)	Miniature pasta in any of various shapes, including stars, rings, alphabets, seeds/teardrops	Soups, buttered (as side dish or cereal for childern)
Penne (quills or pens)	Same as mostaccioli	With hearty sauces
Rice noodles	Noodles in various widths (up to 1/8 inch); rice sticks are long, straight ribbons; rice vermicelli is very thin; rice flour	Oriental dishes
Rigatoni	Thick, ridged tubes cut in lengths about 1/2 inches	With hearty sauces; baked
Rotelle (wheels)	Spiral-shaped; wheat flour	With medium or hearty sauces
Ruote (cartwheels)	Small, round 6-spoked wheels; *ruotini* are small wheels; wheat flour	With hearty sauces; *ruotini:* soup
Soba (Japanese)	Noodles the approximate shape and thickness of *fedeli* or *taglarini;* buckwheat flour	Oriental dishes, including soups, hot and cold noodle dishes
Somen (Japanese)	Long, thin, noodles; resemble *tagliarini;* wheat flour	Oriental dishes, including soups,
Spaghetti (little strings)	Solid, round strands ranging from very thin to thin; very thin spaghetti may be labeled *spaghettini;* wheat flour	With oil, butter, marinara, seafood, or other thin sauces
Tagliatelli	Same as fettuccine; may be mixed plain and spinach noodles, called *paglia e fieno* (straw and hay)	With rich, hearty sauces
Tubetti lunghi (long tubes)	Medium-small (usually about as thick as elbow macaroni), tubular, may be long or cut in lengths of about and inch; *tubettini* are tiny tubes.	With medium and hearty sauces; *tubettini:* soups
Udon (japanese)	Thick noodles, similar to somen; wheat flour	Oriental dishes
Vermicelli	Very fine cylindrical pasta, similar to capellini; wheat flour	With oil, butter, or light sauce
Ziti (bridegrooms)	Medium-sized tubes; may be ridged (rigati); may be long or cut in approximately 2-inch lengths *(ziti tagliate)*; wheat flour	With hearty sauces; baked

Review Your Learning 2.1

1. The two continents that are native homes of the potato (not yam) are North America and:
   a. Europe.
   b. Asia.
   c. South America.
   d. Africa.

2. Potatoes exposed to light may develop a greenish color. This means they contain:
   a. chlorine.
   b. solanine.
   c. starch.
   d. fiber.

3. Whole grains should be kept no more than:
   a. one week.
   b. two weeks.
   c. three weeks.
   d. four weeks.

4. Describe what happens to a grain when it is milled.

5. How should dried legumes and pasta be stored?

Cooking Potatoes

AFTER STUDYING SECTION 2.2, YOU SHOULD BY ABLE TO:

- Identify and describe different types of potato.
- Using a variety of recipes and cooking techniques, prepare potatoes.

The potato is one of the most popular vegetables because it is inexpensive and versatile. Many cooking methods, including boiling, steaming, baking, sautéing, en casserole, deep-frying, and puréeing, can be applied to produce a number of preparations with special flavors, textures, and appearances. (These cooking techniques can be reviewed in *Chapter 4: Kitchen Basics* of *Becoming a Foodservice Professional, Year 1.)* Different potato varieties will produce different results.

Types of Potatoes

You may think that all potatoes are the same. However, potato varieties differ in starch and moisture content, shape, and skin color. That's why different varieties

KEY TERMS

- All-purpose potato
- Chef's potato
- En casserole
- Idaho potato
- Latke (LAHT-key)
- Lyonnaise (LEE-on-AZE)
- Multiple-stage technique
- New potato
- Russet potato
- Single-stage technique
- Sweet potato
- Yam

produce a different end product. The starch content of any potato increases with age.

Sweet potatoes, yams, and russet potatoes are suited to baking, puréeing, and frying because they are high in starch and low in moisture.

Exhibit 2.7
Sweet potatoes range in color from light tan to brownish red.

Sweet potatoes are tubers whose thick skin ranges in color from light tan to brownish red. As you may remember from *Chapter 9: Fruits and Vegetables* in *Becoming a Foodservice Professional, Year 1*, tubers are fat, underground stems capable of growing a new plant. Sweet potatoes have an orange, mealy flesh that is very high in sugar. Sweet potatoes are best suited to boiling, baking, and puréeing. They are a popular ingredient in breads, pies, and even puddings. Unlike the russet or chef's potato, sweet potatoes are available canned in a sweet, sugary sauce.

Yams are very similar to sweet potatoes. They originated in Asia, and are less sweet than sweet potatoes. Yams range in color from creamy white to a deep red. Often, yams and sweet potatoes are used interchangeably.

Russet potatoes are often referred to as **Idaho potatoes.** They are the standard white baking potato. Their skin is generally a brownish-red color, and their flesh is mealy and white. Russets, or Idaho potatoes, are excellent for baking and frying. They are available in many shapes and sizes.

Exhibit 2.8
Russet and all-purpose potatoes.

Unlike russet potatoes, **chef's** or **all-purpose** potatoes are usually drier and less starchy than russet potatoes. These potatoes are also often less expensive than russet potatoes. Because chef's potatoes are usually irregularly shaped, they are most suited to preparation in which the final shape of the potato is not visually important, such as mashing, puréeing, in salads, scalloped or casserole dishes, soups, braising, and sautéing.

New potatoes are small, immature red potatoes that are harvested when they are very small—less than 2 inches in diameter. Unlike other baking potatoes, new potatoes are high in moisture and sugar, but have a low starch content. They are good to use in any preparation where the potato must keep its shape. For example, boiling and steaming are the best cooking methods to use to bring out their natural sweetness and fresh flavor.

Cooking Potatoes

There are two categories for cooking potatoes: single-stage and multiple-stage techniques. In the **single-stage technique,** potatoes are taken directly from the raw state to the finished state by using one cooking method. Boiled and baked potatoes are examples of single-stage techniques.

Potatoes prepared using a **multiple-stage technique** are prepared using more than one cooking method before they are a finished dish. One example of potatoes prepared using the multiple-stage method is **Lyonnaise** (LEE-on-AZE) potatoes. In this recipe, the potatoes are precooked, sliced, then fried with onions.

Everyone should eat baked potatoes! Why? Because they are superstars. Not only are they good-tasting, but they are also good for you. Cooking potatoes with their skin allows them to retain maximum nutrients. They are high in fiber, vitamins, and minerals, so eat them on a regular basis.

Boiling is one of the easiest methods of cooking potatoes. In addition, boiling is often the first step for other preparations, such as puréed potatoes. To boil potatoes, place washed potatoes in a pot of cold water with enough liquid to cover them. Bring the water to a boil and simmer until they are done. To test for doneness, pierce the potato with a fork. If the fork slides easily through the potato, it means the potato is done. The boiled potato can then be served immediately, or held for up to an hour.

Steaming is an especially good cooking method for new potatoes because of their high moisture content. New potatoes should be steamed until they are very tender. Like boiled potatoes, they can be served right away, or held and used with another dish.

Unlike boiled and steamed potatoes, *baked* potatoes are always served in their skins. The best baking potatoes are Idaho or russets. There are a variety of ways to bake potatoes. Wrapping potatoes in foil prior to baking keeps the skin soft, but makes the inside less fluffy. Rubbing the potato with oil keeps the skin soft while allowing the inside to get soft and fluffy. Baking with no foil or oil leaves the skin crisp.

No matter how they are baked, all potatoes should be scrubbed clean and pierced with a fork before they are placed in the oven. Piercing the potato with a fork will allow heat and steam to escape and prevent the potato from exploding. Baked potatoes should be cooked directly on an oven rack or sheet pan and served immediately.

Exhibit 2.9
Wrapping potatoes in foil before baking keeps the skin soft.

Did You Know?

When tin foil is wrapped around a potato and then placed in an oven, the potato isn't baked—it is steamed! The foil traps the heat and moisture from the potato as it cooks, creating a steaming effect.

En casserole potato dishes combine peeled and sliced raw potatoes with heavy cream, sauce, or uncooked custard and are then slowly baked in a buttered pan. Often the dish is topped with bread crumbs, butter, grated cheese, and broiled briefly to give it a golden-brown color. These potatoes are excellent for banquet service because they can be divided into individual portions very easily and can be held without losing quality.

Chef's potatoes are the best for *sautéing*. Sautéed potatoes should have a crisp, evenly browned exterior with a tender interior. Sauté the potatoes in oil or butter, stirring or flipping them frequently until they are golden brown. For best results, they should be served immediately.

FUN FOOD
FACT

Tips for Crispy French Fries and Potato Chips

To get really crisp fried potatoes, cut the potatoes in the desired shape, soak them in cold water, and refrigerate them for about one hour. Drain and dry them before frying. This process removes much of the potatoes' starch and allows them to fry to a crispier texture.

Another popular method of cooking potatoes is *deep-frying*. It is used to make French fries, cottage fries, steak fries, and many other fried potato dishes. Russet potatoes are best suited for deep-frying because of their low moisture content. Most potatoes prepared in deep fat should be *blanched* (cooked briefly in a lower temperature frying fat [325°F]) and refrigerated until service time. At service time, they are fried in fat heated to 350–375°F until golden brown. This is done in two stages because of the long cooking time. When they are done, drain them on a paper towel. Deep-fried potatoes cannot be held and should be served immediately.

Potato pancakes are made with grated potatoes and other ingredients, and are pan-fried to a crispy brown. They are traditional in many Eastern European cuisines, particularly in American-Jewish cooking, where they are called **latkes** (LAHT-keys). Latkes are traditionally served with apple sauce and sour cream.

Puréeing potatoes is another way to prepare potatoes. *Puréed* potatoes are important as the basis of many popular dishes, including mashed or whipped potatoes, duchesse potatoes, and potato croquettes.

Exhibit 2.10
French fries are a popular way to cook potatoes.

Puréed, whipped, and mashed potatoes are first boiled, steamed, or baked before they are combined with other ingredients or mashed. They may be held for service in a bain-marie or steam table. Puréed potatoes that are to be used in other dishes can be refrigerated for several hours.

Whenever possible, cook potatoes in their skins to retain their nutrients. Cut and peeled potatoes should be completely covered in a liquid to prevent discoloring.

Exhibit 2.11
Whole red potatoes are served boiled.

Review Your Learning 2.2

1. What happens when a potato is baked in aluminum foil?
   a. The foil causes the potato to become discolored
   b. The inside becomes less fluffy
   c. It requires a longer baking time than an unwrapped potato
   d. It shrinks when removed from the oven

2. You can prevent peeled and cut potatoes from discoloring by placing them in a(n):
   a. liquid.
   b. oven.
   c. refrigerator.
   d. freezer.

3. When preparing to boil potatoes, put potatoes in water that is:
   a. luke-warm.
   b. warm.
   c. cold.
   d. hot.

4. If you were making sautéed potatoes, what is the best type of potato to use?
   a. New potatoes
   b. Chef's potatoes
   c. Russet potatoes
   d. All-purpose potatoes

5. Discuss single-stage and multiple-stage techniques for cooking potatoes. How are they different? Give some examples of potatoes cooked each way.

2.3

SECTION 2.3

Cooking Legumes and Grains

AFTER STUDYING SECTION 2.3, YOU SHOULD BE ABLE TO:

- Identify and describe different types of grains and legumes.
- Using a variety of recipes and cooking techniques, prepare grains and legumes.

Grains and legumes are concentrated sources of nutrients, good-tasting, inexpensive, and readily available. They're full of protein, fiber, vitamins, and minerals.

KEY TERMS

- Arborio (ahr-BORE-ee-oh)
- Pilaf (PEEL-ahf)
- Risotto method (ree-SO-to)

Grains and legumes must be cooked:

- to change their textures so they can be chewed and digested easily;
- to develop their flavor; and
- to remove dirt, dust, or other natural substances that can be harmful to humans.

Cooking Legumes

Legumes must be rinsed carefully and, in some cases, soaked before cooking. Legumes can be placed in a large colander or sieve and rinsed well with cold running water to remove any dust or dirt particles. They should then be placed in a large pot with cold water. Any legumes that float to the surface should be discarded.

Why must you always cook legumes and grains before eating them? To develop their flavor, to remove harmful substances, and to make them easy to chew and digest. Cook them so they are firm to the bite.

Soaking legumes before cooking is not required but it does shorten the cooking time. The tough seed coatings of legumes don't absorb water quickly. If they are cooked without having been soaked first, they may not become soft even after cooking. Exhibit 2.12 shows the time requirements for soaking and cooking dried legumes.

Legumes can be soaked overnight in cold water or by using a quick method in which the legumes are boiled briefly and then soaked in the hot water for one hour. Legumes can only be boiled, and are done when they are very tender.

Exhibit 2.13
Variety of dried beans.

Exhibit 2.12
Soaking and cooking times for dried legumes.

Type	Soaking Time	Cooking Time
Adzuki beans	4 hours	1 hour
Black beans	4 hours	1½ hours
Black-eyed peas	n/a	1 hour
Chickpeas	4 hours	2-2½ hours
Fava beans	12 hours	3 hours
Great Northern beans	4 hours	1 hour
Kidney beans	4 hours	1 hour
Lentils	n/a	30-40 minutes
Lima beans	4 hours	1-1½ hours
Mung beans	4 hours	1 hour
Navy beans	4 hours	2 hours
Peas, split	n/a	30 minutes
Peas, whole	4 hours	40 minutes
Pink peas	4 hours	30 minutes
Pinto beans	4 hours	1-1½ hours
Soybeans	12 hours	3-3½ hours

The typical American cowboy and cowgirl diet consisted of chili, baked beans, and sourdough biscuits. The early pioneers planted herbs, onions, and peppers along the trail so they would always have a supply of fresh herbs on hand to spice up their meals!

Cooking Grains

Like legumes, grains should be soaked before they are cooked. For example, when whole grains such as barley and buckwheat are soaked, the water softens the outer layer, or bran. This makes them easier to cook. There are several ways to cook grains, including steaming, pilaf, and risotto.

Steamed grains are cooked in a double boiler with a perforated bottom over simmering or boiling liquid. Properly steamed grains should be tender to the bite and have a good flavor.

Pilaf (PEEL-ahf) is a technique for cooking grains in which the grain is sautéed briefly in oil or butter, then simmered in stock or water with various seasonings. In the pilaf method, the grain is first heated in a pan, either dry or with oil, and then combined with hot liquid and cooked in the oven or on the stove top. The grains will be tender, remain separate, and have a pleasing, nutty flavor. To give rice a particular flavor or color, add vegetable or fruit juice to the liquid. Use of an acid, such as tomato juice, may increase the cooking time up to 15 minutes

The risotto (ree-SO-to) method is usually used with one special short grain rice, **arborio** (ahr-BORE-ee-oh). Risotto has a very creamy consistency when it is finished because of the starch that is released from the arborio rice as it is cooked. This starch makes the finished

Exhibit 2.14
Lentils come in many different colors.

product sticky and creamy. In the **risotto** (ree-SO-to) **method,** the rice is stirred constantly as small amounts of hot liquid, usually flavored broth or water, are added and absorbed. The starch in the rice is released gradually during the cooking process, producing a creamy texture. The best risotto has a porridge-like consistency (sticky and creamy) and can be served as an appetizer or main entrée.

Exhibit 2.15
Pilaf is a flavorful accompaniment to shish kebabs.

Review Your Learning 2.3

1. What should you do with grains or legumes that float to the top of the rinse water?
   a. Prepare them first
   b. Throw them away
   c. Parboil them
   d. Rinse them again

2. In the pilaf method, cook the rice until it is:
   a. thick.
   b. soupy.
   c. crunchy.
   d. tender.

3. Why are grains and legumes rinsed before cooking?
   a. To remove dust and dirt
   b. To give them more flavor
   c. To make them more tender
   d. To make them cook faster

4. Steamed grains should be:
   a. mushy.
   b. tender.
   c. gummy.
   d. slightly hard.

5. Bring in a recipe from a cookbook, magazine, etc., for cooking a grain. What cooking method is used in the recipe?

SECTION 2.4

Cooking Pasta and Dumplings

AFTER STUDYING SECTION 2.4, YOU SHOULD BE ABLE TO:

- Identify and describe different types of pasta.
- Using a variety of recipes and cooking techniques, prepare pasta.

Pasta and dumplings are important elements of most cuisines because they are made from inexpensive, staple ingredients, and they can be used in many dishes—appetizers, entrées, salads, and even desserts.

Pasta and dumplings are prepared from a dough or batter that includes a starch, such as flour or potatoes, and a liquid. Additional ingredients may be used to add shape, color, texture, and flavor. The basic pasta dough recipe produces a stiff dough that can be stretched, rolled into thin sheets, and cut into desired shapes.

KEY TERMS

- **Al dente (ahl DAN-tay)**
- **Dumpling**
- **Gnocchi (nee-YO-key)**
- **Resting stage**
- **Spaetzle (SPAYT-z-le)**

Exhibit 2.16
Fresh pasta made by hand.

No one knows for sure where pasta originated. Some believe that the explorer Marco Polo brought it to Venice from China around A.D. 1300, but Italians passionately believe that people ate pasta during the time of Ancient Rome, around A.D. 1000.

Cooking Pasta

There are many differences between fresh pasta and dried pasta. Fresh pasta cooks very quickly. The pasta is done when it feels firm to the bite, or **al dente** (ahl DAN-tay). Because fresh pasta cooks so quickly, there is little reason to cook it in advance. However, cooked fresh pasta can be held for short periods for banquet and buffet service, then reheated by placing it in a wire basket and dipping it briefly in a pot of boiling water.

Cooking dry pasta does take longer than cooking fresh pasta. Like fresh pasta, it should be cooked al dente and served as soon as possible. However, dried pasta can be held for a longer period of time.

From Bugs Bunny macaroni to regular thin spaghetti, pasta comes in a wide array of colors, shapes, and sizes. The choice is yours and it's practically endless. But don't overcook. Otherwise, you'll end up with mushy macaroni!

Exhibit 2.17
A variety of dried pastas.

Fresh pasta dough uses four simple ingredients: eggs, salt, olive oil, and bread flour. Often, fresh herbs, spices, and vegetables are added for flavor and color. When vegetables are added to the mixture, they must be as dry as possible before they are mixed into the dough. Fresh herbs must be chopped or finely minced.

When mixing pasta dough, the most important stage is the **resting stage.** If the

Exhibit 2.18
Two of the basic ingredients for fresh pasta dough: eggs and flour.

dough is not sufficiently relaxed, it will be difficult to roll the dough into thin sheets. Pasta dough should be smooth and elastic, and slightly moist to the touch. When the dough has rested 15-30 minutes, it is ready to be rolled out into thin sheets.

Fresh, uncooked pasta can be held under refrigeration for a day or two, or it can be frozen. If it is to be stored longer, the pasta should be dried and stored in the same manner as commercially prepared dried pasta.

Any sauce served with pasta must be the right consistency to complement the type of pasta. For example, long, flat pastas, such as fettucine and linguine, are best served with smooth light cream sauces. Tube and twisted pastas are paired with heavier sauces, such as thick tomato and meat sauces, because they catch the sauce.

It's also important to pair the sauce with a pasta's particular flavor. For example, the delicate flavor of fresh pasta should be paired with a light cream or butter-based sauce, while heartier meat sauces are better for dried pastas. Filled pastas need only a very light sauce because a heavy sauce would overpower or conflict with the flavor of the filling.

Exhibit 2.19
Tortellini is a stuffed pasta with either meat or cheese filling.

Cooking Dumplings

Dumplings are made from doughs or batters, while others have bread and potatoes as their main ingredients, and are usually shaped into small round balls. The only way to test the doneness of dumplings is to cut into one of them. Dumplings should never have a doughy, uncooked interior.

Exhibit 2.20
Asian dumplings (potstickers).

Dumplings can be cooked in a variety of ways—simmered, steamed, poached, baked, pan-fried, deep-fried, and broiled. Simmered or poached dumplings are quite popular. In fact, most dumplings are initially cooked by poaching. After they have been poached, they can be finished in any of the ways mentioned above.

Slight additions or changes can transform pasta dough into a dumpling batter for **spaetzle** (SPAYT-z-le), small German dumplings, or breadlike dumplings that are tasty in stews. **Gnocchi** (nee-YO-key) are small potato dumplings served in Italian cuisine.

Review Your Learning 2.4

1. What are the two basic ingredients in any fresh pasta dough recipe?
   a. Starch and liquid
   b. Herbs and spices
   c. Vegetables and sugar
   d. Meat and starch

2. What does the term "al dente" mean when it is used to describe pasta?
   a. Soft to the bite
   b. Mushy to the bite
   c. Crisp to the bite
   d. Firm to the bite

3. Which of the following is a dumpling?
   a. Rotini
   b. Gnocchi
   c. Latke
   d. Linguine

4. How can you refresh cooked pasta before serving?
   a. Place it in the refrigerator
   b. Place it in the freezer
   c. Place it in ice-cold water
   d. Place it in hot water

5. Explain what sauces are best suited to certain types of pastas.

Flashback

CHAPTER 2

SECTION 2.1: SELECTING AND STORING POTATOES, GRAINS, LEGUMES, AND PASTA

- Potatoes, grains, and pastas are tasty, nutritious, and filling, and they have become an important part of the contemporary menu.
- Potatoes should be firm and relatively smooth.
- Any potatoes with black or green spots, mold, large cuts, or sprouts are unacceptable.
- Potatoes should be stored in a cool, dry place at temperatures ranging from 55°F to 60°F (12.8°C to 15.6°C). The maximum storage period for Idaho, russet, and all-purpose (chef's) potatoes is 30 days; new potatoes should be stored no longer than one week.
- Always discard potatoes if you have any doubts about their freshness or food safety.
- Grains, meals, and flours are all stocked in the professional kitchen.
- **Whole grains** are grains that have not been **milled.**
- **Stone-ground** grains retain more of their nutrients.
- Whole grains have a shorter shelf life than milled grains and should be purchased in quantities that can be used within three weeks.
- Grains and dry pastas should be carefully inspected when they are delivered.
- Store dry goods in an area that is dry, ventilated, and accessible. All dry goods should be placed above floor level on shelves.
- Whole grains should be stored in the refrigerator, or even the freezer.
- **Legumes** are seeds from pod-producing plants.
- Dried legumes have many uses in cooking, from salads and appetizers to main courses and desserts.
- Dried beans can be kept for one to two years, however, they are best when they are used within six months of purchase.
- Beans and peas are also available fresh, canned, or frozen.

- Legumes should be stored in cool, dry, well-ventilated areas, away from light and excessive heat.
- Always discard any beans or peas that appear moldy, damp, or wrinkled.
- Dried pastas and noodles are essential convenience foods because they store well, cook quickly, and provide a base or accompaniment for many popular dishes.

SECTION 2.2: COOKING POTATOES

- The potato is one of the most popular vegetables because of its versatility and wide appeal.
- A wide range of cooking techniques, including boiling, steaming, baking, sautéing, en casserole, deep-frying, and puréeing, can produce a number of preparations with special flavors, textures, and appearances. Different potato varieties will produce different results.
- **New potatoes** have a high moisture and sugar content, and a low starch content. This makes them perfect for steaming or boiling whole.
- Boiling is one of the easiest methods of cooking potatoes and is the first step for other preparations, such as potato croquettes.
- Potatoes cooked in their skins retain more nutrients. There are two categories of potato cookery—single-stage and multiple-stage techniques.
- In the **single-stage technique,** potatoes are taken directly from the raw state to the finished state by using one cooking method.
- Potatoes prepared in the **multiple-stage technique** undergo one or more cooking methods before they are a finished dish.

SECTION 2.3: COOKING LEGUMES AND GRAINS

- Cooking grains and legumes changes their textures so they can be chewed and digested easily and develops their flavor.
- Grains and legumes must be rinsed carefully to remove any dust or other particles.
- Any grains or legumes that float on the surface should be discarded.
- Soaking is not essential but it does shorten the cooking time.
- Grains should not be held long after cooking.

- Cooked legumes may be held for a few days after cooking if they are cooled and stored under refrigeration in their cooking liquid.
- There are several ways to cook grains, including steaming, **pilaf,** and **risotto.**
- The risotto method is usually used for one special short grain rice, **arborio.**
- Legumes can only be boiled.
- Grains are done when they are tender to the bite; legumes are done when they are very tender, with no hard core at the center.

SECTION 2.4: COOKING PASTA AND DUMPLINGS

- Pasta and dumplings are made from inexpensive, staple ingredients and can easily be used in appetizers, entrées, salads, and even desserts.
- Pasta and dumplings are prepared from a dough or batter that always includes a starch, such as flour, meal, or potatoes, and a liquid. Additional ingredients may be added to change the dish's shape, color, texture, and flavor.
- The basic pasta dough recipe produces a stiff dough that can be stretched, rolled into thin sheets, and cut into desired shapes.
- Fresh pasta cooks very quickly and should be cooked until it is **al dente,** or firm to the bite.
- Fresh, uncooked pasta can be held under refrigeration for a day or two, or it can be frozen.
- If it is to be stored longer, the pasta should be dried and stored in the same manner as commercially prepared dried pasta.
- The accompanying sauce that is served must be the right consistency to complement the shape and flavor of the pasta.
- Filled pastas need only a very light sauce.
- **Dumplings** can be cooked in a variety of ways, depending on their type—simmered, steamed, poached, baked, pan-fried, deep-fried, or boiled.
- The only way to test the doneness of dumplings is to cut into one of them.
- Slight additions or changes can transform pasta dough into a dumpling batter for **spaetzle,** or breadlike dumplings that are tasty in stews.

PROFILE

Alexis Edwards

Innkeeper
The Whitlock Inn
Marietta, Georgia

The lodging industry is a really fun industry to be a part of. Every day I am introduced to many new people and interesting situations. The variety of people I meet is wonderful—the guests bring the world to the inn. Sometimes I feel like I get to travel without even going anywhere!

There will always be a need for the lodging industry because people will always travel, whether it is for work or for fun. Guests stay at the inn for many different reasons—vacation, business, weddings. It's my job to make sure they enjoy themselves and are comfortable.

Being able to handle a lot of different tasks is really important in my job as innkeeper. I'm responsible for greeting and checking in guests, taking care of daily accounting procedures, overseeing my employees, and managing the overall upkeep of the inn. I also work with caterers and florists for special functions like holiday parties and weddings.

It's really important to be familiar with all aspects of the operation. I did an internship where I did a little bit of everything, from preparing breakfast, doing the night audit, and even cleaning. It was hard, but it gave me a great appreciation for my own work at the Whitlock Inn. Even though my employees do things like clean and audit, I understand how these jobs are done and can fill in when I'm needed. There is no such thing as a typical day here. Every day is different, with different challenges and situations.

The lodging industry fills a need, and that need is to make people comfortable when they are away from home. I enjoy the fact that I don't have to wait to see the effects of my work. I know at the end of every day that my work has reached people. I was surprised at how much work it takes to run an inn, but the work is always interesting and *very* rewarding.

CHAPTER 3

The Lodging Industry

Understanding Lodging

AFTER STUDYING SECTION 3.1, YOU SHOULD BE ABLE TO:

- Trace and explain the earliest types of lodging establishments in America.
- Give an overview of career opportunities in the lodging industry.

KEY TERMS

- Administrative department
- Back-of-the-house
- Front-of-the-house
- Lodging property
- Service department

Whether they're called hotels, motels, suites, resorts, or bed and breakfasts, **lodging properties** all have one basic thing in common—they provide temporary housing to overnight guests for a price.

A Brief History of Lodging in the U.S.: Planes, Trains, and Automobiles

The lodging industry in the United States has always been strongly influenced by changes in transportation. As stagecoach routes were established in the mid-1600s, coaching inns became popular resting places where travelers could expect a meal and a bed for the evening. Although these inns resemble today's lodging facilities, it wasn't until the 1700s that American inns really began to combine food and beverage service with lodging.

The year 1794 saw the opening of the City Hotel in New York City, the first building in the U.S. designed specifically as a hotel. The property inspired the construction of other pioneering establishments, and American innkeepers continued to build bigger and better equipped lodging properties throughout the 1800s. The Tremont House, the first of the grand hotels, was built in Boston in 1828. It was the first hotel to offer private rooms with locking doors.

With the invention of the railroad in 1825, inns, taverns, and foodservice facilities located near railway stations began to grow. Travelers could now reach remote areas from coast to coast by rail. Several famous resorts developed as a result of this growth in the rail industry, including the Hotel del Coronado near San Diego, California, and the Greenbriar Resort in West Virginia.

Near the turn of the century, Conrad Hilton, who was a banker in New Mexico, purchased his first hotel, the Mobley, in Cisco, Texas. Hilton was very successful at operating this hotel and purchased several other hotels in the area. Other famous hotels were built during the early part of the twentieth century, including the Ritz Carlton in Boston, the Plaza in New York City, and the Stevens Hotel (now the Chicago Hilton and Towers) in Chicago.

During the Depression in the 1930s, several hotel properties across the country closed. The cause is simple to understand. People could afford to travel when the economy was healthy, but most Americans did not travel when the economy was depressed. Hotel properties were expensive to run, and without enough people staying in them, they could not cover their costs.

Exhibit 3.1
During World War II, the lodging industry experienced high occupancy rates because of war-related travel.

During World War II in the 1940s, the lodging industry prospered. Many people were traveling for war-related reasons. No new hotels were being built because all construction materials and labor were devoted to the war efforts. Therefore, finding an empty hotel room was difficult for travelers. Hotels experienced extremely high occupancy rates—usually at least 90%.

In the 1950s, the increased availability and popularity of the automobile, together with a new interstate freeway system, made cross-country vacations a popular option for many American families. The first motels sprang up along highways across America, offering travelers a convenient place to bathe, sleep, and eat before getting back on the road.

In 1958, transportation technology soared to new heights, as commercial airlines became a popular and increasingly economical way of traveling. Builders turned their eyes toward land near airports as the next new place to situate their hotels, motels, and foodservice facilities.

And in the future? Count on the lodging industry to keep a close eye on how people are getting from here to there.

Give It A Try...

Many of this country's biggest hotel chains were started by young entrepreneurs at the beginning of the 20th century. Can you name the hotels they founded?

- ***Conrad Hilton***
- ***Howard Johnson***
- ***Cesar Ritz***
- ***William Waldorf Astor & John Jacob Astor IV***
- ***J. W. Marriott and J. W. Marriott, Jr.***

Lodging Operations Organization

Lodging properties come in all shapes and sizes, from small, roadside motels, where owners oversee all operations, to large, full-service hotels employing hundreds of people.

There are many ways to organize departments within a lodging operation. One common method is to categorize each

Exhibit 3.2
In the 1950s, a car and the open road were all a family needed to plan a cross-country vacation. About ten years later, commercial airlines made long-distance travel much less time-consuming.

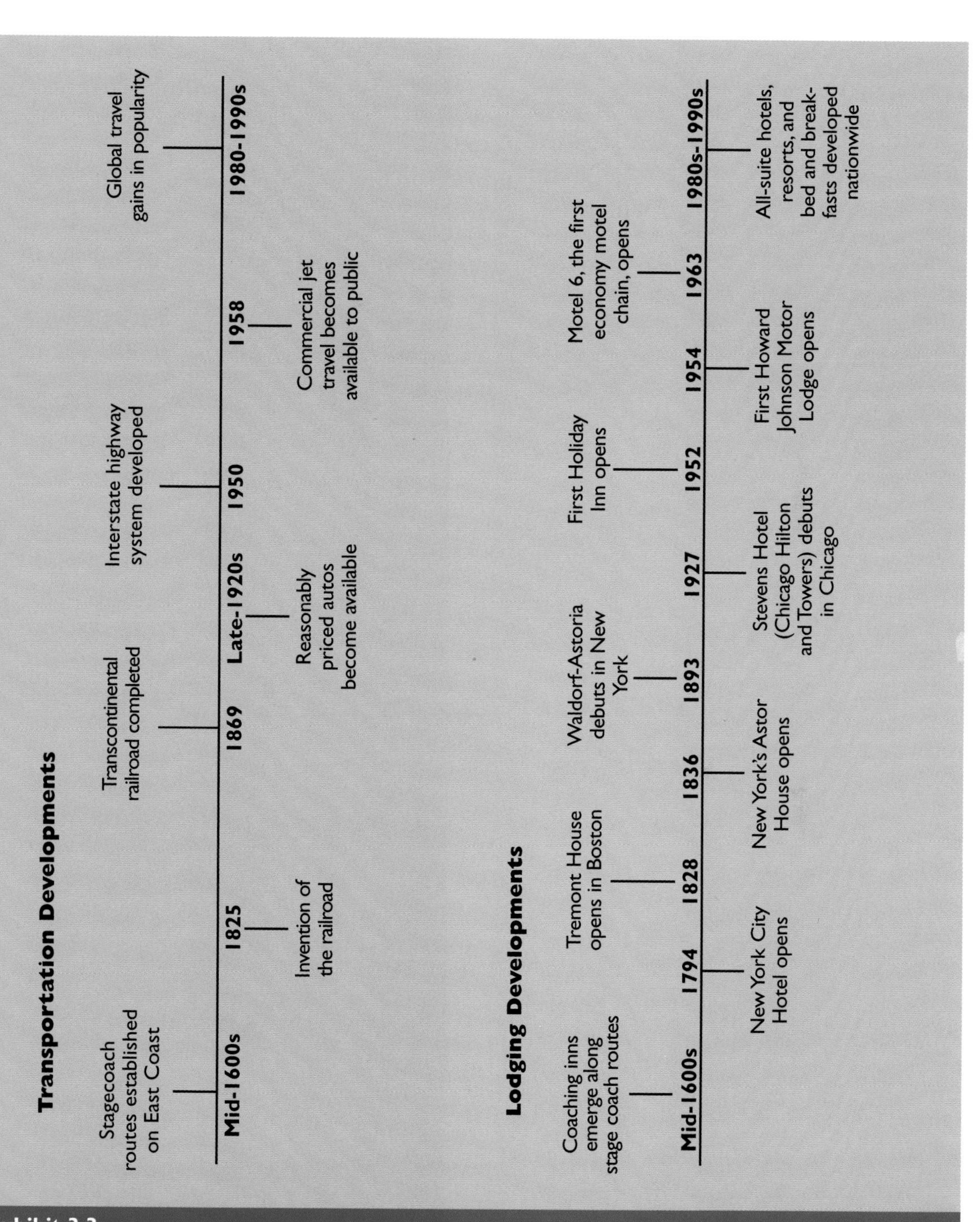

Exhibit 3.3
Where transportation goes, lodging is sure to follow.

Exhibit 3.4
Front-of-the-house employees, such as this room service attendant, come in direct contact with guests.

area as front-of-the-house or back-of-the-house. **Front-of-the-house** employees are those who come into direct contact with guests. **Back-of-the-house** employees operate behind the scenes, supporting front-of-the-house areas in a variety of ways.

A typical lodging operation can also be divided between its administrative departments and service departments. **Adminis-trative departments** manage the business responsibilities such as accounting, human resources and training, and marketing and sales. **Service departments** are responsible for serving the guests directly—by providing quick and easy check-ins; clean, safe, and well-kept facilities; and meeting guests' other needs to keep them comfortable.

A quick overview of the departments in a lodging operation is included here, but we will explore them in more detail in Section 3.3

Administrative Departments

General Management—The general manager (GM) is the person-in-charge of the lodging establishment. The GM directs staff, oversees all department operations, ensures guest satisfaction, and is responsible for increasing the operation's profits. The assistant GM, executive housekeeper, and other management employees report directly to the general manager.

Exhibit 3.5
Human resources personnel often are responsible for employee training programs.

Accounting and Financial Management—This area keeps track of overall profits, records sales, and calculates costs. While accounting staff routinely manage accounts receivable (money coming in) and financial reporting and control, they may also prepare operating statements, conduct cost studies, and forecast industry trends.

Human Resources—In an industry as labor-intensive and service-oriented as lodging, hiring and keeping quality employees are key. Human resources personnel not only recruit, select, and train qualified applicants, but evaluate performance as well. They are also responsible for administering federal, state, and local labor laws and overseeing the operation's benefits program.

Marketing and Sales—Marketing and sales are largely responsible for generating the property's sales. They do this by making sure that their lodging facility and its services are well-suited to their customers' needs. Marketing and sales employees are constantly working to learn what type of services guests want and are willing to pay for. This knowledge helps them develop marketing and sales plans that can increase an operation's profits. Encompassing general sales, group sales, banquet sales, and advertising, people working in marketing and sales need to have a thorough knowledge of all aspects of the lodging operation.

Exhibit 3.6
A good first impression at the front desk can set the tone for an enjoyable stay

Service Departments

Front Office—Often described as the "nerve center," the front office represents what a lodging establishment is to most guests. For this reason, it's vital that front office employees have good people skills and know the importance of quality service. In addition to greeting and communicating with guests, front office employees handle check-in, checkout, and reservations; they also manage rooms, resolve complaints, and provide guests with information.

Housekeeping—In addition to maintaining property, housekeeping personnel are responsible for keeping rooms guest-ready and ensuring that accommodations are clean and safe. *According to studies conducted among business and leisure travelers, room cleanliness is the number one factor in choosing a lodging facility.*

Engineering and Facility Maintenance—Engineers and facility maintenance workers keep the physical building in good running order. Electrical, heating, plumbing, ventilation, air conditioning, lighting, refrigeration, and fire prevention systems all fall within this department's responsibilities. They also maintain the operation's mechanical equipment.

Security—Depending on its size, a lodging facility may employ a number of security personnel, including a director, watchmen, guards, and detectives. In addition to protecting guests, fellow employees, and property, security staff is also responsible for developing and following all emergency procedures, as well as maintaining security alarm systems.

Food and Beverage—The food and beverage department is one of the most demanding areas of lodging operations. As with the front office department, employees in food and beverage need good people skills and a commitment to quality. The food and beverage director oversees the kitchen, dining room, and lounge, as well as banquet and room service. The director's other responsibilities include supervising and scheduling employees, monitoring product cost-control, and composing menus.

Exhibit 3.7
Food and beverage departments are usually profit centers for lodging operations.

Review Your Learning 3.1

1. Historically, the lodging industry has been closely tied to the ________ industry.
   a. baking
   b. shipping
   c. leisure
   d. transportation

2. What mode of transportation was invented in the early 1800s?
   a. Railroads
   b. Busses
   c. Commercial airlines
   d. Cars

3. During which decade in U.S. history did the lodging industry experience the closing of many hotels?
   a. 1920s
   b. 1930s
   c. 1940s
   d. 1950s

4. In the 1950s, the extensive development of __________ encouraged the development of roadside motels.
   a. railroads
   b. coach lines
   c. commercial airlines
   d. the interstate highway system

Continued on next page

5. If you wanted to improve your ability to be friendly with strangers, you might want to take a class in:
   a. speech communication.
   b. computers.
   c. biology.
   d. math.

6. Which of the following lodging departments is *not* an administrative department?
   a. Marketing and sales
   b. Front office
   c. Human resources
   d. General management

7. The term *front-of-the-house* is most closely related to which of the following?
   a. Administrative
   b. Behind the scenes
   c. Guest service
   d. Back office

8. Which of the following provide temporary housing to overnight guests for a price?
   a. Overnight investments
   b. Lodging properties
   c. Retail properties
   d. Administrative departments

3.2

SECTION 3.2

Organization of the Lodging Industry

AFTER STUDYING SECTION 3.2, YOU SHOULD BE ABLE TO:

- Describe the differences between leisure and business travelers.
- List the characteristic types of lodging operations.
- List and discuss elements that differentiate one lodging establishment from another.
- Identify national organizations that rate commercial lodging establishments, and list factors used in making their rating judgments.
- List several different services offered by lodging operators.

Two Types of Travelers

People travel away from home for a variety of reasons. Some may be attending out-of-town conventions, others are visiting relatives or traveling abroad to experience a foreign culture. Depending on their reasons for staying at a lodging property, all of these

KEY TERMS

- All-suite property
- Amenity (a-MEN-i-tee)
- Bed and breakfast
- Business travelers
- Economy lodging
- Full-service property
- Hotelier (OH-tell-YAY)
- Leisure travelers
- Luxury property
- Meeting and convention hotel
- Mid-priced facility
- Resort (re-ZORT)

guests fall under one of two categories: leisure travelers or business travelers.

Although both types of guests seek clean, comfortable, and safe accommodations, business and leisure travelers expect different things from a lodging property. **Leisure travelers** often want to "get away from it all." They're on vacation and they're eager to do fun things like shopping, fine dining, sightseeing, attending sports events, or simply finding the time to relax.

Many lodging properties cater to specific leisure travelers by offering services or activities designed especially for them. Some facilities, for example, sponsor programs for children; others are geared toward adults, providing guests with social activities or on-site recreational or health facilities.

Exhibit 3.9
Seven reasons people become leisure travelers.

What's Your Leisure?

- Visit friends or relatives
- Visit cultural attractions or historically significant places
- Visit natural landmarks
- Participate in recreational activities
- Attend special events
- Celebrate religious holidays or festivals
- Improve health through relaxation

Business travelers stay at lodging properties for business-related reasons. They represent the majority of guests for most lodging establishments. Recognizing and catering to their needs are essential to the success of many properties.

Typical business travelers spend most of their time working. In addition to well-lit

Exhibit 3.8
Leisure travelers may travel just to relax, or to visit natural landmarks.

work spaces and telephones, they often need modems for personal computers, copiers, and fax machines, as well as meeting and banquet facilities. Many business travelers expect 24-hour room service, valet parking, and a secure lodging operation. While women business travelers—a significant part of the corporate travel market—need the same general services as their male counterparts, they tend to favor establishments that emphasize security.

Lodging properties depend on attracting both leisure and business travelers. Most establishments look to fill their rooms with business travelers Monday through Thursday, while concentrating on leisure travelers for their weekend bookings. This strategy keeps unoccupied rooms—also known as *vacancies*—to a minimum.

Although business and leisure travelers expect different services when traveling away from home, they have one thing in common for sure. *According to numerous studies, the most important factor considered when selecting a lodging facility is room cleanliness.* This is true regardless of the type of traveler. Other amenities and services are important, but not as important as staying in a clean room.

Exhibit 3.10
Business travelers need access to technology and business services on the go.

At Your Service: Lodging Establishments for All

Lodging properties can be classified in many ways: by the level of service provided, the rates charged, the amenities offered, or any combination of these or other factors. An **amenity** (a-MEN-i-TEE) is a service or facility within the lodging operation that guests may use or enjoy without having to leave the hotel.

Lodging amenities range from restaurants, lounges, and parking garages to newsstands, boutiques, barber shops, dry cleaners, and florists. Amenities add value to the guests' experiences by satisfying their needs in a convenient manner. By putting these facilities within easy reach of their guests, lodging operators increase the satisfaction of their customers.

The differences in facilities, however, are ultimately a reflection of the type of guest each aims to serve. Again, business and leisure travelers differ in their needs at a full-service property. While business travelers are attracted by such extras as banquet and meeting facilities, all guests enjoy clean, well-decorated rooms, and high-quality service.

Full-service properties, for example, cater to travelers in search of a wide range of conveniences. They offer larger rooms, well-trained staff, and feature plenty of amenities, which may include swimming pools, room service, and cable television. They also have amenities such as meeting and banquet rooms.

Luxury properties are hotels that offer top-of-the-line comfort and elegance. While often considered a part of the full-service sector, luxury hotels take service and amenities to new heights of excellence. The rooms are spacious and well-decorated and may feature luxurious extras like bathrobes. Other amenities found at luxury properties include gift shops, boutiques, and a variety of restaurants and lounges. These establishments are often aimed at wealthy travelers and corporate executives.

Unlike luxury hotels, **economy lodging** offers clean, low-priced accommodations primarily to traveling salespeople, senior citizens, and families with modest

Exhibit 3.11
A room at a full-service property offers more than just a bed, but may not provide as many amenities as are found in a luxury property.

Did You Know?

Standard rooms at luxury hotels are usually priced at several hundred dollars a night, and their most expensive suites can often go for well over $1,000 a night.

incomes. To maintain low rates, these properties employ small staffs and provide limited amenities. Guest rooms usually have one or two double beds, as well as a bathroom with clean towels and soap. In return for doing without the extras offered at full-service or luxury properties, guests enjoy sanitary, fully-furnished accommodations at budget prices.

Mid-priced facilities fall somewhere between the full-service and economy sectors. They are designed for travelers who want comfortable, moderately priced accommodations. Also known as *tourist-class* properties, mid-priced facilities provide private baths, on-premises food and beverage service, and simple decor.

The fastest growing segment of the lodging industry includes **all-suite properties.** These offer apartment-style facilities at mid-market prices. Featuring a living room and dining room, at least one bedroom and bathroom, and a kitchenette, each all-suite unit provides guests with about 500 to 800 square feet of space (versus 300 to 400 square feet in a standard hotel room).

A Blast From the Past

Founded in 1962, Motel 6 is the oldest economy chain in the United States. Its business philosophy was summed up in one of its original advertisements:

> *Has the whole idea of motels gotten out of hand? Motels were invented as an alternative to the bother and expense of a hotel. Someplace simple, where you could drive right up to the door and have a nice functional little room for the night without taking out a bank loan to do it. But today many motels are just a little simpler and slightly plainer than Buckingham Palace...At Motel 6 our idea of a motel room is more like the original idea...What you get at Motel 6 is what you need—without spending the bankroll.*

While all-suite establishments appeal to different people for different reasons, all guests enjoy the at-home atmosphere and the extra space that these properties provide for both work and relaxation. The roominess is also a draw for traveling families, since parents and children can spread out as if they are staying in an apartment instead of a hotel room.

Sparing no expense, **resorts** (re-ZORTS) feature extensive facilities for vacationers who are looking for recreational activities and entertainment. Appealing to specific types of guests, some resorts provide programs for singles only, families with children, couples only, or senior citizens. Other establishments focus on a particular area of interest, such as golf, tennis, scuba diving, or health.

Often located in beautiful vacation areas, resorts usually have distinct tourism seasons. While resorts cater primarily to vacationers, many rely on conventions to keep vacancy rates low year-round. Resorts, however, enjoy only a small part of the business travel market.

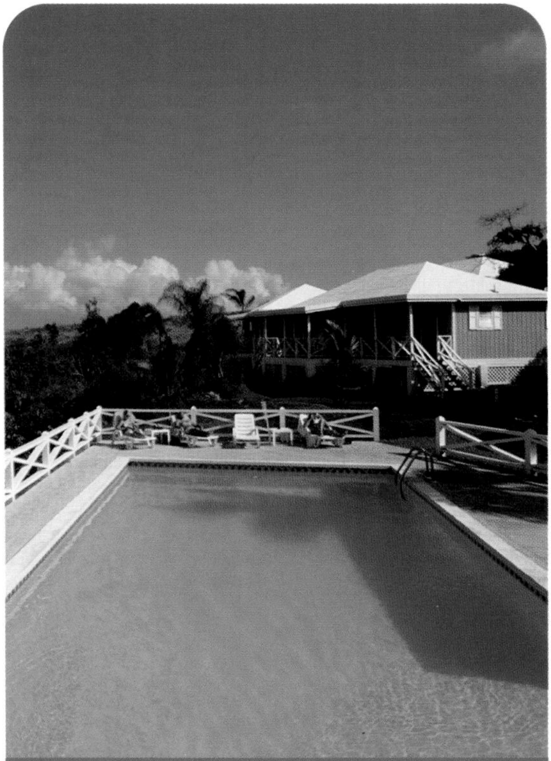

Used with permission from the Educational Institute of the American Hotel and Motel Association.

Exhibit 3.12
Resorts offer leisure travelers several options for recreation and relaxation.

Bed and breakfasts are a type of lodging property catering to guests looking for quaint, quiet accommodations with simple amenities. Bed and breakfasts are usually privately-owned homes converted to have several guest rooms. Often guests may share bathrooms with other guests staying at the bed and breakfast. Bed and breakfasts are usually found off the beaten path in areas with tourist or natural attractions.

At bed and breakfasts, guests are served breakfast during a specified time in a small dining room. They usually do not serve lunch or dinner, but may offer special hours for teas or cocktails in the afternoon. Bed and breakfasts are different from other lodging properties because the owner usually lives on the property and manages its day-to-day operations.

Many lodging properties are constructed specifically to accommodate conferences and conventions. Specializing in large gatherings and exhibitions, a typical **meeting and convention hotel** may host as many as 100

The Whitlock Inn, Marietta, Georgia. Photo by George Clark.

Exhibit 3.14
Bed and breakfasts, also called B&Bs, offer travelers quaint, relaxed accommodations with a personal touch.

conventions per year. They are usually connected to or very near convention halls and arenas.

Businesspeople attending conventions often prefer these hotels because they provide conference and meeting rooms in the same building. In addition to emphasizing food and beverage service and meeting and banquet rooms, many convention hotels also offer secretarial services and access to desktop computers, photocopy and fax machines, and audiovisual equipment.

Many convention hotels also feature extensive recreational facilities. These amenities are all designed to make a conventioneer's stay as comfortable and productive as possible.

Exhibit 3.13
Examples of hotels and chains in each lodging segment. How are they different from each other? How are they similar?

Luxury
- Ritz-Carlton
- Waldorf-Astoria
- Four Seasons

Economy
- Travelodge
- Budgetel
- Red Roof Inn
- Motel 6

Mid-priced
- Holiday Inn
- Radisson
- Howard Johnson

All-suite
- Embassy Suites
- Marriott Suites
- Comfort Suites

Full-service
- Westin
- Hyatt
- Hilton
- Sheraton

Meeting and Convention
- Las Vegas Convention Center
- Hilton
- Atlanta Marriott Marquis

Bed and Breakfasts
- Independent operators

Resorts
- Disney World-Epcot Center
- Club Med

LOCATION, LOCATION, LOCATION

Location is one of the most influential factors contributing to the success of a lodging facility. It helps determine the mix of leisure and business travelers an establishment will serve.

Businesspeople, for example, prefer hotels close to their destinations and transportation. Vacationers, on the other hand, often look for facilities close to tourist or cultural attractions or tucked away in more remote areas. In general, there are five location categories for lodging properties.

Airport facilities were originally constructed to accommodate flight crews and air travelers whose flights were delayed or canceled. To attract both local businesspeople and large groups attending conventions, **hoteliers** (OH-tel-YAYS), which are owners or managers of lodging properties, began to add banquet and meeting facilities to their standard offerings. Today, airport properties offer quality facilities that save guests travel time to and from the airport.

Downtown properties serve primarily business travelers and conventioneers. During the workweek, downtown facilities put professionals close to convention and meeting locations; at night, guests are close to entertainment and cultural events found in most cities.

Downtown facilities tend to charge higher room rates than those in outlying areas because they are located on costly real estate. Most downtown facilities have higher occupancy during the week and much lower occupancy on the weekend.

In the 1950s, people began to move from the city to its outlying areas where land and housing were less expensive. This population shift brought about a need for suburban lodging.

Suburban properties originally provided accommodations for travelers who wanted to attend downtown events but didn't want to spend the night in the city. They also provided lodging for guests visiting suburban locations to attend special events such as holiday celebrations, weddings, and reunions.

Today, many suburban establishments feature banquet facilities and meeting rooms in an effort to attract local professionals who travel to the suburbs for business purposes.

Roadside motels are located near major highways. These highway lodging operations meet the needs of vacation and business travelers alike. Roadside motels were created in the 1950s and 1960s with the growth of the interstate highway system. These motels accommodate guests who typically stay an average of just one night.

Resorts are often located in popular vacation areas. As a result, most resort establishments have distinct tourism seasons, which usually match periods of good weather. Resort complexes are often built far from cities and transportation routes, so many resorts must have large storage facilities for supplies, as well as expanded areas for laundry, food, and maintenance services.

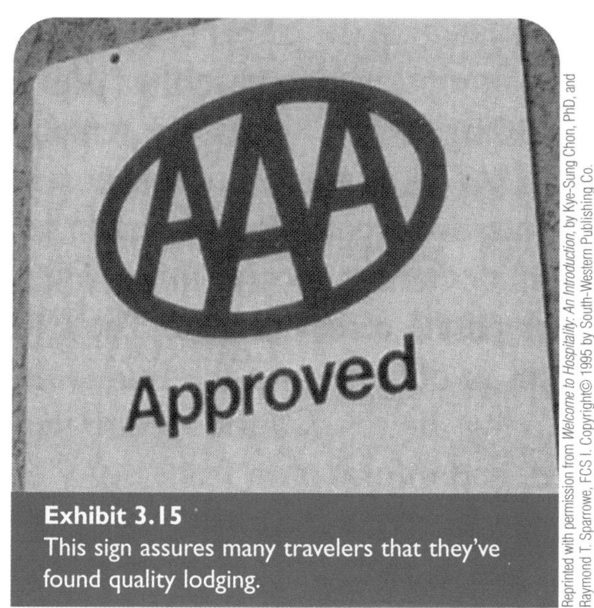

Exhibit 3.15
This sign assures many travelers that they've found quality lodging.

Facility Rating Systems

To distinguish one lodging property from another, several organizations rate the quality of lodging establishments. The American Automobile Association's (AAA) *Tour Book* is the most widely recognized rating service in the United States. Distributed to members of the AAA, the guide uses a diamond system in judging overall quality.

- ♦ Functional accommodations that comply with minimum standards; meet basic needs of comfort, privacy, cleanliness, and safety
- ♦♦ Noticeable enhancements over ♦ properties in terms of decor and/or quality of furnishings
- ♦♦♦ Marked upgrade in services and comfort, with additional amenities and/or facilities
- ♦♦♦♦ Excellent properties offering a high level of service and a wide variety of amenities and upscale facilities
- ♦♦♦♦♦ Exceptional establishments providing the highest level of luxury and service

Exhibit 3.16
A review of the types of lodging facilities and what they offer.

Type of Lodging Property	Features and Amenities
Economy	Smaller, simple rooms. Amenities are limited but may include such necessities as irons and ironing boards and convenient check-out options.
Mid-priced	Larger, simple rooms. Amenities may include a restaurant, in-room coffee makers, and small meeting rooms.
Full-service	Larger, decorated rooms. Amenities may include a swimming pool, room service, cable television, a restaurant or lounge, and meeing and banquet rooms.
Luxury	Spacious, deluxe rooms with features such as bathrobes and complimentary toiletries. Amenities may include laundry services, gift shops, hair stylists, boutiques, and a variety of restaurants and lounges.
All-suite	Suites that include kitchenettes and living areas apart from the sleeping area. Amenities may include laundry services and work-out areas.
Meeting and Convention	Larger rooms with tables or desk areas for working and fax and computer hook-ups in the room. Amenities may include office or secretarial services, large meeting rooms with audio-visual equipment, and banquet facilities.
Resort	Larger rooms with a relaxed decor. Amenities may include pools and sun decks, water sports, tennis courts, night clubs, several restaurants and lounges, and services such as massages and beauty treatments.
Bed and Breakfast	Quaint rooms with a personal touch. Amenities may include private bathrooms, complimentary breakfast, and personal attention.

The AAA looks at many factors when judging properties, including the following.

- Management and staff
- Housekeeping
- Maintenance
- Room decor and furnishings
- Bathrooms
- Guest services and facilities
- Soundproofing
- Security
- Parking
- Exterior appearance

The *Mobil Travel Guides* are another major American rating resource. The *Mobil Travel Guides* rate thousands of properties with a five-star system:

★	Good, better than average
★★	Very good
★★★	Excellent
★★★★	Outstanding—worth a special trip
★★★★★	One of the best in the country

The *Mobil Travel Guides* rate facilities by looking at the quality of the building and its furnishings inside, maintenance, housekeeping, and overall service. The top rating is very difficult to achieve, with fewer than 100 properties being awarded five stars each year.

Review Your Learning 3.2

1. On a separate sheet of paper, indicate which type of traveler—business **(B)** or leisure **(L)**—would find the features listed below most important.

   a. Meeting rooms available
   b. Programs for children
   c. Near shopping areas
   d. Location close to the airport
   e. Shuttle bus to theme park
   f. Kiddie swimming pool
   g. Shuttle bus to convention center
   h. Located close to a city's cultural attractions
   i. Twenty-four hour room service
   j. Modems for computers in each room

2. For the following types of properties, provide an example of:
   a. a specific guest each aims to serve.
   b. amenities or services that might attract this type of guest to the property.

   - Economy
   - All-suite
   - Resort
   - Meeting and convention hotel

3. ___________ facilities are often constructed far from cities and transportation routes.
   a. All-suite
   b. Downtown lodging
   c. Resort
   d. Economy

Continued on next page

4. As part of the full-service segment, which of the following properties cater to wealthy travelers and corporate executives?
   a. All-suite
   b. Economy
   c. Full-service
   d. Luxury

5. Which of the following hotels is most likely to provide conference and meeting rooms and secretarial services?
   a. Economy
   b. Meeting and convention
   c. Luxury
   d. All-suite

6. A florist shop that operates in a hotel's lobby is known as a(n):
   a. amenity.
   b. hotelier.
   c. all-suite.
   d. full-service.

7. Since they rely primarily on business travelers, which of the following hotels typically experience low occupancy rates on weekends?
   a. Resort
   b. Downtown
   c. Economy
   d. Luxury

8. Which of the following factors *doesn't* the AAA consider when rating a lodging property?
   a. Management and staff
   b. Room decor
   c. Guest services and facilities
   d. Proximity to major cultural attractions

Career Opportunities in the Lodging Industry

AFTER STUDYING SECTION 3.3, YOU SHOULD BE ABLE TO:

- Identify career opportunities in the hospitality industry and list the qualifications commonly sought by hospitality employers.
- List and describe activities associated with front office operation.
- List and describe tasks performed by the housekeeping department.
- List and describe duties performed by the engineering and facilities maintenance department.

KEY TERMS

- Assistant general manager
- Bell captain
- Chief engineer
- Concierge (con-see-AIRJ)
- Controller
- Convention manager
- Convention sales manager
- Desk clerk
- Executive assistant manager
- Executive housekeeper
- Food and beverage director
- Front desk manager
- General manager (GM)
- Human resources (HR) director
- Marketing director
- Management information systems (MIS) supervisor
- Night auditor
- Reservations manager
- Resident manager
- Room attendant
- Security chief

Developing a Career in the Lodging Industry

The U.S. lodging industry has many fulfilling jobs to choose from. Opportunities for quick advancement are common in this industry. While people without high school diplomas find jobs in lodging, the more education you have, the better the position you're likely to find—and the higher the wages you'll earn as you climb the job ladder.

Certificate and diploma programs are offered by high schools and business, career, and technical institutes. In addition, hundreds of hospitality administration and hotel management degree programs are available at community and four-year colleges across the country. Subjects such as speech communication, computers, psychology, accounting, law, math, and hospitality business will give you the skills you need to enter the profession.

With the growth of international business and widespread world travel, knowing a second language often gives you a competitive edge in this field. Many students study or work abroad to better learn a second language.

Most lodging operations have extensive company-sponsored training programs for their new employees. In addition to education and work experience, associations and professional trade organizations offer programs and events that can help you further your career. Seminars and trade shows are great places to get to know your industry colleagues on both a social and professional level.

While most lodging establishments perform the same basic functions, the number and type of employees at each property will depend on property size and guest services offered, as well as many other factors. As we discussed in Section 3.1, the departments in a lodging operation are broken into two broad categories—administrative and service. Now let's take a closer look at the people and responsibilities within these departments.

Administrative Departments

General Management

The **general manager (GM)** is responsible for the overall performance of a lodging establishment and its employees. General managers usually have a bachelor's degree in hotel management or a related field and at least 10 years of work experience in the lodging industry. Leadership is the most important quality a GM can bring to the job, as he or she directly supervises employees throughout the facility.

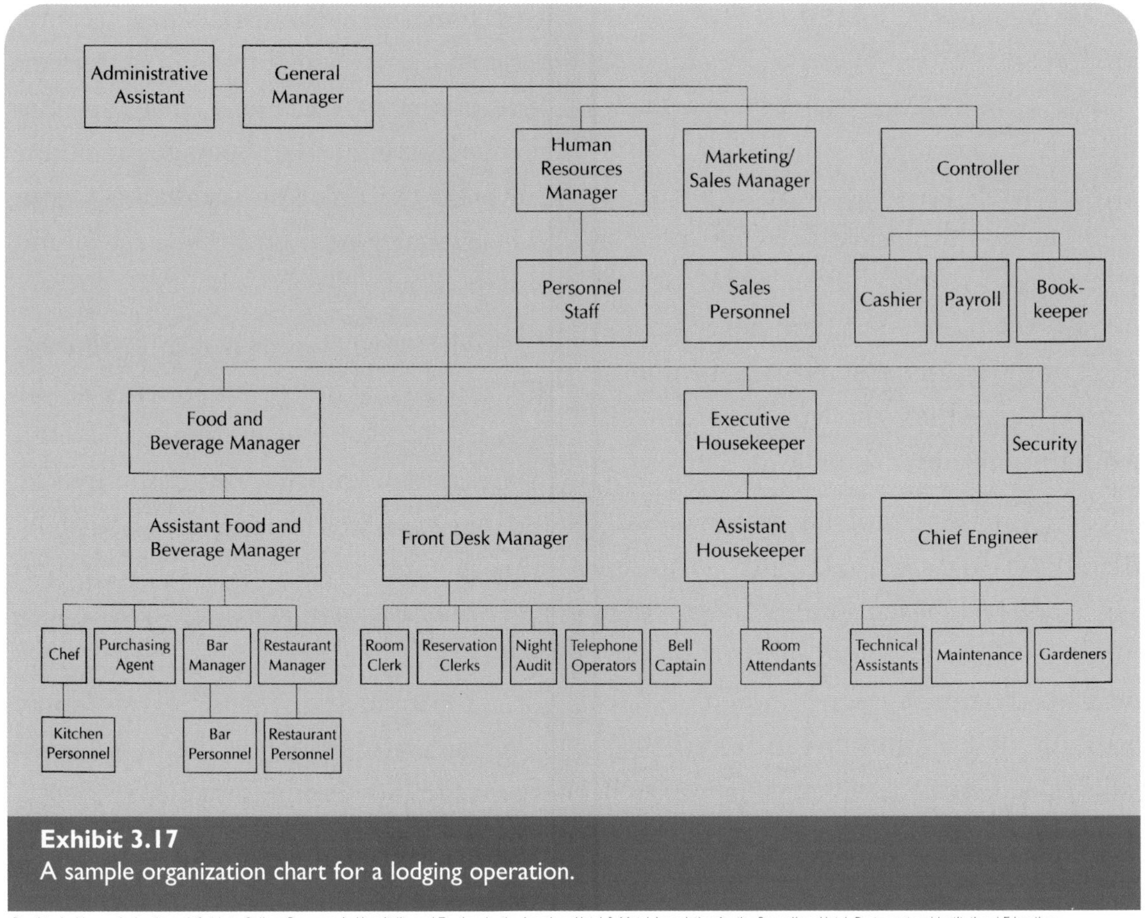

Exhibit 3.17
A sample organization chart for a lodging operation.

Reprinted with permission from *A Guide to College Programs in Hospitality and Tourism*, by the American Hotel & Motel Association for the Council on Hotel, Restaurant and Institutional Education. Copyright© 1993, by John Wiley & Sons, Inc.

Along with leadership, the GM provides the vision that helps the organization compete and succeed in the industry. In addition to directing and communicating, the GM's managerial skills include planning, staffing, organizing, and controlling.

The **assistant general manager** helps carry out the GM's plans and serves as a liaison between management and staff. The assistant GM continually checks to see how well his or her employees are performing their responsibilities. Smaller facilities often don't employ an assistant GM; in such cases, department heads report directly to the general manager.

Other managers report to the GM and/or Assistant GM as well. The **resident manager** supervises front office operations

Exhibit 3.18
Weekly meetings allow the assistant GM to stay informed of a hotel's daily operations.

and reservations and is responsible for emergencies twenty-four hours a day when the GM is not on duty. In larger hotels, the resident manager often lives in an apartment in the hotel itself. The **executive assistant manager** is responsible for all room rentals. Also answering directly to the GM and assistant GM are the executive housekeeper and the reservations manager, who are each responsible for running all or part of a service department.

Accounting and Financial Management

Often referred to as "the back office," the accounting department oversees all the financial activities of the lodging property. The **controller** manages the accounting department, participates in long-term financial planning, and provides daily financial reports to management. The GM depends on the controller to provide information about the financial operations of the establishment, including investment opportunities and insurance costs. The controller usually has a college degree, along with experience in both accounting and the hotel industry.

Smaller facilities often share the accounting responsibilities among the GM, a night auditor, a secretary, and an outside accountant. In contrast, full-service properties may employ many specialists, including a credit manager, an operations analyst, and a payroll manager. Many large properties now employ a **management information systems (MIS) supervisor,** a computer specialist responsible for solving computer-related problems and making sure computer systems are running as efficiently as possible.

All facilities, regardless of size, usually employ clerks and cashiers, who issue checks, keep records, post sales, and compute wages and salaries. These positions require backgrounds in bookkeeping or accounting, as well as computer literacy.

Human Resources

The human resources department oversees one of the most important elements of the lodging operation: its employees. The **human resources (HR) director** is responsible for interviewing, selecting, recruiting, training, and evaluating performance of the operation's staff. In addition to creating plans to motivate staff, providing pay increases, and establishing employment policies, the HR director is responsible for handling employee complaints, the employee benefits program, and the administration of all labor laws. While larger properties often enjoy the expertise of a full-time HR director, smaller establishments usually divide the job among department heads.

Marketing and Sales

The marketing and sales department generates business for a lodging property. They sell rooms and facilities by creating contracts with guests, businesses, and people involved in the travel industry. The **marketing director** is responsible for generating new business, organizing special events, and conducting market research. The director also reviews the needs of existing markets, keeps an eye on the competition, and works with other departments to create in-house promotions.

Full-service establishments usually have many other specialists in the marketing and sales department. The **convention manager,** for example, plans meetings, determines rates, and sells the facility's banquet services, while the **convention sales manager** brings in the business by promoting the establishment as a site for conferences, seminars, and meetings. Many larger properties also have positions such as tour and travel sales manager and corporate sales manager.

The advertising and public relations (PR) branch of the marketing and sales department plays a vital role in attracting customers to the lodging facility. Through advertising campaigns and effective public relations, these employees are able to attract new customers to the lodging property.

Service Departments

Front Office Operations

The front office is the heart of all lodging properties. It has four main responsibilities.

- Check-in
- Reservations
- Information
- Checkout

Heading the department is the **front desk manager.** He or she prepares budgets, maintains cost-control systems, and forecasts room sales. A good communicator

Exhibit 3.19
Front desk staff often provide guests with their first impression of a facility.

and supervisor, the front desk manager oversees a team of people who have more direct contact with guests than any other department.

The **desk clerk** greets and registers guests, and performs all check-in functions, including selecting and blocking rooms, verifying information for advanced reservations, and providing details of room rates and availability. After registering guests, the desk clerk checks to make sure the room is ready to be occupied; he or she then assigns the rooms, provides keys or key cards, and provides any information that may be important for guests to know (i.e., check-out times, courtesy breakfast hours, etc.)

In addition to check-in, front desk staff members hold rooms for guests who will be arriving some time in the future. Reservations employees take incoming requests for accommodations, note special circumstances, and track room inventories. While reservations are handled by the manager or front desk clerk at small facilities, large establishments often have a **reservations manager,** who oversees the reservations function and manages a number of full-time reservationists.

The **bell captain** is an important member of the check-in staff, and manages a number of employees, including bellhops, door attendants, and valet parking crew members. Along with staff members, the bell captain carries luggage, explains hotel services and room features, and provides guests with information about the lodging establishment.

Once guests have arrived and settled in, many seek specific information about a variety of things. Although front desk personnel often answer questions and handle special requests, a **concierge** (con-see-AIRJ) specializes in providing a wide range of information services. The concierge answers questions, books restaurant reservations, makes arrangements for car rentals, obtains theater tickets for guests, and much

Exhibit 3.20
The bell captain is responsible for managing bellhops, door attendants, and valet parking crew members.

more. To perform all of these activities, the concierge must be graceful under pressure, as well as creative and organized.

When guests check out, the front desk clerk verifies the final amount owed, posts recent charges, and assists guests in making payments. In addition to performing all checkout related tasks, the desk clerk must be especially courteous to ensure that guests will return to the establishment.

Did You Know?

The word *concierge* comes from the French. In France, it is used to describe someone who attends to the entrance of an apartment, providing security and light janitorial help.

Finally, the front desk usually has a night auditor on staff. Just like it sounds, the **night auditor** works the evening shift, posting charges not recorded during earlier shifts and balancing daily financial transactions. A background in accounting is useful for this position.

Housekeeping

Housekeeping is one of the most important departments in a lodging property, and is often one of the largest. Surveys point to cleanliness as a major factor in determining whether or not guests will come back to a hotel or motel.

Housekeeping works closely with front office personnel, notifying them when rooms have been cleaned and are ready for new guests. Cleaning a room involves changing bed and bath linens, vacuuming, dusting, cleaning bathrooms, emptying all trash, replenishing supplies, checking televisions and lights to ensure that they're working, and restocking refrigerators and bars. The housekeeping department also maintains public areas such as hallways, lobbies, administrative offices, outside areas, and meeting rooms.

The **executive housekeeper** oversees the department by hiring, training, scheduling, and directing staff; purchasing

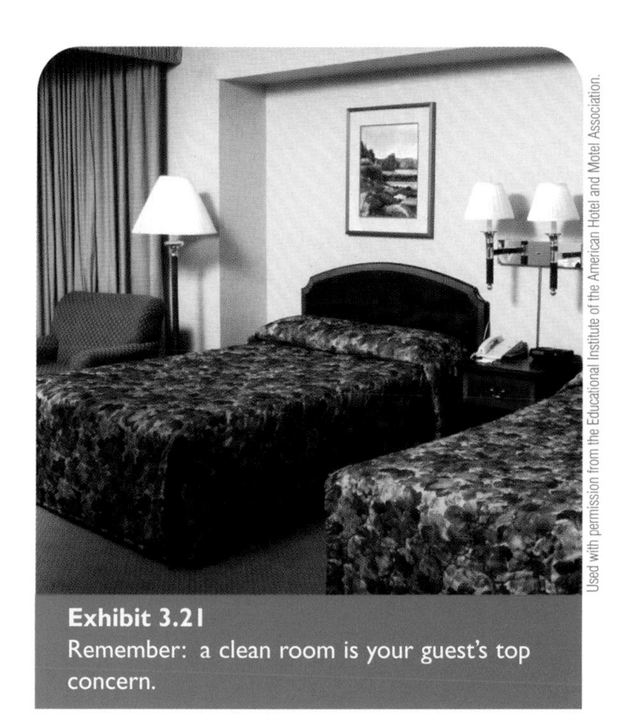

Exhibit 3.21
Remember: a clean room is your guest's top concern.

and maintaining an inventory of cleaning supplies and equipment; and setting cleaning priorities. The executive house-keeper may also supervise the lost and found, laundry services, and maintenance functions.

Large establishments usually have at least one assistant and several inspectors or floor supervisors, all of whom work under the direction of the executive housekeeper. These people check to make sure that **room attendants**—employees who actually clean guest rooms—perform their job consistently and efficiently.

Engineering and Facility Maintenance

Guests can quickly become frustrated or even angry if elevators break down or air conditioning stops working. The engineering and facility maintenance department ensures that all mechanical systems are safe and in proper working order. At small establishments, the department may only consist of a handyman. At larger properties, a chief engineer usually supervises a department of painters, plumbers, electricians, carpenters, locksmiths, and mechanics.

The **chief engineer** plans and organizes the tasks to be carried out by the department. Administrative duties include budgeting, coordinating and supervising

Exhibit 3.22
Smaller lodging establishments often hire outside contractors to make repairs when needed instead of keeping someone on staff.

Exhibit 3.23
No matter how fancy a lodging establishment is, a clean room is at the top of guests' wish lists.

Lodging Property Characteristics (in order of importance)

Type of lodging	*Business travelers*	*Leisure travelers*
Economy	1. Clean rooms 2. Convenient location 3. Safety and security	1. Clean rooms 2. Safety and security 3. Room rates
Mid-price	1. Clean rooms 2. Convenient location 3. Reputation for good service	1. Clean rooms 2. Safety and security 3. Reputation for good service
Luxury	1. Convenient location 2. Clean rooms 3. Reputation for good service	1. Clean rooms 2. Reputation for good service 3. Safety and security

From a study conducted for the Dial Corporation by Dr. B.J. Knutson of the School of Hospitality business, Michigan State University.

repair and maintenance orders, and negotiating contracts. In addition to heating and air conditioning, the chief engineer oversees the maintenance of facility lights, fire fighting equipment, refrigerators, plumbing, and electrical systems.

Chief engineers often train other employees to conserve energy and save on utility costs. They also provide advice about equipment maintenance and environmental control. Along with a high school diploma, the chief engineer should have an excellent knowledge of how machinery works; further education in heating and air conditioning systems, electrical repair, and plumbing; and several years of work experience.

Security

The security department's emphasis is on *preventing* problems rather than simply detecting them. This area aims to protect guests from crime, fire, and unsafe conditions, as well as to protect the establishment from theft and property damage. Although the security department is specifically charged with these duties, security is the responsibility of all lodging employees.

Large establishments may have a security chief, along with a number of professionally trained security officers, watchpeople, house detectives, and security system specialists. Many facilities also hire private, off-duty police officers .

The security chief usually has extensive law enforcement training. Working with the director of human resources, the **security chief** works to minimize theft. The security chief also provides ongoing training programs with other departments to educate employees in fire and other safety procedures.

Security chiefs train security officers to spot people who might cause problems. The department is constantly on the lookout for suspicious or unusual activities. Some properties place guards in visible locations where they can see everyone who enters and leaves the facility, while other establishments use plain-clothes officers as guards.

Exhibit 3.24
Security chiefs take many different steps to ensure the safety of their guests, including using cameras to monitor the property.

Food and Beverage

The **food and beverage director** supervises the most labor-intensive department of a full-service lodging operation. In addition to managing the formal dining room, coffee shop, and lounge, the director also manages the hotel's banquet, catering, and room service.

When it comes to actually handling and producing food, the executive chef works with a sous chef and other chefs to provide quality meals and refreshments for the hotel's guests.

In addition to being an accomplished cook, the executive chef should be an effective manager. Many establishments also have a food production manager, as well as stewards, who supervise the washing of dishes, glasses, and cutlery.

Other employees of the food and beverage department are similar to those found in any foodservice operation. They include servers, hosts and hostesses, bussers, dishwashers, and cashiers.

Review Your Learning 3.3

Match each lodging position title on the left with its corresponding job function on the right.

1. Assistant general manager
2. Chief engineer
3. Night auditor
4. Room attendant
5. Human resources director
6. Convention manager

a. Develops employee benefits programs
b. Sells the property's banquet services
c. Performs daily guest room cleaning
d. Serves as liaison between GM and staff
e. Posts charges not recorded during earlier shift
f. Trains employees on how to conserve energy

7. International lodging operations often are especially interested in hiring young people who know:
   a. a second language.
   b. American customer service practices.
   c. world history.
   d. how to carry heavy luggage.

8. Which of the following skills should a supervisor have in order to directly supervise employees throughout the facility?
   a. Bookkeeping
   b. Accounting
   c. Leadership
   d. Sales

3.4

SECTION 3.4

Property Management Systems and Room Rates

AFTER STUDYING SECTION 3.4, YOU SHOULD BE ABLE TO:

- Compare and contrast the different property management systems used for front office and reservations.
- Describe the use of forecasting and overbooking in reservations management.
- Given a set of numbers, calculate room rates using the Hubbart formula.

General Management

Computers are essential to most modern lodging operations. **Property management systems (PMS)** are computer software programs that are designed specifically for the lodging

KEY TERMS

- Block
- Block-out
- Central reservation system (CRS)
- Guest folio (FOE-lee-oh)
- Hubbart formula
- No-shows
- Overbook
- Post
- Property management system (PMS)
- Rack rate
- Room inventory
- Rooms forecast
- Understays
- Yield management

industry. They improve efficiency for employees and managers alike. For front desk clerks, for example, a PMS computer program eliminates the need to perform the same tasks over and over. For managers, a PMS provides fast and accurate information and allows for improved control over the operation.

While property management systems are extremely valuable to the front desk department, other departments in a lodging property use the computer system too. A PMS can connect accounting systems, reservations and registration databases, housekeeping room status records, and marketing research to help departments throughout the operation better coordinate activities with one another.

Exhibit 3.25
Computers help link the many departments of a lodging property together.

Guest Account Management

Customer service and satisfaction are the goals of every lodging establishment. A PMS helps managers reach these goals by providing a variety of guest account management programs. When a guest checks in, the property management system allows the front desk clerk to open a guest account. This account includes a variety of information about the guest, including name, address, length of stay, and accommodation preferences. The account also sets up a **guest folio** (FOE-lee-oh)—a record of guest charges and payments.

When guests stay at a hotel, they don't want to have to pay cash every time they buy something inside the hotel. Instead, they want these charges to be added to their guest folio as they occur, so that they can pay them all at once when checking out. A PMS lets employees throughout the facility **post,** or record, charges on that account at the time and place where the transaction takes place.

Once entered in the PMS, these transactions can be added together by the night auditor, so that final bills can be ready for guests when they check out in the morning. When a guest is ready to leave, a PMS makes checkout easier by prompting the front desk clerk to check the balance, post any late charges, and accept payment from the guest.

Today, most guests indicate whether they will pay in cash or by credit card when they register. The increased use of credit cards by guests, together with a PMS, provides other options to the standard front desk checkout. Many lodging operations now feature electronic checkout systems that allow guests to use their in-room television remotes to review their folios, then check themselves out. Other operations slip a final copy of guests' folios under their doors early on the morning of checkout. The guests review their folios, and if they're correct, they simply confirm their method of payment to finish their checkout.

Exhibit 3.26
Charges such as long distance phone calls are charged to a guest's folio.

Rooms Management

Today's computer software lets front desk employees know whether or not a room is available for occupancy with the touch of a button. Two lodging property departments—front office operations and housekeeping—determine whether or not a room is available.

If a room is available for renting, the reservationist will designate it as being *open*. *Confirmed* indicates that a room has been reserved and will be held until a certain time—usually until 4:00 p.m. or 6:00 p.m. *Guaranteed* rooms, on the other hand, have usually been prepaid by the guest with a credit card. A *guaranteed* room will be held until guests arrive, no matter how late. Finally, *repair* status notes a room that is unavailable because of maintenance work.

The housekeeping department uses different terms to provide some additional information about a room's availability. A room is usually described as being *occupied* or *available*. Other descriptions include *stayover* (the guest won't be checking out of the room on the current day), *on change* (the guest has checked out, but housekeeping hasn't cleaned the room yet), and *out of order* (the room is unavailable because of a mechanical problem).

Room status reports help every department of a lodging property. By noting status labels, housekeeping personnel know which rooms need cleaning, night auditors can verify which rooms have been rented, engineers can plan for maintenance or remodeling, and marketing and sales employees can book upcoming conventions.

Exhibit 3.27
Departments throughout a lodging property depend on correct, up-to-the-minute room information.

Room Status Designations

Reservations	*Housekeeping*
■ Open	■ Occupied
■ Confirmed	■ Available
■ Guaranteed	■ Stayover
■ Repair	■ On change
	■ Out of order

Reservations Management

A property management system allows lodging establishments to manage a steady flow of customers coming to their properties. With PMS programs for reservations, confirmation, deposits, and cancellations, a front desk clerk simply types in the name of a guest with a reservation, and the system automatically prints out all applicable records.

If a lodging property is part of a larger chain of businesses, its PMS is usually linked to a nationwide **central reservation system (CRS)** that guests access through a toll-free telephone number. To make reservations using the CRS, guests simply call the number to speak with an operator at the central reservation office. This operator has access to the room inventory at all participating facilities. **Room inventory** refers to the total number of rooms that a property has to sell. With this information, the CRS operator can help guests make reservations quickly and easily.

There are many advantages to connecting a property's PMS to the CRS of its chain or franchise group. Since the CRS is able to automatically determine what rooms are available, local front office employees spend less time

Exhibit 3.28
Toll-free numbers and computerized CRS networks have made making a reservation simple.

handling individual reservations. Some systems are even connected to airline CRSs, allowing travel agents to create air and hotel packages for their customers. This ability reduces the work that lodging property employees once did and can serve to increase lodging business through travel agencies. You will learn more about travel agents and their jobs in *Chapter 11: Tourism and the Retail Industry*.

Once a reservation has been received, a room is blocked in room inventory. When you **block** a room, you automatically remove it from the available status in the reservations system. If a property has no vacancies for a particular night, the PMS simply won't process a request for that date. Many systems will alert CRS operators of other facilities in the area that do have available rooms.

In order to anticipate room inventory levels, a manager can do a **rooms forecast.** Using a PMS, the manager can look at the establishment's occupancy rate over a specific time period. The rooms forecast allows the front office manager to determine projected revenues and make decisions about rates and reservations. Other departments also depend on this forecast in order to manage the property's finances, schedule labor, plan improvements, renovate rooms, and order supplies.

Forecasting is essential for achieving the goal of 100% occupancy. In order to recover from late cancellations and **no-shows,** which are guests that make reservations and do not arrive, many establishments regularly **overbook,** or accept reservations for more rooms than are available, by forecasting the number of walk-ins, no-shows, stayovers, and understays. **Understays** are guests who leave before their anticipated date of departure.

Think About It

What can guests do to make sure that a room will be ready for them at a hotel that regularly overbooks?

Yield Management

Yield management allows management to change room rates as the demand for rooms varies. By analyzing the demand for rooms in the past, forecasting demand in the future, and adjusting rates as demand changes, management maximizes profit from both guest room sales and property services. Running an effective yield management system requires a well-trained front office staff, and sometimes, the help of a computer system.

There are two main yield management strategies: one for when demand for rooms is high and the other for when demand is low. In a high-demand period, lodging properties rent rooms only to those willing to pay higher rates. They also limit availability of low-rate rooms, or require minimum lengths of stay. One method management uses to encourage guests to commit to a minimum number of nights is called **blocking-out.** If demand is very high and a reservation request falls in a blocked-out time period, it is refused unless the guest is willing to stay for the entire period.

In a low-demand period, management often go to cheaper, promotional rates to attract guests. Another low-demand strategy is to seek business from price-sensitive customers (e.g., senior citizens, off-season tourists), or to promote low-cost packages to local clientele.

Exhibit 3.29
GMs use yield management strategies to maximize profits whether business is busy or slow.

Yield Management Strategies

Demand	Strategy
High	■ Raise rates ■ Limit cheaper rooms ■ Block-out to ensure minimum lengths of stay
Low	■ Lower room rates ■ Seek business from price-sensitive markets ■ Promote local weekend rate packages

Setting Room Rates

Selling room space is the primary way that a lodging property makes money. Room rates vary considerably depending on a variety of factors, including construction and real estate costs, level of luxury, and type of bedding offered. In setting room rates, management must consider projected sales estimates, market competition, price sensitivity, and many other factors.

There are many methods for setting room rates. Most, however, should be used only as guidelines. The general rule-of-thumb method suggests that room rates should be set at $1 for every $1,000 of construction costs. If a new hotel is built at $50,000 per room, for example, the room rate should be initially established at $50 per night.

The **Hubbart formula** helps managers set rates using four main factors.

1. *Operating expenses,* which are the costs of running the establishment.
2. *Desired return on investment (ROI),* which is the money a business hopes to make.
3. *Other income,* which is earned in various departments in the establishment (such as catering or food and beverage).
4. *Projected room sales,* which can be forecasted using historical information or other research.

The Hubbart formula for setting room rates is:

$$\frac{(\text{Operating expenses} + \text{Desired ROI}) - \text{Other income}}{\text{Projected room sales}} = \text{Room Rate}$$

If, for example, operating expenses are $3,000,000; desired ROI $2,000,000; additional income $300,000; and projected room sales $100,000; the room rate should be set at $47.

$$\frac{(\$3,000,000 + \$2,000,000) - \$300,000}{\$100,000} = \$47$$

Lodging properties establish rate categories to attract specific customers. The **rack rate** is the highest rate category. It is the figure quoted when guests request rate information and is usually applied to those who don't fall into a particular category. *Special rates and package deals are always lower than the rack rate.*

Corporate rates, for example, are set for businesspeople. To qualify for the rate, participating companies must sometimes agree to book a minimum number of rooms during a specific time period. Similarly, group rates are applied to organizations that book a large number of rooms. These rates are offered to associations and groups that host meetings, seminars, or conferences at the property.

In-season rates match periods of large demand and tend to be fairly high. Off-season rates, on the other hand, reflect low demand. To increase occupancy levels, many properties create package rates, promotional discounts that often include accommodations, use of recreational facilities, and access to special events. Properties that rely on business travelers suffer from low occupancy on weekends. These establishments will often advertise special weekend packages that can consistently generate income. Lodging establishments have a variety of other rates as well, as shown in Exhibit 3.30.

Exhibit 3.30
Different room rate categories.

- *Complimentary (free) rates* provide no income for lodging establishments but promote goodwill among property managers, local dignitaries, and others.
- *Government rates* are given to government employees and are usually based on a contract between a lodging property and a government agency.
- *Airline/agent rates* are discounts for airline employees or travel agents. The rates are generally not valid when hotels are fully booked.
- *Day rates* apply to guest rooms used for a part of the day only.
- *Weekly rates* are sometimes offered to guests staying for one week or more.
- *Family rates* allow children under a certain age to stay in their parents' room for free.
- *Educational rates* help educators who are often on limited expense accounts.
- *Local business rates* provide both a discount and guaranteed availability to preferred businesses in the community.

Review Your Learning 3.4

1. Which of the following is *not* an advantage for lodging properties that use property management systems (PMS)?
   a. Eliminates the need for front desk clerks to perform the same tasks over and over
   b. Provides fast and accurate information for managers
   c. Lets customers pay for each item bought separately
   d. Allows departments to better coordinate activities with one another

2. A guest uses his in-room TV remote to check out. This convenient checkout procedure is made possible through the lodging property's:
   a. PMS.
   b. CRS.
   c. Hubbart formula.
   d. point-of-sale.

3. The highest rate category is the:
   a. rack rate.
   b. group rate.
   c. corporate rate.
   d. off-season rate.

4. Which of the following room status designations are part of the reservations system (R) and which are part of the housekeeping system (H)?
   a. Confirmed
   b. Stayover
   c. On change
   d. Guaranteed

Continued on next page

5. For each of the designations in question 4, write a short, one-sentence description of each status on a separate sheet of paper.

6. Which of the following is used to check that a room can be reserved for a customer?
   a. Rack rate
   b. Room inventory
   c. Rooms forecast
   d. Point-of-sale

7. Which of the following is *not* a strategy for high-demand yield management?
   a. Raise rates
   b. Limit cheaper rooms
   c. Block-out to ensure minimum lengths of stay
   d. Promote local weekend rate packages

8. Use the Hubbart formula to set a room rate given the following information:
   Projected room sales: $100,000
   Desired return on investment: (ROI) $3,000,000
   Operating expenses: $4,000,000
   Other income: $600,000

9. Which rate category would most likely apply to vacation travelers reserving a hotel room during the high-season?
   a. Complimentary rate
   b. Government rate
   c. Rack rate
   d. Local business rate

Flashback

CHAPTER 3

SECTION 3.1: UNDERSTANDING LODGING

- The lodging industry has historically been impacted by changes in transportation.
- The invention of stagecoaches, trains, automobiles, the interstate freeway system, and airplanes have all influenced the evolution of lodging properties.
- During the Depression in the 1930s, several hotel properties across the country closed because of decreased travel business.
- During World War II in the 1940s, the lodging industry prospered from war-related travel.
- In the 1950s, the first motels sprang up along highways across America.
- In 1958, commercial airlines became a popular and increasingly economical way of traveling.
- **Front-of-the-house** employees come into direct contact with guests; **back-of-the-house** employees maintain systems or support front-of-the-house areas.
- Lodging facility departments can be classified as administrative or service.
- **Administrative departments** include general management, accounting and financial management, human resources, and marketing and sales.
- **Service departments** include front office operations, housekeeping, engineering and facility maintenance, security, and food and beverage.

SECTION 3.2: ORGANIZATION OF THE LODGING INDUSTRY

- Lodging property guests can be either leisure travelers or business travelers.
- Many establishments cater to specific **leisure travelers** by offering special services or activities, like programs for children, social activities, and health facilities.
- **Business travelers** often need access to office equipment and business services, like computers, fax machines, and copiers, as well as meeting and banquet facilities.

- Lodging properties differ substantially according to the type of guests they aim to serve.
- **Full-service** properties cater to travelers in search of comfortable accommodations with added amenities, such as swimming pools and room service.
- **Luxury properties** are top-of-the-line, full-service operations that offer both comfort and elegance at a premium price.
- **Economy lodging** provides clean, fully-furnished rooms at budget prices.
- **Mid-priced facilities** target guests seeking comfortable, moderately priced accommodations.
- **All-suite properties** offer apartment-style facilities with an at-home atmosphere.
- **Resorts** feature extensive facilities for vacationers looking for recreational activities and entertainment.
- **Bed and breakfasts** are usually privately-owned homes converted to have several guest rooms. Bed and breakfasts are different from other lodging properties because the owner usually lives on the property and manages its day-to-day operations.
- **Meeting and convention hotels** are constructed specifically to accommodate large exhibitions and their attendees, as well as business travelers.
- Location is one of the most influential factors contributing to the success of a lodging facility. Establishments can be distinguished by their location: airport, downtown, suburban, highway, and resort properties are the main divisions.
- Several guide books rate establishments based on a variety of criteria.
- The American Automobile Association's (AAA) *Tour Book* uses a five-diamond system in judging overall quality. It is the most widely recognized rating system in the United States.
- The *Mobil Travel Guides* assess thousands of properties with a five-star system. Obtaining a five-star rating is very difficult; only about 100 properties receive this superior rating on average each year.

SECTION 3.3: CAREER OPPORTUNITIES IN THE LODGING INDUSTRY

- Formal education, on-the-job experience, ability to speak a second language, and membership in professional trade organizations can all help employees develop a career in the lodging industry.

- Most lodging facilities perform the same basic functions, but the number and type of employees at each establishment depend on property size and several other factors.
- The **general manager (GM)** is responsible for the overall performance of a lodging establishment and its employees.
- The **assistant GM** serves as a liaison between management and operations.
- Managed by the **controller,** the accounting department oversees all of the financial activities of the lodging property.
- Focusing on employees, the human resources department is responsible for the entire staffing function and the administration of personnel. It is managed by the **human resources (HR) director.**
- Headed by the **marketing director,** the marketing and sales department generates business by selling rooms and facilities.
- Marketing and sales department specialists include a **convention manager,** a **convention sales manager,** a tour and travel sales manager, and a corporate sales manager.
- The advertising and public relations branch of the marketing and sales department creates promotional campaigns to attract customers to the lodging property.
- The front office is responsible for check-in, reservations, information, and checkout.
- The **desk clerk** executes all check-in and checkout functions.
- Reservations employees take incoming requests for accommodations, note special circumstances, and track room inventories.
- The **bell captain** oversees bellhops, door attendants, and valet parking crew members.
- The **concierge** specializes in providing a wide range of information and customer services.
- The **night auditor** posts charges to guest's folios not recorded during earlier shifts.

- Housekeeping is responsible for the cleaning and upkeep of all guest rooms and public areas.
- Under the direction of the **executive housekeeper,** floor supervisors monitor guest room cleaning performed by **room attendants.**
- Managed by the **chief engineer,** the engineering and facility maintenance department ensures that all systems are safe and in proper working order.
- The chief engineer focuses on preventive maintenance and energy savings.
- The security department aims to protect guests from crime, fire, and unsafe conditions and to safeguard the establishment from theft and property damage.
- The **security chief** and a staff of watchpeople, house detectives, and security officers are constantly on the lookout for suspicious or unusual activities.
- The **food and beverage director** supervises the most labor-intensive department of the lodging operation.
- Food handling and production are managed by the executive chef, who is assisted by a sous chef and a crew of other chefs and attendants.
- Other employees of the food and beverage department are similar to those found in any foodservice operation. They include servers, hosts and hostesses, bussers, dishwashers, and cashiers.

SECTION 3.4: PROPERTY MANAGEMENT SYSTEMS AND ROOM RATES

- **Property management systems (PMS)** are computer software programs designed specifically for the lodging industry.
- A PMS allows front desk personnel to coordinate activities with other employees throughout the establishment.
- A PMS provides programs for reservations, confirmation, deposits, and cancellations.
- When a guest checks in, a PMS enables the desk clerk to open a guest account.
- A PMS allows employees to **post** charges to **guest folios** at the time and place the transactions take place.
- A PMS also allows for in-room video checkout and quick payment method confirmations.

- Room status indicates whether or not rooms are available.
- Reservations status designations include *open, confirmed, guaranteed,* and *repair;* housekeeping status labels are *occupied, available, stayover, on change,* and *out of order.*
- Lodging properties that are part of a larger chain usually have their PMS linked up to a nationwide **central reservation system (CRS).**
- This central reservation system is able to directly and automatically determine room availability for all of its participating properties.
- A CRS operator has access to the room inventory at all participating facilities.
- **Room inventory** refers to the total number of rooms that a property has to sell. CRS operators use this information to help guests make reservations quickly and easily.
- Once a reservation has been received, a room is **blocked** in room inventory.
- The **rooms forecast** allows management to determine projected revenues, manage the property's finances, schedule labor, plan improvements, and order supplies.
- **Yield management** is the process of changing room rates as the demand for rooms varies.
- There are yield management strategies for both high and low demand.
- The general rule-of-thumb method for setting room rates suggests that prices should be set at $1 for every $1,000 of construction costs.
- The **Hubbart formula** sets room rates based on operating expenses, desired return on investment, other income, and projected room sales.
- Lodging properties establish various rate categories to attract specific customers.
- The **rack rate** is the highest rate category.
- Special prices are extended to specific guests through corporate, group, weekend, government, airline/agent, day, weekly, family, educational, and local business rates.

Customer satisfaction is important to the success of every foodservice operation. This unit focuses on making any operation customer-friendly: customer-appealing service styles, customer-pleasing desserts, and customer-targeted marketing techniques.

UNIT 2

Amy Risk

Service Captain
Spiaggia
Chicago, Illinois

Guests at Spiaggia have very high expectations of the service they'll receive here. We have a very good reputation for providing excellent food and service. Being an award-winning restaurant, even out-of-town visitors expect this and are willing to pay for it. My goal is to have every guest want to return.

I know when we're providing good service by guests' reactions. I "read" them. I ask questions. If they're not pleased—not really surprised and delighted by our exceptional service—I find out what I can do to personalize it and impress them.

I'm always prepared to go out and give great service. Every captain goes through three weeks of intensive training before we go solo on the floor. We know the menu down to every ingredient. We learn every job on the floor from experienced servers before we're made captain of our team. But it doesn't stop there; it's a continual learning process. We have a lot of items on our menu, plus daily specials. I'm always learning.

A strong team is important, and teamwork between servers, maître d', and managers is very important too. You have to have good interpersonal skills. You have to put guests at ease.

My advice to new servers is: Don't be afraid of your guests. You can't be shy about talking to strangers. Don't hide, show your personality! Once you're comfortable doing that, the job becomes fun and very profitable.

CHAPTER 4

The Art of Service

4.1

SECTION 4.1

Traditional Service Staff and Service Styles

AFTER STUDYING SECTION 4.1, YOU SHOULD BE ABLE TO:

- Demonstrate the similarities and differences between American, French, English, Russian, and quick-service styles.
- Describe and demonstrate tableside preparations such as carving meats and slicing desserts.
- Describe traditional service staff, and list the duties and responsibilities of each.

The phrase "art of service" means, in its simplest form, being able to help people enjoy themselves. Many factors contribute to creating good service in the hospitality industry—from the service styles and tools used, to knowing how to sell to customers and handle complaints effectively. The more you know about what excellent service is, the more fun it is to be a part of the restaurant industry.

KEY TERMS

- American service
- Apprentice
- Captain
- English service
- Flambé (flahm-BAY)
- French service
- Front waiter
- Guéridon (gay-ree-DAHN)
- Headwaiter
- Maître d'hotel (MAY-tra doe-TELL)
- Quick-service
- Russian service

Exhibit 4.1
Excellent service is a learned skill.

Service Organization

Many large, full-service restaurants have a formal service organization, or group of servers, that performs service-related tasks. Every one of the servers in the front-of-the-house must work together to ensure that guests enjoy themselves.

One of the people involved in the formal service organization is the **maître d' hotel** (MAY-tra doe-TELL), who is responsible for the overall management of service. The **headwaiter** is responsible for service in a particular area, such as a banquet room or dining room, while the **captain** is responsible for a server area of usually 15 to 25 guests, and is assisted by one front waiter or an apprentice. Working with the captain, the **front waiter** has only 1 to 2 years of experience. An **apprentice** is a server in training.

No matter how an operation organizes its employees, it is important that each person know their role and their specific tasks and responsibilities.

Service Styles

There are also a number of service styles an operation can use, depending on its menu, theme, and decor. They are quick-service, American service, French service, English service, and Russian service.

Quick-service is an easy and fast way to dine and typically involves no servers. Instead, guests help themselves to food set up in food bars, or order at a counter. Other forms of quick-service include drive-through service, buffet service, carry-out service, vending service, and cafeteria service.

In **American service,** food is portioned onto plates in the kitchen by employees, and brought directly to the guests' table by the server. The meal is complete on one plate. American service has quickly been adopted by many operations because it is one of the easiest service styles and uses the fewest tools and utensils.

In **French service,** servers serve guests from a tableside cart, called a guéridon (gay-ree-DAHN). A **guéridon** holds food

Exhibit 4.2
Cafeteria service is quick-service dining.

or liquid items that will be served to guests, as well as serving dishes and other utensils the servers and guests may need. Unlike American service, French service is more formal and the most labor-intensive style. In French service, the finishing touches of the food are done at the table, often creating quite a spectacle.

Both English and Russian service styles serve food in bowls and platters. In **English service,** bowls and platters of food are placed on the table and a seated host or hostess places the food onto plates. These plates are then passed to each guest. This style is not often used in the United States, except in some clubs and for private parties.

Russian service is the most formal service style, in which all food preparation is done in the kitchen. The bowls and platters of food are then brought to guests at the table. Servers using the Russian style of service hold the bowls and platters as they serve the food to each guest.

Service Techniques

There are times when the final meal preparation steps are finished at the guests' table. The most common table-side techniques are those for carving meats, poultry, and fish. A roast bird (like chicken or turkey) is carved at the table by first removing one leg, cutting apart the drumstick and thigh, then removing the wings and slicing the breast meat. Boneless cuts of meat, such as a beef tenderloin, are held down with the back of a fork so that juices are not lost, and cut at an angle to look bigger. Leg of lamb, poached fish, and salmon are also impressive when carved at the table.

Sometimes a service technique is used mainly to impress guests. For example, often specific items are **flambéed** (flahm-BAYed) by pouring alcohol on them and lighting them on fire. This creates a quick burst of controlled flame, and usually causes guests to take notice! Since it is done quickly, flambéing does not affect the food's taste and is done mostly for show. Foods like *Bananas Foster* and *Cherries Jubilee* are usually flambéed.

Review Your Learning 4.1

On a separate sheet of paper, match the service style on the right with its correct definition on the left.

1. Food is portioned onto plates in the kitchen and brought to the table.
2. Used in most fast-food or quick-service operations.
3. Food is served in bowls and platters and seated host or hostess places food onto guests' plates.
4. The meal is served from a guéridon with finishing touches done at the table.
5. Food is brought to guests in bowls and platters, which are held by servers as the servers serve the guests.

a. French
b. English
c. Quick-service
d. American
e. Russian

6. In a formal foodservice organization, the captain is:
   a. responsible for service in a specific area, like a banquet room.
   b. responsible for overall service in the restaurant.
   c. a server in training.
   d. responsible for a service area in the operation, usually 15–25 guests.

7. Which of the following techniques is often done at the guest's table side?
   a. Carving meats, like roast turkey or chicken
   b. Deep-frying potatoes
   c. Sautéeing vegetables in vegetable oil
   d. Boiling water for pasta

8. Which of the following definitions describes an apprentice in the foodservice organization?
   a. Hostess in training
   b. Chef in training
   c. Server in training
   d. Owner in training

4.2

SECTION 4.2

Service Tools and Utensils

AFTER STUDYING SECTION 4.2, YOU SHOULD BE ABLE TO:

- Identify the types of dining utensils: knives, forks, spoons, glasses, and china, and explain specific uses for each.
- Identify various server tools and the correct way to stock a service station.

KEY TERM

- **Service station**

One of the contributing factors in the art of good service is knowing and understanding the various server tools and utensils used in an operation. Being prepared both as a server and a foodservice organization will help ensure guest satisfaction.

Exhibit 4.3
The service station keeps many important items close at hand.

Service Tools

In full-service restaurants, servers usually carry many different service tools with them. They may carry a hand towel, matches, a corkscrew, change, a pen, and an order pad. These items are helpful to have on hand because servers use them so often.

The **service station** is the area in the operation where additional items are kept, like napkins, silverware, cups and saucers, condiments, menus, and water glasses.

Having these items in a service station prevents servers from having to go into the back-of-the-house to get them and is a good way to keep much needed utensils close by.

Silverware

Knowing the many types of silverware that an operation uses is critical. Specific utensils are used for certain foods, and each table must be set accordingly. The variety of knives, forks, and spoons used in any given operation is huge. Some of the most necessary and widely used utensils are discussed in the next few paragraphs.

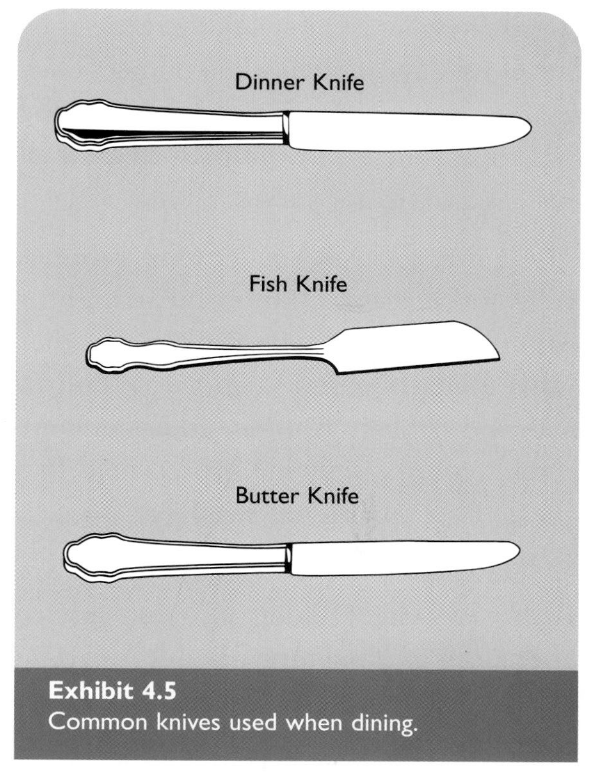

Exhibit 4.5
Common knives used when dining.

Exhibit 4.4
A butter knife can be used to spread soft cheese.

As shown in Exhibit 4.5, there are basic knives used most often when dining. They are dinner knife, the butter knife, and the fish knife. The *dinner knife* is used for all entrées and main courses.

A *butter knife* is smaller than a dinner knife and is used to butter bread and for cutting breakfast foods, fruit, and other softer foods. The *fish knife* is used only to fillet and cut fish. Another common knife is the *steak knife,* which is presented to a guest who has ordered steak.

A number of different forks are also used when dining in a full-service operation, as shown in Exhibit 4.6. The *dinner fork* is used to eat main courses, vegetables, and pasta. The *salad fork,* smaller than the dinner fork, is used not only for salads, but for appetizers, desserts, fruit, smoked fish, and other delicate foods. A *fish fork,* as its name suggests, is used only for eating fish. The small, thin *snail fork* and *lobster fork* are used only to eat those shellfish and the small, round *oyster fork* is served with both oysters and clams. When dessert arrives, it will often be served with a *cake fork.* It is used to eat cakes, tortes, pies, and pastries. With only three tines, it is delicate enough for even the sweetest dessert!

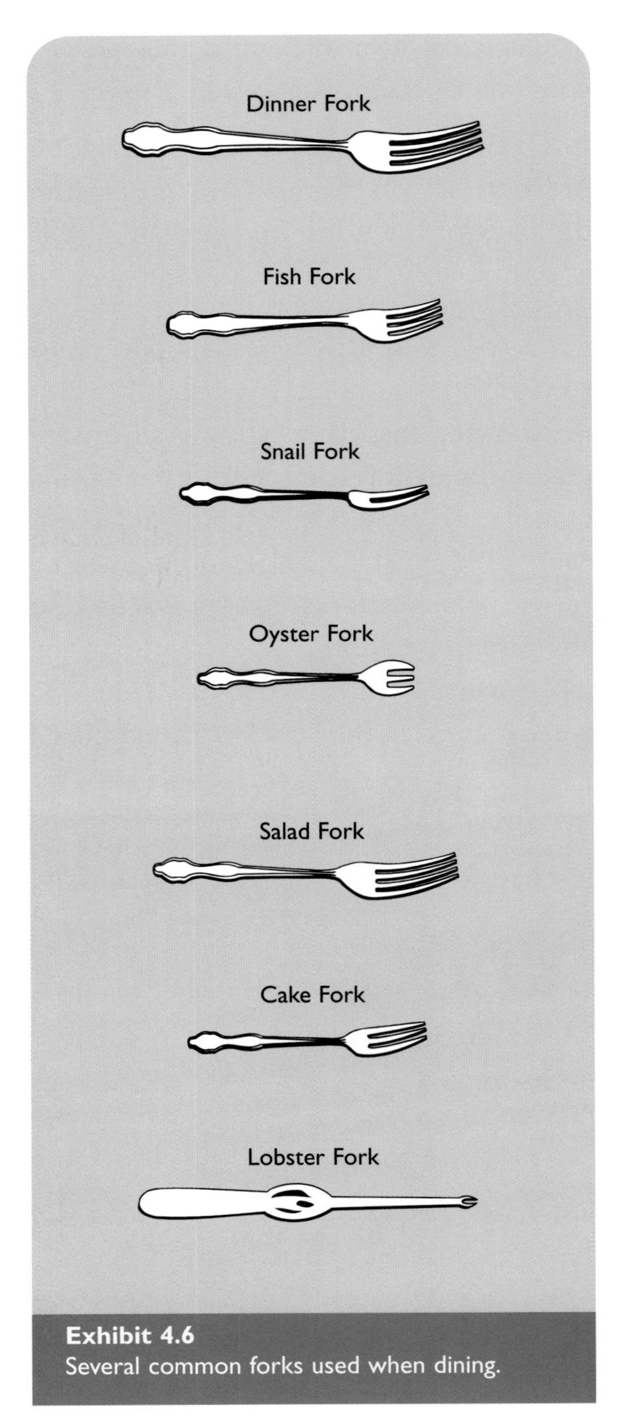

Exhibit 4.6
Several common forks used when dining.

Just as with knives and forks, there are different spoons to match different courses and foods. Exhibit 4.7 lists some of these spoons. The *soup spoon,* which is the largest spoon, is often served with pastas, as well as soup. A *sauce spoon* is used with dishes served with sauce on the side. A *coffee spoon* is smaller than a soup or sauce spoon, and is not only served with coffee, tea, and hot chocolate, but can be used for fruit cocktails, grapefruit, and ice cream.

An *espresso spoon* is much smaller than a coffee spoon, and matches small espresso cups. The *sundae* or *iced tea spoon* has an especially long handle to stir large glasses of tea, or dip into a deep and chocolaty sundae. A *grapefruit spoon* has jagged edges for carving into the grapefruit. The tiny *teaspoon* is served with desserts, soups in small cups, snails, and melon.

Special Serving Utensils

Servers use different serving utensils when they serve food to guests. As shown in Exhibit 4.8, large *serving spoons* are used to serve many items, like casseroles and vegetables. *Pastry tongs* are used to serve individual pastries, such as cream puffs and small cakes. *Cake* and *pie servers* come in many shapes to match the size of the piece of cake, or pie. This keeps the dessert from breaking apart as it is served.

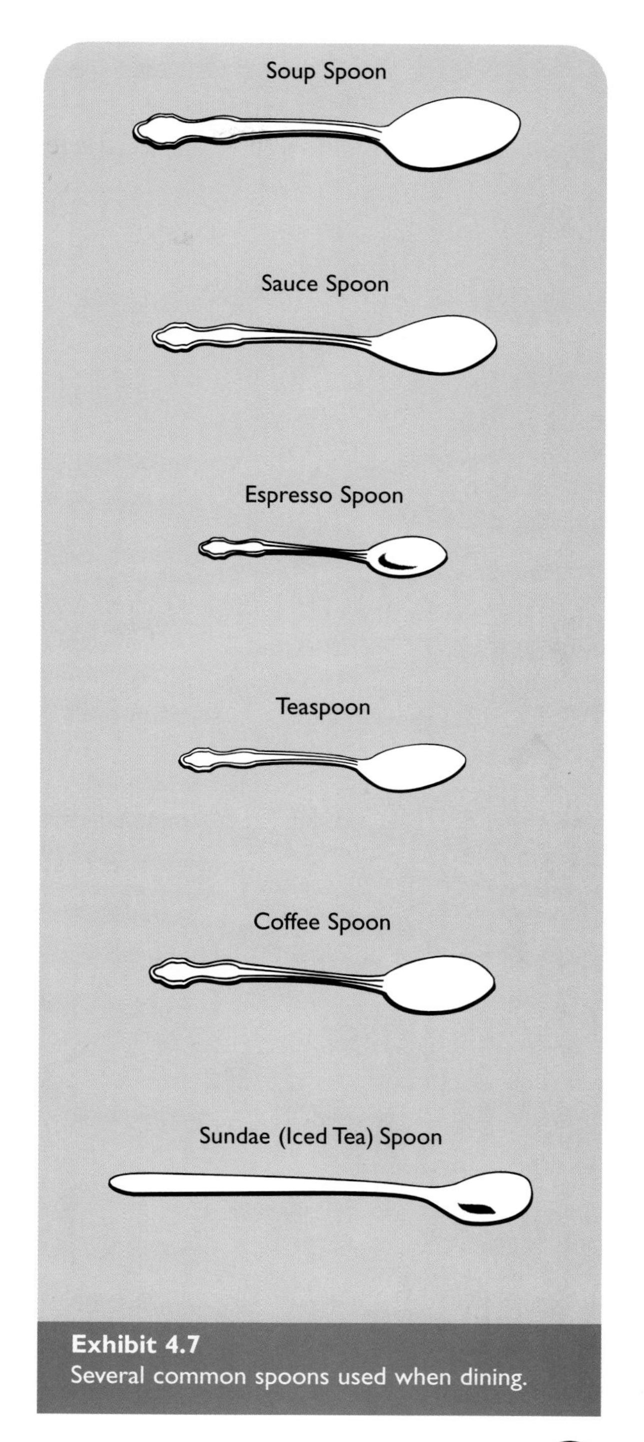

Exhibit 4.7
Several common spoons used when dining.

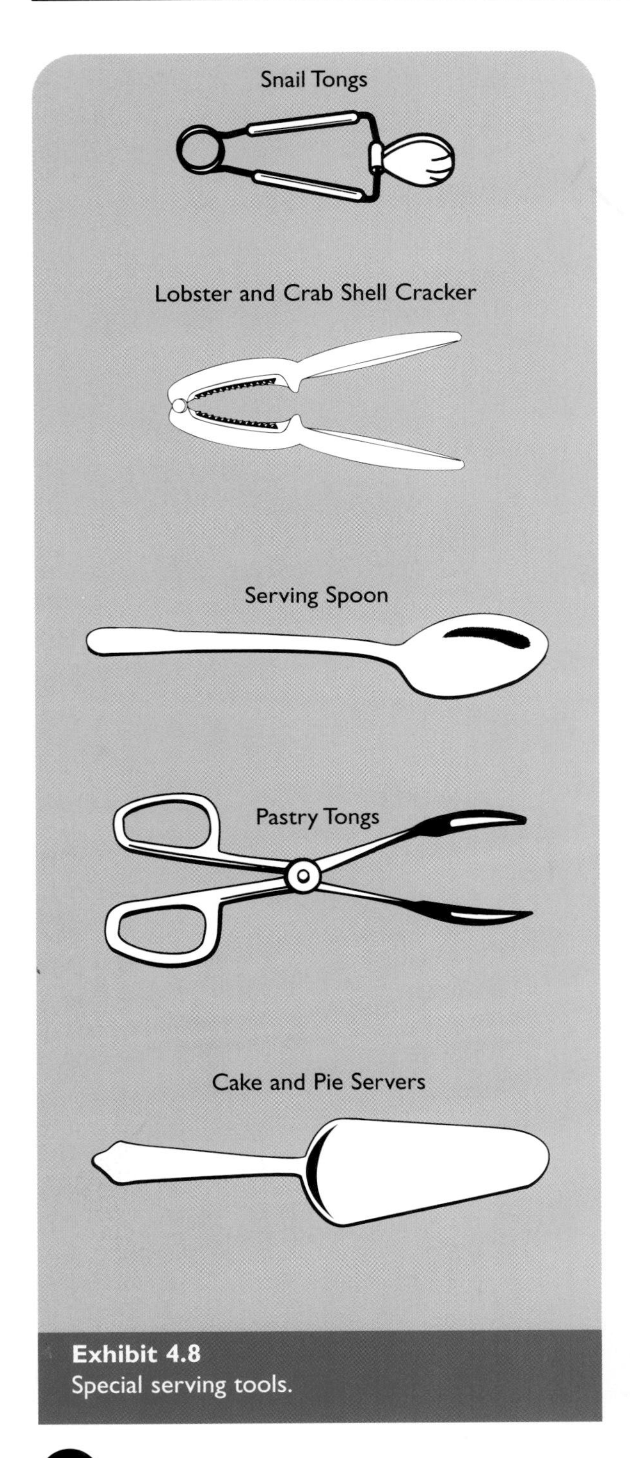

Exhibit 4.8
Special serving tools.

Other utensils are used for foods that are a bit more difficult to eat. For example, *snail tongs* are a specialized utensil used for holding a snail shell so the snail can be removed. Since the shells of lobsters and crabs are hard and thick, a *shell cracker* is used to crack them.

Cups and Glassware

Drinking glasses come in many shapes and sizes, and often use either clear glass, or thicker, solid ceramic. Generally, if a drink is cold, like soda, water, or iced tea, it will come in a clear glass. Hot drinks, like coffee, tea, and cocoa, are served in mugs made from thick glass, or ceramic. This helps drinks stay hot. Exhibit 4.10 shows different types of drinking glasses, and the beverages they hold.

Exhibit 4.9
Hot drinks, like coffee, are usually served in thick mugs.

Exhibit 4.10
Drinking glasses.

Chinaware

Perhaps the most important part of the table setting is the china. Like glasses, cups, and silverware, plates have adapted to fit the various types of food we eat. Exhibit 4.11 shows examples of chinaware. We are all most familiar with the dinner plate. A *dinner plate* is 10 to 12 inches across, and is used for all kinds of main courses and meals, and as a base plate for smaller plates and bowls. A *salad plate* is much smaller than a dinner plate (7 or 8 inches across). It is used for desserts and appetizers as well as salads, and as a base plate for gravy and sauce boats, and sundae glasses. Besides being used for bread, a *bread plate* can be used as a base for jams and other condiments that may easily spill. A *soup plate* is flat around the edge, but has a dip in the center to hold soup, pastas, and even mussels, shrimp, and clams. The *soup bowl* is smaller and deeper with no flat edge, and unlike the soup plate, is used only for soup.

Exhibit 4.11
Standard chinaware.

Though the pieces mentioned here can be served with many foods, there are a number of china pieces used for only one purpose. For example, a *tureen* is a large covered bowl used to serve soup. The *snail plate* has six or twelve indentions for holding snails. A *gravy boat* has a special lip, or spout to prevent spilling when pouring the sauce onto the plate. A *finger bowl* is a small bowl filled with water used to clean the fingers after eating, especially with messier meals such as shellfish and ribs.

Exhibit 4.12
Bowls that are properly garnished make a pleasing presentation for soup.

Review Your Learning 4.2

1. Which of the items below do servers commonly carry?
   a. Knife
   b. Corkscrew
   c. Pen
   d. Rubber band
   e. Order pad
   f. Extra credit card
   g. Hand towel

2. Which of the following items is **NOT** found in a service station?
   a. Cups and saucers
   b. Dinner plates
   c. Menus
   d. Silverware

3. A salad fork can also be used for:
   a. thick soups and creams.
   b. meats and shellfish.
   c. appetizers, desserts, and other delicate foods.
   d. pasta and pizza.

4. Explain what a finger bowl is, and what it is used for.

SECTION 4.3

Serving the Meal

AFTER STUDYING SECTION 4.3, YOU SHOULD BE ABLE TO:

- Demonstrate setting and clearing items properly.

Exhibit 4.13
Different restaurants use different table settings.

Traditional Setting

Every operation has its way of setting a table. However, there are several items that can be found in virtually all the place settings mentioned in this section. In a traditional table setting, the napkin is set in the middle of the setting; the dinner knife is set to the right of the setting with its sharp edge facing the middle of the setting; a spoon is set to the right of the knife; the dinner fork is set to the left of the setting; a water or wine glass is set above the right side of the setting; and a bread plate is set to the left of the setting.

French, Russian, and American Place Settings

While many restaurants use this traditional setting, other full-service operations use a specific place setting that matches its service style. For example, the French, Russian, and American service styles all have different place settings.Exhibit 4.14

Exhibit 4.14
French, Russian, and American place settings.

shows some examples of what French, Russian, and American place settings look like.

As you can see, many of the utensils used in the more unique service styles and settings are also found in the traditional service setting. Though differences may be small, it is important to recognize the various table settings available, and to use the most appropriate one.

Setting and Clearing Tables

Not only are servers responsible for properly setting the table, but they must know how to remove items from the table while guests are still seated. This is important so servers are not in the guests' way and don't interrupt their meal.

Certain tasks should be performed at either the left side, right side, or in front of guests. Some tasks that are performed at the guests' left side are presenting and serving from platters, serving salad and bread, and cleaning the table of extra utensils and crumbs. Also, anything served from the left should be removed from the left.

Setting and clearing plates, changing flatware, and pouring beverages are all done at the guests' right side. However, there are some exceptions to the rule. At corner tables, guests are served so as to disturb them as little as possible. This means serving from whichever side is most convenient. At rectangular tables, servers should stand at the head of the table when opening wine, taking orders, and assisting them with the menu. This is done so all seated guests can see the server.

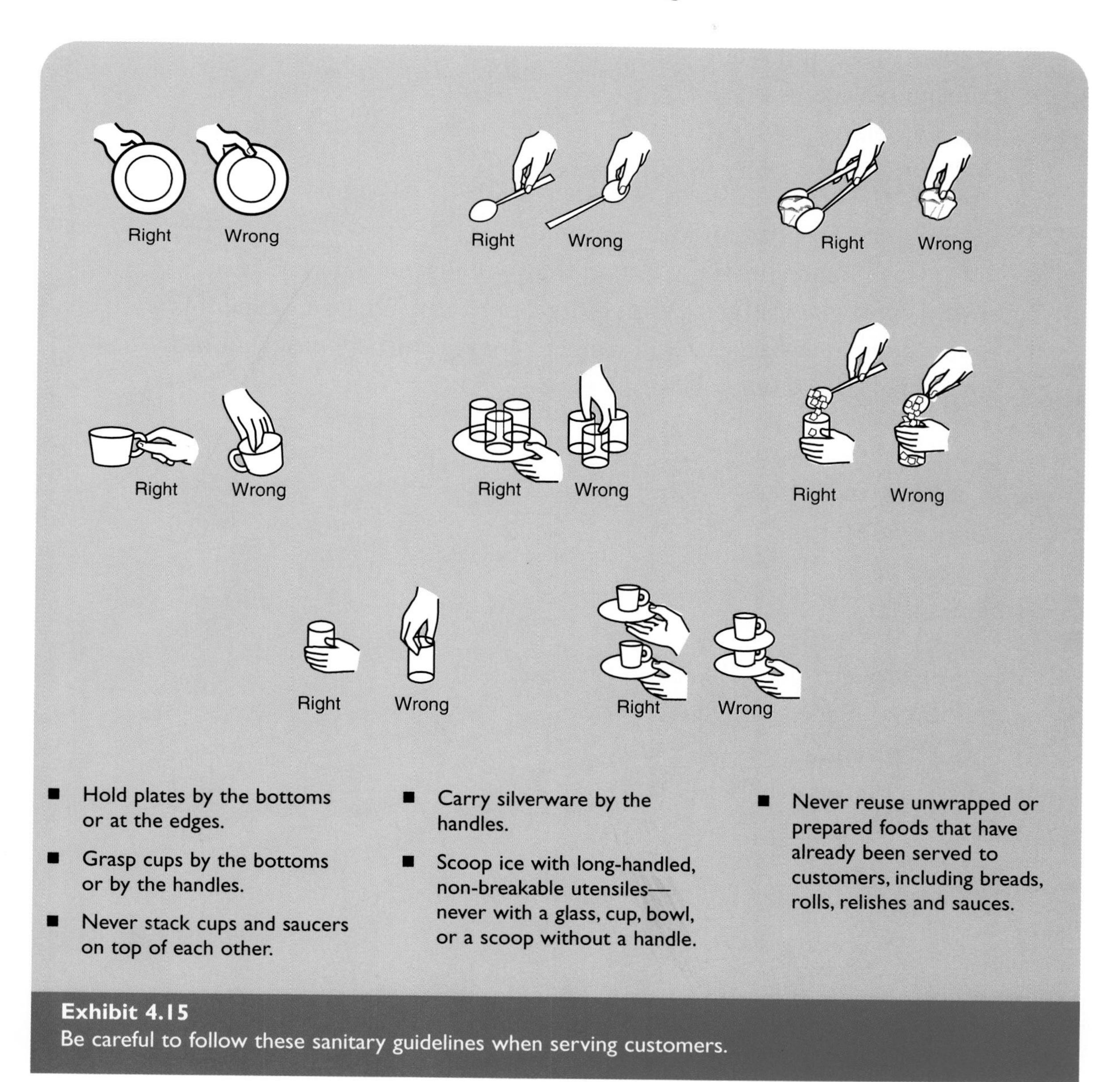

Exhibit 4.15
Be careful to follow these sanitary guidelines when serving customers.

Review Your Learning 4.3

1. Which of the tasks below are done from the guests' right side?
   a. Changing silverware
   b. Serving bread and salad
   c. Pouring beverages
   d. Clearing plates
   e. Presenting and serving from platters

2. When using tableware, employees should:
   a. never wash hands before working; they will just get dirty anyway.
   b. always carry glasses by the rim; more can be carried at one time this way.
   c. never touch a surface that will come in contact with a guest's mouth.
   d. always stack cups when carrying them.

3. In traditional table settings, the ______________ goes in the center of the setting.
   a. water goblet
   b. soup spoon
   c. butter knife
   d. napkin

4. Most full-service operations use a variation of the:
   a. traditional place setting.
   b. French place setting
   c. Russian place setting.
   d. English place setting.

5. What are the exceptions to the rules when serving guests from the right or left?

4.4

SECTION 4.4

Suggesting Items and Guiding Guests through the Menu

AFTER STUDYING SECTION 4.4 YOU SHOULD BE ABLE TO:

- Dramatize ways of describing and recommending menu items to guests.

KEY TERM

- **Suggestive selling**

Exhibit 4.16
Guests welcome good service in a friendly atmosphere.

From the moment you meet a customer, you are representing the operation through your actions, attitude, and appearance. Giving good customer service should make your job enjoyable, and is the perfect way to ensure that guests return.

Giving good customer service isn't always as simple as it seems. But there are some steps to take to make sure that you are doing your best. Focus on the customer, and show that you will meet customers' needs immediately, or as fast as you can. Following up with customers to make sure they enjoyed their meal is also very important guest communication. As guests are coming or going, a friendly hello or goodbye will make them feel welcome and eager to return.

Suggestive selling is a cost effective way to promote an operation's products and services. The server has an extremely important role in suggesting items to guests, selling individual menu items, and increasing check and tip averages. It starts with the way servers take orders. Instead of asking, "Would you like an appetizer?" ask, "Can I bring you an order of our fresh mozzarella with sliced tomatoes and fresh basil? It's delicious, and it won't fill you up before your meal." Most guests welcome recommendations and will be more than willing to try specialties.

Using active and descriptive words to describe foods is a great way to suggestively sell menu items. Make items sound appetizing by using words like *sweet, juicy, mouth-watering,* and *rich.* For example, "Our Belgian waffles are made with Grade A fresh eggs, whole wheat flour, and milk, and are served hot from the griddle, topped with plump fresh strawberries and pure whipped cream or vanilla ice cream."

Exhibit 4.17
Customers appreciate knowledgeable and helpful servers.

Once customers have placed an order, let them know they've made a good decision by saying something like, "Excellent choice, sir. The salmon is very fresh today, I think you'll really like it." This makes customers feel good about their decision, and they will look forward to the meal.

Another aspect of suggestive selling is using the organization's promotional plans or daily specials to ensure guest satisfaction, and increase check totals. It is acceptable, and recommended, to mention these "deals" right from the start of the meal. Suggesting entrée specials, fruity drinks, hot appetizers, and savory desserts will only enhance the guest's dining experience.

You will learn more about suggestive selling in *Chapter 6: Marketing and the Menu.*

Review Your Learning 4.4

1. Which of the following are ways to give good customer service?
   a. Letting customers sit at the table for a long time without any service
   b. Following up with customers to see if they enjoyed their meal
   c. Sharing with customers your personal information
   d. Letting customers leave without saying goodbye

2. Suggestive selling is a way to:
   a. force guests to order only what you like.
   b. recommend items that are not selling to make the chef happy.
   c. sell individual menu items and increase check totals.
   d. convince guests to order the most expensive thing on the menu to increase the check total.

3. Which of the following responses will help guests feel good about their menu choice?
   a. "Great choice, ma'am. The tortellini is fresh, and has excellent flavor."
   b. "Hopefully you'll like the catfish. We've recently had some complaints about it, but I think it is OK today."
   c. "I like the ribeye steak myself, but not everyone enjoys that cut of meat."
   d. "Tofu stir-fry? Are you sure?"

4. Describe either a dish you have eaten at home or one you have prepared in class. Use suggestive selling techniques to sell this dish to your classmates.

4.5

SECTION 4.5

Handling Customer Complaints

AFTER STUDYING SECTION 4.5, YOU SHOULD BE ABLE TO:

- Dramatize methods of effectively resolving customer complaints.

Preventing Customer Service Problems

There will always be occasions when things go wrong and a customer is unhappy. Most customers who complain are not troublemakers; they can help find and correct problems. The great majority of customers who are dissatisfied never complain to the operation, but they will tell an average of 10 other people about their bad experience. This is bad for business. Complaints are a valuable key to knowing what customers want.

If a guest is dissatisfied, the first step is to find out what the problem is and fix it as soon as possible. This way the customer knows that his or her business is valued. By doing this, it is possible to win the customer back. Statistics show that a customer whose complaint is handled well will remain a loyal customer for many years to come.

It is much easier to prevent problems before they occur than to fix them after they make a customer unhappy. The best way to prevent most complaints is for all employees to do their jobs well. Being ignored by servers; being rushed or kept waiting; substandard food; or unsanitary conditions anywhere in the operation are all common reasons why guests may be unhappy with service and the meal.

Recognizing Problems

The important thing is recognizing when a customer is upset so the problem can quickly be solved. Some problems are easy to recognize, especially when a customer is shouting and demanding something. However, most problems are more difficult to recognize because the large majority of customers will not shout, or even complain, if they are unhappy.

Customers need to be asked if everything was enjoyable. Rather than asking, "Was everything OK?" ask, "Did you enjoy the red snapper?" If there is any sign that the guest is unhappy with the service or meal, encourage the customer to reveal the problem.

Some of the more subtle signs of an irritated guest are looking annoyed, not finishing a meal, avoiding eye contact, or saying unconvincingly that everything was just "OK." Be aware of these signs, and ready to help solve the problems.

Exhibit 4.18
Making sure that guests are happy begins the minute they walk in the door.

Handling Complaints

Once an unhappy guest has been discovered, the next step is to deal with the problem in a timely and considerate manner. It is traditionally held that the customer is always right. Although this is not necessarily true, even when the customer is wrong, the customer is still the customer. This means that customers are the only reason the operation is in business, and they deserve to be treated respectfully and professionally, even when their demands seem unreasonable. The majority of customers with complaints often do have a valid reason for being upset.

Plan ahead for possible problems. If a problem does arise, remember the following guidelines for handling complaints.

1. *Stay calm.* Under all circumstances, you must maintain self-control and a professional manner.
2. *Listen carefully*. Take time to hear what the customer is saying. If the customer is angry, allow the customer to vent their anger. Do not interrupt them. All customers want and deserve to be listened to.
3. *Empathize.* Look at the situation from the guest's point of view.

4. *Don't become defensive.* Don't take customers' complaints personally or feel threatened by an angry guest. Face the problem together.
5. *Never ignore a dissatisfied guest.*
6. *Don't hide behind your job description.* Never brush off a guest by saying, "Sorry, that's not my job."
7. *Don't blame the customer for what he or she is complaining about.*
8. *Don't try to prove that you are right and the customer is wrong.*
9. *Don't pass the buck or blame other employees.* There are a few exceptions to this point. For example, when dealing with an intoxicated guest, the situation might be handled by blaming company policy or the law when cutting off service of alcohol.
10. *Accept responsibility.* Customers are generally not interested in excuses and explanations. Accept responsibility for solving the problem—on behalf of the operation—and apologize sincerely for any inconvenience.
11. *Find a solution.* A dissatisfied customer whose problem is solved promptly is likely to become a loyal repeat visitor. Checking back within five minutes after a meal is served will catch problems early. Ask the customer for suggestions for a possible solution and offer options. Solutions may be as simple as having the chef re-cook an item, giving a guest a free dessert or beverage, or reducing the amount of the bill.
12. *Follow up.* Be sure the customer is satisfied with the solution by following up with them.

Exhibit 4.19
Handling a complaint well may help you earn a customer for life.

Managers should be notified of all customer complaints. This helps the whole operation take corrective action so the problem won't happen again. Customers appreciate it when managers apologize and show concern. In extreme cases, a follow-up written note of apology is appropriate.

Review Your Learning 4.5

1. On a separate sheet of paper, indicate which of the following are the most common reasons guests become unhappy with service.
   a. Being rushed or kept waiting.
   b. Being given too much food on their plate.
   c. Being seated right away.
   d. Unsanitary conditions in the operation.

2. If a guest is avoiding eye contact with the server, it probably means he or she is:
   a. too full to finish the meal.
   b. unhappy with the service and the meal.
   c. very pleased with the meal, but busy eating.
   d. pleased with the meal, but too shy to look at the server.

3. When handling complaints, be sure to:
   a. blame it on another employee. It's always someone else's fault.
   b. tell the guest you can do nothing about it. After all, you didn't cook the meal.
   c. listen carefully to the complaint. There just may be a really good reason.
   d. keep your stand, no matter what. You've been there longer and know more than the guest.

4. The majority of customers who are dissatisfied:
   a. never return; they complain to their friends and family instead.
   b. never complain to their friends and family, but keep it to themselves.
   c. always complain to the operation and demand compensation.
   d. always write letters of complaint to the operation.

5. Why should employees tell managers about all customer complaints?

Flashback

CHAPTER 4

SECTION 4.1: TRADITIONAL SERVICE STAFF AND SERVICE STYLES

- The traditional service staff includes a **maître d'hôtel, headwaiter, captain, front waiter,** and **apprentice.**
- There are a number of service styles used today, including **American, French, Russian, English,** and **quick-service.**
- Some full-service techniques are done at guests' tables, including carving meats like roast bird, lamb, and fish, and **flambéing.** Sometimes a **guéridon** is used at the tableside.

SECTION 4.2: SERVICE TOOLS AND UTENSILS

- Servers should always carry a hand towel, matches, corkscrew, change, a pen, and order pad.
- **Service stations** should be set up with napkins, silverware, cups and saucers, condiments, menus, water glasses, and anything else that will help servers serve guests.
- There are four main knives used while dining: *dinner knife, butter knife, fish knife,* and *steak knife.*
- The main forks used while dining are *dinner, salad, fish, cake, snail,* and *oyster fork.*
- Many different spoons are also used. They are the *soup spoon, teaspoon, sauce spoon, coffee spoon, espresso spoon, sundae spoon,* and *grapefruit spoon.*
- Other utensils are *snail* and *pastry tongs* and *shell crackers.*
- Basic chinaware consists of *dinner, salad,* and *bread plate,* and a *soup plate* and *bowl.* More specialized pieces include a *tureen, snail plate, gravy boat,* and *finger bowl.*

SECTION 4.3: SERVING THE MEAL

- When setting and clearing tables, the following should be done from the guest's left side: present platters, serve from platters, hold platters, serve salad, serve bread, clean the table, clear anything served from the left.

- The following should be done from the guest's right side: set and clear plates, change flatware, pour beverages, and present bottles.
- For corner tables, serve guests whichever way is the easiest. At rectangular tables, servers should stand at the head of the table when assisting with the menu, taking orders, and opening bottles of wine.

SECTION 4.4: SUGGESTING ITEMS AND GUIDING GUESTS THROUGH THE MENU

- Some ways to give good customer service are to focus on the customer, meet the customer's needs, welcome them, and say "good bye," and follow up to make sure they enjoyed their meal. Good listening skills are also important to good customer service.
- **Suggestive selling** is the important role the server has in suggesting items to guests. This is done by fully describing food items, and using promotions to increase sales and please the guests.
- Suggest items like appetizers, drinks, and desserts consistently throughout the meal. If customers are having a difficult time deciding what to order, do not force them to decide.

SECTION 4.5: HANDLING CUSTOMER COMPLAINTS

- Customers get an overall impression of a foodservice operation from its employees. Every time a customer comes in contact with an employee the opportunity is created to keep that customer for life.
- The following are some examples of what may make a customer unhappy about service: ignoring them, rushing them, keeping them waiting, serving substandard food, allowing unsanitary conditions anywhere in the operation, and behaving indifferently or rudely.
- An irritated guest may display the following: a look of annoyance, not finishing a meal, avoiding eye contact, and unconvincingly saying everything is all right.
- Customers are the main reason for being in business. They deserve to be treated with respect.
- Always handle customer complaints as professionally as possible, by listening, staying calm, and finding a solution to the problem.
- Managers should be notified of all customer complaints, even when they are handled well.

Shari Carlson

Owner
Dessert Dreams
Irving, Texas

My first job in the foodservice industry was as a waitress while going to college. While waiting tables, I became friends with the chef and started working part time in the kitchen preparing simple salads and cold prep items. I discovered that I really liked working in the kitchen. To develop my skills and start a career in the culinary arts, I joined an apprenticeship program coordinated by the American Culinary Federation (ACF) and the Texas Chefs Association (TCA). I worked in all areas of the kitchen during my apprenticeship, but enjoyed the bake shop the best. After completion of the program I started as an assistant pastry chef at the Hyatt Regency in Dallas. I then moved to the Hyatt in Fort Worth as a pastry chef.

After four years as a pastry chef, I decided to open my own company that would supply high quality pastries to upscale hotels and restaurants. I started out by renting space in the kitchen of a country club. I used the kitchen in the very early hours of the morning and completed all my work before most of the kitchen staff arrived to start their day. Networking through the ACF/TCA affiliation led to the rapid expansion of my business. I soon moved into my own operation and have been in business ten years.

My day starts at 5:00 am with a review of the day's production sheets and any additional orders that have arrived overnight. I then set mise en place and staff schedules. Now I supervise staff and handle various other small business functions rather than working in the kitchen all the time. But I still make time to research new recipes and create the menu!

I compete in various culinary competitions and have been on culinary teams that have won awards in Germany, France, and Ireland. I also teach culinary arts part time at El Centro College in Dallas.

For anyone wishing to start a career in culinary arts, I recommend getting a job with a well respected and helpful chef. The only way to determine if you will enjoy making a career in culinary arts is by working in a kitchen. The hours are long and the environment is hot and very strenuous. But, it is also very exciting, and I have found it to be very rewarding, both personally and professionally.

CHAPTER 5

Desserts and Baked Goods

Bakery Products

AFTER STUDYING SECTION 5.1, YOU SHOULD BE ABLE TO:

- Identify and use common ingredients in baking.
- Identify and describe types and roles of strengtheners, shortenings, sweeteners, flavorings, leaveners, and thickeners.
- Calculate ingredient weights using baker's percentages.
- Convert recipes to a new yield.

Baking is a science, requiring exact measurements, proper handling of ingredients, and the right equipment to ensure quality baked products. Nearly all bakery products are prepared using a common list of ingredients that fall into seven categories.

- Strengtheners, such as flour and eggs
- Shortenings, such as butter and oils

KEY TERMS

- Air
- All-purpose flour
- Baker's percentage
- Baking powder
- Baking soda
- Bread flour
- Cake flour
- Caramelization
- Creaming method
- Extract
- Ferment
- Flavoring
- Foaming method
- Formula
- Gluten (GLOO-ten)
- Leavener
- Liquid
- Pastry flour
- Shortening
- Sift
- Strengthener
- Sweetener
- Thickener
- Yeast

- Sweeteners, such as sugars and syrups
- Flavorings, such as vanilla and nuts
- Chemical, organic, and physical leaveners, such as baking powder, baking soda, yeast, and steam
- Thickeners, such as cornstarch, flour, and eggs
- Liquids, such as water, milk, cream, eggs, honey, molasses, and butter

In baking, **strengtheners** provide stability and ensure that the baked item doesn't collapse once it is removed from the oven. Flour is a main ingredient used in baking. There are four basic types of wheat flour: bread flour, all-purpose flour, cake flour, and pastry flour.

Bread flour, as its name suggests, is a strong flour that is used for making breads, hard rolls, and any product that needs high gluten for a strong texture. **Gluten** (GLOO-ten) is a protein found in bread flour. The more yeast doughs are mixed, worked, and kneaded, the more the gluten becomes elastic and stretchy. When baked, it helps provide the firm structure and a light, even texture, needed in bread production.

All of the ingredients that go into creating a bakery product add nutritional content, from the butter or eggs used as a liquid, to the flavorings that may include nuts, spices, and extracts. Together, these basic ingredients provide great taste and nutritional value.

Cake flour has a low-gluten content and has a very soft, smooth texture and a pure white color. Cake flour is used for cakes and other delicate baked goods. Pastry flour is not as strong as bread flour and not as delicate as cake flour. **Pastry flour** is used for baking cookies, pie pastry, some sweet yeast doughs, biscuits, and muffins. It feels like cake flour, but has the creamy color of bread flour.

All-purpose flour falls between pastry and bread flour, and is good to use in cookies, biscuits, and general production work.

Shortening is another necessary baking ingredient that makes baked goods moist, adds flavor, and keeps the baked item fresh longer. Any fat, such as oil or butter, acts as a shortening in baking. The more thoroughly mixed the fat, the more it will affect the item's overall texture. Fats that are rubbed or rolled into doughs tend to separate the dough into large layers, creating a flaky texture. When the fat is thoroughly creamed together with the other ingredients, the resulting texture of the baked item will be smooth, soft, and more cake-like.

Sweeteners include refined sugars, molasses, brown sugar, corn syrup, honey, and malt syrup (usually used in yeast breads). Sweeteners add flavor to baked goods. They also help the shortening blend with other ingredients, and make the product soft and tender. When the product is baked, the heat causes the sugar to turn a light brown color. This process is called **caramelization,** and occurs whenever sugar is used as an ingredient in baked items.

Leaveners are necessary in baking because they allow the dough, or batter, to rise. Leaveners fall into three categories: chemical, organic, and physical. Baking soda and baking powder are the main chemical leaveners; yeasts comprise the organic leaveners; the basic physical leaveners are air and steam.

Exhibit 5.1
Honey is one type of sweetener used in baked goods.

Baking soda and baking powder are both chemical leaveners. They act much in the same way that yeast does. **Baking soda** (sodium bicarbonate) releases carbon dioxide gas when mixed with a liquid and an acid. For example, baking soda will leaven a batter when mixed with an acid such as lemon juice or buttermilk. Other, less reliable reactants are honey, molasses, cocoa, or chocolate. Because heat is not necessary for the leavening process to occur, the item must be baked right away to prevent the gases from escaping and leavening the item too soon.

Baking powder is a very versatile leavener. It is a mixture of baking soda and an acid, and an inactive material, like starch. Because there is acid in the baking powder, there does not need to be any acid in the batter for leavening to take place. Leavening occurs when liquid and heat are added.

Yeast, an organic leavener, is a microscopic plant used often in baking. When yeast is mixed with carbohydrates (such as sugar and flour) it **ferments,** or produces carbon dioxide gas and alcohol.

The release of carbon dioxide gas and alcohol causes the bread dough to rise (leavens it). It's important to measure all leavening agents very carefully. Even small changes can produce major defects in baked products.

Introducing **air** into the batter is another way to leaven the baked item. The air expands during baking and leavens (or raises) the product. There are two methods used to introduce air into batter: creaming and foaming. In the **creaming method,** fat and sugar are beaten together. Creaming is most often used in cake and cookie making. In the **foaming method,** eggs are beaten, with or without sugar. Whole egg foams are used in sponge cakes, while egg white foams are used in angel food cakes, meringues, and soufflés.

Eggs are a high protein food that are easily contaminated by salmonella. When working with eggs, make sure they are fresh and have been properly stored before using them.

Thickeners include gelatin, flour, arrowroot (a powdered starch made from a tropical root), cornstarch, and eggs. **Thickeners,** combined with the stirring process, determine the consistency of the finished product. For example, custard cooked over direct heat and stirred constantly will result in a sauce; the same custard recipe cooked in a bain-marie (which is a water bath used to cook foods gently by surrounding the pan with simmering water) without stirring will set into a firm custard that can be sliced.

Flavorings, such as spices, salt, and extracts, affect a baked item's taste and color. Spices used most often in baking are cinnamon, nutmeg, mace, cloves, ginger, caraway, cardamom, allspice, anise, and poppyseed. Salt plays an important role in baking. It improves the texture of breads and controls how yeast acts (ferments) in bread doughs. **Extracts** are flavorful oils taken from such foods as vanilla, lemon, and almond. A few drops of extract will greatly enhance the flavor of baked goods. Flavorings need to be measured accurately so that the flavor of the spice or extract will not overwhelm the flavor of the finished baked product.

One of the most important elements used in baking is liquid. The liquid used in baking can be water, milk, cream, molasses, honey, or butter. **Liquid** is used in baking to provide moisture to the product and to allow the gluten to properly develop. Water is the most basic and common form of liquid used in baking. Often, milk products such as whole milk, buttermilk, cream, or dried milk, are used. Milk provides the baked product with flavor, nutritional value, and texture. Honey, molasses, eggs, and butter also act as a liquid in baking by contributing moisture to the baked item, as well as a unique taste and texture.

Milk is one of nature's most nutritious foods. Packed with vitamins and minerals, such as calcium, iron, potassium, and vitamin A, it really is a nutritional powerhouse!

Baker's Percentages

Standardized recipes, or **formulas,** for bakery products are set up a bit differently than those for other items. Proportions for each ingredient are given in the form of percentages. Flour is always given a proportion of 100 percent, and all other ingredients are given percentages in relation to the flour. This is known as **baker's percentages.** In this way, recipes can be converted to give larger or smaller yields by changing ingredient amounts that keep proportions and percentages the same. The formula for baker's percentages is expressed like this:

$$\frac{\text{Weight of ingredient}}{\text{Weight of flour} \times 100\%} = \%\text{ of ingredient}$$

Exhibit 5.3 shows a formula for soft rolls using baker's percentages. The formula also shows the various directions given in a bake shop recipe, such as mixing, how long the yeast should ferment, scaling and baking temperature.

Once you understand baker's percentages, it's easy to calculate the weight of any ingredient or to convert a formula to a new yield. For example, if a formula calls for 20% sugar and you are using 10 pounds of flour, how much sugar do you need by weight? Change the ingredient percentage to decimal form by moving the decimal point two places to the left. Then, multiply the weight of the flour by this decimal to get the weight of the ingredient.

Example: 20% = 0.20

10 lb flour × 0.20 = 2 lb sugar

To convert a formula to a new yield, change the total percentage to decimal form by moving the decimal point two places to the left. Then, divide the desired yield by this decimal figure to get the weight of the flour. If necessary, round off this number to the next highest figure. Use the weight of flour and remaining ingredient percentages to calculate the weights of the other ingredients.

Exhibit 5.2
Making more or less of a recipe is easy when you understand baker's percentages.

Dry ingredients must be sifted before they are incorporated, or mixed, into the dough or batter. **Sifting** adds air to flour, cocoa, and confectioner's sugar, removing lumps and filtering out any impurities. Check recipes carefully to see whether ingredients are to be scaled before or after sifting.

Baking pans must be properly selected and prepared. The correct shape and size are important to ensure that the baked item's texture and appearance are correct. Delicate batters must be baked in pans that are liberally greased and floured. This is done by first greasing the pan, then dusting flour into the pan,

Exhibit 5.3
Formula for soft rolls.

Ingredient	U.S. measure	Metric measure	Percentage
Water	1 lb 4 oz	600 g	45%
Yeast	2 oz	60 g	4.5%
Bread flour	2 lb 12 oz	1300 g	100%
Salt	1 oz	30 g	2.25%
Sugar	4 oz	125 g	9%
Nonfat milk powder	2 oz	60 g	4.5%
Shortening	2 oz	60 g	4.5%
Butter or margarine	2 oz	60 g	4.5%
Eggs	4 oz	120 g	9%
Yield	5 lb 1 oz	2420 g	183%

Mixing:	Straight dough method. 10–12 minutes at second speed.
Fermentation:	1½ hours at 80°F (27°C)
Scaling and makeup:	16–20 oz (450–600 g) per dozen rolls.
Baking:	400°F (200°C)

covering all the greased surfaces. Excess flour can be removed by lightly tapping the pan upside-down on the work surface. The baking pans used for lean doughs very often are dusted with cornmeal, while angel food cakes are baked in completely grease-free tube pans.

It's very important not to overload the oven during baking, since the air won't be able to circulate and properly bake the items. Once the baked item has been removed, it must be cooled on a rack in the baking pan.

Richer doughs, such as croissants, Danish, muffins, and some cakes, can be reheated in a microwave oven. Many times, cakes are prepared in advance and frozen. Always thaw baked goods at room temperature.

Review Your Learning 5.1

1. Strengtheners are important in baked products because they:
   a. ensure the baked product won't collapse when it is removed from the oven.
   b. make sure the dough rises properly in yeast breads.

2. Shortening is important in baked products because it:
   a. gives the crust a nice, brown color.
   b. makes baked goods tender and moist.

3. Leaveners are important in baked products because they:
   a. give baked goods moisture and flavor.
   b. allow dough, or batter, to rise.

4. What do flavorings add to baked goods? What are some common flavorings used in baking?

SECTION 5.2

Yeast Breads

AFTER STUDYING SECTION 5.2, YOU SHOULD BE ABLE TO:

- Differentiate between lean doughs, rich doughs, sponge doughs, and sourdoughs, and give examples.
- Proof bake shop items.
- Mix yeast dough using the straight mix method.
- Prepare and compare yeast breads.

Yeast breads are divided into two categories, lean doughs and rich doughs. **Lean doughs** are made with flour, yeast, and water. Breads made from lean dough tend to have a chewy texture and a crisp crust. French bread and hard rolls are examples of lean doughs.

Rich doughs are made with the addition of shortening or tenderizing ingredients such as sugars, syrups, butter, eggs, milk, and cream. When these ingredients are introduced, they change the bread's overall texture, as well as the way the dough

KEY TERMS

- Knead (need)
- Lean dough
- Oven spring
- Proof
- Rich dough
- Sourdough
- Sponge
- Sponge method
- Straight mix method

Exhibit 5.4
Lean dough breads include hard rolls, French bread, and wheat breads.

Exhibit 5.5
Rich dough breads include Danish and croissants.

is handled. Rich doughs should have a cake-like texture after baking. Parker House rolls, cloverleaf rolls, soft rolls, and Danish are examples of rich doughs.

Exhibit 5.6
The straight mix method.

- Combine all ingredients in a bowl.
- Mix the dough until it starts to catch.
- Knead the dough until it is smooth and springy.
- Remove the dough to an oiled bowl.
- Let it rise.
- Punch it down.
- Remove it to a floured workbench.
- Shape and place the dough in pans.
- Let it rise.
- Bake.

The straight mix method and the sponge method are the most common methods used to mix yeast breads. The straight mix method can be used for all types of doughs—lean, rich, and sponge.

When using the **straight mix method** to mix dough, all ingredients can be combined at the same time. See Exhibit 5.6 for the steps involved in the straight mix method. The yeast may be mixed with warm water first, at a temperature of 138°F (59°C). After mixing the dough, it must be kneaded until it is elastic and smooth. To **knead** (need) dough is important because it develops the gluten in the dough, and gives the dough the "stretch" and "give" it needs to develop the proper texture.

Like the straight mix method, the **sponge method** is also used to mix yeast batters. The first stage of this method involves mixing the yeast, liquid, and half of the flour to make a thick batter called a **sponge.** After the sponge rises and doubles its size, the remaining fat, salt, sugar, and flour are added. The dough is kneaded and left to rise. Breads made with the sponge method have a lighter texture and more unique flavor than breads made using the straight dough method.

Exhibit 5.7
Made with a starter, sourdough bread has a unique and tangy flavor.

Helpful Hints for Baking Bread

- **If the baked item tastes strongly of yeast, the dough was not allowed sufficient time to proof before baking or too much yeast was used.**
- **Doughs without sufficient salt will have a bland flavor.**
- **If the dough is pale after baking, it is either not completely baked or has been baked at too low a temperature.**

When using fresh yeast, keep it refrigerated until it is to be used. It should look creamy and white, and have a fresh, yeasty smell. If the yeast has a sour odor, or is brown and has a slimy film, discard immediately. Using only the freshest yeast will ensure a quality baked product.

Sourdough is another type of bread that is made with yeast batter. However, sourdough breads are leavened with something called a starter, a mixture of water, yeast, and all-purpose flour, that has been fermented until it has a sour smell (usually overnight).

Once yeast dough has been mixed and left to rise, punch it down by pushing the dough down in a few places. This will expel the carbon dioxide and redistribute the yeast evenly.

Once the dough is in the pan, it must be **proofed,** or allowed to rise a second time. Proofing, the final rise of the yeast product before baking, should be between 95°F and 115°F (35°C and 46°C). The product should continue proofing until it is about twice its original size and bounces back when lightly touched.

Once the product is placed in the oven, it will rise quickly. **Oven spring** is the sudden and quick rise of the product as the heat from the oven causes gases in the product to grow and expand.

The doneness of a baked good is determined by its color, size, and the sound it makes when thumped with a finger (it should make a deep, hollow sound).

Alert! Alert! Be very careful to wear oven mitts when removing hot pans and cookie sheets from the oven. Keep hot pans at arm's distance, and place on a cooling rack to allow the items to properly cool.

After cooling, breads can either be sliced immediately or stored. Most breads can be held for a short time on parchment-lined trays or in baskets. For longer storage, wrap cooled bread in plastic wrap. Most yeast breads can be frozen for longer storage. After they have thawed, reheat breads before service. Some items, such as hard rolls and Italian bread that are made from lean doughs, can stale quickly. These items can be reheated in convection ovens before service to maintain their quality.

There are 10 basic steps in making yeast breads. Here are the steps and a brief description of each.

1. *Scaling ingredients.* All ingredients must be measured accurately.
2. *Mixing and kneading ingredients.* During mixing, the ingredients are combined, the yeast is distributed, and the gluten is developed. The dough is kneaded to further develop the gluten, until the dough is smooth and elastic.
3. *Fermentation.* During fermentation, the yeast acts on sugars and starches in the dough to produce carbon dioxide and alcohol. Carbon dioxide gas gets trapped in the gluten.
4. *Punching down.* The dough is gently folded down to expel and redistribute gas pockets in the dough. Punching also relaxes the gluten and evens the temperature.
5. *Portioning.* Divide the dough into pieces of uniform weight, according to the product you are making. Weigh portions on a portion scale to ensure uniform size and weight.

6. *Rounding*. After portioning, shape the dough into smooth, round balls. The outside layer of gluten becomes smooth. This holds in the gases and makes it easier to shape the dough.

7. *Shaping*. Dough can then be shaped into a variety of forms, depending on the desired type of bread.

8. *Proofing*. Proofing is the final rise of the shaped yeast dough just before baking. The dough is kept in a warm, draft-free area, or in a proofing box, and allowed to double in size.

9. *Baking*. Load the ovens carefully because proofed doughs are fragile until they become set by baking. Common baking temperatures are between 400°F and 425°F (204.4°C and 218.4°C). A golden brown crust color normally indicates the loaves are done.

10. *Cooling and storing*. Loaves should be removed from their pans and placed on racks to allow air circulation. Yeast products should be cooled at room temperature. For storage, wrap cooled breads in moisture-proof bags to retard staling. Breads must be thoroughly cool before wrapping or moisture will collect inside the bags.

Review Your Learning 5.2

1. Which of the following ingredients make up lean doughs?
   a. Flour, yeast, and water
   b. Flour, shortening, and water
   c. Yeast, shortening, and flour
   d. Yeast, shortening, and water

2. What are the various methods used to mix yeast breads?

3. What are some examples of breads made from rich dough?

4. Kneading is important in making dough because it:
   a. evenly distributes the flour.
   b. thoroughly incorporates air into the dough.
   c. develops the gluten, giving the dough "stretch" and "give."
   d. evenly distributes the shortening.

5.3

SECTION 5.3

Quick Breads, Cakes, Pastries, Pies, and Cookies

AFTER STUDYING SECTION 5.3, YOU SHOULD BE ABLE TO:

- Prepare different types of quick breads and cake batters.
- Identify the main functions of icings and determine which are best suited for different baked goods.
- Prepare and describe steamed puddings and dessert soufflés.
- Prepare pie dough using the 3-2-1 method.
- State in your own words the procedure for baking blind.
- Describe roll-in dough, phyllo dough, and pâte à choux.
- Prepare cookies using various makeup methods.

KEY TERMS

- 3-2-1 dough
- Baking blind
- High-ratio
- Icing
- Pâte à choux (paht ah SHOE)
- Phyllo dough (FEE-low)
- Profiterole (pro-FEET-uh-roll)
- Quick bread
- Roll-in dough method
- Sheet method
- Soufflé (soo-FLAY)
- Steamed pudding
- Two-stage method

Quick breads and cakes are all popular snack and dessert items and are usually easy and quick to make. Quick breads and cakes use the same mixing methods, so we'll discuss them together.

Quick breads, such as biscuits, scones, and muffins, differ from yeast breads. As their name suggests, quick breads can be prepared faster. **Quick breads** use chemical leaveners rather than organic ones, and therefore, don't require a rising period.

Exhibit 5.8
Muffins and biscuits are popular quick breads.

There are four basic methods for preparing quick bread and cake batters.

1. As discussed in Section 5.2, all ingredients are combined at once and blended into a batter using the straight dough method. Corn bread and blueberry muffins are examples of quick breads made with the straight dough method.
2. In the creaming method, fat and sugar are creamed together to produce a very fine crumb and a dense, rich texture. A yellow butter cake is an example of a cake using the creaming method.
3. The **two-stage method** is used to prepare high-ratio cakes. **High-ratio** cakes are so named because they contain a higher amount, or ratio, of sugar and liquid to the flour in the recipe. In the two-stage method, the emulsified shortening, which spreads easily, is combined with the dry ingredients. One half of the liquid is then added and blended. The remaining liquid is gradually added to the mixture. High-ratio cakes made using the two-stage method have a very fine crumb, and are quite moist. Devil's food cake is one popular item prepared with the two-stage method.
4. In the foaming method, a foam of whole eggs, yolks, or whites provides the structure for cakes with the lightest texture, such as angel food and chiffon cakes.

Make sure the eggs being used are fresh and have been properly stored. Eggs left in the shell should be refrigerated at 40°F (4.4°C) for a maximum period of one week.

The mixing technique for biscuits (known as the biscuit method) differs from the four mixing methods mentioned above. Instead of combining all the ingredients at once, a fat is rubbed, or cut, into the flour until the mixture is mealy, or bumpy, in appearance. This produces a stiff batter with a slightly chewier texture than that of more cake-like items. Sometimes this batter is kneaded very briefly because the dough will be tough if overworked.

Icings (frostings) are sweet coatings for cakes and other baked goods. Icings have three main functions.

- They improve the keeping qualities of the cake by forming a protective coating around it.
- They contribute flavor and richness.
- They improve appearance.

It's important to always use top-quality flavorings and ingredients for icings, so that they will enhance the cake rather than detract from it. Icing should be light and delicate, and not overwhelm the flavor of the cake. In general, use heavy frostings with heavy cakes and light frostings with light cakes. For example, to frost an angel food cake with a heavy fudge icing would cause the cake to collapse.

Exhibit 5.9
Decorated cakes are always a creative addition to a party or special occasion.

Puddings, Custards, and Dessert Soufflés

Steamed puddings and dessert soufflés are made of batters that require special handling. **Steamed puddings** are more stable because of the greater percentage of eggs and sugar in the batter. Baked custard and crême caramel are examples of steamed puddings.

Soufflés rely more on egg whites and are not as stable. **Soufflés** (soo-FLAY) are lightened with beaten egg whites and then baked. Baking causes the soufflé to rise like a cake. Chocolate soufflé and almond soufflé are examples of dessert soufflés. See Exhibit 5.10 for the steps involved in making a soufflé.

Exhibit 5.10
How to make a dessert soufflé.

- Prepare a base according to the recipe and have it at room temperature.
- Coat the molds with butter and sugar.
- Add any desired flavoring to the base.
- Whip the egg whites to a medium peak and fold them into the base.
- Fill the molds and level the tops.
- Bake the soufflé on a sheet pan in a hot oven.
- Serve them immediately with the appropriate sauce.

Exhibit 5.11
This beautiful apple pie is fresh from the oven.

Pies, Croissants, and Pastries

Pies, croissants, and Danish pastries are all popular baked goods. Pies are made using a basic pie dough called **3-2-1 dough.** It is called this because it is made of three parts flour, two parts fat, and one part water (by weight). When it is properly made, the crust is flaky and crisp. Exhibit 5.12 shows how to make pie dough. It is important to use pastry flour and work the dough as little as possible. Both the fat and liquid should be cold when mixed into the dough. The fats used are shortening, butter, or lard, and the liquid is usually water, milk or cream. If milk or cream are used instead of water, decrease the amount of fat in the overall formula.

In general, pies are baked just until they begin to take on a golden color. If they begin to brown too much before they are done baking, top the pie loosely with aluminum foil near the end of the baking process.

Exhibit 5.12
Making pie dough.

- Dissolve the salt in water.
- Cut the fat into the flour.
- Add the cold water and mix together.
- Chill the dough.
- Turn the dough out onto a floured work surface.
- Roll out the dough.
- Cut the dough and fill the pie pan.
- Bake or fill, add a top crust, and bake.

Helpful Hints for Pies

- **If the dough has been rolled out unevenly, the thicker portions may appear moist, indicating that the dough is not fully baked.**
- **The dough should be flaky. If the dough has been underbaked, the texture may be gummy or rubbery. If it has been overbaked, the crust may be tough.**
- **Lard gives a very flaky crust, while shortening gives a more mealy crust.**

One great way to make pies more nutritious is to use fresh quality fruit, like strawberries, cherries, blueberries, and peaches. Fruits contain many vitamins and minerals, such as vitamin A, fiber, carbohydrate, and potassium.

Many pies use fruit fillings. These fillings are prepared using sliced and peeled fresh fruit that is either poached with a liquid or allowed to cook as the entire pastry bakes. Cornstarch, tapioca, or arrowroot may be added to thicken the fruit filling. Lower-grade fruits can be used in baked pies and puddings.

Baking blind is the procedure for preparing a pre-baked pie shell. The dough is prepared, rolled out, and fitted into the pan, then pierced in several places with a fork. The pastry is then covered with parchment paper and baked with an empty pie pan on top of it.

While 3-2-1 dough is used for making pie crusts, the **roll-in dough method** is used for Danish, croissant, and puff pastry. See Exhibit 5.13 for making roll-in dough. Proper mixing methods, rolling techniques, and temperature control are necessary to produce a flaky, quality product. The dough must be rolled out into a large rectangle. The dough is then folded over in thirds, rolled again, and folded the appropriate number of times. A few guidelines will help you work with this dough.

- Keep the dough chilled.
- Use a sharp knife when shaping and cutting edges.
- Do not run the roller over the dough's edge.
- Chill puff pastry items before baking them.
- Save puff pastry scraps for use in other smaller items.

Other doughs, such as phyllo and pâte à choux, are commonly used. **Phyllo dough** (FEE-low) is used to prepare baklava, a dessert made of thin pastry, nuts, and honey. **Pâte à choux** (paht ah SHOE) is made by combining water or other liquid, butter, flour, and eggs into a smooth batter. Some familiar desserts that use pâte à choux include eclairs, cream puffs, and **profiteroles** (pro-FEET-uh-rolls), which are small round pastries made from pâte à choux filled with ice cream.

Exhibit 5.13
Making roll-in dough.

- Combine ingredients, usually shortening, flour, and water.
- Loosely blend the dough.
- Shape into a ball.
- Roll into a rectangle
- Fold into thirds and roll again, based on recipe.

Cookies

Cookies should be colorful and appetizing. Due to their high sugar content, cookies are best when they are baked in convection ovens.

There are seven makeup methods for cookies.

- *Dropped*—Dropped cookies, such as chocolate chip and oatmeal, are made from a soft dough and dropped from a spoon or scoop onto the cookie sheet.
- *Bagged*—Bagged cookies, made by forcing soft dough through a pastry bag, include ladyfingers, macaroons, and tea cookies.
- *Rolled*—Rolled cookies are made more often at home than in commercial kitchens because they take a lot of work. These cookies, including decorated sugar cookies and shortbread, are cut from a stiff dough that has been rolled out on a baking board.
- *Molded*—Molded cookies are molded by hand into any shape from a stiff dough. Peanut butter cookies are examples of molded cookies.
- *Icebox*—Icebox cookies are made from dough that has been rolled into logs and chilled, to be sliced just before baking. Butterscotch icebox cookies and chocolate icebox cookies are examples.

In the 1930s, Ruth Wakefield, owner of the Toll House restaurant, cut a bar of Nestle semi-sweet chocolate into small pieces and mixed them in her butter cookie dough. She expected the chocolate to melt into the dough. Much to her surprise, these chocolate bits kept their shape. These "mistake" cookies, known as Toll House cookies, became very popular, and in 1939 the Nestlé company bought Wakefield's recipe and began packaging Nestlé semi-sweet chocolate chips especially for Toll House cookies.

- *Bar*—Bar cookies are made by baking three or four bars the length of the baking pan, which are then sliced into small bars.
- *Sheet*—Brownies are usually made using the **sheet method,** in which the batter is poured into the entire baking pan and then sliced into individual squares or rectangles after baking. Other types of cookies prepared with the sheet method include butterscotch brownies or blondies.

Exhibit 5.14
Ladyfingers are a common type of bagged cookie.

Review Your Learning 5.3

For questions 1–3, select the answer that best completes each statement.

1. Baking blind is:
   a. used only for roll-in doughs.
   b. preparing a pre-baked pie shell.
   c. preparing a homemade pie shell.
   d. used only with doughs made with the straight mix method.

2. In general, pies are baked:
   a. until they begin to get a golden brown color.
   b. for at least 90 minutes.
   c. until the filling spills out onto the crust.
   d. for at least 30 minutes.

3. Pâte à choux is often used as a dough for:
   a. Danish.
   b. profiteroles.
   c. baklava.
   d. French rolls.

4. Which of the following is the method used to prepare corn bread and blueberry muffins?
   a. Two-stage method
   b. Straight mix method
   c. Steaming method
   d. Foaming method

5. For each cookie listed on the left, select the appropriate makeup method on the right. Some makeup methods will not be used.

Cookie
Chocolate Chip
Decorated Sugar Cookies
Ladyfingers
Brownies
Peanut butter

Makeup Method
a. Sheet
b. Molded
c. Icebox
d. Ice box
e. Bagged
f. Rolled

SECTION 5.4

Chocolate

AFTER STUDYING SECTION 5.4, YOU SHOULD BE ABLE TO:

- Explain how chocolate is made, including chocolate liquor, cocoa butter, and cocoa powder.
- Demonstrate how to store chocolate properly.
- State in your own words how to temper chocolate.

KEY TERMS

- Bloom
- Chocolate liquor
- Cocoa butter
- Cocoa powder
- Nib
- Tempering

FUN FOOD FACT

The Aztecs of Mexico had been enjoying chocolate for centuries before the first chocolate mill was opened in the United States in 1765. Chocolate is still popular in Mexican cooking and is the main ingredient in a popular sauce, mole (moe-lay) used on many nonsweet main courses.

Chocolate is produced from cocoa beans picked from cacao trees. We usually think of chocolate as a sweet, used in cookies, candies, cakes, and other desserts. However, chocolate is very versatile and can be used in many main dishes.

To make chocolate, the cocoa beans are roasted. The outer shells are loosened and the beans are cracked into smaller pieces, called **nibs.** Nibs are the basis of all cocoa products. The cocoa beans are then crushed into a paste that is completely

Chocolate, often regarded as a "bad" and unhealthy food, really is not so bad after all. Eaten in moderation, it provides quick energy and has often been called the perfect food. 1.5 ounces of pure milk chocolate contains 6g of protein, 2.4g of vitamin A, 9g of riboflavin, and 9g of calcium.

unsweetened, called **chocolate liquor.** The chocolate liquor is processed for a smooth, fine texture. When the chocolate liquor is pressed, the result is **cocoa butter.** The cocoa solids are ground into **cocoa powder.** Cocoa butter can be combined with chocolate liquor to make eating chocolate, or flavored and sweetened to make white chocolate. Exhibit 5.17 at the end of this section describes some various chocolate products.

To store chocolate, wrap it carefully, and keep it in a cool, dry, well-ventilated area. Do not refrigerate chocolate. Refrigeration causes moisture to condense on the surface of the chocolate. In hot, humid weather, however, refrigeration or freezing may be necessary to prevent flavor loss.

Sometimes a white coating, called **bloom,** appears on the surface of the chocolate. The bloom indicates that some of the cocoa butter has melted and then recrystallized on the surface. This has no effect on the quality. When it is properly stored, chocolate will last for several months. When cocoa powder is stored in tightly sealed containers in a dry place, it will keep almost indefinitely.

Chocolate must be handled very carefully when using it in cooking. Chocolate contains two distinct types of fat that melt at different temperatures. Chocolate is

Fudge was popular in the early 1900s at women's colleges in the Northeast. It was reportedly cooked over gaslight as an excuse for parties after "lights-out" curfew. The standard formula was 3 squares unsweetened chocolate, 2 cups sugar, and 1 cup cream.

Exhibit 5.15
Chocolate comes in many colors, shapes, and forms.

melted in a process called **tempering** (melting the chocolate by heating it gently and gradually) to ensure that both fats will melt smoothly, harden evenly, and have a good shine. In the tempering process, the chocolate is chopped into coarse pieces and placed in a stainless steel bowl over water simmering over a very low heat. *It is important that no water gets into the chocolate.*

When melting chocolate on the stove, make sure that you remain a safe distance from the stovetop. Wear oven mitts to protect your hands from the heat, and keep all loose clothing and hair pulled back and away from the stove.

Once the temperature of the chocolate reaches 105°F (40.6°C), remove it from the heat. More chocolate pieces are then added and stirred until the temperature drops to 87°F (30.6°C). It is then placed on the heat to raise the temperature to 92°F (33.3°C). Make sure that the tempered chocolate does not become grainy or scorched. If it does, it must be discarded. Tempered chocolate will coat items with an even layer and then harden into a shiny shell. To coat a food item, dip the item directly into the tempered chocolate, or place it on a rack over a clean tray, and pour the chocolate over it. Tempered chocolate can be piped out into designs with a parchment cone for decoration or can be used as a glaze.

Chocolate was officially introduced to the United States when John Hannon, an Irish immigrant, brought cocoa beans from the West Indies into Dorchester, Massachusetts, and started milling them. The first notice of the sale of cocoa and chocolate in America appeared March 12, 1770, in the Boston Gazette and Country Journal.

Exhibit 5.16
Chocolate must be tempered to make chocolate sauce.

Exhibit 5.17
Chocolate and related products.

Type	Description	Purchase Form
Chocolate liquor	Chocolate-flavored portion of the chocolate; obtained by grinding and liquefying chocolate nibs	(See *chocolate, unsweetened*)
Cocoa butter	Vegetable fat portion of chocolate; removed for cocoa; added for chocolate	Plastic at room temperature
Cocoa	Chocolate from which all but 10%–25% of the cocoa butter has been removed	Bulk and cans
Cocoa, Dutch process	Cocoa from which all but 22%–24% of the cocoa butter has been removed; treated with alkali to reduce its acidity	Bulk and cans
Cocoa, breakfast	Cocoa with at least 22% cocoa butter	Bulk and cans
Cocoa, low-fat	Cocoa with less than 10% cocoa butter	Bulk and cans
Cocoa, instant	Cocoa that has been pre-cooked, sweetened (usually about 80% sugar), and emulsified to make it dissolve more easily in liquid; may have powdered milk added	Bulk and cans
Chocolate, unsweetened (bitter/baking)	Solid chocolate made with about 95% chocolate liquor, 5% cocoa butter, and 5% sugar and other flavorings	Blocks or bars
Chocolate, bittersweet	Solid chocolate made with 35–50% chocolate liquor, 15% cocoa butter, and 35%–50% sugar; interchangeable with semi-sweet chocolate; may have added ingredients, such as nuts, fillings, stabilizers, emulsifiers, and/or preservatives	Blocks, bars, chunks, and chips
Chocolate, semi-sweet	Solid chocolate made with about 45% chocolate liquor, 15% cocoa butter, and 40% sugar; interchangeable with bittersweet chocolate; may have added ingredients	Blocks, bars, chunks, and chips

Exhibit 5.17 (CONTINUED)
Chocolate and related products.

Type	Description	Purchase Form
Chocolate, sweet	Solid chocolate made with 15% chocolate liquor, and 70% sugar, may have added ingredients	Blocks, bars, chunks, and chips
Chocolate, milk	Solid chocolate made with 10% chocolate liquor, 20% cocoa butter, 50% sugar, and 15% milk solids; may have added ingredients	Blocks, bars, chunks, and chips
Chocolate, coating (couverture)	Solid chocolate made with 15% chocolate liquor, 35% cocoa butter, and 50% sugar; high-fat content makes it ideal for coating candy, pastries and cakes	Blocks, bars, chunks, and chips
Confectionery coating	Solid artificial chocolate made with vegetable fat other than cocoa butter; usually contains real chocolate flavoring in chocolate-flavored types; other flavors available	Blocks, bars, chunks, and chips
Chocolate, white	Solid chocolate made with cocoa butter or other vegetable fats, sugar, milk solids, and vanilla; contains no chocolate liquor; may contain artificial yellow color and/or other added ingredients	Blocks, bars, chunks, and chips
Chocolate syrup	Chocolate or cocoa, sugar, and/or other sweeteners, water, salt, other flavorings	Bulk, bottles, and cans
Chocolate sauce	Same as chocolate syrup but thicker; may have added milk, cream, butter, and/or other thickeners	Bulk, bottles, and cans
Carob	A dark-brown, somewhat chocolate-like flavoring produced from the carob bean; unsweetened carob is somewhat sweet, so it requires less added sugar than chocolate (about ¾ usual amount)	Blocks, bars, chunks, and powder

Review Your Learning 5.4

1. A white coating that sometimes appears on the surface of chocolate is called:
   a. crystal.
   b. bloom.
   c. cocoa powder.
   d. chocolate dust.

2. Cocoa beans that are crushed into a paste and left unsweetened are called:
   a. cocoa butter.
   b. chocolate liquor.
   c. cocoa powder.
   d. chocolate nibs.

3. Properly stored in a cool, dry, well-ventilated area, chocolate will keep for several:
   a. days.
   b. weeks.
   c. months.
   d. years.

4. If tempered chocolate becomes grainy or scorched, the chocolate must be:
   a. immediately discarded.
   b. immediately immersed in a cool bath of ice water.
   c. reheated to 105°F (40.6°C).
   d. reheated to 92°F (33.3°C).

Dessert Sauces, Creams, Fruit Desserts, and Tortes

AFTER STUDYING SECTION 5.5, YOU SHOULD BE ABLE TO:

- Explain how crème anglaise, pastry creams, and Bavarian creams are made, and how they are used in desserts.
- List the steps used to prepare poached fruits and tortes.

KEY TERMS

- **Bavarian cream**
- **Crème anglaise (krem an-GLAY)**
- **Curdle**
- **Genoise (zhen-WAAHZ)**
- **Pastry cream**
- **Poached fruit**
- **Sabayon (sa-by-ON)**
- **Torte**

Dessert Sauces

Sauces are used to add flavor, moisture, and eye appeal to desserts. Vanilla sauce, also known as crème anglaise, is a classic accompaniment to soufflés and steamed puddings. **Crème anglaise** (krem an-GLAY) is a light vanilla-flavored custard sauce made from milk, egg yolks, and sugar. It is a delicate sauce that must be handled carefully. See Exhibit 5.18 for the procedure for making crème anglaise.

Exhibit 5.18
Making crème anglaise (vanilla sauce).

- Carefully scale or measure all ingredients.
- Heat the milk or milk/cream combination with some of the sugar to just below a boil.
- Combine the eggs with the remainder of the sugar.
- Temper (gently heat) the eggs with the hot milk and return the tempered eggs to the pan.
- Stirring constantly, cook the sauce over low heat, or pour the tempered egg mixture into custard cups and bake in a bain-marie until the custards are set.

It is especially important to have all the necessary equipment assembled before preparing the sauce. If the sauce begins to overheat or **curdle** (develop lumps), it can still be saved by straining it immediately into a container set in an ice-water bath.

Exhibit 5.19
Puff pastry with fruit and whipped cream makes a beautiful and tasty dessert.

Other popular sauces include caramel, butterscotch, chocolate, and fruit sauces. Any of these sauces can be prepared in advance; however, sabayon is one sauce that is too delicate to be made ahead and held. **Sabayon** (sa-by-ON) is a fragile foam of egg yolks, sugar, and Marsala wine. It is whipped constantly as it cooks over simmering water until it becomes thick and light.

Creams

Pastry creams are more dense than custards and are frequently used as the filling for pastries such as eclairs. These creams may also be used as a soufflé base. Eggs, sugar, flour or cornstarch, milk, and/or cream are cooked together into a very thick, smooth mixture. Pastry cream, as a basic preparation, is part of the mise en place for many kitchen desserts. Exhibit 5.20 shows how to make pastry cream.

Exhibit 5.20
Making pastry cream.

- Combine the flour and part of the sugar; blend them well to remove all lumps. Add the eggs and/or egg yolks to the mixture.
- Heat the milk with the remainder of the sugar to just below a boil.
- Temper the egg mixture with one-third of the hot milk mixture. Return the tempered egg mixture to the pot.
- Bring the pastry cream to a second boil, stirring it constantly.

Thomas Jefferson is credited with making French food popular in the United States. During his years as the American ambassador to France, he developed a taste for French food, and upon his return home, he brought back a French chef and many European recipes. Some of his favorite French desserts were chocolate dishes and ice cream served in a hot pastry shell.

Delicate **Bavarian creams** are made by combining three basic ingredients: vanilla sauce, gelatin, and whipped cream. The vanilla sauce is combined with the dissolved gelatin. This mixture is then cooled over an ice-water bath until it mounds slightly when dropped from a spoon. Whipped cream is then folded into the mixture and poured into molds. Exhibit 5.21 shows how to make Bavarian Cream. Bavarian creams may be used as single items, or as fillings for a variety of pastries.

Exhibit 5.21
Making Bavarian cream.

- Prepare a vanilla sauce. Flavor as desired.
- Combine the vanilla sauce with gelatin that has been dissolved.
- Cool the vanilla sauce over an ice-water bath until it mounds slightly when dropped from a spoon.
- Fold whipped heavy cream into the Bavarian and pour it into prepared molds. Chill the Bavarian for several hours before serving.

Fruit Deserts

Poached fruits include favorites such as Peach Melba and Pears Belle Hélène. Fruits to be poached should be firm enough to hold their shape during cooking. Good fruits to use for poaching are apples and pears. In poaching, the fruit is combined with the liquid, which is usually a mixture of sugar, spices, and wine. The fruit and liquid are then heated together until the fruit is tender. The fruit is fully poached when the skin is easily pierced with a fork. The greater the amount of sugar in the poaching liquid, the more firm the end result will be.

Exhibit 5.22
Pears are good for poaching because of their dense texture.

Tortes

A **torte** is an elegant, rich, many-layered cake often filled with buttercream or jam. A **genoise** (zhen-WAAHZ), French sponge cake, is normally used in preparing a torte. It is split into layers, and each layer is then topped with the buttercream or jam filling. The layers are placed back together, and the entire cake is coated with simple syrup and then frosted.

Review Your Learning 5.5

1. Match each definition on the left with the correct dessert on the right. Some desserts will not be used.

   Also known as crème anglaise.
   Made by splitting a genoise into layers.
   Fragile foam of egg yolks, sugar, and Marsala wine.
   Peach Melba is an example of this type of dessert.
   Frequently used as filling for eclairs.

   a. Crème anglaise
   b. Genoise
   c. Poached fruit
   d. Torte
   e. Sabayon
   f. Pastry cream

2. Bavarian cream is made from:
   a. whipped gelatin, milk, and crème anglaise.
   b. whipped cream, gelatin, and sabayon.
   c. gelatin, pastry cream, and milk.
   d. gelatin, whipped cream, and crème anglaise.

3. Pastry creams are part of the mise en place for many desserts, and are used as filling for:
   a. eclairs.
   b. croissants.
   c. Danish.
   d. tortes.

4. Good fruits to use for poaching are:
   a. bananas and pears.
   b. apples and peaches.
   c. pears and apples.
   d. bananas and berries.

5. Which of the following best describes a torte?
   a. Ice cream served in a hot pastry shell
   b. Elegant, rich, many-layered cake filled with jam
   c. Dense custard
   d. Rich, single-layered cake covered with buttercream

Flashback

CHAPTER 5

SECTION 5.1: BAKERY PRODUCTS

- Baking is a science in which exact measurements and proper handling of ingredients and equipment are essential to ensure quality baked products.
- Nearly all bakery products are prepared using a common list of ingredient types.
- **Strengtheners** provide stability and make sure that the baked item doesn't collapse once it is removed from the oven. The binding properties of **gluten,** a protein found in flour, are responsible for a light, even texture in the finished product.
- **Sweeteners** give the baked goods moisture. The **caramelization** of sugar is responsible for the attractive brown color that appears on most baked items.
- **Leaveners** introduce air into products and fall into three categories: chemical, organic, and physical.
- **Baking soda** and **baking powder** are the main chemical leaveners.
- **Yeast** is an organic leavener.
- Steam and **air** are the basic physical leaveners.
- **Thickeners** include gelatin, flour, arrowroot, cornstarch, and eggs. Thickeners, combined with the stirring process, determine the finished product's properties.
- **Liquids** are needed in baking to provide moisture to the product and allow the gluten to expand. The liquid may be water, milk, cream, molasses, honey, or butter.
- Baking pans must be properly selected and prepared. The correct shape and size are important to ensure that the baked item's texture and appearance are correct.
- Delicate batters must be baked in pans that are liberally greased and floured.

- Lean doughs very often are dusted with cornmeal, while angel food cakes are baked in completely grease-free tube pans.
- Avoid overloading the oven. Once the baked item has been removed from the oven, it must be cooled properly on a rack in the baking pan until it is sufficiently cooled.

SECTION 5.2: YEAST BREADS

- Yeast breads are divided into two categories—lean doughs and rich doughs.
- **Lean doughs** are made with flour, yeast, and water.
- **Rich doughs** are made with the addition of shortening or tenderizing ingredients such as sugars, syrups, butter, eggs, milk, or cream.
- **Proofing** is done before the yeast is added to the other ingredients.
- **Sponge** and sourdough starter are two types of yeast batter. Sponge is used with certain flours, such as rye and oat, that are low in gluten; sourdough is leavened with a fermented starter instead of, or in addition to, fresh yeast.
- The one technique used for mixing yeast dough is the **straight mix method,** where all ingredients can be combined at once.
- The **sponge method** is another method for mixing yeast batters. Breads made with the sponge method have a light texture and unique flavor.
- **Sourdough** breads are leavened with a starter made from water, yeast, and all-purpose flour that has been fermented.
- Once the dough is in the pan, it must be bench proofed.
- The doneness of a baked good is determined by its color and size and the sound it makes when thumped with a finger.

SECTION 5.3: QUICK BREADS, CAKES, PASTRIES, PIES, AND COOKIES

- Quick breads, such as muffins and biscuits, differ from yeast breads.
- **Quick breads** use chemical leaveners and do not require a rising period.
- There are four basic methods for preparing **batters.**
- **Straight mix method**—all ingredients are combined at once and blended into a batter.

- Creaming method—fat and sugar are creamed together for an exceptionally fine crumb and dense, rich texture.
- **Two-stage method**—used to prepare high-ratio cakes. The dry ingredients are combined with all of the shortening and half of the liquid until smooth, then the remaining wet ingredients are gradually added.
- Foaming method—a foam of whole eggs or their yolks or whites provides the structure for cakes with the lightest texture, such as angel food and chiffon cakes.
- **Icings** or frostings are sweet coatings for cakes and other baked goods and have three main functions:
  - —Improve the keeping qualities of the cake.
  - —Contribute flavor and richness.
  - —Improve appearance.
- Biscuits, scones, and soda breads are quick breads. Batter is stiff, almost a dough, that produces a texture slightly chewier than that of the more cake-like muffins.
- **Steamed puddings** and dessert **soufflés** are made of batters that require different handling.
- Steamed puddings are more stable because of the greater percentage of eggs and sugar in the batter.
- Soufflés rely much more on egg whites and are not as stable.
- Basic pie dough is sometimes called **3-2-1 dough** because it's made of three parts flour, two parts fat, and one part water (by weight).
- Pie crust is flaky and crisp—use pastry flour and work the dough as little as possible.
- **Baking blind** is the procedure for preparing a pre-baked pie shell.
- **Roll-in doughs** are used for Danish, croissants, and puff pastries. Proper mixing methods, rolling techniques, and temperature control are necessary to produce a flaky, quality product.
- Other doughs, such as **phyllo** and **pâte à choux,** are commonly used.
- **Phyllo dough** is used to prepare baklava and is a very lean dough.
- **Pâte à choux,** used for eclairs and cream puffs, is made by combining water, butter, flour, and eggs into a smooth batter.

- Cookies should be colorful and appetizing. Because of their high sugar content, cookies are best when they are baked in convection ovens. There are seven makeup methods for cookies: dropped, bagged, rolled, molded, icebox, bar, and sheet.

SECTION 5.4: CHOCOLATE

- Chocolate is a delicate ingredient that must be handled with care.
- Chocolate contains two distinct types of fat that melt at different temperatures.
- For smooth, even handling, chocolate is melted in a process called **tempering.**
- Tempered chocolate will coat items with an even layer and then harden into a shiny shell.

SECTION 5.5: DESSERT SAUCES, CREAMS, FRUIT DESSERTS, AND TORTES

- Sauces are used to add flavor, moisture, and eye appeal to desserts.
- Vanilla sauce, also known as **crème anglaise,** is a classic accompaniment to soufflés and steamed puddings. It is a delicate sauce that must be handled carefully.
- **Pastry creams** are more dense than custards and are frequently used as the filling for pastries such as eclairs. Eggs, sugar, flour, milk, and/or cream are cooked together into a very thick, smooth mixture.
- **Bavarian creams** are made by stabilizing a vanilla sauce with gelatin, combined with whipped cream and beaten egg whites. They may be used as single items, or as fillings for a variety of pastries.
- **Poached fruits** include such favorites as Peach Melba and Pear Belle Hélène.
- Fruits to be poached must be firm enough to hold their shape during cooking.
- A **torte** is an elegant, rich, many-layered cake using a **genoise,** a French sponge cake, and often filled with buttercream, jam, or other fillings.

Al Hansen

Manager
Chi-Chi's
Schaumburg, Illinois

To run a successful restaurant, you have to know how to market and promote your restaurant. It's one of the most important things you can learn in school. And to run a successful promotion, you have to know your customers. Our goal is to have 80% of our customers come back as repeat business. I get information two ways. I spend about 75% of my time every day in the front of the house, talking to our guests. I make small talk, I find out what businesses they're in, where else they go when they go out, what they like and don't like about our place.

We also hold quarterly focus groups with frequent guests to talk about the quality of our food and service. We ask questions like, How's our salsa? Do you like the chips? How do our margaritas compare to the ones down the street? Even though we're part of a chain, I really manage this operation as though it were an independent restaurant. Ours is the only Chi-Chi's with this particular clientele.

I work very closely with vendors to help me promote their products. They have so much to offer, and my showing an active interest in working with them really helps us work together for both our benefit.

We have a form posted on a bulletin board specifically for eliciting employees' ideas for new promotions. We promise them a response on every idea within 72 hours, and employees whose ideas are used get $50. We use about half the ideas they come up with. We also hold regular meetings where we discuss new promotions so all employees are well prepared. We offer employee incentives—money, T-shirts, tickets to sports events. Our most popular incentive is when we let the highest seller make his or her own schedule for the month.

We track and evaluate every promotion we run. We collect sales histories for comparison, set goals, and compare. We always know how well something worked, and whether it's worthwhile to do something similar in the future.

Upselling is the last promotional tool we focus on. It's the icing on the cake, and it's generally something that our more experienced servers are comfortable doing and that they can do successfully. Servers must know all the basics, everything about the menu and the operation, before they can upsell. We track all of our items, and we hold server contests and incentives to stimulate suggestive selling.

CHAPTER 6

Marketing and the Menu

6.1

SECTION 6.1

What Is a Menu?

AFTER STUDYING SECTION 6.1, YOU SHOULD BE ABLE TO:

- Define à la carte, table d' hôte, California, du jour, and cycle menus.
- Organize the information on a menu.

KEY TERMS

- À la carte (AH le CART) menu
- California menu
- Commercial
- Cyclical menu
- Du jour menu
- Limited menu
- Menu content
- Noncommercial
- Table d´hôte (TAH-bull DOT) menu

What is a menu? For customers, a menu is a list that describes the food and drink offered by a foodservice establishment. For the foodservice manager, however, the menu is a strategic tool that defines the purpose of the establishment and every phase of its operation.

The menu is essential to an operation's success for two reasons. First, the menu is an important working tool used by managers to plan, organize, operate, and control back-of-the-house operations. Second, it is a published announcement of what the restaurant has to offer.

The Menu as a Tool

A menu is the most important document that defines the purpose, strategy, market, service, and theme of an operation. It also defines the type of employees and servers the establishment requires, as well as the amount of training all employees will need. A menu should help sell items to customers by offering choices that will please a variety of tastes.

Think of the menu as a production plan that governs almost every part of a food-service operation. The menu is a guide to purchasing, a work order for the professional chef in the kitchen, and a service schedule for employees. The menu is also the most important advertisement for the restaurant or foodservice operation. It is the only place that lists and describes every item offered by the operation, along with the price, presented in an attractive format.

Before writing a menu for an establishment, the menu planner must know the important characteristics of the operation.

Exhibit 6.1
A menu is a very important communication tool.

- Who are the customers?
- What types of food and service do they expect?
- What is the purpose of the operation? For example, is it a seafood restaurant? A pancake house? A college cafeteria?
- Are the food and beverage items needed for the menu readily available and at the proper cost?
- Can the menu items be prepared in an appealing way?

Answering these questions helps menu planners know the goals of the menu they are planning, and determine which kinds of menus meet those objectives. They understand their foodservice operation and know the type of customers they are serving. Unless managers have this knowledge, the menu (and the operation) will fail. One important point to remember: no operation can afford its menu to do some things well but other things poorly.

Menus are planned differently depending on whether the foodservice operation is commercial or noncommercial. The **commercial** segment includes any type of operation that sells food and beverages for profit, such as full-service restaurants, quick-service chains, recreational and sports centers, and hotel restaurants. When planning a commercial restaurant menu, it is a working document for foodservice personnel to follow, and a promotional and marketing tool to attract and communicate to customers.

Noncommercial establishments are generally those operations that operate food services to support the actual purpose of the establishment. Some examples include schools, colleges, airlines, and hospitals. Menus are equally important in noncommercial establishments because they must be developed to control costs, meet the overall objectives of the institution, and make the operation efficient.

Restaurants and foodservice operations use different types of menus to serve a variety of needs depending on the occasion. Many operations use special menus for breakfast, brunch, holidays, teas, parties, and formal dinners.

The Order of Courses

Most menus organize foods according to the order in which they are eaten.

- Appetizers and soups

Exhibit 6.2
Types of menus.

The major types of menu are:

À la carte (AH le CART)

This menu offers food separately at separate prices; that is, each item is listed separately on the menu with its own price.

Cyclical

This menu, normally used by institutional food services, is made up for a certain time period, and then it is repeated. Cycles usually vary from three to seven or more days. The menu should contain enough variety so diners are not aware of repeating food choices.

California

This menu lists all meals available at any time during the day. This type of menu—printed on heavy stock and often laminated—originated in California to suit different patron eating schedules.

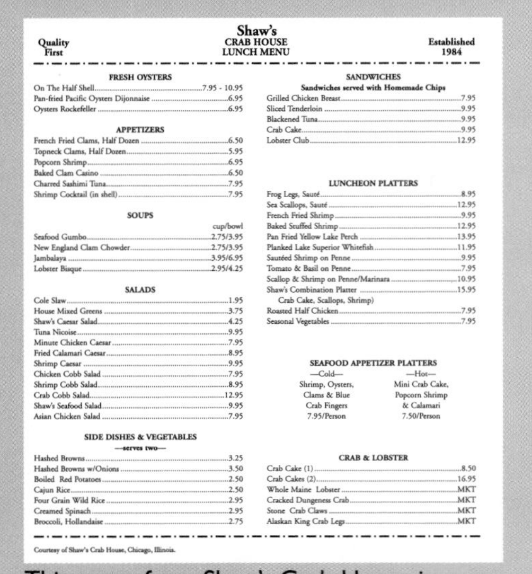

Quality First

Shaw's
CRAB HOUSE
LUNCH MENU

Established 1984

FRESH OYSTERS

On The Half Shell .... 7.95 - 10.95
Pan-fried Pacific Oysters Dijonnaise 6.95
Oysters Rockefeller 6.95

APPETIZERS

French Fried Clams, Half Dozen 6.50
Topneck Clams, Half Dozen 5.95
Popcorn Shrimp 6.95
Baked Clam Casino 6.50
Charred Sashimi Tuna 7.95
Shrimp Cocktail (in shell) 7.95

SOUPS

cup/bowl
Seafood Gumbo 2.75/3.95
New England Clam Chowder 2.75/3.95
Jambalaya 3.95/6.95
Lobster Bisque 2.95/4.25

SALADS

Cole Slaw 1.95
House Mixed Greens 3.75
Shaw's Caesar Salad 4.25
Tuna Nicoise 9.95
Minute Chicken Caesar 7.95
Fried Calamari Caesar 8.95
Shrimp Caesar 9.95
Chicken Cobb Salad 7.95
Shrimp Cobb Salad 8.95
Crab Cobb Salad 12.95
Shaw's Seafood Salad 9.95
Asian Chicken Salad 7.95

SIDE DISHES & VEGETABLES
—serves two—

Hashed Browns 3.25
Hashed Browns w/Onions 3.50
Boiled Red Potatoes 2.50
Cajun Rice 2.50
Four Grain Wild Rice 2.95
Creamed Spinach 2.95
Broccoli, Hollandaise 2.75

SANDWICHES
Sandwiches served with Homemade Chips

Grilled Chicken Breast 7.95
Sliced Tenderloin 9.95
Blackened Tuna 9.95
Crab Cake 9.95
Lobster Club 12.95

LUNCHEON PLATTERS

Frog Legs, Sauté 8.95
Sea Scallops, Sauté 12.95
French Fried Shrimp 9.95
Baked Stuffed Shrimp 12.95
Pan Fried Yellow Lake Perch 13.95
Planked Lake Superior Whitefish 11.95
Sautéed Shrimp on Penne 9.95
Tomato & Basil on Penne 7.95
Scallop & Shrimp on Penne/Marinara 10.95
Shaw's Combination Platter 15.95
Crab Cake, Scallops, Shrimp)
Roasted Half Chicken 7.95
Seasonal Vegetables 7.95

SEAFOOD APPETIZER PLATTERS

—Cold—	—Hot—
Shrimp, Oysters, Clams & Blue Crab Fingers	Mini Crab Cake, Popcorn Shrimp & Calamari
7.95/Person	7.50/Person

CRAB & LOBSTER

Crab Cake (1) 8.50
Crab Cakes (2) 16.95
Whole Maine Lobster .... MKT
Cracked Dungeness Crab .... MKT
Stone Crab Claws .... MKT
Alaskan King Crab Legs .... MKT

Courtesy of Shaw's Crab House, Chicago, Illinois.

This menu from Shaw's Crab House is an example of an à la carte menu.

- Sandwiches (sandwiches can be offered before or after salads)
- Salads
- Entrées
- Vegetables
- Desserts
- Beverages

Foods within a major classification should be prepared using a variety of cooking methods, such as poaching, roasting, grilling, frying, and baking. Tastes, textures, and seasoning should also be varied for contrast to meet the tastes of a variety of customers.

Entrées can be divided by beef, pork, chicken, lamb, veal, ham, shellfish, fish, pasta, egg, cheese, and vegetarian dishes. Balance should be maintained in the choice of vegetables, sauces, and potatoes used to complement entrées. For example, if a menu contains ham and chicken, an offering of sweet potatoes or yellow winter squash is a good balance. Four to six vegetables, including potatoes, should meet most menu needs. Salads and salad dressings also should reflect balance and variety.

Exhibit 6.2 (CONTINUED)
Types of menus.

Du jour

From the French for "of the day," this menu offers different foods each day. The phrase can be used to describe the soup of the day (soup du jour), fish of the day, etc.

Limited

This menu offers few selections. It is used often by quick-service restaurants and cafes.

Table d'hôte (TAH-bull DOT)

This menu offers a complete meal or several items grouped together for a single price. In this way, an establishment can limit the number of combinations that may be ordered. This type of menu may offer a choice between some items, like soup or salad, and a choice of desserts. À la carte items may be added by the guest.

Charlie Trotter's

¢¢¢¢

Grand Menu Degustation 75.00

Smoked Maine Salmon with Petite Lobster-Tomato Salad & Chilled Smoked Salmon Broth

or

New York State Foie Gras & Oxtail Terrine with Arkansas Short Grain Rice Salad,
Sherry Wine Vinaigrette & Yellow Bell Pepper Juice
Grilled Hamachi with Peeky Toe Crab & Cardamom Infused Carrot Juice

or

Potato Wrapped Veal Sweetbreads with Soy-Bacon Vinaigrette & Shiitake Mushroom Essence
Hawaiian Spot Prawns & Hand-Harvested Sea Scallop with Spring Pea Shoots,
Cashews & Spicy Coconut Milk Broth

or

Belgian Endive, Frisee, Roasted Hazelnuts, Goat Cheese, Japanese Pears & Dried Mission Figs
Gulf of Maine Swordfish with Caramelized Walla Walla Shallots, Artichokes,
Olive Oil Poached Tomato, Basil & Black Olives

or

Duck Confit with Lamb's Tongue, Mushroom & Pig's Feet Ragout & Szechwan
Peppercorn Infused Reduction
Spicy Seared Yellow-Fin Tuna with Morel Mushrooms, Black-Eyed Peas,
Sweet Peas, Celery Root Coulis & Veal Stock Reduction

or

Texas Baby Antelope Saddle with Rosemary Polenta, Ratatouille & Thyme Reduction

¢¢¢¢

This Evening's Progression of Desserts

Courtesy of Charlie Trotter's, Chicago, Illinois

A successful table d'hôte menu from Charlie Trotter's.

Exhibit 6.3
Cyclical menu.

Monday, 9/13	Portion
Chili with Beans & Cheese	1 c
Mixed Greens Salad	½ c
Cherry Apple Juice	6 oz
Sesame Crackers	8
Peanut Butter Cookie	1
Low Fat Milk	½ pt

Tuesday, 9/14	Portion
Vegetable Pizza	1 Slice
Seasoned Green Beans	½ c
Fresh Apple	½ c
Low Fat Milk	½ pt

Wednesday, 9/15	Portion
Cheese Burger/Bun	3.5 oz
French Fries	½ c
Chilled Peaches	½ c
Low Fat Milk	½ pt

Thursday, 9/16	Portion
Sliced Turkey	4 oz
Whipped Potatoes	½ c
Garden Peas	½ c
Raisin Spice Bar	1 ser
Low Fat Milk	½ pt

Friday, 9/17	Portion
Lasagna	3 oz
Apple Sauce	½ c
Sweet Corn	½ c
Sourdough roll	1
Low Fat Milk	½ pt

The number of desserts on the menu depends on customers' tastes and past sales. Some operations may need to serve only ice cream or sherbet to satisfy their customers. Others may need to combine these with a limited number of pies or cakes; puddings and fruit can be added to extend dessert selections.

For specific meals and occasions, managers rely on customer preference and costs to determine what items should be included on the menu.

Several factors must be considered in developing a menu, including:

- physical layout of the facility, including space for storage, preparation, and service areas;
- skill level and number of employees;
- availability of food;
- customers' needs;
- customers' expectations of the menu offerings and prices; and
- profit margin.

How do menu planners determine the menu content? **Menu content** refers to the selection of food items in each menu category. A well-balanced menu is important for a successful operation. Menu planners develop the menu content by using a five-step process that results not only in a printed menu, but also in a group of alternate items that can be used as specials. These five steps are outlined in Exhibit 6.5.

In the first step, all the items that could possibly be included in a particular menu category are listed. Any items on the list that may be difficult to purchase, prepare, or serve are eliminated in the second step. The list is further reduced to those food items that would be suitable to the restaurant's cuisine or theme in the third step. Next, items that fall within a predetermined price range and that the restaurant's staff can prepare well are chosen. In the fifth step, final selections are made for each category on the printed menu.

Exhibit 6.4
Menu guidelines.

Breakfast menus:

- Can contain à la carte and table d'hôte items.
- Table d'hôte offerings should include a continental breakfast (juice, bread, and a hot beverage) that is placed prominently on the menu.
- Breakfast menus typically have eight categories of food: fruits and juices; cereals; eggs, alone or combined; omelets; meats; pancakes, waffles, and French toast; toast, rolls, bagels, and hot breads; and beverages.

Brunch menus:

- Combine items found on breakfast and lunch menus.
- The main dish should be substantial—omelets, soufflés, small steaks, etc.
- Fruit juice or fruit should be offered as well as hot breads, fruit salad, vegetables, and a beverage choice.

Lunch menus:

- Offer à la carte combinations, such as a sandwich and beverage; or soup, salad, and dessert with beverage.
- À la carte offerings should be permanent but also present daily offerings. The permanent menu could offer sandwiches, smaller portions of dinner items, salads, fountain items, and desserts.

Afternoon menus:

- Use specials and snack-type foods to appeal to afternoon-free customers, retired people, shoppers, part-time workers, and senior citizens.

Dinner menus:

- More specialty items are appropriate than on other menus, with decor and service to match.
- Introduce interesting choices to the standard fare of main dish, potato, vegetable, salad, dessert, and beverage.
- Ethnic foods should be authentic, but still appeal to American tastes.

Exhibit 6.5
Steps to developing menu content.

1. List all possible items.
2. Eliminate items.
3. Tailor items to fit customers, cuisine, and theme.
4. Choose items within the price range that can be prepared well.
5. Make final selections for the printed menu.

Review Your Learning 6.1

1. Find the correct words from Section 6.1 to complete the following sentences.
   a. The ________________ is an important tool that helps servers sell food to customers and helps managers plan their purchasing and production systems.
   b. Hardee's, TGI Friday's, a hotel restaurant, and a local pizzeria are called ________________operations because they sell food in order to make a profit.
   c. Your school cafeteria is a ________________ foodservice operation because it supports the school and isn't open to the public.
   d. On a(n) ________________ menu, items are listed separately, at separate prices.
   e. The ________________ , or main course, is the featured attraction of the meal.
   f. Most menus organize foods in the order that people ________________.
   g. ________________ is a combination of breakfast and lunch.
2. Which type of menu groups several food items together for one price?
3. How often does a du jour menu change?

Designing and Analyzing the Menu

AFTER STUDYING SECTION 6.2, YOU SHOULD BE ABLE TO:

- Write and lay out a menu.
- Use sales information to analyze how menu items are selling.

The menu is the foodservice operator's opportunity to entice the customer and is the primary selling tool in most restaurants. The two main functions of a successful menu are *communicating* and *selling*.

A menu's design should reflect the restaurant's character and atmosphere and distinguish it from the competition. An appealing menu contains a variety of

KEY TERMS

- Average contribution margin achievement rate
- Clip-on
- Contribution margin
- Contribution margin proportion
- Cover stock
- Dog
- Fonts
- Laminated
- Menu analysis
- Menu analysis worksheet
- Menu contribution margin
- Menu mix
- Menu mix percentage
- Plowhorse
- Puzzle
- Star

items developed according to market factors and customer preferences. Menu copy should be descriptive, whetting customers' appetites and encouraging them to order menu items.

Menu Design

No matter how well the menu is planned and priced, it must be clearly and attractively presented so that customers can easily and quickly read and understand the items. The menu's appearance must make a favorable impression on customers and help the restaurant reach its goals.

While a menu planner does not need to be a graphic artist, it is helpful to understand basic design concepts to create attractive menus. Knowing what it takes to produce an attractive-looking menu will help you in working with professional menu printing companies, which can provide original design, copywriting, layout, and printing services.

Proper layout of food items and creative use of color will enhance a menu's eye appeal. A heavy cover paper, called **cover stock,** helps protect the menu's inner pages. **Laminated** cover stock is protected with a plastic coating that keeps menus clean and reduces wear and tear from frequent handling. Some menus use clip-ons for emphasis. A **clip-on** is a temporary attachment to a menu used to announce special items.

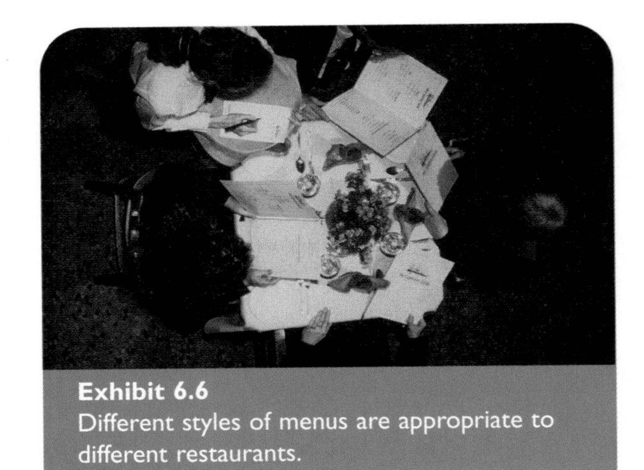

Exhibit 6.6
Different styles of menus are appropriate to different restaurants.

The shape and form of a menu can boost sales. For example, a menu featuring seafood may be in the shape of a fish; a child's menu can be in the shape of a clown or other character whose picture is on the front cover. There are many ways to emphasize menu items. They can be as simple as a change from small type to larger type or using all capital letters. Setting special food items in a decorative box on the menu page can also attract attention.

A menu's format—the spacing, weight (darkness) of the printed letters, page design, color contrasts, and other design factors—make the menu easy for customers to read. Different styles of type (called

fonts) can be used to show certain settings or to emphasize particular food items. A menu, like a person, has a personality. As a marketing tool, it should reflect the e stablishment's atmosphere and theme. Well-designed menus are pleasing to read, are easy to understand, and successfully represent the foodservice establishment.

Analyzing Menus

Menu analysis helps managers make decisions about keeping, cutting, or adding menu items. Prices, the market, food costs, seasonal factors, and where items are placed on a menu all influence a menu's performance. A **menu analysis worksheet** shows how each item contributes to profitability, allowing managers to evaluate menus. By categorizing items according to their listed results, managers can make adjustments to the menu.

Analyzing a menu can be done manually, but today most operations use various computer programs. However, a computer will only be as accurate and helpful as the information you enter into it. Following are twelve steps managers often use to determine the success of menu items. The information is then transferred to a worksheet. Look at Exhibit 6.7, the Menu Analysis Worksheet for The Holly House Restaurant, as you practice these twelve steps.

1. List all items on the menu.
2. Determine the number of each item sold in a specific time period (usually a month). This number is called the item's **menu mix.**
3. Determine each item's **menu mix percentage** by dividing its menu mix by the total number of items sold in that period.

$$\text{Menu mix \%} = \frac{\text{Menu mix (number of an item sold)}}{\text{Total number of items sold}}$$

4. Categorize each item's menu mix percentage as either high or low (according to standards set by management).
5. List each item's selling price.
6. Determine each item's standard food cost.
7. Determine each item's **contribution margin** by subtracting its standard food cost from its selling price.

Contribution margin =
Selling price – Standard food cost

8. Determine the **menu contribution margin** by adding each item's contribution margin (step 7) and menu mix (step 2).

Menu contribution margin =
All contribution margins + All menu mixes

Exhibit 6.7
Sample menu analysis worksheet.

Sample: Menu Analysis Worksheet

Restaurant: THE HOLLY HOUSE **Meal Period:** DINNER **Date:** July 6

(A) Menu Item Name	(B) # Sold/ Menu Mix	(C) Menu Mix %	(D) Item Food Cost	(E) Item Selling Price	(F) Item Contribution Margin (E - D)	(G) Menu Costs (D × B)	(H) Menu Revenues (E × B)	(L) Menu Contribution Margin (F × B)	(P) Contribution Margin Category	(R) Menu Mix % Category	(S) Menu Item Clasification
LOBS. TAIL	150	5%	5.31	12.95	7.64	796.50	1,942.50	1,146.00	HIGH	LOW	PUZZLE
P. RIB (20 OZ)	60	2%	5.29	11.50	6.21	317.40	690.00	372.60	HIGH	LOW	PUZZLE
NY STRIP	360	12%	4.31	10.50	6.19	1,551.60	3,780.00	2,228.40	HIGH	HIGH	STAR
T. SIRLOIN	510	17%	3.71	9.50	5.79	1,892.10	4,845.00	2,952.90	HIGH	HIGH	STAR
SHRIMP PL.	210	7%	3.49	8.50	5.01	732.90	1,785.00	1,052.10	HIGH	LOW	PUZZLE
RED SNAPPER	240	8%	2.71	6.95	4.24	650.40	1,668.00	1,017.60	LOW	HIGH	PLOWHORSE
P. RIB (12 OZ)	600	20%	3.37	7.50	4.13	2,022.00	4,500.00	2,478.00	LOW	HIGH	PLOWHORSE
CHICKEN DIN.	420	12%	1.54	4.95	3.41	646.80	2,079.00	1,432.20	LOW	HIGH	PLOWHORSE
CH. SIRLOIN	90	3%	2.26	5.50	3.24	203.40	495.00	291.60	LOW	LOW	DOG
TENDERLOIN TIPS	360	12%	2.21	5.25	3.04	795.06	1,890.00	1,094.40	LOW	HIGH	PLOWHORSE
	N					I	J	M			
Column Totals:	3000					9,608.70	23,674.50	14,065.80			

Additional Computations:

$K = I/J$: $\frac{9{,}608.70}{23{,}674.50} = 0.4059$

$O = M/N$: $\frac{14{,}065.80}{3{,}000} = \$4.69$

$Q = (100\%/\text{items})\ (70\%)$: $\left(\frac{100\%}{10}\right)(70\%) = 7\%$

Courtesy of Hospitality Financial Consultants, Okemos, Michigan.

9. Determine each item's **contribution margin proportion** by dividing its contribution margin (step 7) by the menu contribution margin (step 8).

$$\text{Contribution margin proportion} = \frac{\text{Contribution margin}}{\text{Menu contribution margin}}$$

10. Categorize each item's contribution margin as high or low according to its relationship to the **average contribution margin achievement rate.** This rate is found by dividing the menu contribution margin (step 8) by the total number of items sold (step 2).

$$\text{Average contribution margin achievement rate} = \frac{\text{Menu contribution margin}}{\text{Total number of items sold}}$$

11. Classify each menu item in relation to the others. Here are popular terms used for this classification.

    Dog—low menu mix percent, low contribution margin

    Puzzle—low menu mix percent, high contribution margin

    Plowhorse—high menu mix percent, low contribution margin

    Star—high menu mix percent, high contribution margin

12. Make decisions for each item based on all of the previous information. Such decisions might be to retain, reprice, reposition, or replace items.

Review Your Learning 6.2

1. Why is it important to have a well-designed menu?
2. What are the two main functions of a successful menu?
3. Give some examples of how a menu's shape can match the theme or look of a restaurant.
4. A quick-service restaurant sold 21,248 total items last month, including 3,419 chocolate milkshakes. Each chocolate milkshake cost $0.45 and sold for $1.29.
   a. What was the menu mix for chocolate milkshakes?
   b. What was the menu mix percentage for chocolate milkshakes?
   c. What is the contribution margin for chocolate milkshakes?
   d. If it turns out that the chocolate milkshakes have a high menu mix percentage but a low contribution margin, what will they be classified as (a dog, puzzle, plowhorse, or star)?

6.3

SECTION 6.3

What Is Marketing?

AFTER STUDYING SECTION 6.3, YOU SHOULD BE ABLE TO:

- Distinguish among and discuss basic marketing concepts such as product-service mix, marketing mix, and market trends.

KEY TERMS

- Communication mix
- Contemporary marketing mix
- Intangible (in-TAN-je-BUL)
- Market
- Market trends
- Marketing
- Marketing mix
- Presentation mix
- Product-service mix
- Service

The foodservice industry provides a service. A **service** means an intangible product sold or purchased in the marketplace. **Intangible** (in-TAN-je-BUL) means something that cannot be touched or held. You may have thought food service meant only preparing a tangible product—food. You are partly correct. However, because that tangible product depends so much on the people who prepare, serve, or package it, the foodservice industry is considered a service industry.

How does a restaurant or foodservice operation let people know about its great food and service? Effective marketing is the answer. In today's competitive environment, foodservice operations that meet and exceed customer expectations will be the most successful. To do this, it is important to understand the basics of marketing. Marketing is the first activity necessary for any successful business.

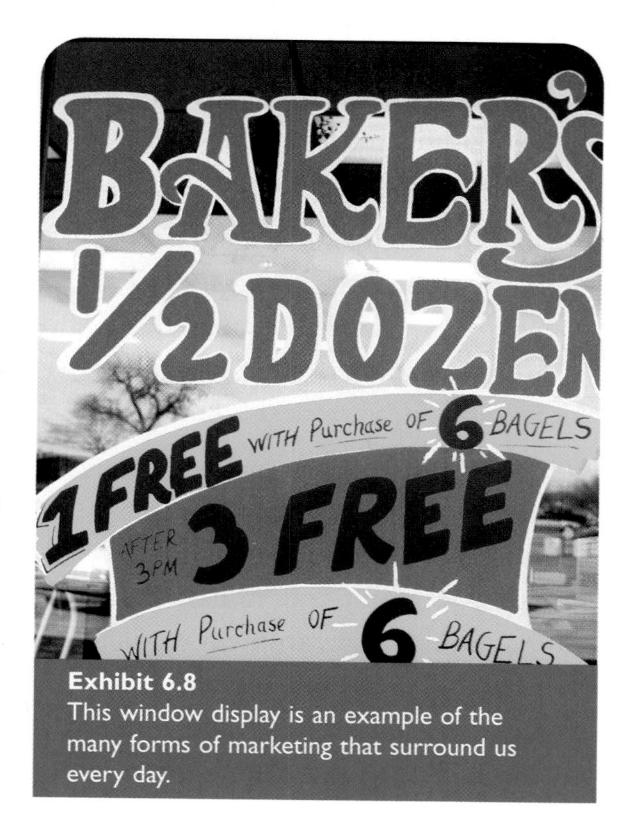

Exhibit 6.8
This window display is an example of the many forms of marketing that surround us every day.

Every day we come in contact with some form of marketing—selling, advertising on TV, radio, or in magazines, coupons, free samples—just to name a few. But none of these activities alone is marketing. Only when several are combined, along with other activities such as research, product development, and pricing, can the end result be called "marketing." To be a successful marketer requires paying close attention to industry trends, customer feedback, and being able to "go with the flow."

So what exactly is marketing? **Marketing** is the communication and plan for taking a product or service to market. **Market** means a group of people (customers) with specific, similar needs and wants. Marketing shows you how to find the right customers, and then how to sell your product or service to them. For example, your high school does marketing when it promotes the school band and athletic teams. Participating students might wear identifying T-shirts, and posters or signs reminding you of the event may be prominently displayed in the school gym, cafeteria, or library/media center.

The goal of marketing is to identify customers' wants and needs and then to satisfy them. When a product or service is marketed properly, very little selling is needed. Customers already think that they want or need the product or service. All that is necessary is someone to provide it.

At first you may think that since the need to eat already exists, all someone has to do is open a restaurant and people will automatically come, since people already need and want food. This is not the case. Competition in the foodservice industry makes it necessary for foodservice managers to use marketing skills to attract customers.

Here is what foodservice managers do to market their operations:

- **Determine what customers want.**
- **Create a product-service mix to satisfy customers. The product-service mix is all of the products and services offered by an operation, such as food, beverages, atmosphere, party facilities, customer service, and personal attention to guests.**
- **Promote and sell the product-service mix at the profit needed to run the operation and pay its employees. Or, in a noncommercial or institutional operation, at a high enough price to break even, or cover all costs.**

Basic Marketing Concepts

Following are some common marketing terms and concepts that will help you understand the nature of marketing and how it works in food service.

The Marketing Mix

Until recently, the **marketing mix** meant the four P's: product, place, promotion, and price. But the foodservice industry today uses a special formula called the contemporary marketing mix. The **contemporary marketing mix** includes:

- **Product-service mix**—All the food, plus services, like takeout and delivery, offered to customers.
- **Presentation mix**—All the things that make the operation look unique, like the building, the furniture, decorations, and servers' uniforms.
- **Communication mix**—All the ways an operation communicates to its customers: through its menu, TV and radio, newspapers and magazines, customer surveys, and other means.

It is important to remember that no marketing mix can ever be permanent. Some factors are always changing, such as customer preferences, industry trends, competition, and government regulations. One factor, however, never seems to change—customers continually demand and appreciate top-quality service.

Consumers and Market Trends

Foodservice operators and managers must be aware of market trends. Some broad **market trends** that have a big impact on the foodservice industry are consumers' changing attitudes and tastes in food, and political issues such as recycling and the environment.

Operators and managers must constantly be able to make improvements in their marketing strategies by observing and quickly reacting to market trends.

Review Your Learning 6.3

1. Give some examples of marketing that you have seen in your school.

2. List some trends you have noticed in your school cafeteria. For example, is there a salad bar or taco bar? More healthful foods, such as fresh fruit or yogurt?

3. Name two new brand-name products. What marketing activities have you seen used to introduce them to customers (for example, TV commercials and billboards)?

4. Complete the following sentences by choosing the correct word or phrase from Section 6.3.
   a. A restaurant's building, furniture, decorations, and other things that make it look unique are part of its ________________ mix.
   b. The way a restaurant talks and listens to customers, for instance, through its menu, is called its ________________ mix.
   c. All of the food and services a restaurant offers to its customers is called its ________________ mix.

5. Things that are intangible are things that you cannot touch or hold with your hands. Which of the following things are intangible?
   a. Good service
   b. A hamburger
   c. Dishes
   d. A server's smile
   e. The way people feel about your restaurant
   f. A menu
   g. A parking lot
   h. The reasons people have for going out to eat
   i. Tables and chairs
   j. A manager's personality

6.4

SECTION 6.4

Looking at the Market

AFTER STUDYING SECTION 6.4, YOU SHOULD BE ABLE TO:

- Outline the components of a marketing plan.
- Identify and collect local area or market segment information.

KEY TERMS

- Demographics
- Experimental method
- Focus group
- Marketing plan
- Market research
- Marketing strategy
- Observational method
- Sampling
- Survey method

With the increasing competition among foodservice operations, it is even more important to have on-target marketing strategies. A **marketing strategy** is a specific plan to achieve the organization's objectives for doing business. Effective marketing strategy starts with planning. Although planning can be very time consuming, good decisions can't be made without it.

The Marketing Plan

A **marketing plan** is a list of the important steps to sell a product or service to customers. The following twelve steps are necessary in an effective marketing plan. All the steps should be performed by a team, not by one manager working alone.

1. Gather information from various reliable sources. The most reliable source is the operation's own customers, employees, and community. Other secondary sources include

trade journals, trade shows, and government offices.

2. Establish objectives for the organization. These objectives should clearly state what is to be accomplished during a set timetable, who is responsible, and how the results will be evaluated.
3. Examine the organization's strengths, weaknesses, opportunities, and the competition.
4. Examine the product or service's strengths, weaknesses, and competition.
5. Develop several marketing strategies.
6. Evaluate the pros and cons of each strategy.
7. Select the best strategy.
8. Develop an action plan, with a deadline, to carry out the best strategy.
9. Put the plan in action and observe how it is working.
10. Evaluate the action plan. How successful was it?
11. Evaluate feedback from customers and employees. Surveys are good ways to get feedback.
12. Modify the plan as necessary.

Gathering Market Information

The first step in the marketing plan is to gather information. To make effective marketing decisions and avoid costly mistakes, it is important to always look at relevant information about the foodservice industry, its customers in general, and its customers in the community. This information, which refers to people's ages, sex, incomes, occupations, locations of home or office, lifestyles, business patterns, and tastes, is called **demographics.**

How can managers find this information? Through **market research.** Hiring a professional market research firm is one way to do this, but it can be expensive. Three less expensive sources for gathering information about a foodservice operation include:

- sales figures,
- employees, *and*
- guests.

To be useful in making important marketing decisions, the information must be objective, logically organized, and useful. There are various ways to plan market research.

- The **experimental method** tries out different services or products to groups of people. For example, a chain foodservice operation might test various new menu items with different groups of people around the country. A smaller restaurant might invite several regular customers to come in and try new appetizers. The operation would have a preview of guest responses before determining which products to add to the menu permanently.

Researching Properly

- State the research goal clearly.
- Decide what sources you will use.
- Make a plan for doing the research.
- Collect the information you need.
- Analyze the information you've gathered.
- Summarize your results and reach a conclusion(s).

- The **observational method** involves observing how consumers behave toward a product or selling approach. For example, a manager might instruct servers to suggest appetizer items in three different ways. The servers keep a record of how successful (or unsuccessful) each approach is during the course of three weeks. The manager then trains all the servers to use the most successful approach.
- The **survey method** gathers information through telephone surveys or a questionnaire sent in the mail. For example, if a restaurant wanted to know how customers felt about its new serving hours on weekends, the operation could send a questionnaire or call a representative number of customers.
- **Sampling** involves testing a small group of people (called a **focus group**), and based on their feelings or tastes, the product or service is launched. For example, before introducing a new recipe for chewy cherry brownies to the school cafeteria, you might first serve them to a small group of people to get their reaction.

Exhibit 6.9
Sampling a focus group is one way of gathering market information.

Review Your Learning 6.4

1. How would you begin to market a new product, chewy cherry brownies, in your school cafeteria?
2. Which of the four methods (experimentation, observation, survey, sampling) would you use to gather information about the cafeteria market? Why did you choose that method?
3. List five questions you would include in a survey to determine whether students would support a cafeteria dessert bar.
4. What questions would you ask a focus group of students to get their opinion on the selection of a band for a school dance?

6.5

SECTION 6.5

Making Sense of Market Information

AFTER STUDYING SECTION 6.5, YOU SHOULD BE ABLE TO:

- Describe how markets are commonly segmented.
- State predictions of market demand by forecasting.

KEY TERMS

- Forecasting
- Market demand
- Market segmentation
- Positioning
- Unique selling proposition (USP)

Once you have the essential information about your market (customers) you must figure out the best way to use that information to match your product or service with customers' needs. Market segmentation, product-service mix positioning, and pricing help you do that.

Market Segmentation

What is market segmentation? Why is it important in marketing planning? **Market segmentation** means breaking down the potential market of customers into smaller groups of similar individuals. In other words, the big market is made up of smaller groups of people who share common characteristics. Segmenting the market provides you with more detailed consumer information. The more you know about your customers, the more successful you will be.

There are five basic ways to break down or segment the market:

- *Demographic segmentation* includes people's ages, incomes, marital status, sex, size of households, and education.
- *Geographic segmentation* includes where the consumers live and work, which will affect their needs and wants.
- *Product usage segmentation* analyzes the "heavy users" of a product or service.

Exhibit 6.10
Studying people's lifestyles will tell you the types of products they are likely to buy. What might this consumer be interested in buying?

- *Benefit segmentation* looks at information about what consumers expect from using a product or service.
- *Lifestyle segmentation* looks at consumers' activities, hobbies, interests, and opinions.

The information in market segments helps organizations target specific groups of customers. For example, if you are trying out a new product, then benefit segmentation may provide the most useful information. If an advertising or sales promotion theme is being decided, then lifestyle segmentation may be the best choice. One of the greatest benefits of market segmentation is that it makes it easy to develop a unique marketing program for each segment.

Positioning the Product-Service Mix

Positioning answers the question: Why would a consumer want to choose your product over the competitor's? **Positioning** means planting in the mind of the consumer a clear, specific identity for a product or service. Successful positioning gives the product or service a distinctive image that distinguishes it from competing products or services. For example, when you say "Campbell's," what do you naturally think of? Soup. What do you think of when someone says "Xerox?" Photocopying. What about when you think of McDonald's and Burger King? Hamburgers? Action figures? A bargain? The best products and services are those that position themselves through one simple idea.

How can companies decide how to position their services or products? Make it clear: What are you selling?

The first rule of getting any message across: Keep it simple.

Three key points should be considered when developing positioning. First, find out how customers view the operation. What impressions come to mind when someone says "Blue Parakeet Café?" Fantastic food? Good value for the money? Great place for a party? Family restaurant?

Second, list all the benefits offered by the operation. Some examples might be the freshest seafood in town, the best chocolate cake, the most beautiful waterfront view, etc.

Third, what is the operation's unique selling proposition? A **unique selling proposition,** or **USP,** is something distinctive about the operation's product or service that makes it stand out from the competition. For example, the chewy cherry brownies that you want to serve in the school cafeteria are different from the other brownies because you are baking them fresh, right in front of the students. Your brownies are fresher and have a delicious cherry flavor and texture—that's your USP.

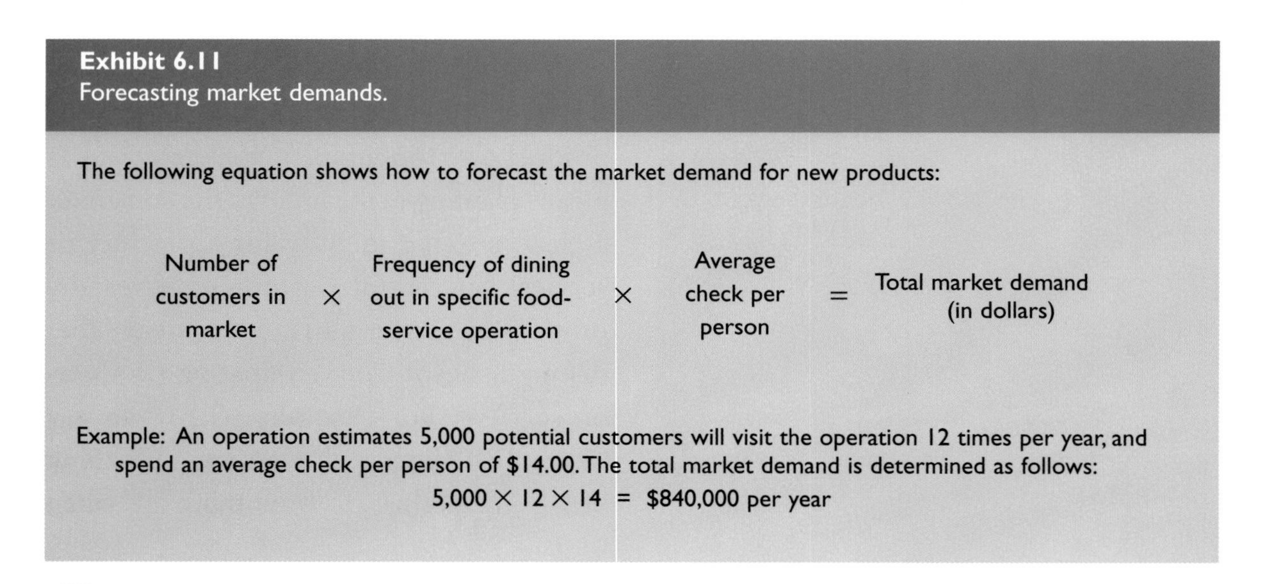

Exhibit 6.11
Forecasting market demands.

The following equation shows how to forecast the market demand for new products:

Number of customers in market × Frequency of dining out in specific foodservice operation × Average check per person = Total market demand (in dollars)

Example: An operation estimates 5,000 potential customers will visit the operation 12 times per year, and spend an average check per person of $14.00. The total market demand is determined as follows:

5,000 × 12 × 14 = $840,000 per year

Exhibit 6.12
How much should you charge? Here is a basic pricing formula.

Formula:

1. How much does it cost to produce this product?
2. What overhead expenses need to be included in the price of the product?
3. What is the sum of the two? This is the minimum price you should charge for the product.
4. What is the amount of (fair) profit you want to make on each product sale?
5. Add your profit to the sum in step number 3.
6. Now you have an initial price for your product. Is it comparable to your competitors? Will customers pay it?
7. Ask customers for feedback!

Example:

- It costs $1.70 to produce a tuna melt sandwich with French fries at a quick-service restaurant called The Sandwich Shack.
- The overhead expenses are low—about $0.30 per sandwich for labor and utilities.
- The sum of these two is $2.00. This is the minimum that should be charged for the sandwich in order to cover all expenses.
- The fair profit desired on each sandwich is about 25% of the cost, or approximately $0.50.
- The price should then be at least $2.50 per sandwich.
- Since Jimmy's drive-in (located one block away) sells the same sandwich for $3.75, The Sandwich Shack can raise its price to $2.95 and local customers will still consider it a great deal!

How Big is Your Market?

How can you find out the size of your market or how many customers are likely to buy your product or service? You are looking for the **market demand,** which means the number of potential customers who have the money and desire to purchase your product or service. For example, how many people who eat in the school cafeteria will want to buy your chewy cherry brownies?

There are two ways to predict market demand: by using past sales histories, and by forecasting. **Forecasting** is estimating ahead of time what sales will be while considering other conditions that will affect planning and food production. In the example of the chewy cherry brownies, looking at the cafeteria's past sales of brownies can give you a general idea of how many brownies you can expect to sell. Exhibit 6.11 shows an example of forecasting.

How Much Should You Charge?

Pricing a product or service can be tricky. On one hand, prices should cover costs and bring in a profit, but they should not be so high that people won't want to pay them.

One important point about pricing *any product* or *service* is that the customer must see the product or service as something of value. If the price seems too low or too high for the quality that customers are looking for, they won't buy it. Remember, "If it seems too good to be true, it probably is," but high prices scare some customers away.

In the example of the chewy cherry brownies, if they are priced significantly lower than the existing brownies, students may be skeptical and instead buy the same brownies as before. If they're priced too high, students might not think they're worth it. You must know your customer. Start by asking, "What would I pay?" and "What would my customers pay?"

Top-Notch Customer Service

Guest satisfaction has a direct and immediate impact on a restaurant's sales volume. While comment cards are important, too often the information is supplied only by highly motivated guests who bother to fill them out. To see how satisfied customers are with the operation's food and service, keep track of customers' spoken compliments and complaints; count repeat customers; follow up complaints or compliments by phone or by letter; and look at sales figures regularly for patterns.

Review Your Learning 6.5

1. Name five examples of popular brand-name products and describe how they are positioned in the market.
2. Name three popular brands of soft drinks. What is the unique selling proposition (USP) for each?
3. Using your school cafeteria as an example, how would you forecast the total market demand for the new chewy cherry brownies discussed in this chapter?
4. Using a favorite family recipe, how would you position it for sale in your school cafeteria?

SECTION 6.6

Sales Promotions and Public Relations

AFTER STUDYING SECTION 6.6, YOU SHOULD BE ABLE TO:

- Create and write a restaurant promotion.
- Define public relations.

KEY TERMS

- Internet
- Personal selling
- Point-of-sale display
- Public relations
- Sales promotion
- Suggestive selling
- Web site

Promotions and public relations are ways to interact directly with customers. Promotional activities can be very creative and fun. For example, foodservice operations have offered toys in special kids' meals, awarded free trips, and offered new cars in special sweepstakes or games. An effective public relations program is something every company needs. Public relations are a good way for customers, the community, and the media to get to know the organization and its products and services.

Planning a Successful Promotional Campaign

Sales promotion is a sales technique that offers consumers an extra incentive to take fast action, either to buy the product or to ask for further information. Promotions are important because they can help reinforce an advertisement's message and boost sales.

Exhibit 6.13
Promoting a new menu is very important to its success.

Promotional techniques include **point-of-sale displays** (table tents, posters, or other attention-getting devices located at the foodservice operation), brochures, sampling, special discounts, coupons, premiums, contests, sweepstakes, and frequent diner programs.

The growth of the Internet has created a new outlet for sales promotion. The **Internet** is a worldwide computer network that brings information to anyone with access to an Internet connection. Many restaurants now have a **web site,** a place on the Internet that advertises the restaurant and includes information such as driving directions, restaurant hours, and menus. Other web sites include guides to locating restaurants by location or type of food and restaurant reviews.

Like all forms of marketing, promotions need careful planning. The following are key elements for an effective promotions plan for a foodservice operation.

- Select a specific group of customers.
- Determine what you want these customers to buy or do (for example, choose new appetizers, try the restaurant's new brunch service, or order the special of the day).
- Choose a promotional technique that will persuade your customers to buy your product or service.
- Set a budget.
- Select the type of advertising that will support the promotion.
- Develop a timetable for each phase of the promotion.

Exhibit 6.14
Table tents are an effective point-of-sale display.

- Explain to employees how the promotion works.
- After putting the plan in motion, monitor results.

Personal Selling

Personal selling, also called **suggestive selling,** is a cost-effective way to promote an operation's products and services. It does not require any additional spending since servers are already hired and trained, and the menu items are already available. There are benefits to employees too, such as increased tips and job satisfaction.

Servers who are trained in personal selling offer guests the full range of products and services available. They don't pressure guests into ordering the most expensive menu items. For example, a server might say, "Good evening. May I suggest that you start with our new shrimp appetizer? The shrimp are lightly broiled in a spicy marinade and served with an orange salsa."

The Power of Public Relations

Public relations are on-going activities that involve managing an operation's relationships with consumers, media, communities, governments, suppliers, employers, and all other public groups. Through news releases, public appearances, and sponsorship of community events, foodservice operations can form a favorable public image. For example, helping to sponsor the local Special Olympics or supporting the local library through a raffle promotes a positive image in the community.

Review Your Learning 6.6

1. Using one of your favorite foods, write two examples of how you would practice suggestively selling it to your classmates.
2. Think of a successful promotion you've seen, such as two-for-one hamburgers at a fast-food chain, and explain briefly why you think it was or was not successful. The promotions can be related to foodservice or to any other industry.
3. You have been selected to head a public relations campaign to promote your school in the community. List three ideas that you would include in your campaign to enhance your school's image.

Flashback

CHAPTER 6

SECTION 6.1: WHAT IS A MENU?

- A menu is the most important document that defines the purpose, strategy, market, service, and theme of an operation.
- The menu is an important working tool used by managers to plan, organize, operate, and control back-of-the-house operations.
- The menu is a published announcement of what the restaurant has to offer customers in the front-of-the-house.
- The menu is a guide to purchasing, a work order for the professional chef and a service guide for employees.
- Before writing a menu for an establishment, the menu planner must know the characteristics of the operation.
- Good menu planners know the goals of the menu they are planning and determine which kinds of menus meet those objectives.
- Menus are planned differently depending on whether the foodservice operation is **commercial** or **noncommercial.**
- Restaurants and foodservice operations use different types of menus depending on the occasion.
- Many operations use special menus for breakfast, brunch, holidays, teas, parties, and formal dinners.
- The major types of menus include: **à la carte, table d'hôte, du jour, limited, cyclical**, and **California.**
- Many menus organize foods according to the order in which they are eaten, such as appetizers and soups; sandwiches (sandwiches can be offered before or after salads); salads; entrées; vegetables; desserts; and beverages.
- Foods within a major classification should be prepared using a variety of cooking methods, such as poaching, roasting, grilling, frying, and baking. Tastes, textures, and seasoning should be varied to meet a variety of tastes.
- The ordinary menu probably needs at least five or six entrées, but some specialty restaurants may only have one or two. For specific meals and occasions,

managers rely on customers' preferences and costs to determine what items should be included on the menu.

- Several factors must be considered in developing a menu, including:
  - —physical layout of the facility, including space for storage, preparation, and service areas;
  - —skill level and number of employees;
  - —availability of food;
  - —customers' needs;
  - —customers' expectations of the menu offerings and prices; and
  - —profit margin.

SECTION 6.2: DESIGNING AND ANALYZING THE MENU

- The menu is the foodservice operator's opportunity to entice the customer. Products are sold effectively and profits are maximized through the menu.
- An appealing menu contains a variety of items developed according to market information and customer preferences.
- No matter how well the menu is planned and priced, it must be presented clearly so that customers can quickly understand the items, leading to satisfactory sales.
- Menu design creates an identity and distinguishes a restaurant.
- **Menu analysis** helps managers make decisions about keeping, cutting, or adding menu items.
- A **menu analysis worksheet** shows the extent to which items contribute to profitability, allowing managers to evaluate menus.

SECTION 6.3: WHAT IS MARKETING?

- Foodservice operations let people know about great food and service by using effective marketing.
- **Marketing** is the communication and plan for taking a product or service to market.
- A **market** means a group of people with specific, similar needs or wants.
- The goal of marketing is to identify customers' wants and needs and then to satisfy them.
- When a product or service is marketed properly, very little selling is needed.
- For food service, the **marketing mix** refers to three elements: **product-service mix, presentation mix,** and **communication mix.**

- For foodservice managers, marketing means creating the product-service mix to satisfy determined customer needs and promoting and selling the product-service mix at the established profit.
- Various factors, such as customer preferences, industry trends, competition, and government regulations, can change the marketing mix.
- Foodservice operators and managers must constantly be able to change their marketing strategies by observing and quickly reacting to market trends.

SECTION 6.4: LOOKING AT THE MARKET

- A **marketing strategy** is a specific plan to achieve the organization's objectives for doing business.
- The **marketing plan** is a list of the important steps an organization must follow to successfully show and sell a product or service to customers.
- The first step in the marketing plan is to gather information about the foodservice industry and customers by conducting market research.
- **Demographic** information about guests, such as their age, sex, income, occupation, location of home or office, lifestyle, business patterns, and tastes, is essential for foodservice operators.
- Commonly used ways of market research include the **experimental method, observational method, survey method,** and **sampling.**

SECTION 6.5: MAKING SENSE OF MARKET INFORMATION

- **Market segmentation** means breaking down the potential market of customers into smaller groups of similar individuals.
- Demographic segmentation, geographic segmentation, product usage segmentation, benefit segmentation, and lifestyle segmentation are basic ways to segment the market.
- One of the greatest benefits of market segmentation is that it makes it easy to develop a unique marketing program for each segment.
- **Positioning** the product-service mix means planting in the minds of consumers a clear, specific identity for a product or service.
- Successful positioning gives the product or service a distinctive image that distinguishes it from competing products or services.

- The operation's **unique selling proposition** or **USP** is essential in positioning.
- **Market demand,** or the number of potential customers who have the money and desire to purchase your product or service, can be predicted by using previous sales records or by forecasting.
- The formula for **forecasting** market demand is:

  Total market demand (in dollars) = Number of customers in market × Frequency of dining out in specific foodservice operation × Average check per person

- In pricing any product or service, it is essential that the customer see the product or service as something with value; never sacrifice quality for a low price.
- Guest satisfaction has a direct and almost immediate impact on the restaurant's sales volume.

SECTION 6.6: SALES PROMOTIONS AND PUBLIC RELATIONS

- Promotions and public relations are ways to interact directly with customers.
- **Sales promotions** are important because they reinforce an advertisement's message and boost sales.
- Promotional techniques include **point-of-sale displays,** brochures, sampling, special discounts, coupons, premiums, contests, and frequent diner programs.
- Many operations have **web sites** on the **Internet** to promote their establishments.
- An operation needs an organized promotions plan within its marketing plan.
- **Personal selling,** also called **suggestive selling,** is one of the most cost-effective ways to promote an operation's products and services.
- Effective personal selling can boost an operation's image, as well as enhance employee benefits such as increased tips and job satisfaction.
- **Public relations** activities involve managing an operation's relationships with consumers, media, communities, governments, suppliers, employers, and all other public groups.
- An effective public relations program is something every company needs in order to enhance its image and make its products and services visible.
- Organizations get publicity by sending press releases to the media.

To succeed in business, every foodservice operation must control costs. This unit focuses on managing the purchasing process, properly cooking expensive food items, and accurately accounting for costs.

UNIT 3

PROFILE

José Laboy

General Manager
Red Lobster
Hillside, Illinois

I received my bachelor's degree in Restaurant, Hotel, Institutional, and Tourism (RHIT) Management from Purdue University. While attending college, I owned and operated a vending company that traveled to the various outdoor summer activities in and around Chicago to sell refreshments. From my earliest experiences in the foodservice industry, I learned the importance of purchasing and inventory control.

After I graduated from Purdue University, I began working as a manager-in-training for Red Lobster. Because the main product, seafood, is very delicate, highly perishable, and expensive, the underlying principle during training is controlling the purchasing and inventory of seafood. It is important to order the correct amount to meet the needs of your customers without ordering too much that may have to be thrown away.

Red Lobster has a number of systems to help its managers control purchasing and inventory. The unit's computer system monitors deliveries and production schedules, and gives me a projected inventory and suggested amounts of products to buy. The manager has the final say about ordering and must take into account situations like holidays, traffic construction, or other events that might increase or decrease normal customer counts. Once the product has been received, it is important to monitor its progress through the operation to ensure quality, security, and profits.

The restaurant industry offers great opportunities. It is one of the few businesses left where you can start at an entry-level position and, through your ability and hard work, become a manager or even own your own restaurant. The one thing that you must remember throughout your career no matter what position you are in, is to treat your fellow workers with respect. It is only though teamwork that a restaurant can be successful.

CHAPTER 7

Purchasing and Inventory Control

SECTION 7.1

What Is Purchasing?

AFTER STUDYING SECTION 7.1, YOU SHOULD BE ABLE TO:

- Explain the relationship between primary and intermediary sources and retailers.
- Explain the differences between formal and informal buying and the formal bidding process.
- List factors that affect food prices.

Some people may think that foodservice purchasing is like shopping—you just make a list of things you need, pick them out, and poof!—food and

KEY TERMS

- Bids
- Buyers
- Channel of distribution
- Commissary
- Cooperative (co-op) buying
- Distribution
- Economies of scale
- Form value
- Formal purchasing method
- Franchise
- Informal purchasing method
- Intermediary sources
- Place value
- Primary sources
- Purchasing
- Quotes (kwotes)
- Retailers
- Service value
- Supply and demand
- Time value
- Transportation value
- Vendor

equipment are delivered. Foodservice managers know better, however. For them, **purchasing** is the careful process of selecting from many choices, making sound decisions, and developing solid relationships with vendors. A **vendor** refers to any company that sells things to a restaurant. Vendors include both goods suppliers (produce, meat, or dairy companies) and service suppliers (window washers, landscapers, or exterminators).

In a small restaurant, the owner or manager usually makes all the purchases. In a large operation there may be one person whose main job is to buy food, supplies, and equipment. In general, people who do the purchasing are known as buyers. **Buyers** order all the food, beverages, supplies, and equipment for the operation. A buyer must know everything about the restaurant—from the items on the menu and their current prices, to the restaurant's anticipated

Exhibit 7.1
Buyers need people skills, organizational skills, and good math skills.

Exhibit 7.2
Three different examples of purchasing.

Giotto's Italian Restaurant

As the third-generation manager of this popular family restaurant, Karen Diminico learned purchasing from one of the best buyers in the business. She can still remember helping her father check the produce delivery every morning before she left for school. Years later, it's Karen who runs the show as the owner, manager, and main buyer of Giotto's. She orders every food item, supply, service, and piece of equipment that the restaurant needs. Her control over the business is typical of most independent foodservice operations.

Karen's two brothers each operate their own versions of Giotto's in the suburbs. A few years back, the three businesses began combining their orders to get lower prices from their suppliers. This type of working together is often called **cooperative buying,** or **co-op buying** for short.

KowaBurga

With over 350 locations throughout the midwest, KowaBurga is a highly successful fast-food chain. Like other chains, KowaBurga benefits from its **economies of scale**—the savings that a multi-unit business creates for itself by sharing the cost of purchasing expenses. In KowaBurga's case, its size allows the company to maintain a central **commissary**—a distribution warehouse that provides goods to each individual location. A director of purchasing is responsible for keeping the commissary filled with products that the 350 KowaBurga operations use. When a KowaBurga location in one city needs hamburger, the store manager simply contacts the commissary to place an order.

Sonny's Morning Café

Eight years ago, Alonzo bought the franchise rights to Sonny's Morning Café, a popular chain of breakfast-based restaurants. A **franchise** is a legal business relationship in which an independent owner buys the right to use a company's name, products, and logo. Many fast-food chains have used franchise agreements with local owners to grow as quickly as possible. Some more famous examples are Boston Market, McDonald's, and KFC. In a franchise foodservice operation like Sonny's Morning Cafe, Alonzo can choose to buy from a central commissary run by the franchise or any supplier that meets the company's standards.

volume of business. They must also understand federal and state regulations that oversee food quality, production, processing, labeling, transportation, and safety.

Managing an efficient and successful foodservice operation calls for buyers with a thorough understanding of the purchasing process. Let's take a look at Exhibit 7.2 to see how three very different foodservice operations go about their purchasing.

The Flow of Food to Restaurants

How does food get from the farm to the restaurant? **Distribution** refers to the journey products make as they move from where they are grown or raised to their final destination in a restaurant. Many businesses are involved in this effort. A **channel of distribution** includes the particular businesses that buy and sell a product as it makes its way from its original source to a retailer. The channel of distribution for a crate of tomatoes is different than the channel for a box of cereal. See Exhibit 7.3 for an example of how a channel of distribution works.

There are three main layers in any channel of distribution.

- **Primary sources**—Here's where you'll find the farmers and ranchers who raise produce and livestock. This group also includes manufacturers (businesses that make products like kitchen equipment from raw materials)

Exhibit 7.3
Channels of distribution.

Primary Sources
Farmers
Ranchers
Manufacturers
Distillers

Intermediaries
Wholesalers
Distributors
Suppliers

Retailers
Restaurants
School cafeterias
Caterers

and distillers (businesses that produce alcoholic beverages from raw materials like grapes and grains).

- **Intermediary sources**—These include wholesalers, distributors and suppliers. These various businesses are sometimes referred to as *middlemen* because they don't actually alter the products in any way. Instead, these businesses buy products from primary sources and sell them to their final destination: the retailer.
- **Retailers**—All restaurants are considered retailers because they sell their products directly to the public. Most foodservice operations only deal directly with primary sources when they are buying new equipment or locally grown specialty foods.

> **Think About It...**
>
> **A truck driver who delivers fresh produce to restaurants belongs to which layer on the channel of distribution?**

Formal and Informal Purchasing

Hotels, large restaurants, and chains like KowaBurga use the formal purchasing method to order goods and services. In the **formal purchasing method,** buyers prepare purchase specifications for the items they want. (We'll learn more about specifications in Section 7.2.) These specifications are then sent to several suppliers for bids. **Bids** are specialized, written price lists created for the restaurant by a supplier.

Smaller operations like Giotto's use an **informal purchasing method.** When Karen Diminico needs a new supplier, she simply asks for verbal price quotes from a variety of suppliers before making a decision. A **quote** (kwote) is a verbal notice of a price that a supplier gives to a buyer during the purchasing process. Regardless of the system used, buyers must consider a number of factors before choosing a vendor.

Prices

Buyers must also understand the economic factors that can affect a product's price as it moves through the distribution system (see Exhibit 7.4).

- **Time value** refers to the price retailers pay for the convenience of selecting the time of delivery from suppliers.
- **Form value** is the price savings created when a buyer purchases bulk quantities of food instead of individually portioned servings. As a result, blocks of

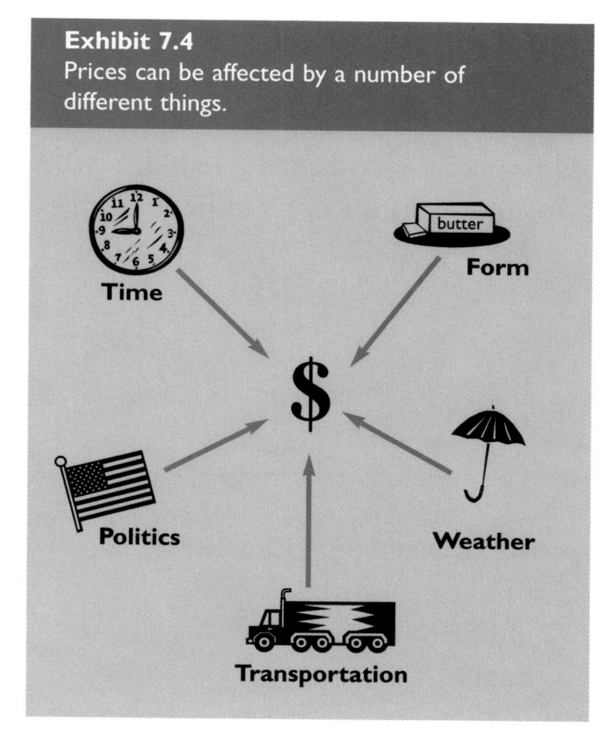

Exhibit 7.4
Prices can be affected by a number of different things.

butter cost less than individual pats because less packaging and processing goes into making the block of butter.

- **Place value** refers to the differences in price of a product depending on where it needs to be shipped. Delivering fresh fish from New England to a supermarket in Kansas City is more expensive than having that same fish delivered to a store on the Atlantic coast.
- **Transportation value** refers to the cost of choosing a quick but expensive form of transport to get your goods delivered. Shipping seafood by air is much more expensive than by truck, but the increased price may be worth the added freshness of the product.
- **Service value** refers to different services that a vendor provides to its customers. This could include customer services that make ordering easier, such as a 24-hour, toll-free number, or it might include things that streamline kitchen prep, like precoring lettuce or providing special cuts of meat. These services often result in higher prices paid for an item, but this higher price is often offset by reduced food preparation costs.

Less obvious factors can affect food prices as well. Political efforts both in this country and abroad often affect price. When Congress tries to block the import of cheaper Mexican oranges to protect American orange growers from going out of business, restaurants pay a higher price for American oranges.

Weather can also impact food prices. A bad coffee crop in Brazil will decrease the supply of coffee beans. While the supply decreases, the number of buyers who want these goods remains the same. As a result, the price of coffee goes up. This imbalance is an example of an economic reality known as **supply and demand.**

Supply and demand can also drive prices down. Strawberries sold in June are less expensive than those sold in January because June is the time of year when most farmers' crops are ready for picking. In January, only warm climates like California or Florida are able to grow the crop, and the price of the fruit goes up.

Review Your Learning 7.1

1. An independent owner buys the rights to use a large chain's company name, products, and logo. This legal relationship is known as a(n):
   a. commissary.
   b. chain.
   c. independent owner.
   d. franchise.

2. A ____________ is another name for a supplier.
   a. buyer
   b. vendor
   c. purchasing agent
   d. retailer

3. Which of the following demonstrates the channel of distribution for a tomato as it makes its way from the farm field to a caterer's cooler?
   a. Intermediary source—retailer—primary source
   b. Retailer—primary source—intermediary source
   c. Primary source—intermediary source—retailer
   d. Vendor—buyer—retailer

4. Suppliers, vendors, distributors, and wholesalers are all ______________ in the channel of distribution.
   a. buyers
   b. retailers
   c. intermediary sources
   d. franchises

Continued on next page

5. Written-out bids are a normal part of which purchasing method?
   a. Formal purchasing method
   b. Channel of distribution
   c. Informal purchasing method
   d. Cooperative buying

6. Anthony operates a small road-side hot dog stand. He calls up two or three meat suppliers and asks them for their current hot dog prices. This is an example of:
   a. cooperative buying.
   b. informal purchasing method.
   c. channel of distribution.
   d. economies of scale.

7. You go shopping late in the summer and notice that the price of tomatoes is really low. Which of the following ideas best explains why this happens?
   a. Supply and demand
   b. Form value
   c. Transportation value
   d. Political events

8. A buyer at Arnold's Steak House realizes that she could spend far less money on beef if her restaurant bought large sides of beef and cut them up into individual portions in-house. She is recognizing what type of value?
   a. Transportation value
   b. Time value
   c. Form value
   d. Service value

9. A produce supplier starts up a 24-hour electronic order-taking machine for its retail customers. This is an example of ___________ value.
   a. form
   b. service
   c. time
   d. transportation

7.2

SECTION 7.2

Standard Ordering Procedures

AFTER STUDYING SECTION 7.2, YOU SHOULD BE ABLE TO:

- Develop a specification list for items based on inventory information.
- Write purchase orders for items to be purchased.

KEY TERMS

- Grades
- Organic produce
- Packers' brand
- Purchase order
- Requisition form (WREK-kwi-ZI-shun)
- Specifications (specs)

Before the manager or buyer can purchase food or equipment, it's important to know exactly what the restaurant needs and then explain those needs clearly to a vendor or supplier. This information is usually provided to suppliers on a product specification form.

SPECIFICATIONS

Specifications, or **specs,** describe the characteristics of products and services that an operation wants to buy. Exhibit 7.5 shows some sample specifications. The details suppliers need in order to provide a buyer with an accurate bid or quote include:

- exact name of the product;
- cost;
- quantity;
- size;
- acceptable waste;

- U.S. quality grade;
- package type and size;
- preservation method;
- color;
- form;
- trade association standards;
- buyer's inspection procedure; and
- general instructions (notes about the menu, budget, and service style that the restaurant intends to use).

Twenty years ago, when most restaurants used canned fruits and vegetables regularly, it was easy to order them. However, with today's health-conscious consumer, more and more restaurants feature fresh, high-quality produce in their

Exhibit 7.5
Sample specifications.

	Hamburger	**Turkey**	**Eggs**	**Butter**
Name	Hamburger, IMPS no. 136	Turkeys, Beltsville, fresh-killed	Eggs, fresh, in shell	Butter, sweet cream
Amount needed	150 lb (1200 patties)	80 lb	Two cases (1 lot)	400 lb
Grade	From US Select (Top)	US Grade A, ready-to-cook, young toms	US AA	US Grade A (93 score)
Packaging	2 oz patties, frozen; packed in 25 lb lots, layer packed with wax paper separators	Wrapped in polyethylene and air exhausted, two to a carton, delivered at 40°F (4.4°C) or less but not frozen	30 doz paper cartons	5-lb packs, 72 pats per lb
Price	Price per lb net	Price per lb net	Per dozen	Per pound
Misc.	Conform to all IMPS requirements: only from chucks, rounds, flanks, or shanks; deliver at 0°	Minnesota grain-fed birds each between 24 and 26 lb, no tolerance permitted over or under internal temperature	Size large, min. wt. net per case 45 lb; no dozen shall weigh more than 25 oz nor less than 23 oz	Pats shall be individually separated by wax paper and layer packed; deliver over two-month period in lots under 40 lb each

meal line-up. As you learned in *Chapter 11: Fruits and Vegetables* of *Becoming a Foodservice Professional, Year 1,* fruits and vegetables come in a number of different varieties. It is therefore necessary to know the exact name of the product you want. Some restaurants use only organic produce. Unlike conventionally grown produce, **organic produce** is grown without the use of pesticides (chemicals that kill insects that feed on produce) or herbicides (chemicals that kill weeds). This trend poses new challenges for foodservice operators.

To ensure that standards for your restaurant are met it is also necessary to only purchase foods that have passed inspection by the US Department of Agriculture (USDA). Inspection of meat, poultry, and eggs is mandatory and is done to ensure safety and wholesomeness. Grading is a voluntary service paid for by packers, and is done to show the level of quality in food items. Exhibit 7.7 shows the federal inspection and grade stamps.

Exhibit 7.6
Some restaurants use only organically grown produce.

Did You Know?

Upton Sinclair's 1906 novel, *The Jungle*, shed light on the unsanitary conditions found in Chicago's meatpacking industry. It created a public outcry over food safety, which in turn led to the creation of the Food and Drug Administration, or FDA.

When ordering, be sure to remember the different grades used to determine a food's quality. **Grades** are labels given to foods to help buyers quickly know what level of quality they are receiving. You may have noticed that while the U.S. Department of Agriculture (USDA) has set quality grade standards for most food items, each category uses different terminology. The best beef is *Prime,* while the highest quality milk products are *Grade A.* Other grades include *US Extra Fancy* for highest quality fruits and vegetables, and *US Grade A Fancy* for highest quality canned products.

Fresh fish is *not* subject to a mandatory inspection system by the federal government. Instead, many suppliers participate in a voluntary federal quality program. Fish that pass this program's grading criteria are awarded the Packed Under Federal Inspection (PUFI) seal.

Another grading system is the packers' brand. A **packers' brand** is a packing company's own personal grading system. These are the most familiar brands among fresh produce suppliers. A packers' brand usually places a high value on consistency and quality. Some buyers believe that packers' brands are more specific and consistent than government grades.

Exhibit 7.8
Using a packers' brand often assures buyers of a consistent level of quality.

Exhibit 7.7
Federal inspection and grading stamps.

The meat industry also has a self-regulating system that provides uniform information for both buyers and suppliers. It is called the Institutional Meat Purchase Specifications (IMPS). This identification system allows buyers to select the type of meat, cut, and other details by number. The numbers are published in the *Meat Buyer's Guide,* along with a picture and description of the meat.

Well-written specs prevent buyers from receiving low-quality or wrong items. However, it is possible to write specs that are too rigid. Demanding an out-of-season melon may force a supplier to ship by air and greatly increase the price. As a result, a good supplier could be eliminated. Instead, you may wish to review your menu, or allow for substitutions. While some substitutions will have little impact on overall quality, it is important to remember that customers easily notice slight variations in dairy products. Accepting a low-fat cheese or lower quality ice cream will greatly affect the restaurant's image and may result in reduced sales.

Purchase Orders

A **purchase order** is a legally binding written document that details exactly what the buyer is ordering from the vendor. Buyers place purchase orders in a number of ways. Some buyers phone in an order, others use a computer modem, and still others fax their orders. Exhibit 7.9 shows a sample purchase order.

Every purchase order should include:

- name of operation, address, and phone number;
- buyer's name;
- name of supplier, address, and phone number;
- supplier's contact person;
- date of the order;
- desired date of receipt/how long the purchase order is good;
- shipping method;
- quantity;
- brief description of item;
- size of item;
- unit price;
- total price for all items;
- total price for entire order (including sales tax, shipping, and any other special charges); and
- any special information regarding the item or delivery.

Exhibit 7.9
Sample purchase order.

Ordered By:	Blue Parakeet Café 55 East Palm Drive Ocean View, FL 32174 Phone: 303/339-1772 Contact: Lisa Bluebell	**Purchase Order** **Purchase Order No. 3247**
To:	Tom's Top Produce 16625 Westview Avenue Ocean View, FL 32174 Phone: 303/545-9100 Attn: Tom Overhill	

Date	Good Thru	Account No.	Terms
9/12/99	10/12/99	658430-C	Net 30 Days

Item	Description	Quantity	Unit Price	Extension
1	Cases of Boston Lettuce, US Fancy	10	$18.00	$180.00
2	Cases of US No. 1 California Avocados	3	27.00	81.00
3	Cases of Broccoli, US Fancy	2	4.00	8.00
4	Cases of Carrots, US Extra No. 1	24	12.00	288.00
5	Carton of Cucumbers, US Fancy	1	5.00	5.00
6	Case of Red Tomatoes, US No. 1	1	5.00	5.00
			Subtotal	567.00
			Tax (7%)	39.69
			Shipping (5%)	28.35
Authorized Signature	Lisa Bluebell		**Total**	$635.04

Keeping track of all this information helps the buyer control products and services. Purchase orders are generally less detailed than specs, but remember: purchase orders are legal contracts between buyers and suppliers.

Requisition Forms

Occasionally, expensive new equipment will need to be purchased. In large foodservice organizations, approval must be obtained before the buyer can order the item. If the chef believes that a deep-fat fryer should be replaced, the chef must first fill out a **requisition form** (WREK-kwi-ZI-shun) that lists the item or service needed and send it to company headquarters. Once approval has been received, the buyer can then place the order.

Review Your Learning 7.2

1. Which standard purchasing form describes in detail the characteristics of products and services that an operation wants to buy?
   a. Purchase order
   b. Inventory sheet
   c. Specifications form
   d. Invoice

2. Why is it important for a buyer who's considering several different vendors to write a good set of specs?
   a. Keeps the competition guessing
   b. Lets supplier know exactly what the buyer wants
   c. Helps expand inventory
   d. Forces suppliers to give the buyer the lowest price

3. Some suppliers develop their own grading system that surpass even federal grading standards. These grading systems are known as:
   a. packers' brands.
   b. USDA requirements.
   c. general guidelines.
   d. Institutional Meat Purchase Specifications (IMPS).

Continued on next page

4. Which written form spells out exactly what the buyer agrees to purchase from the supplier?
   a. Requisition form
   b. Invoice
   c. Purchase order
   d. Credit memo

5. Which of the following written forms should be used to order an infrequently requested item, such as a new deep fryer?
   a. Requisition form
   b. Spec list
   c. Purchase order
   d. Inventory sheet

6. Ben Dare, a restaurant buyer, doesn't want to take the time to properly fill out a spec list for his restaurant. If he gives a vague spec list to his suppliers, which of the following problems is likely to occur?
   a. His suppliers will charge him more for the extra time used to figure out his spec list
   b. He'll receive more product than what he requested in his purchase order
   c. He increases the chance that he'll receive low-quality or wrong items from his suppliers
   d. His order will not be delivered on time

7. Why is it important to double-check a purchase order before giving it to a supplier?

8. Which government department is responsible for grading food items like eggs and poultry?
   a. NASA
   b. CIA
   c. USO
   d. USDA

7.3

SECTION 7.3

Making Purchasing Decisions

AFTER STUDYING SECTION 7.3, YOU SHOULD BE ABLE TO:

- Explain how production records influence purchasing decisions.
- List the criteria for selecting appropriate suppliers.

Before making any purchasing decisions, the buyer must know the operating budget and needs of the restaurant. In *Chapter 12: Controlling Foodservice Costs* of *Becoming a Foodservice Professional, Year 1,* we learned how to create an operating budget and set up an inventory control system. Buyers use these inventory records to determine the immediate needs of a foodservice organization and to calculate future sales.

Effective Forecasting

How does the buyer or manager predict the future? While no method is absolutely certain, foodservice **forecasting** is basically a highly educated guess of what products

KEY TERMS

- "As purchased price (AP) price"
- Consulting services
- Convenience foods
- Cost-plus buying
- Daily food cost sheet
- Delivery schedule
- Edible portion (EP)
- Food cost percentage
- Forecasting
- Lead time
- Make-or-buy analysis
- One-stop shopping

Exhibit 7.10
Forecasting is a smart way to predict your purchasing needs.

the buyer thinks will be needed in the future. Buyers and managers use production records to effectively forecast their buying needs.

Production records include:

- production sheets;
- daily food cost sheets; and
- sales mix records.

By combining this information with years of personal experience, buyers can effectively plan their restaurant's purchasing needs.

In most foodservice operations, the chef fills out production sheets for the upcoming weeks. A **production sheet** lists all menu items that will be prepared on a given day. At the end of the day, the chef adjusts the information to reflect actual production and gives the sheets to the buyer. When compiled over a period of time, production sheets become a very important forecasting tool. Exhibit 7.11 shows a sample production sheet.

Buyers also use production sheets to spot signs of **stockouts** (the running out

KEY TERMS (CONTINUED)

- Optimal price
- Overproduction
- Processed foods
- Production records
- Production sheet
- Reciprocal buying
- Sales mix record
- Standing order
- Stockless purchasing
- Stockout
- Substitutions
- Yield

of a menu item), and **overproduction** (the making of too much food). Overproduction often leads to food waste, which affects food cost percentage.

Food Cost Percentage

One of the most important ways managers try to limit food waste is by keeping accurate **daily food cost sheets,** or ongoing records of daily and monthly food costs for an operation. In *Chapter 12: Controlling Foodservice Costs* of *Becoming a Foodservice Professional, Year 1,* you learned that daily food cost is determined by adding all the requisitions from the storeroom and the daily purchases. This number, divided by the daily sales figure, is the daily **food cost percentage.**

Managers use this information to compare costs over a period of time. Most managers try to stay at or below 33%. While minor fluctuations do occur, a large change will quickly identify problems, such as overproduction, food waste, or theft.

Managers also keep **sales mix records** that track each item sold from the menu. This can be done on a daily, weekly, or monthly basis. This record shows which items sell well, called *leaders,* or ones that don't sell well, called *losers.* By recognizing leaders, buyers can safely order those items in volume.

Sales mix records help managers determine an item's popularity. When sales for a popular chicken entrée drop off suddenly, a manager might use the sales mix record to explore possible causes. Does the meal sell better in the summer? Are production problems or poor sales techniques responsible? The sales mix record gives managers clues to answer these important questions.

Evaluating and Selecting Suppliers

Finding a reasonably priced supplier that consistently provides high-quality products is one of the most important tasks for a foodservice buyer or manager.

Suppliers should be evaluated on three main factors:

- supplier services;
- price; and
- product quality.

Supplier Services

Suppliers often provide a variety of services and incentives to get buyers to purchase goods from their company.

Exhibit 7.11
Sample production sheet.

PRODUCTION SHEET

DAY: ______________________ DATE: ______________________

AMOUNT	•ITEM•	LOCATION	TEMP.	TIME	REMARKS
	•REHEATS•				
					EMPLOYEES' CAFETERIA
	•VEGETABLES•				
	Cases of Spinach				
	Pans of Baking Potatoes				

AMOUNT OF RIBS LEFT: ______________________ •OUT AT• ______________________

BAKED POTATOES LEFT: ______________________

AMOUNT OF GREENS LEFT: ______________________

AMOUNT OF SPINACH LEFT: ______________________

GREENS IN WALK-IN ICED: ______________________

FISH PROPERLY ICED: ______________________

STOCKPOTS CHECKED (SIMMER): ______________________

TOTAL NUMBER OF DINNERS: ______________________

GENERAL REMARKS: ______________________

Here's a list of practices that suppliers often make available to their buyers.

- **Cost-plus buying**—The buyer is charged the supplier's costs plus a predetermined markup.
- **One-stop shopping**—The buyer receives a volume discount by purchasing as many items as possible from one supplier.
- **Stockless purchasing**—The buyer purchases a large amount of goods at a discounted price and the supplier agrees to store these goods, delivering them to the buyer as needed.
- **Standing order**—The supplier regularly delivers a predetermined amount of items to the buyer's operation. The necessary amount of goods are delivered to bring stock up to an agreed upon inventory level.
- **Delivery schedule**—The buyer informs the supplier of the day and time for delivery.
- **Lead time**—Refers to the time gap between placing an order and its delivery. Shorter lead times are more convenient for the buyer.
- **Reciprocal buying**—Buyer agrees to do business with only one supplier in exchange for the supplier's commitment to use and recommend the buyer's operation.
- **Substitutions**—Buyer agrees to let the supplier fill purchase orders with an acceptable substitute if the specific product ordered is unavailable.
- **Consulting services**—Buyers appreciate suppliers that provide instructions or information regarding a product, such as handling procedures or safety requirements.

Getting the Best Price

There is a difference between the best price and the best value. In the foodservice industry, buyers want to get optimal prices for goods and services. The **optimal price** is the price that produces the best value to the buyer. Product quality and supplier services are both important parts of optimal prices.

The formula chefs use to determine a vegetable's **edible portion (EP)** amount (food quantity after trimming and preparing) is also used by a buyer to find a product's optimal price. You have already practiced calculating the EP for fruits and vegetables in *Chapter 10: Business Math* of *Becoming a Foodservice Professional, Year 1.* As you remember, the edible portion (EP) cost is found by dividing the **as purchased (AP) price** (price of food purchased before trimming and preparing) by the **yield** (amount of food that is actually served divided by the amount of food purchased). Remember, a low AP price is not a great value if it means a low yield or high EP cost.

Finding the optimal price of **convenience foods** which have been processed in some way to make them quicker and easier to use, must also be determined. Buyers use what is known as a make-or-buy analysis to reach this decision. For example, in a **make-or-buy analysis**, the buyer compares the price of potatoes and the labor involved in mashing them to the price and labor needed to use packaged mashed potatoes. Even when convenience foods cost less, they are not the best buy if they fail to meet the quality standards of the restaurant. **Processed foods** are a more basic type of convenience food and do not require such close pricing scrutiny. Staples such as pasta, spices, and oils are examples of processed foods.

Product Quality

Well-written specifications should guarantee that products meet expectations. However, it is still necessary to keep track of suppliers' reliability. Late deliveries, back orders, and returns on items due to poor quality are problems that can quickly affect the quality of meals being served. Insist on good service from your suppliers. If they can't deliver, there is almost always another supplier who can.

If it becomes necessary to find a new supplier, you should always check the supplier's references. Ask friends in the industry what they think of a supplier's way of doing business. Is the supplier dependable and honest? Does the supplier go the extra mile to take care of their customers? Make sure you do your homework before you give your trust to a supplier.

Exhibit 7.12
Dry pasta is an example of a processed food.

Review Your Learning 7.3

1. Production sheets are generally created by the:
   a. chef or kitchen manager.
   b. busboy.
   c. buyer.
   d. supplier.

2. Which production record provides detailed information about the number of menu items actually produced and served on a given day?
   a. Daily food cost sheet
   b. Spec list
   c. Production sheet
   d. Purchase order

3. Which of the following terms is used to describe the running out of a menu item in a kitchen?
   a. Overproduction
   b. Blank order
   c. Stockout
   d. Forecasting

4. If the average daily food cost for a restaurant open 30 days a month is $240 and its sales for the month are $21,000 what is its approximate monthly food cost percentage?

5. Suppliers should be evaluated on three main factors:
   a. Honesty, sincerity, and punctuality
   b. Product quality, supplier services, and price
   c. Spec lists, grading standards, and food costs
   d. Forecasting, delivery schedule, and production records

6. What's the name of the supplier service in which a delivery person regularly shows up at a restaurant and drops off the amount of goods needed to bring stock up to an agreed upon inventory level?
   a. Supply and demand
   b. Cost-plus buying
   c. Standing orders
   d. Inventory levels

Continued on next page

7. A restaurant buyer looks at the previous day's production sheet and notices that 40 eggplant parmesan portions were made but only ten were served. If this trend continues, will the buyer want to reduce or increase the amount of eggplant she purchases in the future? Why or why not?

8. The leftover eggplant parmesan in question 7 is an example of:
   a. stockouts.
   b. opportunity buys.
   c. edible-portion cost.
   d. overproduction.

9. Two shipments of chicken come into a restaurant. Shipment A has an AP price of $0.50 per pound and a 75% yield percentage. Shipment B has an AP price of $0.55 per pound with an 85% yield. Which shipment had the optimal price?

10. Why is a make-or-buy analysis an important way to reduce AP price?

7.4

SECTION 7.4

Receiving, Storing, and Issuing

AFTER STUDYING SECTION 7.4, YOU SHOULD BE ABLE TO:

- List proper receiving procedures.
- State in words or symbols the proper storage procedures for various foods and beverages.
- State the difference between the periodic order and the perpetual inventory methods.

With nearly 40% of annual revenues being spent on food and supplies, the average restaurant can't afford to let their inventory of goods fall prey to theft or waste. Likewise, the savings generated by even the most careful purchasing can quickly be erased if a restaurant's receiving procedures are sloppy or inconsistent. That's why receiving and storing procedures are so important to a restaurant's long-term success. But what exactly do we mean when we talk about receiving and storing?

KEY TERMS

- First in, first out (FIFO)
- Humidity
- Inventory
- Invoice
- Issuing
- Par stock
- Periodic order method
- Perpetual inventory method
- Pilfering
- Receiving
- Receiving sheet
- Reorder point (ROP)
- Request for credit

Receiving: Initial Delivery

Receiving means inspecting, accepting, and in some cases, rejecting, deliveries of goods and services. The first, and perhaps most important, step in setting up good receiving procedures is to make sure that only employees who have been trained in proper receiving techniques do the job. This is especially true when receiving a meat delivery. As one of the most expensive food items, many restaurants only allow the chef, manager, or a highly trained employee to accept delivery. It may seem like a difficult rule to follow, but it's the key to controlling quality and costs at your operation. If all your trained employees are busy when a delivery shows up, have the delivery person wait.

A written invoice should accompany every delivery. The **invoice** is is the supplier's bill listing the actual goods delivered by the supplier. The person responsible for receiving at the restaurant—the *receiver*—should always check the invoice against the restaurant's original purchase order to make sure that the quantity and cost of the goods hasn't changed. The receiver should also have a copy of the original specs to confirm that the delivery meets the buyer's requirements for quality. Any discrepancies on the invoice should be noted and signed by both the receiver and the delivery person.

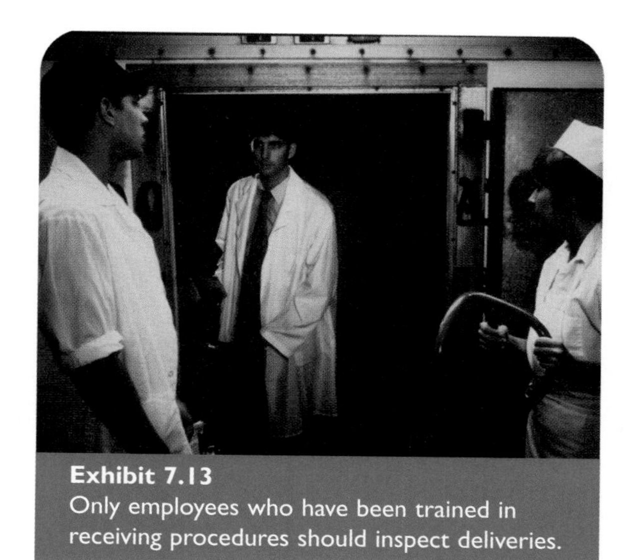

Exhibit 7.13
Only employees who have been trained in receiving procedures should inspect deliveries.

Receiving: Inspection of Goods

What should a receiver look for when a delivery comes in?

- Be alert for extra packaging, including water and ice, that could add to the product weight.
- Always check the lower layers in a package to make sure they are of the same quality as the top layers.
- Examine packages for signs of water damage.
- Check product expiration dates.
- Watch for incomplete shipments.
- Canned foods—Always reject containers that appear swollen, leaky, rusty, dented, broken, or very dirty.

- Dried foods—In addition to the condition of the container, check to see if the food looks moldy, broken up, or unusual in any way.
- Frozen foods—Examine the condition of the container. Keep a sharp eye out for stains or other signs of thawing. Check for freezer burn and if possible, use a thermometer to check the temperature. Frozen foods should be delivered at 0°F (-17.8°C) or below.

If the invoice has an error or some part of the shipment needs to be returned due to poor quality, the receiver should complete a request for credit memo and have the delivery person sign it. A **request for credit** memo is a written record that ensures the operation's account will be credited for the error.

Receiving: Moving Goods into Inventory

Normally, the receiver accepts the delivery and signs or initials the invoice. The goods then move to either the kitchen production area or the storage facility. The delivery date and price are attached to all perishable foods. The receiver should then record each item on a **receiving sheet** or log. Exhibit 7.14 shows an example of a typical receiving sheet.

Exhibit 7.14
Typical receiving sheet. Accurate receiving sheets are crucial to the inventory process.

Date	Time Delivered	Quantity	Invoice #	Supplier	Item Description	Unit Price	Extension	*Direct			**Stores			Other Info.
								Food	Beverage	Nonfood	Food	Beverage	Nonfood	
8/9/99	7:30 a.m.	2.00	00971	Henderson's	Precored head lettuce 25 lb. box	8.75	17.50	1.00			1.00			
8/9/99	6:45 a.m.	1.00	434021	Knicke	Fresh strawberries 15 lb. flat	5.25	5.25				1.00			
8/10/99	2:30 p.m.	3.00	253 Grain	Western	Unbleached baking flour 50 lb. sacks	15.00	45.00	1.00			2.00			
8/11/99	7:20 a.m.	4.00	A2321	Acme	Dishwashing detergent 10 lb. cont.	8.00	32.00			1.00		3.00		

*These columns note goods that go directly to the kitchen prep area, bypassing the main storage area.
**These columns note goods that go into main storage area.

Storing

Proper storage management requires good planning. Your restaurant should have enough space for both perishable and nonperishable foods. Health requirements for storing food items are very exact and cleanliness is essential at all times.

Here are some important points to remember when storing goods:

- Store food in appropriate containers.
- Create proper air circulation around goods by keeping shelves about six inches from the floor, ceiling, and walls.
- Keep foods stored far away from soaps, pesticides, chemicals, etc.
- Try to purchase staples (items for which the demand is constant) in airtight containers.
- Transfer items purchased in unsealed containers into airtight containers to protect them against insects and vermin (small disease-carrying animals, such as lice, fleas, or mice that are difficult to control).
- Use steel shelving for all nonperishables.
- Clean and sweep storage areas daily to eliminate spoiled foods and to discourage insects and vermin.
- Have a professional exterminator come in and spray regularly.
- Store perishable food, such as meat and produce, at their proper temperatures and humidity levels (see Exhibit 7.15). **Humidity** refers to the amount of water moisture in the air or in a contained space such as a refrigerator. Different areas of a cooler have different levels of humidity. Areas close to the cooler's blower have higher humidity levels, while areas away from it have lower humidity levels.

Exhibit 7.15
Food storage temperatures and humidity levels.

Item	Temperature	Humidity Level
Meat and poultry	32°F to 40°F (0°C to 4.4°C)	75% to 85%
Fish	30°F to 34°F (-1.1°C to 1.1°C)	75% to 85%
Live shellfish	45°F (7.2°C)	75% to 85%
Eggs	38°F to 40°F (3.3°C to 4.4°C)	75% to 85%
Dairy products	38°F to 40°F (3.3°C to 4.4°C)	75% to 85%
Most fruits and vegetables	40°F to 45°F (4.4°C to 7.2°C)	85% to 95%

Inventory Procedures

Developing an accurate inventory procedure is the key to effective storage techniques. An **inventory** is a record of all the goods that a restaurant has on hand both in storage and in the kitchen prep area.

The well-managed inventory:

- helps the buyer determine how much stock he or she needs to order at any time;
- helps the buyer take advantage of sale prices when available;
- helps the manager keep food costs low and profits high; and
- allows the manager to better plan for future needs.

Methods of Tracking Inventory

The two most common methods for purchasing nonperishable foods are the periodic order method and the perpetual inventory method. In the **periodic order method,** the entire stock is physically reviewed on a regular basis. From this review, the manager determines the reorder point for each inventory item.

The **perpetual inventory method** uses inventory cards to keep track of what food items are in storage. Items are checked in on inventory cards when they are delivered to the restaurant and checked off as they are issued for use in the kitchen area. These cards are then compiled into a perpetual inventory sheet. A buyer can look at this sheet and easily see which items need to be reordered. Exhibit 7.16 shows a perpetual inventory sheet.

Now let's turn to two other ideas that help buyers in their purchasing decisions—par stock and the reorder point.

Par Stock

Par stock is the ideal amount of an inventory item that should be on hand at all times. In a new restaurant operation, the par stock amounts for many food items will be little more than educated guesses. In time, however, the par stock amount begins to reflect a quantity that neither runs out nor spoils on the shelf. Once par stock is known, the buyer can easily order goods by taking the difference between the par stock figure and the actual amount of stock on the shelves.

For example, let's say a buyer is trying to figure out how many birthday cakes she needs to order. When she receives a weekly cake delivery from her supplier,

Exhibit 7.16
Perpetual inventory sheet.

PERPETUAL INVENTORY SHEET

Date	Order No.	IN	OUT	BALANCE	Date	Order No.	IN	OUT	BALANCE	Date	Order No.	IN	OUT	BALANCE	Date	Order No.	IN	OUT	BALANCE

Remarks				Price
LOCATION	MINIMUM	MAXIMUM	ARTICLE	SIZE OR PART NO.

she knows that her par stock figure is 24 cakes. If 15 cakes are in stock on the day she's placing an order, she know she needs to order 9 cakes.

Par stock − Amount in stock = Amount to be ordered

or

24 - 15 = 9

The par stock amount will change if the suppliers' delivery dates change or the operation's forecasted sales volume increases or decreases.

Exhibit 7.17
Knowing your par stock helps avoid spoilage and running out of food items.

Reorder Point

Another way to ensure that your restaurant always has the proper level of stock on hand is to establish a **reorder point,** or **ROP,** for each item. If the reorder point for 50-pound sacks of flour is two and there are only two sacks left in the storeroom, then the buyer knows that he or she has to order more flour. A reorder point is like a warning bell; it alerts you that you need to order something now.

The reorder point can be used with the par stock figure to help maintain proper inventory when suppliers don't deliver regularly. In our cake example, let's say that the reorder point is 12 cakes. At 15 cakes, the buyer is a few cakes short of the reorder point, but the supplier needs the order today for a delivery two days from now. Assuming that their restaurant goes through 3 cakes a day, the buyer uses the following formula to place her order:

Par stock − Reorder point + Normal usage until delivery = Amount ordered

or

24 - 12 + (3 cakes a day x 2 days) = 18

Managers should decide which inventory tracking method is most appropriate for their operation, then maintain it very carefully to avoid over-purchasing or under-purchasing.

Issuing

All items in the storeroom need to be accounted for when they eventually leave the storeroom and are used in the restaurant. **Issuing** refers to the official procedures employees use when taking an item out of the storeroom and putting it into production. In a standard issuing situation, product requisition forms are filled out by kitchen employees indicating exactly what items are needed and then given to the manager or another appointed employee. Many large restaurants use a formal issuing procedure both as a way to keep accurate inventory records and to prevent pilfering.

Pilfering is the illegal taking of inventory items by employees for their personal use. In the restaurant and hospitality industry, pilfering is both a serious problem and a serious offense. Employees caught pilfering are usually fired. In some more extreme cases, employees have been arrested and convicted of theft.

Employees should observe the first in, first out (FIFO) system of stock rotation, both when the items first go into stock and when they are issued. In the **first in, first out (FIFO)** system, the oldest stock is placed in front of or on top of the newer stock. FIFO makes sure that older items are used before newer items.

Exhibit 7.18
The 10 steps of purchasing.

1. Begin the purchasing process by:
   - reviewing or planning all menus.
   - determining the quality and quantity needed to produce menus.
   - determining purchase amounts needed to maintain par stock levels.
   - reviewing, approving, or writing specifications.
2. Check inventory records to determine supplies on hand and supplies that need to be reordered.
3. Request written price bids or verbal quotes from suppliers.
4. Select the supplier based on three factors:
   - supplier services;
   - optimal price; and
   - product quality.
5. Prepare purchase orders and place the order(s).
6. Use proper receiving procedures when an order is delivered.
   - Review invoice to check quantity, quality, and price of items delivered.
   - Accept delivery and sign or initial the invoice, or reject items and get a request for credit memo.
   - Record each item in the receiving log. Date perishable foods. Remember to save meat and seafood tags in case of a foodborne illness.
7. Store items properly, observing all sanitation guidelines.
8. Store items properly, using the FIFO principle for stock rotation.
9. Have employees fill out requisition forms as supplies are needed.
10. Following par stock guidelines, reorder supplies, and begin the process again.

Review Your Learning 7.4

1. A produce delivery arrives at your back door just minutes before your restaurant's lunch rush. Which is the best thing you can do in this situation?
   a. Stop what you're doing to receive the order even if it means your lunch rush won't go as smoothly.
   b. Ask the delivery person to come back right after your lunch rush.
   c. Have your new employee receive it since he wouldn't be able to handle the rush hour that well anyway.
   d. Just let the produce sit by the back door.

2. What's the name of the form that accompanies every order from a supplier?
   a. Par stock
   b. Purchase order
   c. Invoice
   d. Spec list

3. If an invoice has an error or some part of the shipment needs to be returned due to poor quality, the receiver should complete a(n):
   a. request for credit memo.
   b. purchase order.
   c. invoice.
   d. inventory form.

4. When receiving a shipment of produce, it is especially important that you immediately:
   a. check shipment for spoilage.
   b. check lower layers of packages for bad product.
   c. refrigerate as soon as the shipment has been inspected.
   d. all of the above.

5. The manager at your restaurant checks your restaurant's inventory room every week before she orders. Which type of inventory method is she most likely using?
   a. Periodic order method
   b. Perpetual inventory method
   c. First in, first out (FIFO)
   d. Pilfering

Continued on ne

6. The ideal amount of stock that should always be on hand at a restaurant is known as:
   a. bin cards.
   b. physical inventory.
   c. par stock.
   d. perpetual inventory.

7. The stealing of restaurant food or goods by employees is known as:
   a. perpetual inventory.
   b. cost of doing business.
   c. allowance readjustment.
   d. pilfering.

8. An operation's par stock for tomato juice is 5 cases (12 cans per case). It has 18 cans in inventory and will use 6 by the next delivery date. How many cases should the manager order?
   a. Doesn't need to order any
   b. 12 cans
   c. 4 cases
   d. 5 cases

9. In the foodservice business, FIFO stands for:
   a. Fresh In, Finally Out.
   b. First In, First Out.
   c. the restaurant owner's lovable little dog.
   d. Fresh In, Fresh Out.

Flashback

CHAPTER 7

SECTION 7.1: WHAT IS PURCHASING?

- **Purchasing** is the careful process of selecting and buying goods and services from different vendors.
- A **vendor** refers to any company that sells things to a foodservice operation, including:
  - —Product suppliers (produce, meat or dairy companies)
  - —Service suppliers (window washers, landscapers or exterminators)
- The actual **buyer** of a foodservice operation can be the manager, a supervisor, or someone specially hired to do all the purchasing.
- Buyers purchase all the food, beverages, supplies, services, and equipment in an operation.
- Buyers must know all aspects of their restaurant's business, federal and state regulations, and the ins and outs of the purchasing process.
- The buyer's role can be different depending on whether the restaurant is a smaller independent operation, a chain, or a franchise.
- In smaller operations, the owner/manager usually does all the buying.
- **Cooperative (co-op) buying** refers to the practice of smaller operations joining together to buy items as a group in order to receive a discount.
- Large restaurant chains benefit from **economies of scale**—the savings that a multi-unit business creates for itself by sharing the cost of its various expenses.
- Chains often maintain a central **commissary**—a distribution warehouse that provides goods to each individual location.
- A **franchise** is a legal business relationship in which an independent owner buys the right to use a company's name, products, and logo.
- Franchise owners can choose to buy from a central commissary run by the franchise or any supplier that meets the company's standards.

- **Distribution** refers to the overall movement of products from where they are grown or raised to the restaurant's cooler.
- A **channel of distribution** refers to all the particular businesses that are involved in getting a product from its primary source to a customer.
- There are three main layers of distribution:
  - —**Primary sources** (farmers, ranchers, or manufacturers)
  - —**Intermediary sources** (wholesalers, distributors, or suppliers)
  - —**Retailers** (businesses that sell to consumers)
- Formal purchasing methods are often used by large operations. They require the buyer to develop specifications, request written price bids from several vendors, evaluate the bids, and choose the most appropriate vendor.
- **Informal purchasing methods** require that the buyer receive several verbal **quotes** before selecting the best vendor.
- In choosing a supplier, buyers need to consider several things, including overall prices, product quality, dependability, business stability, service, and value.
- **Prices** can be influenced by numerous factors including **time value, form value, place value, transportation value, service value,** politics, weather, and simple changes in **supply and demand.**

SECTION 7.2: STANDARD ORDERING PROCEDURES

- **Specifications,** or **specs,** are written descriptions of the type of products and services that an operation wants to buy from a supplier.
- Specs give suppliers details about the product needed. Features like the item's exact name, cost and quantity limitations, federal grading guidelines, and color are often noted.
- Fresh produce has become an important purchasing decision because today's consumers are more health conscious.
- In developing produce specs, buyers should state the exact name of the fruit or vegetable desired, packaging and grade requirements, color, ripeness, and intended use.

- **Organic produce** is different from conventionally grown produce in that it is grown without using pesticides or herbicides.
- Inspection of foods by the US Department of Agriculture (USDA) is mandatory and is done to ensure the safety and wholesomeness of foods.
- Grading is a voluntary service paid for by packers that shows the quality of foods.
- Foods like produce, dairy, meat, and eggs are ranked according to a variety of national grading systems.
- A **grade** is a label given to foods to help buyers quickly know what level of quality they are receiving.
- A **packers' brand** is a packing company's own personal grading system. It often exceeds government standards and gives buyers more confidence in the quality they'll receive.
- Fish is *not* subject to a mandatory inspection system by the federal government.
- Many fish suppliers participate in a voluntary federal quality program. Fish that pass inspection are given the Packed Under Federal Inspection (PUFI) seal.
- Institutional Meat Purchase Specifications (IMPS) is an identification system that allows buyers to select the type of meat, cut, and other details by number.
- A **purchase order** spells out exactly what the buyer will purchase from a supplier.
- A **requisition form** is used to obtain authorization to purchase expensive and infrequently ordered items or services.

SECTION 7.3: MAKING PURCHASING DECISIONS

- To make good purchasing decisions, buyers need to consider their operating budget, search out suppliers with the best optimal prices, keep cost-effective amounts of stock in inventory, and insist on suppliers who are dependable.
- Effective **forecasting** comes from years of experience and detailed records of past kitchen production. These records include production sheets, daily food cost sheets, and sales mix records.
- **Production sheets** provide detailed records of menu items produced and served daily.

- Production sheets are used as a purchasing forecasting tool to prevent **stockouts** (the running out of a menu item) and **overproduction** (the making of too much food).
- A **daily food cost sheet** highlights the relationship between daily food sales and the cost of the food needed to generate those sales.
- Buyers use daily food cost sheets to make sure that the food cost percentage stays in line with budget expectations.
- The **sales mix record** shows the amount of each menu item sold over a specified period of time.
- Buyers use the sales mix record to better understand changes in a particular menu item's popularity.
- Suppliers should be evaluated on three main factors: supplier services, price, and product quality.
- A supplier needs to provide the level of product quality as outlined in the buyer's specifications.
- Suppliers often provide a variety of services and incentives to get buyers to purchase goods from their company. Supplier services include **cost-plus buying, one-stop shopping, stockless purchasing, standing orders,** favorable **delivery schedules,** shortened **lead times, reciprocal buying** agreements, flexible arrangements for **substitutions,** and **consulting services.**
- **Optimal price** is the price that produces the best value to the buyer. In addition to an item's price, the optimal price is based on factors like supplier services and product quality.
- Buyers calculate the optimal purchasing price of an item by evaluating its **AP (as purchased) price** in relation to its yield percentage and **EP (edible portion) cost.**
- A **make-or-buy analysis** is the cost of using a convenience food product compared to the cost of making the item from scratch.
- **Convenience foods** are foods that have been processed in some way to make them easier or quicker to use. Canned, frozen, and ready-made foods are all examples of convenience foods.
- **Processed foods** are a more basic type of convenience food. Staples such as dry pastas, spices, and oils are all examples of processed foods.

SECTION 7.4: RECEIVING, STORING, AND ISSUING

- **Receiving** requires inspecting, accepting, and in some cases, rejecting, deliveries of goods and services.
- Effective receiving and storing procedures are a must for any successful foodservice operation.
- Only employees who have been trained in proper **receiving** procedures should ever check in a delivery.
- Usually, only the chef or manager receives meat to ensure that quality, quantity, and price are correct.
- An **invoice** is a written record of the actual goods delivered by the supplier and should accompany every delivery.
- The **receiver** should always check the invoice against the restaurant's original purchase order and product specifications to ensure that product quality, quantity, and price haven't changed.
- When inspecting newly delivered goods, carefully check the quality of the goods. Check for signs of thawing, water damage, and expiration dates.
- Receivers use a **request for credit** memo when they have to return an item due to inferior quality or an incorrect price on the invoice.
- Upon accepting the delivery, the receiver fills out a receiving sheet and moves the new stock into storage.
- The **receiving sheet** notes the amount of goods received and whether they've gone directly into the kitchen production area or the storage facility.
- Proper storage techniques prevent or minimize losses due to pilferage or spoilage.
- Most storage techniques for canned or dry goods involve keeping goods dry, airtight, and free of vermin.
- Temperature and humidity are important concerns for perishable food items like meat and produce. **Humidity** refers to the amount of water moisture in a given space.
- An **inventory** is a record of all the goods that a restaurant has on hand both in storage and in the kitchen prep area.
- The periodic order method and the perpetual inventory method are the two most common methods for purchasing nonperishable foods.

- In the **periodic order method,** the entire stock is physically reviewed on a regular basis.
- In the **perpetual inventory method,** food items are checked in on inventory cards when they are delivered to the restaurant and checked off as they are issued for use in the kitchen area.
- **Par stock** is the ideal amount of an inventory item that should be on hand between deliveries.
- The par stock amount for any item will change if the time between deliveries changes or the operation's forecasted sales change.
- A **reorder point** is a number assigned to each inventory item that alerts the buyer that the item needs to be restocked by the next delivery.
- **Issuing** refers to all the procedures connected to taking stock items out of the storeroom and putting them into production.
- Restaurants use issuing procedures to reduce wastage and pilfering.
- **Pilfering** is the illegal taking of inventory items by employees for their personal use.
- Using the **first in, first out** or **FIFO** system of stock rotation ensures that older items are used before newer items.

Jimmy Gherardi

Chef, Restaurateur, and Public Speaker
Cincinnati, Ohio

I never run out of ideas and ways to involve myself in this industry, and I never get bored. I host a daily nationally-syndicated radio show called *Everybody's Cooking,* which received a 1998 James Beard Foundation nomination. I'm a trained chef and I teach at several culinary schools. I hold seminars and training sessions for large companies like Procter and Gamble and Pepsi. I've even helped develop recipes for Campbell's and other food manufacturers.

My pride and joy is J's, the seafood restaurant I own and operate in Cincinnati. We serve fresh seafood from all over the country. It's flown in every day, and we have to be sure that every delivery is fresh, top-quality, and right for what we plan to do with it. Then, as a chef, I create ways to cook and serve every piece of seafood so that it's presented in the most attractive and delicious way. J's has won many restaurant awards because we give our customers consistently great food and wine and great service.

As a trained chef, I'm a member of the *Chaine des Rotisseurs,* the guild of meat roasters that was founded in France in the Middle Ages. There are so many things to know before you can cut and prepare meat, poultry, and seafood. Every animal and fish has its own characteristics and cooking methods that bring out its flavor. In the larger animals, each cut is suited to different techniques, preparations, marinades, sauces, and accompaniments. Even with all my experience, I never stop learning.

Everything I do is part of my mission to share my love affair with food and wine with others. For anyone willing to work hard and never stop learning, this is the most fulfilling industry you'll ever find.

CHAPTER 8

Meat, Poultry, and Seafood

8.1

SECTION 8.1

Purchasing, Storing, and Preparing Meats, Poultry, and Seafood

AFTER STUDYING SECTION 8.1, YOU SHOULD BE ABLE TO:

- Outline the federal grading systems for meat, poultry, and seafood.
- Describe the various kinds of meat, poultry, and seafood.
- Demonstrate proper procedures for purchasing, storing, and fabricating meat, poultry, and seafood.

PURCHASING, STORING AND PREPARING MEATS

In the foodservice industry, *meats* refer to beef, veal, lamb, mutton, and pork. Serving meat of all kinds is one of the most expensive, yet profitable, areas of business in the foodservice industry. As you can see in Exhibit 8.1, meat consumption is on the rise and is expected to continue for the next decade. Therefore, much care and

KEY TERMS

- Aging
- Boning
- Butterfly
- Crustacean
- Deveining
- Fabricate
- Filleting
- Free-range
- Game meats
- Goujonettes (goo-sha-NET)
- Gutting
- Kosher
- Mollusks
- Mutton

attention should be given to the purchasing, storing, and preparation of meats. When the proper steps are taken, a foodservice operation will make a profit preparing quality meats for its guests.

Purchasing Meats

Meats can be purchased in a variety of forms, from a whole carcass to individual cuts of meat. Selecting which cuts of meat are right for your foodservice operation depends on many things, such as the operation's menu, the size of the operation, and the cost of the meat being purchased. Other factors that influence the quantity and cuts of meat an operation purchases are:

- *Storage*—There must be enough refrigeration and freezer storage to house the meat purchased.
- *Employee skills* and *equipment*—Employees must have the skills and equipment necessary to fabricate large cuts of meat.
- *Cost*—Costs should be considered when purchasing cuts of meat. Is it more economical to purchase large or small cuts of meat?

When purchasing fresh meat it is important to understand the grading systems

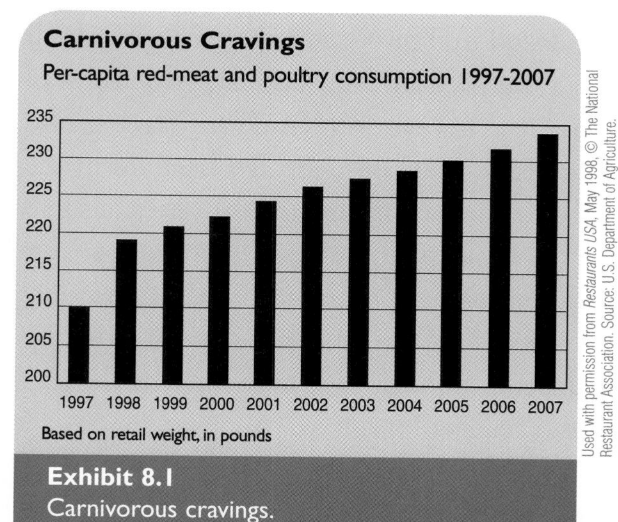

Exhibit 8.1
Carnivorous cravings.

Used with permission from *Restaurants USA*, May 1998, © The National Restaurant Association. Source: U.S. Department of Agriculture.

KEY TERMS

- Offal (OH-fel) meats
- Paupiettes (po-pee-EHT)
- Poultry
- Primal cut
- Quality grades
- Retail cuts
- Scaling
- Shucked
- Silverskin
- Sweetbreads
- Trimming
- Trussed
- Tying
- Yield grade

Exhibit 8.2
There are many factors to consider before meats are purchased.

Meat, poultry, and seafood are considered potentially hazardous foods. Be sure to follow all sanitary procedures when handling these items. Be especially aware of the danger of cross-contamination with raw foods. Check proper storage and handling procedures, and always keep foods out of the dangerous temperature zone of 40°F to 140°F (4.4°C to 60°C).

used during the inspection process. Government inspection of meat is mandatory, or required, and all meats intended for human consumption must pass inspection. The U.S. Department of Agriculture (USDA) has also established voluntary specific quality grades for meat. **Quality grades** are standards given to meats based on their freshness and quality. As you can see in exhibit 8.3, different grading systems are used for each type of meat.

Only beef and lamb have yield grades. The **yield grade** refers to the amount of usable meat after the fat has been trimmed. These grades help purchasers make better decisions about the cuts of meat they buy.

The USDA also publishes an *Institutional Meat Purchasing Specifications* (IMPS) table that describes the different cuts of meat used in the foodservice industry. As you remember from *Chapter 7: Purchasing and Inventory Control,* the table is listed in The Meat Buyers Guide, which is published by the National Association of Meat Purveyors (NAMP). This guide indexes meats numerically; beef are in the 100 series; lamb in the 200 series, and so on. It also includes illustrations and descriptions of each cut listed. It is widely accepted and an invaluable tool in reducing miscommunications between the buyers and sellers of meats.

Exhibit 8.3
Quality grades for meat.

Beef Grades
- Prime
- Choice
- Select
- Standard
- Commercial
- Utility
- Cutter
- Canner

Veal Grades
- Prime
- Choice
- Utility
- Standard

Lamb Grades
- Prime
- Choice
- Good
- Utility

Storing Meats

Sanitary procedures must be followed when storing meats. Meats should be loosely wrapped in air-permeable paper and stored under refrigeration, preferably in a separate unit. Never tightly wrap fresh meats in plastic wrap because this creates a perfect breeding ground for bacteria and will severely limit the shelf life of the product. Separate different types of meats to prevent cross-contamination. Meat stored at the proper temperature

Exhibit 8.4
Proper storage guidelines for meat and meat products.

Frozen Storage of Meats

Meat	Maximum Storage Period at -10° to 0°F (-23.3°C to -17.8°C)
Beef, roasts and steaks	6 months
Beef, ground and stewing	3 to 4 months
Pork, roasts and chops	4 to 8 months
Pork, ground	1 to 3 months
Lamb, roasts and chops	6 to 8 months
Lamb, ground	3 to 5 months
Veal	8 to 12 months
Offal meats (liver, tongue)	3 to 4 months

Refrigerated Storage of Meats

Meat	Maximum Storage Period at 32°F to 36°F (0°C to 2.2°C)	Comments
Roasts, steaks, chops	3 to 5 days	Wrap loosely
Ground and stewing	1 to 2 days	Wrap loosely
Variety meats	1 to 2 days	Wrap loosely
Whole ham	7 days	May wrap tightly
Half ham	3 to 5 days	May wrap tightly
Ham slices	3 to 5 days	May wrap tightly
Canned ham	1 year	Keep in can
Hot dogs	1 week	Original wrapping
Bacon	1 week	May wrap tightly
Lunch meats	3 to 5 days	Wrap tightly when opened
Leftover cooked meats	1 to 2 days	Wrap or cover tightly
Gravy, broth	1 to 2 days	Highly perishable

and under optimal conditions can be held for several days without a noticeable loss of quality. Exhibit 8.4 lists important storage information about various meats—frozen and refrigerated.

Butchering Meats

Before a cut of meat becomes available to a foodservice operation and its customers, several stages of butchering need to take place. After slaughtering, the whole carcass is cut into large sections. The number of sections depends on the type of animal:

- Cattle butchered for beef are cut into four sections. Cattle that are butchered from the age of one day up to 14 or 15 weeks are cut into two halves and sold as *veal,* a meat with a pale flesh and delicate flavor.
- Hogs are slaughtered and cut into two halves in facilities that handle no other type of meat, in order to prevent foodborne illnesses.
- Sheep slaughtered under the age of one year are considered lamb; after that age they must be labeled **mutton.** Lambs are cut directly into primal cuts.

Primal cuts are the primary divisions of meat produced by the initial butchering of animal carcasses.

Aging Meats

Meat must then be **aged** between 48 and 72 hours to allow the muscles to relax. Butchers hang the meat during aging to help lengthen the muscle fibers and increase the tenderness of the meat. When meat is aged for longer periods of time the meat continues to darken and the flavor improves. It also becomes more expensive because the meat loses a significant amount of moisture that reduces its yield.

Fabrication

At the end of the aging period, the carcass is then cut into primal cuts. These cuts also depend on the types of animal. Exhibit 8.5 shows the primal cuts of beef, veal, lamb, and pork. These cuts can then be cut further into roasts or steaks. **Fabrication** is the process of cutting primal cuts into usable portions.

Retail cuts of meat are those cuts that are ready for sale. They can be primal cuts or fabricated portions. The amount of cutting or butchering necessary to prepare a retail cut affects its price. For example, the more time spent cutting or butchering a piece of meat, the more expensive it will be. Foodservice purchasers can choose to purchase retail cuts that are primal cuts and then fabricate them for their own use or buy fabricated portions. The decision is determined by the needs of the restaurant.

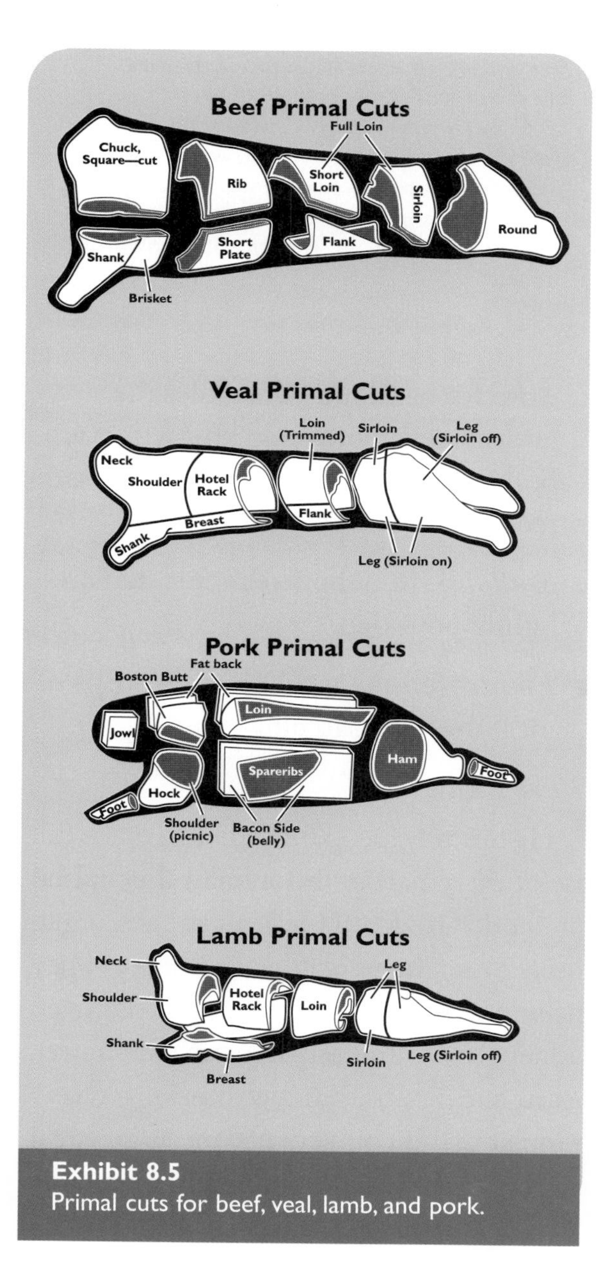

Exhibit 8.5
Primal cuts for beef, veal, lamb, and pork.

Fabricating meat requires practice, but very few tools. A sharp knife and a clean cutting board are all that are needed. Some popular fabrication methods or techniques include tying a roast and trimming and butterflying a tenderloin. Fabrication procedures for beef, veal, lamb, pork, and large game are similar.

Why is it necessary to tie a roast? **Tying** a roast ensures even cooking and keeps the shape of the meat. This is one of the easiest methods of meat fabrication.

Trimming a tenderloin must be done very carefully because it is one of the most expensive cuts. Only the **silverskin,** (the

Exhibit 8.6
A tied roast cooks evenly and keeps its shape.

tough membrane that surrounds the meat), fat, and gristle are removed. First, the fat must be cut away. Then, a chef's knife is used to make an even cut through the center of the meat. Next, the meat is opened using a butterfly cut. **Butterflying** means to cut a piece of meat lengthwise nearly in half so that it opens out and lies flat. This is done to speed up the cooking process by increasing the surface area of the meat.

Buffalo, which almost disappeared, has been reintroduced, as well as *beefalo,* a cross between beef and buffalo. Beefalo meat is slightly sweeter than regular beef and has a much lower cholesterol level. The same general guidelines for purchasing and storing domestic red meats apply to game meats.

Cuts from the boneless loin or tenderloin of beef, veal, lamb, or pork can be made into a variety of menu cuts:

- *Medallions*—small, round pieces molded by wrapping them in cheesecloth
- *Noisettes* (nwah-ZET)—small, usually round portion of meat; the French word for hazelnut. Sometimes the terms "medallions" and "noisettes" are both used to describe small, boneless, tender cuts of meat.
- *Scallops*—thin, boneless cuts that are lightly pounded
- *Emincé* (eh-manss-AY)—thin strips of meat used for sautéing

Exhibit 8.7
Many beautiful and creative dishes come from boneless tenderloin cuts.

Other Meats

Historically, people needed to make full use of every part of the animals they raised for food. **Offal** (OH-fel) **meats** are organ meats from hogs, cattle, or sheep. They include **sweetbreads** (thymus glands), liver, kidney, *tripe,* (muscular stomach lining), heart, and brains. Though no longer very popular in this country, offal meats are great sources of essential vitamins and minerals.

Game meats are from animals that are not raised domestically. They include deer, wild boar, moose, and elk. Many distinctly different dishes are prepared with game meats. However, the same preparation guidelines for red meats apply to game meats.

Kosher meats are specially slaughtered to comply with Jewish dietary laws. In the United States, only beef and veal forequarters, poultry, and some game are used for kosher preparations.

Purchasing, Storing, and Preparing Poultry

Purchasing Poultry

Poultry includes chicken, duck, goose, guinea, squab, turkey, or any domesticated bird raised for the sole purpose of eating. Just as with meat, purchasing poultry depends on factors like storage, employee skills and equipment, and cost. Poultry can be purchased in many forms: fresh or frozen, whole or in pieces, de-boned or bone-in, or ground.

Like red meat, poultry undergoes mandatory government inspection for freshness and quality. The quality grades for poultry, from the highest to the lowest quality are:

- USDA A
- USDA B
- USDA C

Factors that determine grade are: shape of the carcass; ratio of meat to bone; amount of feathers, hair, and down; and number (if any) of cuts or broken bones.

Storing Poultry

All types of fresh poultry should be wrapped loosely and stored under refrigeration between 32°F and 36°F (0°C and 2.2°C) in a separate unit or in a separate part of the cooler. Since fresh poultry has a short shelf life, it should be cooked as soon as possible after it is received. Exhibit 8.8 on the next page shows the acceptable frozen and refrigerated storage periods for poultry.

To prevent cross-contamination, poultry should not come in contact with any other type of meat and should be placed on trays to prevent it from dripping on other foods or onto the floor.

Poultry is a standard menu item at most restaurants. Chicken and turkey are still the most popular types of poultry, however, customer demand is increasing for other birds. One change in menu offerings is the introduction of **free-range** poultry, which are raised in large yards and given a lot of

Exhibit 8.8
Proper storage guidelines for poultry.

Storing Frozen Poultry	**Store at 0°F (-18°C) or lower until ready to thaw**		
Whole chicken, turkey, duck, goose	12 months		
Giblets	3 months		
Cut-up cooked poultry	4 months		

Storing Refrigerated Poultry
Fresh poultry should be used within 2 days of receipt.

Whole chicken, turkey, duck, goose	32°F to 36°F/0°C to 2.2°C	1 to 2 days	Wrap loosely
Giblets	32°F to 36°F/0°C to 2.2°C	1 to 2 days	Wrap separate from bird
Stuffing	32°F to 36°F/0°C to 2.2°C	1 to 2 days	Covered container separate from bird
Cut-up cooked poultry	32°F to 36°F/0°C to 2.2°C	1 to 2 days	Cover

Exhibit 8.9
Quail is an example of a game bird.

space to roam and exercise their muscles. This makes the meat darker in color than other poultry, and gives the meat a slightly different flavor and texture.

Another change is the interest in game birds—wild birds such as partridge, pheasant, squab, duck, goose, and quail that are hunted for sport or food. Many game birds are now raised on farms year-round in conditions similar to those for free-range poultry. These birds are still considered "wild" and are at their best from October through December or January. They should have soft, smooth, pliable skin. The breastbone cartilage should be flexible, as it is for domestic fowl. The flesh should be tender, with a slightly "gamey" taste.

Poultry Fabrication

Domestic poultry is readily available and is less costly than most other meats. When poultry is fabricated, the chef can get the best quality for the best possible price. Also, the trim can be used for stocks, soups, sauces, hors d'oeuvres, and forcemeats. Poultry fabrication includes disjointing and **boning** (separating meat from bones), and cutting a bird into pieces. Fabricating poultry is easier than fabricating other meats because poultry bones are smaller and easier to cut through. Essential tools include a clean work surface, boning knife, and chef's knife.

Breaking down poultry into pieces is a useful technique for both small and large birds. The size of the cut depends on the size of the bird and the method of cooking. Exhibit 8.11 shows how to cut a whole bird into pieces.

Knowing how to disjoint and bone chicken breasts is also an important part of fabricating poultry. Exhibit 8.12 shows how to prepare boneless chicken breasts.

Not all birds are fabricated or cut into smaller pieces. Larger birds are often roasted whole and must be **trussed**—which means the legs and wings are tied to the bird's body—so the entire bird cooks evenly and stays moist.

Exhibit 8.10
The traditional Thanksgiving dinner is one of our favorite ways of eating poultry.

Remember the Steps for Sanitizing

1. Be sure all utensils and cutting boards are cleaned and sanitized before and after working with poultry.
2. Scrape and presoak items, then sort.
3. In the first sink, wash in clean, hot (at least 110°F to 120°F [43.3°C to 48.9°C]) detergent solution.
4. In the second sink, rinse in clear, hot (at least 110°F to 120°F [43.3°C to 48.9°C]), potable water.
5. In the third sink, sanitize items using either a chemical solution or hot water (171°F or 77°C) for 30 seconds. Use a dip basket to allow complete rinsing of items.
6. Air-dry all items. Do not towel dry.

1. Place chicken, breast side up, on a cutting board. Cut skin between thighs and body.

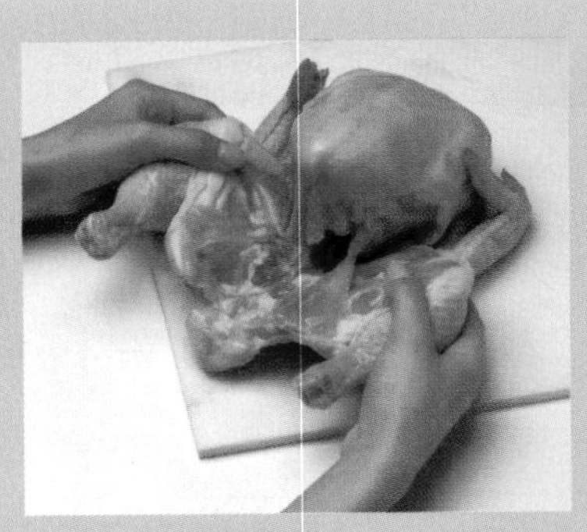

2. Grasping one leg in each hand, lift chicken and bend back legs until bones break at hip joints.

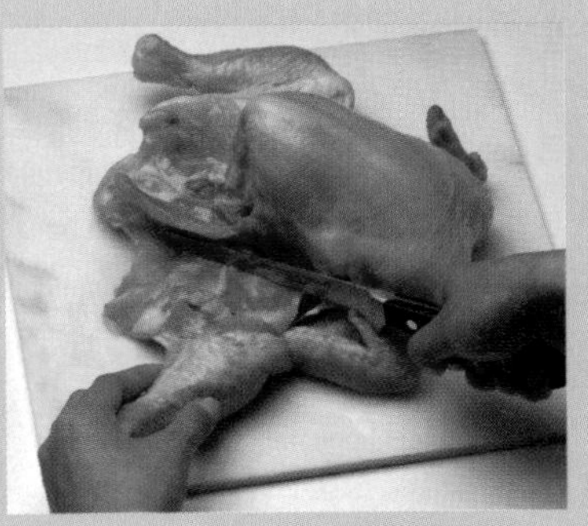

3. Remove leg and thigh from body by cutting (from tail toward shoulder) between the joints, close to bones in back of bird. Repeat for other side.

4. To separate thighs and drumsticks, locate knee joint by bending thigh and leg together. With skin side down, cut through joint of each leg.

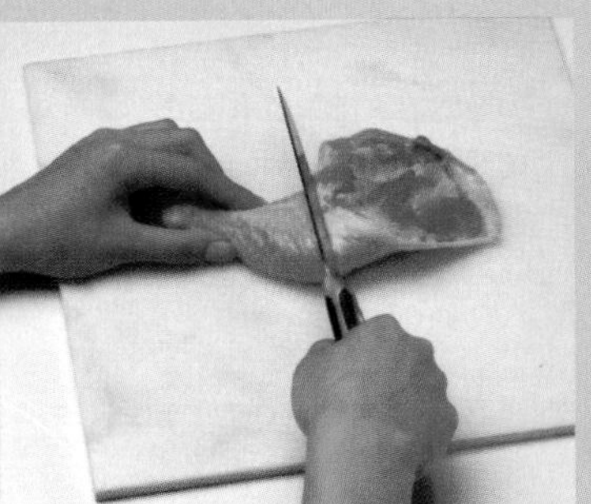

5. With chicken on back, remove wings by cutting inside of each wing just over joint. Pull wing away from body and cut from top down through joint.

6. Separate breast and back by placing chicken on neck end or back and cutting (toward board) through joints along each side of rib cage.

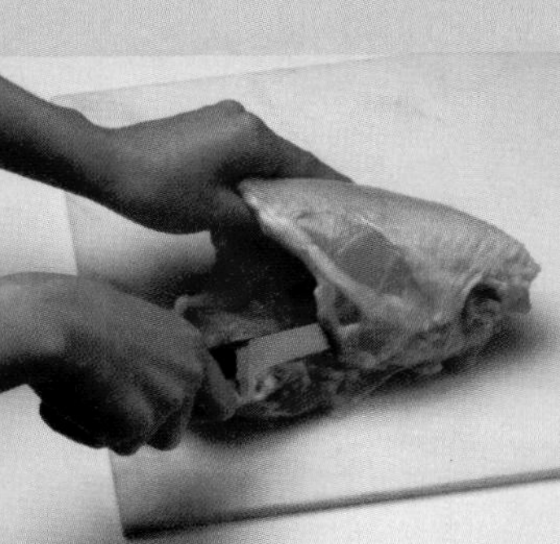

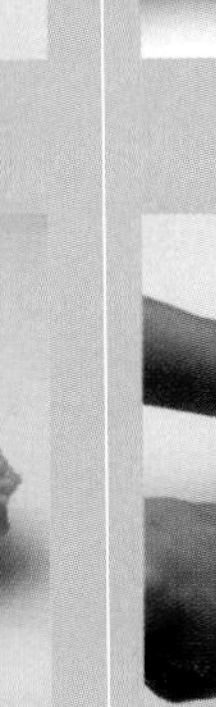

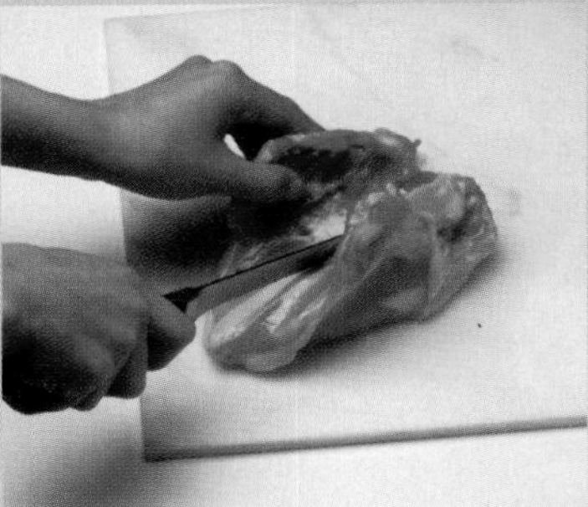

7. To cut breast into halves, place skin side down on board and cut wishbone in two at V of bone.

Exhibit 8.11
Cutting a whole bird into pieces.

Courtesy of Tyson Foods, Inc., Springdale, AR

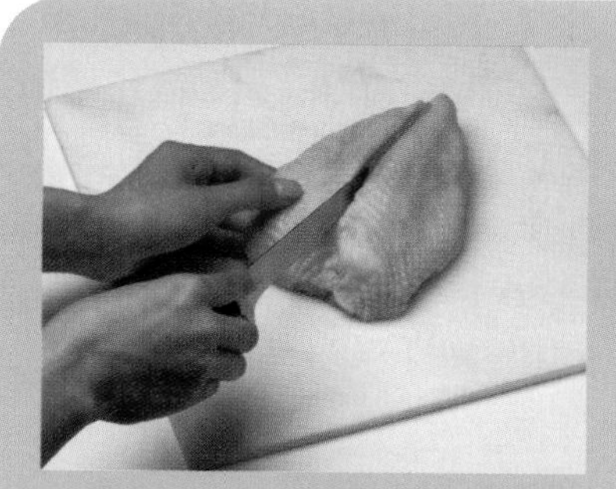

1. Place breast, skin side down, on cutting board with widest part nearest you. With point of knife, cut through white cartilage at neck end of keel bone.

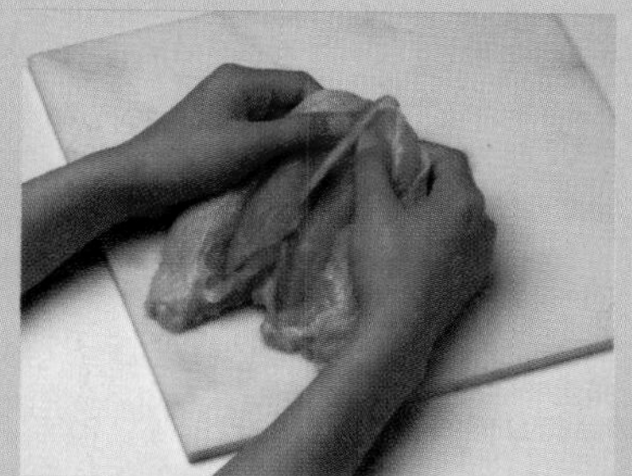

2. Pick up breast and bend back, exposing keel bone.

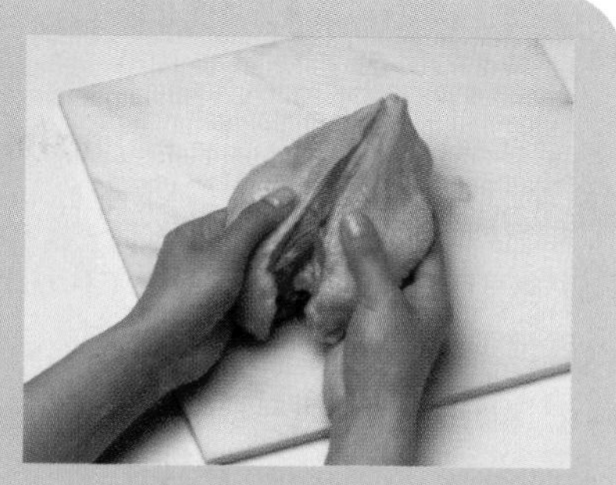

3. Loosen meat from bone by running thumbs around both sides; pull out bone and cartilage.

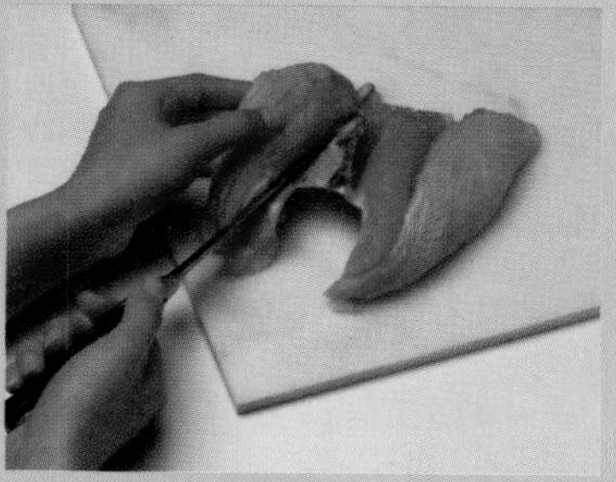

4. Working one side of breast, insert tip of knife under long rib bone inside thin membrane and cut or pull meat from rib cage. Turn breast and repeat on other side.

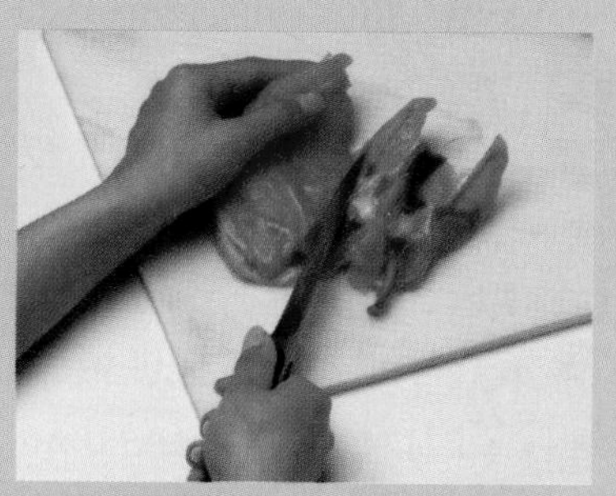

5. Working from ends of wishbone, scrape all flesh away and cut meat from bone. If white tendons remain on either side of breast, loosen with knife and pull out.

Exhibit 8.12
Preparing boneless chicken breasts.

Courtesy of Tyson Foods, Inc., Springdale, AR

The following sanitation rules must be strictly observed in poultry fabrication to prevent cross-contamination.

- Refrigerate poultry when it is not being fabricated.
- Never store uncooked poultry above cooked meats.
- Clean and sanitize the cutting board and all cutting utensils before and after fabrication.
- Store poultry in clean, leak-proof containers.

Purchasing, Storing, and Preparing Fish and Shellfish

Fresh fish and shellfish that are properly prepared and attractively presented can be extremely profitable menu items. They are also a popular appetizer choice. Fish and shellfish are delicate food items that must be purchased, stored, and handled carefully.

Purchasing Fish and Shellfish

As you learned in the previous chapter, fish and shellfish inspections are not required by the federal government. Instead, a voluntary fee-for-service program is available from the United States Department of Commerce (USDC). The Packed Under Federal Inspection (PUFI) stamp means that the product is safe, properly labeled, and has a reasonably good flavor. Because there are so many varieties of fish, only the most common types are graded. After passing the PUFI inspection, fish are given an A, B, or C grade. The top quality (A) products are used in foodservice operations, while B and C grades are usually canned or processed. Exhibit 8.15 shows the five market forms of fish.

Only the freshest, most flavorful fish should be purchased. Even if the product has been stamped for approval and graded, it is still important to check for freshness and quality because fish and shellfish are highly perishable. It's best if an operation can purchase only the amount of fish needed for one or two days. If daily deliveries are not possible, take precautions to ensure fish are fresh. Signs to look for when checking fish and shellfish for freshness and quality are:

- A fresh, clean, "sea" aroma
- Slick, moist skin
- Moist, fresh, flexible with full tail and fins
- Firm and elastic flesh
- Clear and full eyes, gills should have a red or maroon color
- Live crab and lobster should move about; clams, mussels and oysters should be tightly closed

Exhibit 8.13
Fresh fish should have clear, full eyes.

Most shellfish are purchased live and must be checked to make sure they are fresh when received. Shellfish with tightly closed shells indicate they are fresh. Reject any delivery containing open shells. To help ensure safety, the Food and Drug Administration (FDA) requires that all foodservice establishments keep dated shell stock tags from shellfish and crustaceans for 90 days.

There are two basic categories of fish: fin fish and shellfish. Subcategories include flat and round fin fish, and shellfish that are either mollusks or crustaceans. Within these broad categories are many unique kinds of fish and shellfish with a wide range of flavors and textures.

Exhibit 8.14
Classifications and varieties of fin fish and shellfish.

CLASSIFICATION	VARIETIES
Flat	Flounder, sole, halibut
Round	Black sea bass, cod, grouper, haddock, monkfish, ocean perch, red snapper, striped bass, whiting bluefish, mackerel, pompano, salmon, shark, swordfish, tuna, perch, pike, catfish, trout, whitefish
Mollusk	Oysters, clams, mussels
Crustacean	Loster, shrimp, crab

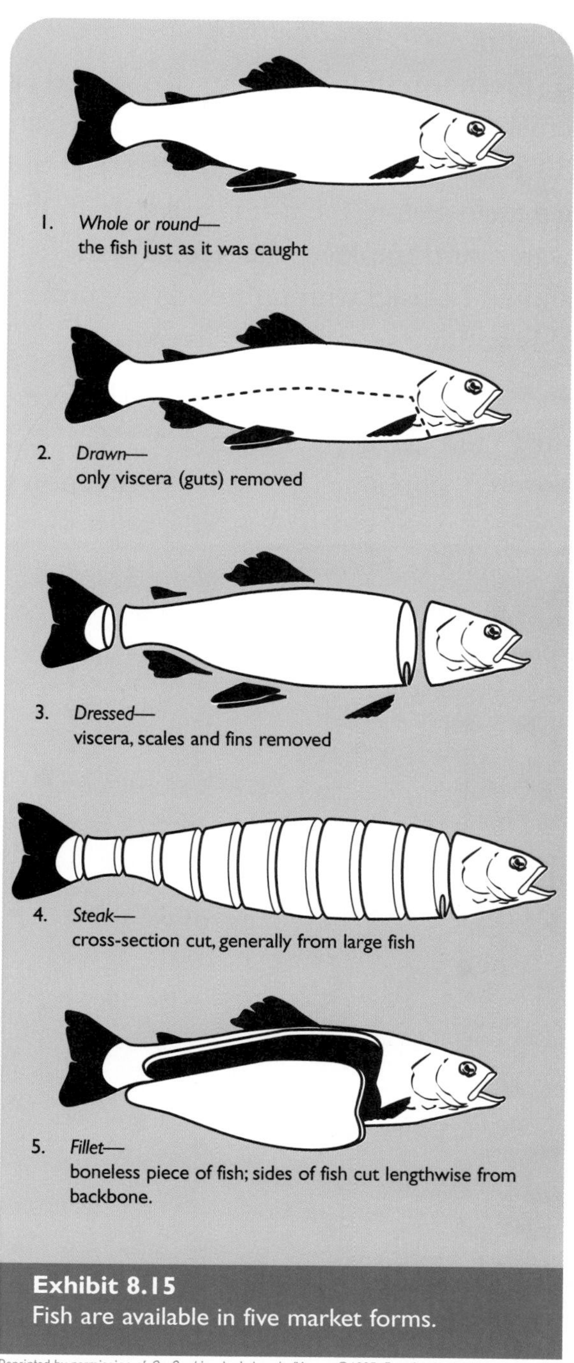

Exhibit 8.15
Fish are available in five market forms.

Storing Fish and Shellfish

Fresh fish should be stored in shaved or crushed ice in a refrigerated unit between 30°F and 34°F (-1.1°C and 1.1°C). If the ice melts before the fish is used, drain the water and replace the ice. Fresh fish should be used within three days—preferably within one day—of delivery.

Exhibit 8.17
Salmon is an example of a round fish.

Fresh shellfish should be stored between 30°F and 34°F (-1.1°C and 1.1°C) in a covered container. Exhibit 8.16 shows preferable temperature and storage periods for fresh and frozen fish and shellfish.

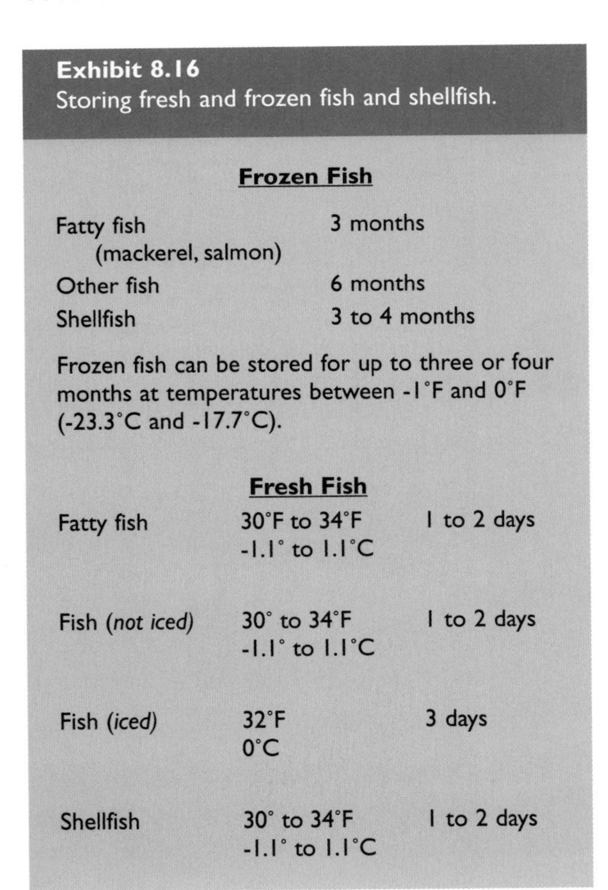

Exhibit 8.16
Storing fresh and frozen fish and shellfish.

Frozen Fish

Fatty fish (mackerel, salmon)	3 months
Other fish	6 months
Shellfish	3 to 4 months

Frozen fish can be stored for up to three or four months at temperatures between -1°F and 0°F (-23.3°C and -17.7°C).

Fresh Fish

Fatty fish	30°F to 34°F -1.1° to 1.1°C	1 to 2 days
Fish (*not iced*)	30° to 34°F -1.1° to 1.1°C	1 to 2 days
Fish (*iced*)	32°F 0°C	3 days
Shellfish	30° to 34°F -1.1° to 1.1°C	1 to 2 days

Fabricating Fish and Shellfish

When fin fish are fabricated, much of the trim can be put to use in a mousseline, filling, canapé, soup, or sauce. Fish fabrication techniques consist of scaling, trimming, gutting, and filleting the fish. Scaling methods are the same for both round and flat fish, but the way you gut and fillet them is slightly different. The tools needed for fish fabrication are a sharp, flexible filleting knife and a clean cutting board.

When **scaling** fish, the scales are scraped off of their skin, usually working from the head to the tail. Once the fish has been scaled and trimmed, it should be gutted.

When **gutting** round fish, a slit is made in the fish's belly and the guts, or insides, are pulled out. Gutting a flat fish is a bit easier. The cuts are made around the head. As the head is pulled away from the body, the guts come away with the head.

Filleting a fish is the step that separates the flesh of the fish from the bones. Flat fish will produce four fillets, while round fish will produce two fillets. It is important to remove all of the bones from the fillet. Exhibit 8.18 shows how to fillet salmon, a round fish.

Once the fish has been filleted, it can be made into various cuts, such as **goujonettes** (goo-sha-NET) or small strips; or **paupiettes** (po-pee-EHT), thin, rolled fillets filled with stuffing; or steaks.

Mollusks and Crustaceans

Unlike fin fish, shellfish do not have bones or a skeletal system. However, they

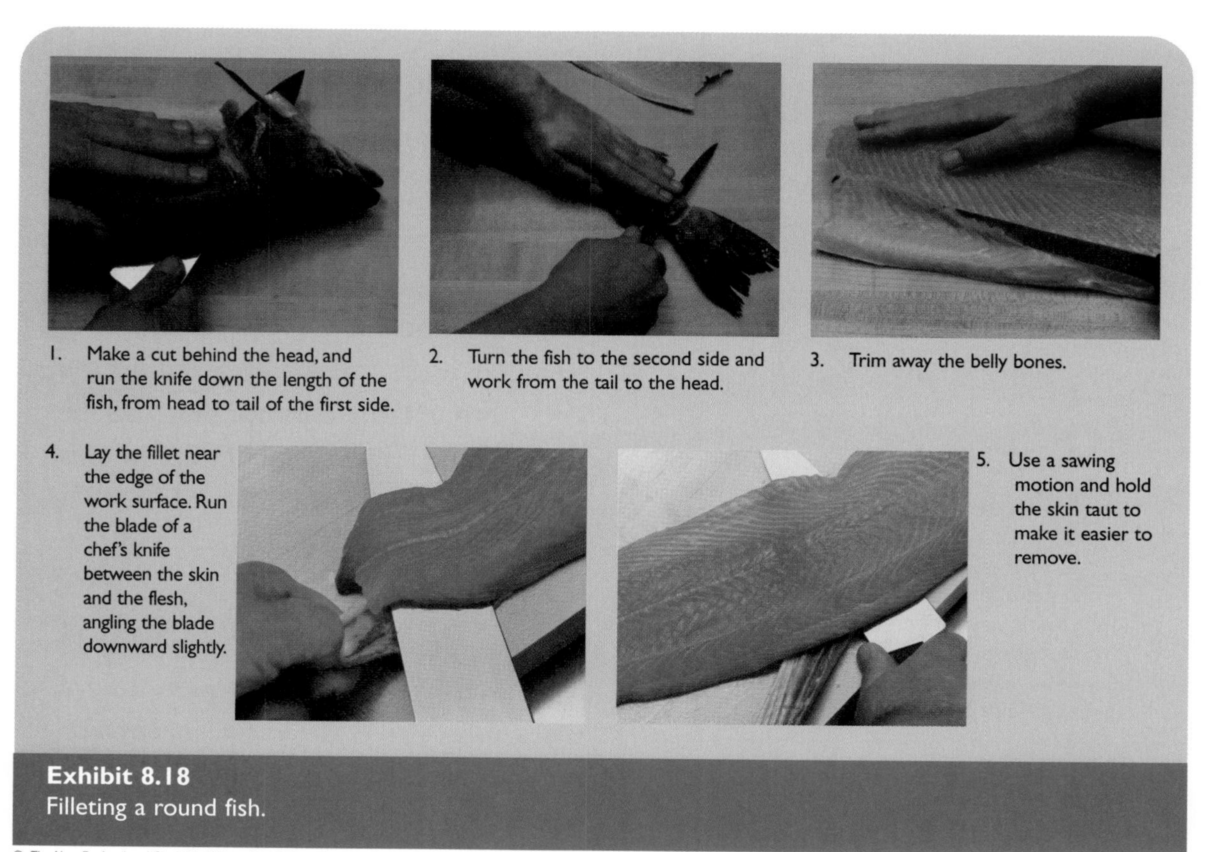

1. Make a cut behind the head, and run the knife down the length of the fish, from head to tail of the first side.
2. Turn the fish to the second side and work from the tail to the head.
3. Trim away the belly bones.
4. Lay the fillet near the edge of the work surface. Run the blade of a chef's knife between the skin and the flesh, angling the blade downward slightly.
5. Use a sawing motion and hold the skin taut to make it easier to remove.

Exhibit 8.18
Filleting a round fish.

do need to be fabricated. There are two classifications of shellfish: mollusks and crustaceans. **Mollusks** are shellfish characterized by a soft, unsegmented body, no internal skeleton, and a hard outer shell, such as clams, oysters, and mussels. **Crustaceans** have segmented shells and jointed legs. Examples include lobster and shrimp.

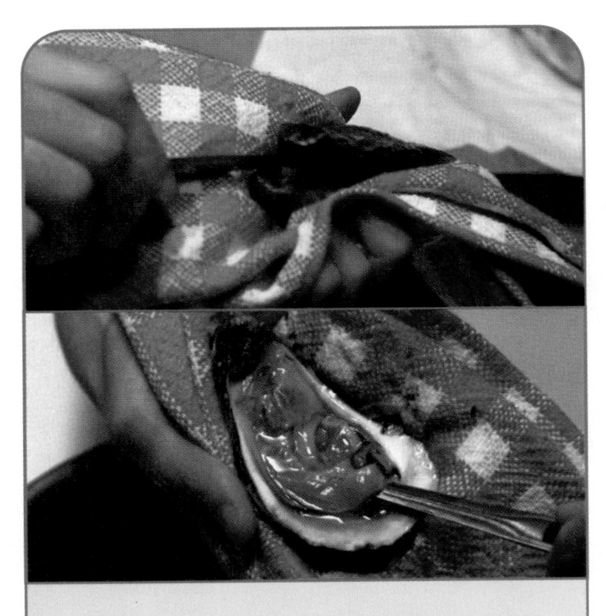

1. Secure oysters for easier handling. Hold the oyster, flatter shell up, with a folded towel and place the tip of the knife near the hinge at the pointed end. Pry and push the tip to bore into the shell until it pops open.
2. Make oysters easier to eat. Run the knife along the inside of the shell and loosen any meat that still clings to it.

Exhibit 8.19
How to shuck oysters.

Courtesy of *Fine Cooking* magazine.

Since clams and oysters are often served on the half shell, it's important not to destroy the shell when they are **shucked,** or removed from the shell. All mollusks should be scrubbed well with a brush under cold running water before being opened. Exhibit 8.19 shows how to shuck an oyster.

When working with lobster, it is easier to remove the meat from the shell when the lobster has been partially or fully cooked. Blanching the lobster lightly in a steam bath, in boiling water, or in a hot oven is all that is necessary to make the flesh easy to remove from the shell.

Shrimp are cleaned by removing the shell and deveining them. **Deveining** is the process of removing a shrimp's digestive tract. Shrimp that has been boiled or steamed in its shell will be more moist and plump than shrimp that has been peeled and deveined before cooking. Exhibit 8.20 shows how to peel and devein shrimp.

More exotic seafood, such as sea urchins, squid, octopus, and eel, have special fabrication techniques. In some cases, protective gloves are necessary to prevent cuts from spiny shells.

Exhibit 8.20
Peeling and deveining shrimp.

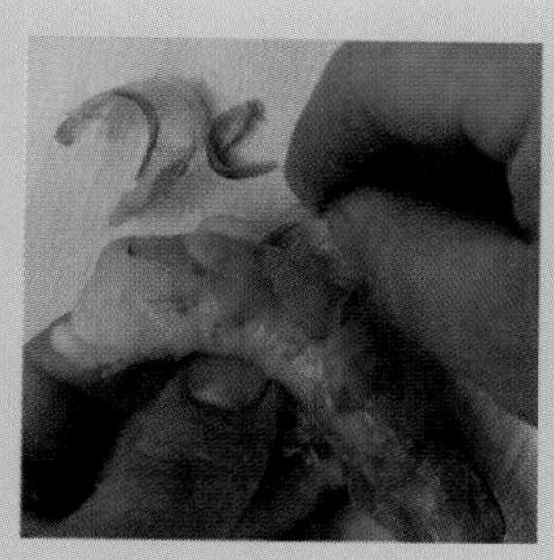
1. Pull away the shell.

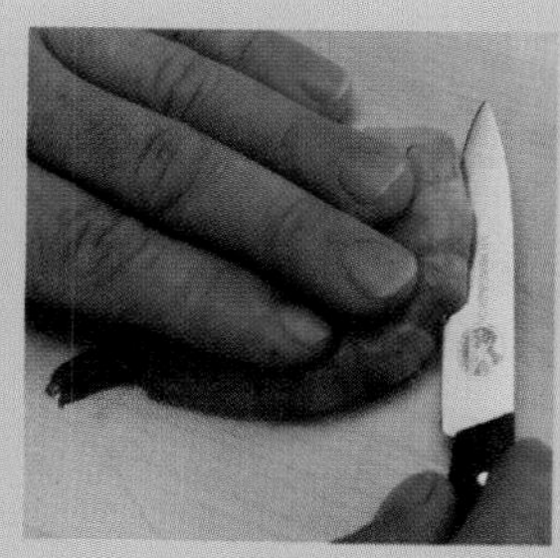
2. Cut along the back vein.

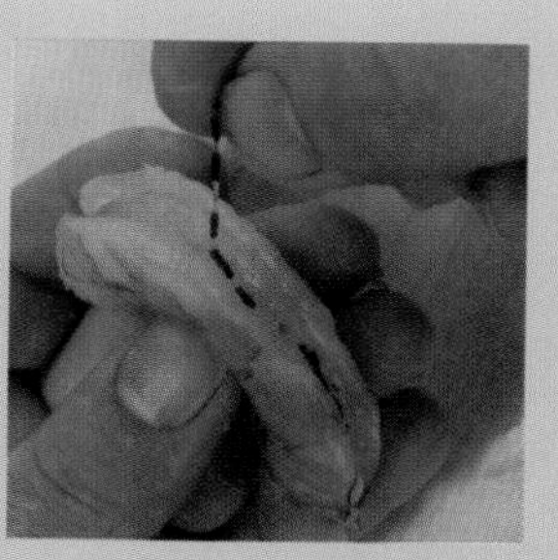
3. Remove the intestinal tract.

Review Your Learning 8.1

Match the term on the left with its description on the right.

1. Fabrication	a. Small, round pieces of meat molded by wrapping in cheesecloth
2. Silverskin	b. Little "nuts" of meat
3. Aging	c. Sheep slaughtered after the age of 1 year
4. Yield grade	d. Working with primal cuts of meat to customize them
5. Veal	e. Cattle that are butchered from the age of 1 day up to 15 weeks
6. Mutton	f. The amount of usable meat after the fat has been trimmed
7. Primal cuts	g. Gives meat a darker color and also makes it more expensive
8. Retail cuts	h. Tough membrane on meat
9. Medallions	j. Leg, loin, rib, and shoulder cuts
10. Noisettes	k. Cuts ready for sale

11. Why is it necessary to tie a roast?

8.2

SECTION 8.2

Cooking Meat, Poultry and Seafood

AFTER STUDYING SECTION 8.2, YOU SHOULD BE ABLE TO:

- Match various cooking methods with different forms of meat, poultry, and seafood.

KEY TERMS

- À point
- Au jus (aw ZHEW)
- Bard
- Bouillabaisse (BOO-ya-base)
- Carryover cooking
- Collagen
- Connective tissue
- Court bouillon (cort boo-YON)
- Deglazing
- Elastin
- En papillote (on paw-pee-YOTE)
- Fumet (foo-MAY)
- Jambalaya (jam-bo-LIE-ah)
- Jus (zhew)
- Jus lié (zhew lee-AY)
- Marbling
- Marinade
- Mirepoix (meer-PWAH)
- Opaque (oh-PAKE)
- Pan gravy
- Seafood Newburg
- Searing
- Trichinosis

Cooking Meats

In *Chapter 4: Kitchen Basics* of *Becoming a Foodservice Professional, Year 1,* you were introduced to the various techniques used to cook foods. Before a chef can determine the right cooking method for a cut of meat, it is necessary to understand the physical composition of the muscle tissue and how it is affected by heat. A good cook must also be aware of the numerous flavorings that can be added when cooking meats.

Meat Composition

Muscle tissue consists of about 75% water, 20% protein, and 5% fat, and is made up of a network of muscle fibers bound together in bundles. Each of the fibers is surrounded by connective tissue. There are two types of **connective tissue:** collagen and elastin. **Collagen** breaks down during long, slow, moist heat cooking, while **elastin** will not break down during cooking and thus needs to be trimmed by hand. You were introduced to this concept in the previous section when you learned how to trim silverskin off of a terderloin.

Exhibit 8.21
Marbling is what makes a steak juicy.

The amount of connective tissue in a muscle increases as the animal ages and the more the animal is exercised. This makes the meat tougher but also more flavorful. Cuts of meat taken from the shoulder and flanks are examples of cuts that have a lot of connective tissue. The tissue that connects the meat to the bone is made of elastin, or gristle, which should be trimmed away before cooking.

The most tender cuts of meat come from those muscle groups that receive the least amount of exercise. They also have more **marbling,** or fat that builds up between the muscle fibers. Tenderloins and roasts from the sirloin are naturally more juicy, because they contain more marbling.

Flavor, Tenderness, and Moisture

The chef's goal while cooking meat is to maximize flavor and tenderness while minimizing the loss of moisture. As heat molecules attack the meat during cooking, the collagen breaks down into gelatin and water. This reduction in collagen increases the tenderness of the meat but at the same time, the loss of moisture dries it out. A tough cut of meat cooked too quickly will still be too tough to serve when done.

Moist-heat methods are generally slower and allow a large amount of collagen to break down while the added water or stock in the pan returns moisture to the roast.

Because the most tender cuts are the most expensive, cooking them in a slow, moist-heat method is not cost efficient since a cheaper cut of meat would produce a quality product and actually offer more flavor. That is why dry-heat methods, which quickly cook meats, are best for naturally tender cuts.

A number of techniques have been developed to impart additional flavor while reducing moisture loss during cooking. Possibly one of the most popular methods is to soak the raw meat in a **marinade**—a liquid made of oil, an acid such as vinegar or wine, and herbs and spices. The acid in the marinade breaks down the collagen along the surface of the meat and allows the flavoring from the aromatics to enter. While marinating, the meat must be refrigerated and turned on occasion to equally distribute the marinade. This method will not turn a tough piece of meat into a tenderloin, but it will improve the flavor of the cooked meat.

Another method used to impart additional flavor is called a dry marinade or spice rub. This is a combination of dry herbs, spices, and salt that will give the exterior of the meat an attractive look and flavorful taste. Caution must be used because the salt, while breaking down the surface structure, also pulls moisture from the meat.

Game meats have much less fat in their muscles than domesticated animals. It may be necessary to **bard** a roast by tying a layer of fat (bacon or pork fatback) around meat and poultry that have little or no natural fat cover, in order to protect and moisten them during cooking. This technique is also used on leaner roasts, such as veal tenderloin.

Exhibit 8.22 lists various cuts of meat and the appropriate methods of cooking them.

Dry-heat Cooking

Meats best suited to the dry-heat cooking methods of broiling and grilling are those that are tender and have enough fat to keep them moist. It is very important to master these two basic cooking techniques. Exhibit 8.24 illustrates how grilled entrées are the most popular menu item today. Examples of recipes using broiling and grilling include shish kebabs and lamb chops.

Meats to be roasted should be tender cuts from the rib or tenderloin. Most of the visible fat should be trimmed to ensure even cooking. While it was once believed that **searing,** or quickly browning the

Exhibit 8.22
Meat cooking guide.

Dry Heat (baking, broiling, grilling, roasting)

Beef	Offal	Lamb	Fresh Pork	Smoked Pork	Veal
Loaf (ground beef)	Liver	Lamb rack	Boston butt	Canadian-style bacon	Chops
Loin strip		Leg	Chops	Loaf (ground ham)	Cutlets (leg)
Outside (bottom) round		Loaf (ground lamb)	Ham (leg)	Ham	Loaf (ground veal)
Rib		Loin	Loin	Shoulder butt	Loin
Round		Rolled shoulder	Rolled shoulder		Rib
Rump butt					Rolled shoulder
Sirloin butt					
Tenderloin					

Moist Heat (simmering, boiling, and combination cooking [braising and stewing])

Beef	Lamb	Fresh Pork	Veal	Offal
Brisket	Breast	Feet	Breast	Kidney
Chuck (all cuts)	Neck	Fresh ham steaks	Leg (round)	Tripe
Flank	Shank	Hocks	Neck	
Heel of round	Shoulder	Picnic	Shoulder	
Neck		Spareribs	Shank	
Ox tails (joint)				
Plate				
Rump butt				
Shank				
Short ribs				
Shoulder clod				
Skirt steak				

surface of the meat over high heat, before roasting would seal in juices, this has been proven untrue. However, searing meat does caramelize the outside of the meat and improve the flavor and appearance of the finished product. A roast can also be seasoned before cooking by marinating, barding, or stuffing.

To cook, the roast should sit uncovered on an elevated rack inside a pan to ensure even cooking. To test for doneness, insert a bi-metallic stemmed instant-reading thermometer at an angle into the thickest part of the meat at any time during the cooking process. Roast meat uncovered until the proper internal temperature is

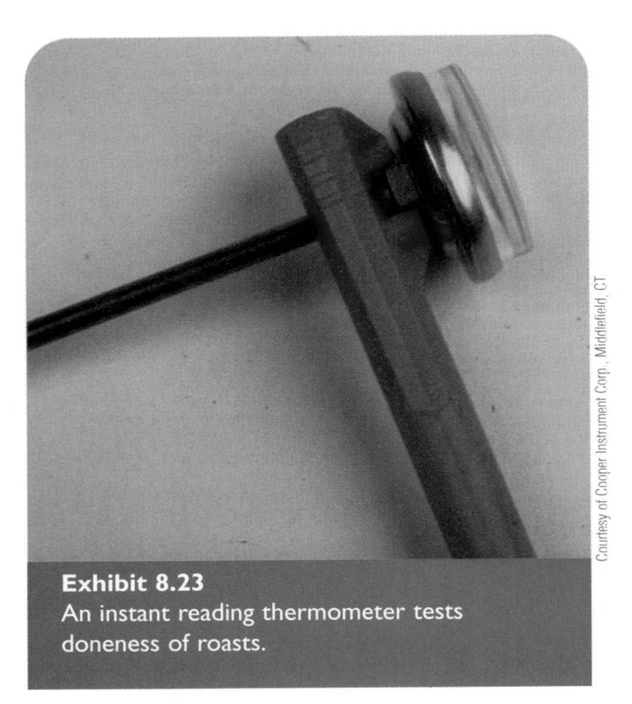

Exhibit 8.23
An instant reading thermometer tests doneness of roasts.

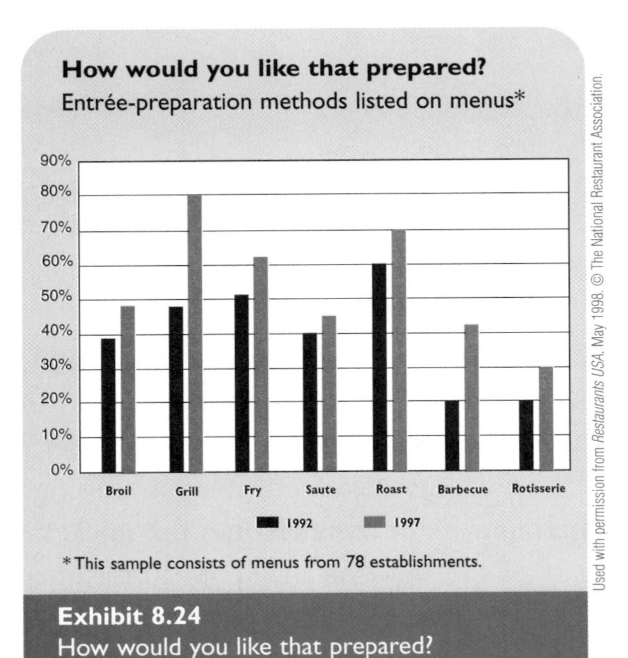

Exhibit 8.24
How would you like that prepared?

reached. Degrees of doneness and internal temperatures are discussed later in this section.

A **mirepoix** (meer-PWAH), a combination of chopped aromatic vegetables—usually two parts onion, one part carrot, and one part celery, can be added to the roasting pan during the final half hour of roasting time to add flavor to the gravy. When finished, the roast should have a golden-brown exterior and an interior that is tender and moist.

Jus (zhew) is a sauce that incorporates drippings released during roasting. Jus is made by deglazing the roasting pan with brown stock or water. **Deglazing** means to swirl a liquid in a pan to dissolve cooked particles or food remaining on the bottom. Foods served with this juice are said to be served **au jus** (aw ZHEW), for example, roast beef au jus. When the jus from the drippings is thickened with arrowroot or cornstarch, it is known as **jus lié** (zhew lee-AY). If a sauce is thickened with a roux incorporating the fat from a roast and additional water or stock, it is called **pan gravy.** Roux will be discussed in greater detail in *Chapter 10: Stocks, Soups, and Sauces.*

Heat retained in cooked foods that allows continued cooking even after the

Exhibit 8.25
Grilled meats are a very popular menu item.

item is removed from the oven is called **carryover cooking.** The larger the item, the greater the amount of heat it will retain. For example, the temperature of a top round of beef may increase as much as 15 degrees.

Dry-heat Cooking with Fats and Oils

Another way to prepare meat is to use dry-heat cooking methods with fats and oils. These methods include sautéing, stir-frying, pan-frying, and deep-frying. Sautéing and stir-frying use a small amount of oil; pan-frying uses a larger amount of oil and a coating. These methods cook meat quickly, use high heat, and require tender, portion-sized or smaller pieces of meat.

Sautéed meats are served with a sauce that is prepared while the food is cooking, or by deglazing the pan after cooking. The sauce is an important element because it contains the food's flavor lost during cooking, introduces additional flavor, and adds moisture. If meat strips are to be sautéed, lightly dust them with flour, and be sure to shake off any excess flour before adding the item to the pan. Flour will help the meat retain moisture and will promote even browning. Beef stroganoff is an example of preparing meat by sautéing.

Meats that are stir-fried are cut into small pieces, with all fat, gristle, or silverskin removed. In stir-frying, food is cooked over very high heat, using little fat or cooking oil. Stir-fried meats should be moist and tender. An example is stir-fried beef with vegetables.

Moist-heat Cooking

Moist-heat cooking techniques produce foods that are delicately flavored and moist with a rich broth. Tougher cuts of meat can be poached, simmered, or boiled. An entire boiled dinner, complete with vegetables and meat, can be cooked in one pot. A New England boiled dinner is one example using the boiling method. Yankee pot roast is an example of cooking with the simmering method.

New Englanders made the boiled dinner so popular that it is named after that region. New Englanders relied on boiled fish dinners, clam bakes, baked beans, succotash, and converted an American Indian pudding into pumpkin pie as a real specialty.

Combination Cooking

The combination cooking methods—braising and stewing—use both dry and moist heat to cook foods that are not very tender. The meat is first seared in hot oil, then slowly cooked with a small amount of liquid in the oven or on the stove. Stewing is very much like braising, except the meat, or other major ingredient, is cut into bite-sized pieces before it is seared.

Determining Doneness

One of the most important steps in cooking meat is determining the doneness. Beef, lamb, and some game meats may be cooked to a wide range of doneness. When cooking beef roasts, the roast is rare when the internal temperature is 130°F (54.4°C). The meat will appear red inside with a thin layer of brown on the outside. At an internal temperature of 140°F to 145°F (60°C to 62.6°C), the roast is medium. The meat will be pink inside with a well-browned surface. The surface of meat cooked to medium is firmer than rare meat. Well-done meat is completely cooked, leaving little or no juice. The cooked surface of the meat is firm and dry, and the internal temperature is 160°F (71.1°). In general, as meat cooks, the exterior should develop a deep brown color. Allow roasts to rest for 15-30 minutes after removing from the oven. This allows less juice to be lost during carving.

White meats, such as veal and pork, should be cooked all the way through but not overcooked. There should be a slight "give" when the meat is pressed with the back of a fork. Care must be taken with thin pieces of meat because they retain heat easily and continue cooking even after they have been removed from the heat source.

As white meat cooks, the meat changes from pink to white or off-white. The meat is generally cooked well done, although many cuts of veal may be considered

Exhibit 8.26
A roast cooked to medium that has rested before carving.

done while still slightly pink in the center. Pork must be cooked long enough to eliminate the danger of **trichinosis**, a disease caused by a parasite that lives in muscle tissue. The United States Food and Drug Administration recommends cooking pork products to an internal temperature of 150°F (66°C).

Cooking Poultry

Dry-heat Cooking

Poultry is especially suited to the dry-heat cooking techniques of grilling, broiling, and roasting. When grilling poultry, it should be cooked through or **à point**, but not overcooked. There should be a slight amount of "give" when the meat is pressed with the back of a fork. Any juices should be colorless. The grilled flavor and aroma should enhance the food, not overpower its natural flavor. One example of chicken prepared using this method is mesquite-grilled chicken breast.

Roasting requires a longer cooking time because this technique is used to cook the whole bird. The bird can be seasoned, stuffed, marinated, barded, and/or seared over direct heat or in a hot oven before roasting. It should then be placed on an elevated rack in a roasting pan so that hot air can reach all sides. Roast the bird uncovered until the desired internal temperature is reached.

Poultry must be cooked until well done (150° to 165°F, or 65.6°C to 73.9°C) to kill all traces of salmonella. Dressing and stuffing for poultry should be baked separately for food safety; however, small birds (Cornish hens and quail) can be stuffed and served as single portions. All sanitation steps must be followed to avoid bacterial growth. The skin should be crisp, creating a contrast with the meat's texture. Roasted herb chicken with natural gravy is one example of using the roasting cooking method.

Dry-heat Cooking with Fats and Oils

Poultry is especially well-suited to dry-heat cooking with fats and oils. These techniques—sautéing, stir-frying, pan-frying, and deep-frying, require tender, portion-size pieces.

Chicken can be combined with a variety of vegetables and other foods to create a tasty stir-fry dish. Marinated chicken should be patted dry before adding it to the cooking oil. One example of using this technique is stir-fried chicken with fresh vegetables and peapods.

One of the most traditional methods for preparing chicken is deep-frying. Chicken that is deep-fried must be naturally tender. Foods prepared by deep-frying are breaded or batter-coated and then boiled in hot fat or oil. The result is a tasty combination of flavors and textures. Always observe sanitation guidelines when you are working with batters.

Moist-heat Cooking

Steaming is a healthy way to prepare poultry because nutrients are not washed, or drawn out of the food during cooking. Steamed poultry is done when it has an evenly **opaque** (oh-PAKE) appearance, which means you should not be able to see through it when done. Also, the flesh offers little resistance when pressed.

Exhibit 8.27
Poultry to be pan fried must be naturally tender.

Simmering and poaching are also excellent ways to prepare chicken. Simmered chicken has a rich, flavorful broth and can be used for soups, creamed dishes, casseroles, and salads.

Combination Cooking

Chicken is a natural ingredient for the combination cooking methods of stewing and braising. These two methods produce dishes with exceptional sauces and flavor concentrations. In addition, these are very healthy choices because the proteins and other nutrients lost from other cooking techniques are retained in the sauce. Mole poblano is one example of poultry prepared with moist-heat cooking.

Cooking Fish and Seafood

Choosing the Right Cooking Method

How can you select the right cooking method for fish? The best way to pair a fish with a cooking technique is to consider the flesh of the fish. For example, mackerel, (an oily fish), cooks best with a dry-heat technique, such as grilling or broiling. Tuna and salmon, which contain a moderate amount of fat, can be prepared using any cooking method. Very lean fish, such as sole and flounder, have the most flavor when they are poached or sautéed.

Dry-heat Cooking

Fatty fish cut into fillets or steaks are the best cuts to bake, broil, and grill. Most fish are baked between 350°F and 400°F (176.7°C and 204.4°C). Larger fish should be baked at the low end of this range so they cook evenly. To retain moistness, fish can be coated with bread crumbs and baked on an oiled or buttered baking sheet.

Dry-heat Cooking with Fats and Oils

Lean fish and shellfish are best when using dry-heat cooking with fats and oils, such as sautéing, stir-frying, pan-frying, and deep-frying. Fish or shellfish should be coated with flour or a breading before cooking in either clarified butter or oil. Small items, such as shrimp and scallops, are extremely delicate and must be quickly sautéed, stir-fried, or pan-fried over very high heat. Larger items require lower heat for even cooking.

When deep-frying, the fish should be very fresh, the fat used to deep-fry should be of high quality, and the item should be served immediately after cooking. Breading the fish before cooking will protect it from the hot fat and provide a crispy coating. Again, it is necessary to follow sanitation rules when working with the batter.

Moist-heat Cooking

Moist-heat cooking techniques—poaching, simmering, and steaming—are excellent ways to cook fish, especially the

Exhibit 8.28
Shrimp should be sautéed in very little oil.

lean varieties. To enhance the flavor of the fish it is often poached in **court bouillon** (cort boo-YON), a stock made of vegetables and an acid such as vinegar or wine. Fish can also be poached in **fumet** (foo-MAY), a rich fish stock made with wine, or it can be simmered in its own juices with a little added liquid.

Shallow-poached fish and shellfish should be opaque. The flesh of oysters, clams, and mussels should show curling on the edges. There should be no white deposits on the flesh of fin fish or shellfish. The finished item should be moist and extremely tender. Any stringiness, dryness, or excessive flaking indicates that the food was cooked too long or at too high a temperature.

En papillote (en paw-pee-YOTE) is one moist-heat cooking technique that is especially suited to fish. In this cooking method, the fish, herbs, vegetables, and/or sauce are encased in parchment paper and steamed in a hot oven. Fish cooked en papillote should be naturally tender. Thicker cuts of fish should first be seared to ensure even cooking.

Example 8.29
Fish served en papillote.

Combination Cooking

Stewing and braising have produced some very popular fish recipes over the years. Some of the best known recipes include **bouillabaisse** (BOO-ya-base), a French seafood stew made with assorted fish and shellfish, onions, tomatoes, white wine, olive oil, garlic, saffron and herbs; **jambalaya** (jam-bo-LIE-ah), a Creole stew from Louisiana made with rice, shellfish, and vegetables, and **Seafood Newburg,** which is lobster, crab, or shrimp in a rich sauce made from butter, cream, egg yolks, sherry, and seasonings.

Review Your Learning 8.2

Identify the cooking techniques below as **A** (dry-heat), **B** (dry-heat cooking with fats), **C** (moist heat), or **D** (combination cooking).

1. Grilling
2. Sautéing
3. Stewing
4. Poaching
5. Braising
6. Stir-frying
7. Broiling
8. Simmering

9. Marinating meats helps to improve the:
   a. age of the beef.
   b. flavor and texture of the meat.
   c. time needed to cook the meat.
   d. exterior appearance of the cooked meat, giving it a darker color.

10. Large birds are often trussed because:
   a. they can easily fit into a roasting pan.
   b. the entire bird cooks evenly and stays moist.
   c. they don't have enough natural fat cover.
   d. it will eliminate the danger of trichinosis.

12. A technique often used with game birds before roasting is:
   a. trimming.
   b. barding.
   c. butterflying.
   d. tying.

13. Roasting requires longer cooking times because:
   a. this method cooks the whole bird.
   b. the oven takes time to reach the desired temperature.
   c. the cooking temeprature is 200°F.
   d. a small amount of fat is used.

14. Bring in your family's favorite meat, chicken, or fish recipe. How long has the recipe been in your family? Where did it come from? What cooking methods are used?

8.3

SECTION 8.3

Charcuterie and Garde-manger

AFTER STUDYING SECTION 8.3, YOU SHOULD BE ABLE TO:

- Identify and describe different types of charcuterie.
- Explain garde-manger and how it relates to charcuterie.

The term **charcuterie,** which in French means "cooked flesh," refers to specially prepared pork products including sausages, smoked hams, bacon, pâtés, and terrines. **Garde-manger** (gard mawn-ZHAY) refers to a kitchen's pantry section where these cold foods are stored and the work area where they are prepared.

Sausages

Traditionally, sausages were ground pork, forced into a casing made from the lining of animal intestines. Today, many

KEY TERMS

- Charcuterie
- Country-style forcemeat
- Emulsified
- Forcemeat
- Galantine (GAL-en-teen)
- Garde-manger (gard mawn-ZHAY)
- Mousseline (moose-uh-LEEN)
- Pâté (pah-TAY)
- Pâté de campagne (pah-TAY de kom-PAN-yuh)
- Pâté en croûte (pah-TAY on kroot)
- Quenelle (kuh-NEL)
- Straight forcemeat
- Terrine (tehr-REEN)

other ingredients are used to make sausages including game, beef, veal, poultry, fish, shellfish, and even vegetables.

There are three main types of sausages: fresh sausages, smoked or cooked sausages, and dried or hard sausages. Fresh sausages are made with raw ingredients that have not been cured or smoked, and must be cooked before serving. *Fresh sausages* include breakfast sausage links and Italian sausages. Polish kielbasa, Mexican chorizo, and French andouille are other examples of fresh sausages.

Exhibit 8.30
There are many types of sausages.

FUN FOOD FACT

Although Germans and other Europeans have eaten sausages wrapped in bread for hundreds of years, the traditional American hot dog was born in St. Louis in 1904. Anton Feuchtwanger, a Bavarian immigrant, originally sold his little sausages from a cart and provided his customers with gloves to hold the hot sausages. When the gloves proved too expensive to give away, Feuchtwanger decided to place the sausages in long, sliced rolls. The name "hot dog" probably derives from the frankfurter's (sausage originating in Frankfurt) and wiener's (a sausage originating in Vienna, or Wein) resemblance to a Dachshund, the small, skinny German dog.

Smoked and *cooked sausages* are made with raw meat products treated with preservatives. German knackwurst, frankfurter, and bratwurst, are examples of smoked and cooked sausages.

Dried or *hard sausages* are made with cured meats, then air-dried under sanitary, controlled conditions. Italian salami and pepperoni are examples of dried or hard sausages.

Forcemeats

A **forcemeat** is a mixture of lean ground meat and fat that is **emulsified,** or forced to combine, in a food grinder and then pushed through a sieve to create a very smooth paste. How did forcemeats get their name? The word forcemeat is from the French word *farce,* which means stuffing. Forecemeats are the main ingredient used to make **pâté** (pah-TAY), a rich loaf made of meat, game, poultry, seafood, and/or vegetables, baked in a mold.

Straight forcemeats are very finely ground, seasoned with herbs and spices, and then cooked in an earthenware mold called a **terrine** (tehr-REEN). The terrine should be cooked in a hot-water bath to an internal temperature of 140°F to 150°F (60°C to 65.6°C). In a **country-style forcemeat,** or **pâté de campagne** (pah-TAY de kom-PAN-yuh), a cured meat is usually the main ingredient. The texture is slightly coarser than in a straight forcemeat, which allows the flavor of the meat to dominate.

Sometimes the forcemeat is wrapped in a paté dough that may contain herbs, spices, or lemon zest. A pâté dough is much stronger than pie dough because it must stand up to the liquid released during cooking. This dish is referred to as a **pâté en croûte** (pah-TAY on kroot).

Inventive chefs have created new recipes, such as Spring Vegetable Terrine, that no longer require meats, but because they are cooked in the same mold, they are still called a terrine.

A forcemeat made of veal, poultry, or fish is called a **mousseline** (moose-uh-LEEN). A mousseline is delicately flavored and lightened with cream and egg whites. The mousseline can be shaped into small dumpling-shaped ovals and poached in a rich stock or court bouillon to make **quenelles** (kuh-nel).

A **galantine** (GAL-en-teen) was traditionally made of chicken forcemeat, but is now made with a number of different meats. The forcemeat is rolled into a round loaf inside the chicken skin, then poached for up to an hour and a half. It is cooled and sliced before serving.

Review Your Learning 8.3

Match the charcuterie specialty on the left with its correct description on the right.

1. Mousseline
2. Quenelle
3. Terrine
4. Galantine
5. Sausage
6. Fresh sausage
7. Smoked sausage
8. Dried or hard sausage
9. Forcemeat
10. Pâté dough

a. Ground meat (usually pork) forced into a casing made of animal intestines
b. Forcemeat made of veal, poultry, or fish
c. Small dumpling-shaped ovals poached in a rich stock
d. Mixture of lean ground meat and fat forced through a sieve
e. Chicken forcemeat rolled in chicken skin and poached
f. Forcemeat rolled in pâté dough and baked in an earthenware mold
g. Crust surrounding a baking forcemeat
h. Sausage made with fresh ingredients that have not been cured or smoked
i. Sausage made with raw meat products treated with preservatives
j. Sausage made with cured meats, then air-dried under sanitary conditions

11. What are some examples of smoked and cooked sausages? What are your favorites?

12. In your own words, what is a forcemeat? What is the difference between a country-style and straight forcemeat?

Flashback
CHAPTER 8

SECTION 8.1: PURCHASING, STORING, AND PREPARING MEAT, POULTRY, AND SEAFOOD

- Purchasing, preparing, and serving meats is one of the most expensive yet potentially profitable areas of a foodservice operation.
- All meat, poultry, and seafood are considered potentially hazardous foods. Always keep meats out of the temperature danger zone of 40°F to 140°F (4.4°C to 60°C).
- Cuts of meat depend on the operation's menu, storage space, available kitchen equipment, and the staff's ability to butcher or fabricate large cuts of meat.
- Beef, veal, pork, and lamb are regulated, inspected, and graded for their quality by the federal government.
- Government inspection of meat is mandatory; grading is optional and is handled by the USDA.
- **Yield grade** is the yield of usable beef or lamb meat after the fat has been trimmed.
- Meats should be loosely wrapped in air-permeable paper and stored under refrigeration, preferably in a separate unit. Never tightly wrap meats in plastic wrap. Separate different types of meats to prevent cross-contamination.
- After slaughtering, carcasses are cut into a number of large sections, depending on the type of animal.
- Cattle that are butchered from the age of one day up to 14 or 15 weeks are sold as veal.
- Hogs are slaughtered and butchered in facilities that handle no other type of meat in order to prevent foodborne illnesses.
- Sheep slaughtered under the age of one year are considered lamb; after that age they must be labeled **mutton.**
- Meat must be **aged** between 48 to 72 hours to allow the muscles to relax.
- Well-aged beef is more expensive because significant moisture and weight loss reduces the ultimate yield

of the meat. It has a darker color, a more intense flavor, and is more tender.

- **Primal cuts** are the primary divisions of meat produced by the initial butchering of animal carcasses.
- Primal cuts for beef are the chuck, brisket, rib, short plate, short loin, flank, sirloin, and round.
- Primal cuts for veal are the neck, shoulder, breast, hotel rack, loin, sirloin, and leg.
- Primal cuts for pork are the jowl, Boston butt, foot, picnic shoulder, belly, spareribs, loin, ham, and fatback.
- Primal cuts for lamb are the neck, shoulder, shank, breast, hotel rack, loin, leg, and sirloin.
- **Fabrication** is the process of cutting primal cuts into usable portions.
- **Retail cuts** of meat are those cuts that are ready for sale. The amount of butchering necessary to prepare a retail cut affects its price.
- Fabrication techniques for meat include **tying** a roast and **trimming** and **butterflying** a tenderloin.
- **Offal** (organ) **meats** include sweetbreads, liver, tripe, heart, tongue, kidney, and brains.
- **Game meats** include deer, wild boar, moose, and elk. The same general rules that determine proper cooking methods for red meat apply.
- **Kosher** meats are specialty slaughtered to comply with Jewish dietary laws.
- **Poultry** refers to chicken, turkey, squab, duck, goose, Cornish hen, quail, and pheasant. All types of poultry should be wrapped loosely and stored under refrigeration, and in a separate unit or at least in a separate section.
- To prevent cross-contamination, poultry should not come in contact with any other type of meat, and should be placed on trays to prevent it from dripping on other foods or on the floor. Poultry should be cooked as soon as possible after being received.
- Poultry is given a mandatory inspection for wholesomeness and may be graded as USDA A, B, or C. It is classified by size and age; the younger the bird, the more tender the flesh will be.
- Factors that determine poultry grade are: shape of the carcass; ratio of meat

to bone; amount of pinfeathers, hair, and down; and number (if any) of tears, cuts, or broken bones.

- **Free-range** birds are raised in large yards and exercised. The meat is darker in color and has a different flavor and texture.
- Game birds include wild birds such as quail, pheasant and squab. Today many game birds are raised on farms all year long. The flesh should be tender, with a slightly "gamey" taste.
- Poultry fabrication includes disjointing and **boning,** cutting a bird into pieces, preparing boneless chicken breasts, and **trussing.**
- Poultry fabrication is easier than for other meats because the bird's bones are smaller and easier to cut through. Sanitation rules must be strictly observed in poultry fabrication to prevent cross-contamination.
- Only the freshest, most flavorful fish should be purchased and then prepared in a manner that highlights the particular taste of the fish.
- Most shellfish are purchased live and must be checked to make sure they are fresh when received. Tightly closed shells indicate freshness. Any delivery containing a large number of open shells should be rejected.
- Shell stock tags must be kept for 90 days.
- The basic categories of fish are fin fish and shellfish.
- There are five market forms of fin fish: whole or round, drawn, dressed, steak, and fillet.
- Fish fabrication techniques include **scaling,** trimming, **gutting,** and **filleting.** Scaling methods are the same for both round and flat fish, but procedures differ slightly for gutting and filleting.
- Flat fish produce four fillets, while round fish produce two fillets.
- Once a fish is filleted, it can be made into various cuts, such as **goujonettes** (goo-sha-NET) or **paupiettes** (po-pee-EHT).
- There are two types of shellfish: **mollusks** and **crustaceans.**
- **Shucking** means removing a mollusk from its shell.
- Shrimp are cleaned by removing the shell and **deveining** them.

SECTION 8.2: COOKING MEAT, POULTRY, AND SEAFOOD

- Muscle tissue consists of about 75% water, 20% protein, and 5% fat, and is made up of a network of muscle fibers bound together in bundles.
- There are two types of **connective tissue: collagen** and **elastin.** The amount of connective tissue increases as the animal ages, and the more the muscle is exercised.
- Match cuts and qualities of meat to the best cooking methods.
- A **marinade** adds flavor, moisture, and tenderness.
- Meat can be cooked in a variety of ways, depending on the tenderness of the cut.
- Meats that are to be prepared using a dry-heat method must be naturally tender.
- A **mirepoix** (meer-PWAH) can be added to a roasting pan during the final hour of cooking.
- The sauce made by **deglazing** the drippings produced during roasting is frequently referred to as **jus** (zhew). Sauce made with a roux incorporating the fat from a roast is called **pan gravy.**
- **Carryover cooking** means the roasted item holds a certain amount of heat that will continue to cook the food.
- Dry heat methods using fats and oils cook meat quickly, use high heat, and require tender, portion-sized, or smaller pieces of meat.
- Sautéed meats are served with a sauce that is prepared while the food is cooking.
- Meats that are stir-fried are cut into small pieces with all fat, gristle, and silverskin removed.
- Moist-heat cooking techniques produce foods that are delicately flavored and moist with a rich broth, which can be served as a separate course or as a sauce base.
- Combination cooking methods—braising and stewing—use both dry and moist heat to cook foods that are less tender.
- Determining doneness is one of the most important steps in cooking meat.
- Roasts should rest for 15–30 minutes before carving.

- Poultry is especially suited to the dry-heat cooking techniques of grilling, broiling, and roasting.
- Roasting requires longer cooking times because this technique cooks whole birds. In roasting, the bird can be seasoned, stuffed, marinated, **barded,** and/or **seared** over direct heat or in a hot oven.
- Dressing and stuffing for poultry are baked separately for food safety; however, small birds (Cornish hens and quail) can be stuffed and served as single portions. All sanitation steps must be followed to avoid bacterial growth.
- When cooking whole birds they must be **trussed**—legs and wings are tied to the bird's body—so the entire bird cooks evenly and stays moist.
- Poultry is also suited to dry-heat cooking with fats and oils: sautéing, stir-frying, pan-frying, and deep-frying. These techniques require tender, portion-sized pieces.
- Deep-fried chicken is breaded or batter-coated and cooked by being completely immersed in hot fat. Chicken that is deep-fried must be naturally tender.
- Steaming is another way to prepare poultry and is healthful, as well as tasty. Steamed foods generally contain a greater proportion of nutrients because water-soluble nutrients are not drawn out during cooking.
- Simmering and poaching are also excellent ways to prepare chicken. Simmered chicken has a rich, flavorful broth and can be used for soups, creamed dishes, casseroles, and salads.
- Chicken is a natural for the combination cooking methods of stewing and braising, which produce dishes with exceptional sauces and flavor concentrations. The proteins and other nutrients lost from cooking the chicken are contained in the sauce.
- The best way to pair a fish with a cooking technique is to consider the flesh.
- Match an oily fish with a dry-heat technique, such as grilling or broiling.
- Fish with a moderate amount of fat can be prepared using any cooking method.
- Very lean fish are most flavorful when they are poached or sautéed.

- Moist-heat cooking techniques and combination cooking methods are excellent ways to cook fish.
- To enhance flavor, fish are often poached in **court bouillion** or **fumet.**
- One moist-heat cooking technique that is especially suited to fish is **en papillote** (on paw-pee-YOTE).
- Fish dishes using stewing and braising techniques include **bouillabaisse, jambalaya** (jam-bo-LIE-ah), and **Seafood Newburg.**

SECTION 8.3: CHARCUTERIE AND GARDE-MANGER

- **Charcuterie** and **garde-manger** refer to special cold meat preparations, including forcemeats, terrines, and sausages.
- Sausages are ground meat, usually pork, forced into a casing made of animal intestines. They may be kept fresh before cooking, or smoked or cured, needing no further cooking.
- Polish kielbasa, Mexican chorizo, and French andouille are examples of *fresh sausages.*
- German knackwurst, frankfurter, and bratwurst are examples of *smoked sausages.*
- Italian salami and pepperoni are examples of *dried* or *hard sausages.*
- **Forcemeats** are lean ground meat and fat emulsions forced through a sieve.
- Forcemeats are the basis for many types of **pâté,** including **pâté de campagne,** and **pâté en croute.**
- Pâté dough is much stronger than pie dough because it must stand up to the liquid released from the pâté during cooking.
- Pâtés are baked in an earthenware mold called a **terrine.**
- **Mousselines** are forcemeats made from veal, chicken, or fish.
- Small dumplings made from mousseline and then poached are called **quenelles.**
- **Galantine** is chicken forcemeat that is rolled into a round loaf inside the chicken skin, poached for up to an hour and a half, and then served cooled and sliced.

Liz Steinhaus

Accountant
Adagio
Chicago, Illinois

If I didn't keep track of money going in and out of our restaurant, we'd be out of business in no time. This is a popular restaurant and nightclub, but that will get you only so far. I put up with the pressure well because I do so many different things during the day, and that keeps me loving my job.

What I love most about Adagio are the people and the fun atmosphere. Restaurants attract diverse personalities. I also like the fact that my hours are flexible, and that I meet a lot of friendly local and out-of-town guests. And, of course, the food's great.

I worked in restaurants during high school and college, where I majored in accounting. I'm responsible for all of the financial operations at the restaurant. I check out servers every day at the end of their shifts. I manage personnel records and the restaurant's health benefits package, and I'm responsible for paying the employees. I pay all of the sales and payroll taxes. I manage accounts payable and accounts receivable, and I oversee inventory control to make sure that we're keeping the highest-quality items on hand and buying them for the best possible price.

If I don't do my job right, there are all sorts of agencies that will charge us high fines or close us down. It's my job to make sure that all personnel policies comply with U.S. Department of Labor standards. I see that all liquor bills are paid on time so our state liquor license isn't taken away. I manage the process for reporting all of the servers' and bartenders' tips.

The information I keep track of and record allows the restaurant's managers and owners to know how the business is doing. I know whether the restaurant is charging the right prices for menu items to ensure a profit, and whether we're paying good prices for quality items. I'll be the first to know if anyone is stealing from our inventories, and whether our sales are up or down.

I use accounting principles every day. Knowing what to do with numbers, which allows you to know whether or not you're making money, is what keeps us in business.

CHAPTER 9

Standard Accounting Practices

9.1

SECTION 9.1

The ABCs of Accounting

AFTER STUDYING SECTION 9.1, YOU SHOULD BE ABLE TO:

- Given a set of figures, apply basic accounting principles to common foodservice scenarios.
- Calculate cost of sales using opening and closing inventory figures.
- Given a set of figures, practice double-entry accounting.

An old business saying goes like this: "To know where you're going, you've got to know where you've been." In any successful business, accounting and financial information plays a big role in letting a company "know where they've been." While many foodservice businesses have accountants who assemble these financial numbers, managers still need to know the

KEY TERMS

- Accounts payable
- Accounts receivable
- Asset
- Bank reconciliation
- Cost
- Cost of sales
- Credit
- Debit
- Depreciation
- Direct cost
- Double-entry accounting
- Expenses
- Indirect cost
- Liability
- Revenue
- T-account
- Transaction
- Trial balance

Exhibit 9.1
It is important for restaurant managers to know basic accounting skills.

basics of accounting to help them make their financial planning, purchasing, and staffing decisions.

Accountants use many words and concepts that are unique to their profession. Exhibit 9.2 describes a number of important accounting terms and principles that foodservice managers need to learn.

Transactions: The Basic Accounting Unit

An accountant's main task is to accurately keep the records of all financial activities of a business. A transaction is the most basic piece of information that an accountant uses. In accounting terms, a **transaction** is when money is exchanged for business reasons. These transactions need to be recorded into a business's

Exhibit 9.2
Standard accounting principles and terms.

Accounts payable	Money that a business owes to other businesses
Accounts receivable	Money that is owed to a business
Asset	Item of value that's owned by a business
Cost	Price paid for goods or services when the goods are received or the services are rendered
Double-entry accounting	System for recording equal debits and credits for every business transaction
Expenses	Cost of items like food, supplies, wages, and insurance that are necessary to run a business
Liability	Debt, obligation, or claim owed by a business
Owners' equity	Total assets minus total liabilities; tells the worth of a business
Profit	Money left when expenses have been subtracted from revenue
Revenue	Money that an operation takes in when it sells products or services

accounting records. A business has transactions with several different groups.

- *Customers*—people who buy things from the business
- *Employees*—people who work for the business
- *Suppliers or vendors*—people who sell products or services to the business
- *Investors/Creditors*—people who lend money to the business
- *Government*— collects taxes from the business

Exhibit 9.3
A transaction happens every time a customer buys something from a business.

Double-Entry Accounting

Almost all accountants use a transaction recording system known as **double-entry accounting** that records equal debits and credits for every business transaction. In any business transaction, a business gets more of one type of asset by giving up another type of asset. For example, when a restaurant buys supplies for its operation, it gives up some of its cash assets and it receives assets in the form of supplies. Double-entry accounting makes sure that both sides of every transaction are recorded, because if one side of the transaction is forgotten, the accounts won't balance when they are added together.

Accountants enter these transactions into charts known as **T-accounts.** As you can see in Exhibit 9.4, the name T-account comes from the fact that the lines that make up each account resemble the letter "T." To understand how this works we first need to look at how debits and credits work.

Think about it...

In this age of ATMs, credit cards, and debit cards, it's easy to think that you already know what the words *credit* and *debit* mean. In accounting, however, these terms are used in ways you may not be familiar with. Although it may seem difficult at first, keep your mind open as you learn how these terms are defined within accounting practices.

Credits, Debits, and T-Accounts

For every transaction, an accountant records an amount as a debit into one record, called an *account,* while the same value is recorded as a credit in another account.

Example: If a manager buys a dishwashing machine for $15,000 cash, the $15,000 figure is listed as a debit in the equipment account, and as a credit in the cash account.

In other words, $15,000 has been taken from the cash account and placed in the equipment account showing how the money was spent. Exhibit 9.4 shows how this transaction is recorded using T-accounts.

Exhibit 9.4
Simple transaction record for a dishwashing machine purchase.

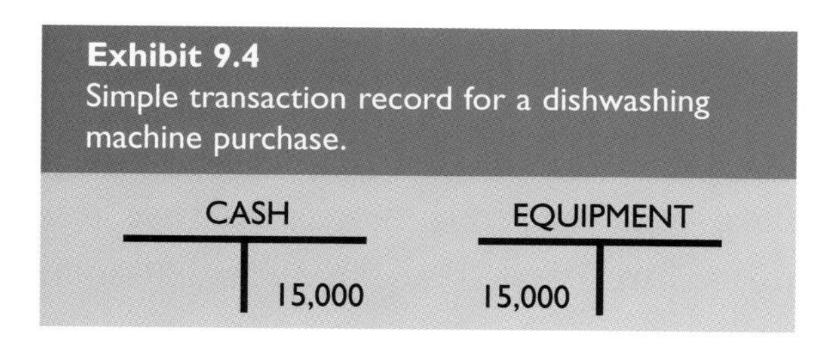

The simplest format for an account is the title, a place to record transactions that increase the account value, and a place to record transactions that decrease the account value. This format is known as a "T- account" because it resembles the letter "T."

As shown in Exhibit 9.5, **debits** are recorded on the left side of the T-account, while **credits** are recorded on the right side. *This is true no matter what type of account is represented by the T-account format.*

Exhibit 9.5
Debits are always recorded on the left side and credits on the right.

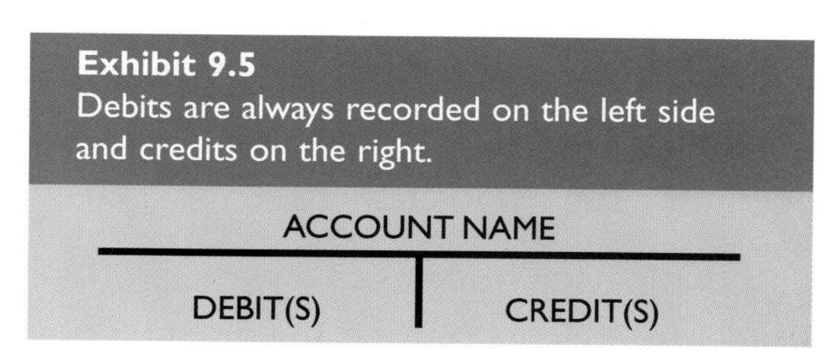

In certain accounts, debits always increase the account value, while credits decrease the account value, and in other account types the opposite is true.

There are five basic types of accounts.

- Asset
- Liability
- Owners' equity
- Revenues
- Expenses

Each type of account can go by several other more specific names. For example, within Asset-type accounts you might find accounts titled "Cash," "Accounts Receivable," or "Inventory." See Exhibit 9.6 for other account titles for these basic types of accounts. Take a look at the second column in Exhibit 9.6 on the next page to see some examples of account titles for other account types.

When recording transactions in Asset and Expense accounts, debits (left side) increase the account balance, while credits (right side) decrease the balance. For transactions being recorded in the Liability, Owners' Equity, or Revenue accounts, the opposite is true.

Let's say a business buys $2,500 of food supplies on credit. One entry of this transaction would be recorded as a debit in an Asset account titled "Food Inventory," and as a credit in a liability account titled "Accounts Payable." In both accounts the balances are increased because debits to asset accounts increase their value, while credits to liability accounts increase their value.

Study Exhibit 9.6 carefully to understand the differences between the main account types.

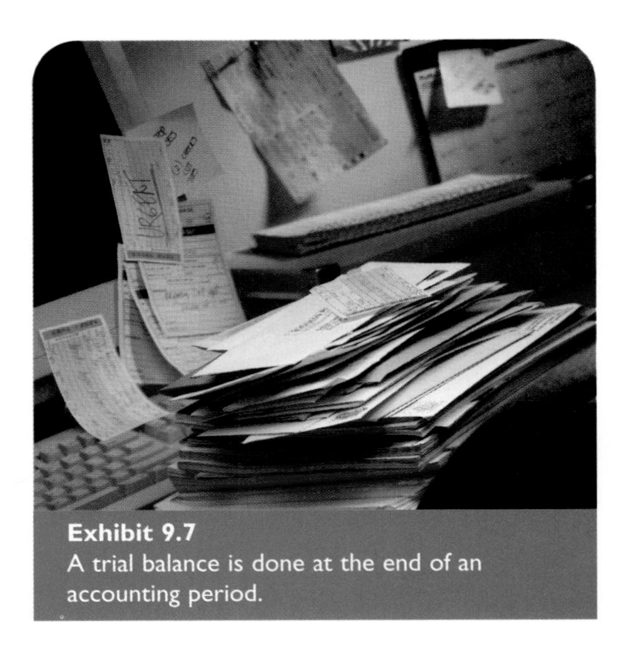

Exhibit 9.7
A trial balance is done at the end of an accounting period.

The Trial Balance

All transactions should be carefully recorded throughout an accounting period. At the end of the period, a trial balance is prepared. A **trial balance** is a procedure used to make sure that total

Exhibit 9.6
The five types of accounts.

Account Type	Examples of Account	Debits (left side)	Credits (right side)
Asset	Cash, Equipment, Supplies	Increase balance	Decrease balance
Liability	Accounts Payable, Mortgage Payable	Decrease balance	Increase balance
Owners' Equity	Retained Earnings, Partner's Capital Balance	Decrease balance	Increase balance
Revenue	Monthly Food Sales, Food Revenue	Decrease balance	Increase balance
Expenses	Wages, Food Inventory	Increase balance	Decrease balance

debits equal total credits. There must be a balance of accounts (debit entries must equal credit entries) for every transaction.

To prepare a trial balance, the debits and credits in each account are added, and the smaller total is subtracted from the larger one to give you the balance for each account. For example, if, in addition to the credit purchase of food supplies, the manager previously mentioned also places two separate advertisements in local magazines for $250 and $600 cash and collects $5,500 in revenue, the transactions would be recorded as shown in Exhibit 9.8.

A trial balance is then taken to make sure that debits equal credits. In other words, the money coming into the business is matched against the money going out of the business. In Exhibit 9.8, the Cash, Advertising, and Food Supplies accounts are added together for a total debit of $8,000. The sum of the Accounts Payable and Revenue accounts comes to $8,000 in credits, so the accounts are balanced.

If total debits and credits didn't balance, then the accountant would need to find where an error in recordkeeping occurred.

Exhibit 9.8
Sample T-account transaction records.

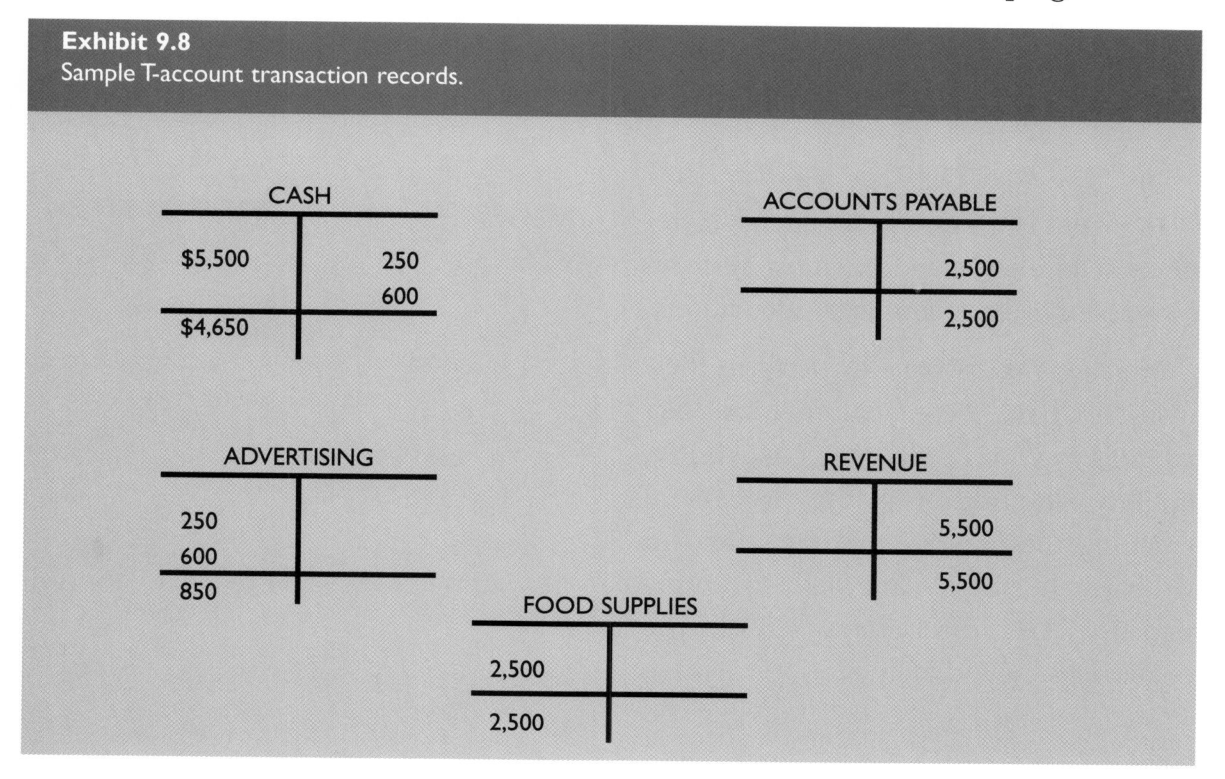

It's important to remember that annual bills, such as rent or insurance, are spread out over twelve months. Other items, such as equipment, are adjusted to show their depreciation over several periods. We'll discuss how depreciation works shortly.

After all accounts are balanced and adjustments are made, the information can be transferred to an income statement and balance sheet (discussed in Section 9.2 and Section 9.3). The accounts for that particular time period are then said to be *closed,* and a new accounting period begins. Once accounts for an accounting period are closed, new transactions shouldn't be added to or subtracted from these accounts anymore.

Basic Accounting Calculations

In order to prepare financial statements accurately, managers must perform a variety of basic accounting calculations.

Managers often have to perform their business's bank reconciliation. Much like balancing your personal checkbook, **bank reconciliation** is the process of matching the bank's monthly statement with your business's internal accounting records. Any differences should be looked into immediately.

One important calculation is an establishment's cost of sales. The **cost of sales** figure reflects the food cost for a given period of time, usually a month. To determine your monthly cost of sales, you'll need to know the following:

- *Opening inventory*—the value of food on hand at the beginning of the month
- *Purchases*—the value of food items purchased during the month
- *Closing inventory*—the value of food on hand at the end of the month

	Opening inventory
+	Purchases
–	Closing inventory
	Cost of sales

Exhibit 9.9
Know your food inventory on the first and last day of the month to determine your monthly food costs.

For example, if the Pine Valley Café begins the month of May with $4,050 in its food inventory, ends the month with $3,890 in inventory, and has purchases totaling $11,380, the cost of sales for May can be calculated as follows:

Opening inventory	$4,050
Purchases	+ 11, 380
	15,430
Closing inventory	– 3,890
Cost of sales	$11,540

In addition to calculating cost of sales, managers must also know how to allocate direct and indirect costs. In general terms, **cost** is the price paid for goods or services when the goods are received or the services are rendered.

A **direct cost** is an expense, such as food purchases, that is the responsibility of a specific department. In a large-scale foodservice operation with several different departments, direct costs are distributed among all the departments that directly use the goods or services purchased. If a restaurant buys 30 cases of tomatoes, and both the dining room and catering departments use them, then the direct cost of these tomatoes would be assigned to both departments.

Indirect costs are expenses that are not easily charged to any one specific department. These expenses, such as advertising, utilities, and administrative costs, are usually spread out among the departments, based on each department's percent of total revenue. **Revenue** is a word accountants use to describe money

Apply It Now

Alexander's Restaurant began December with $4,765 worth of products in its food inventory, ended the month with $2,690 worth of products in inventory, and had receipts showing a total of $4,950 in purchases. Determine the operation's cost of sales for December. Bonus question: What is opening inventory for January?

Exhibit 9.10
Direct costs, such as food purchases, may be distributed between the dining room and the banquet department.

that a department takes in when it sells its products or services. Take a look at Exhibit 9.11 to see the revenue figures for three departments in an operation.

Exhibit 9.12 shows how to determine the share of indirect costs that each department should be responsible for. Multiply the total indirect cost by a department's percent of total revenue. For example, administrative costs (an indirect cost) total $54,200, and the banquet department contributes 23% of the total revenue, it should pay 23% of the indirect cost, which is $12,466.

THINK OF IT THIS WAY...

If you share an apartment with a roommate, but you only make ten percent of the long-distance phone calls on the phone bill, you should only pay ten percent of the long-distance bill. You benefit from having the telephone hooked up, but your usage of the phone is much less than your roommate's.

DEPRECIATION

Most foodservice operations own a large number of physical assets. As defined in Exhibit 9.1, an **asset** is an item of value that's owned by a business. Some assets like cash and credit extended to customers are known as paper assets—their value is

Exhibit 9.11
How three different departments contribute to total revenue.

Department	Revenue	Percent of Total Revenue
Dining room	$884,300	46%
Banquet	432,100	23%
Catering	590,000	31%
Total	$1,906,400	100%

Exhibit 9.12
Each department pays for their fair portion of the indirect costs.

Department	Indirect Costs		Percentage of total revenue		Share of Cost
Dining room	$54,200	×	0.46	=	$24,932
Banquet	54,200	×	0.23	=	12,466
Catering	54,200	×	0.31	=	16,802
Total					**$54,200**

recognized on paper. Another type of asset—physical assets—includes things such as buildings, equipment, furniture, accessories, and supplies. The value of these assets decreases over time, but each asset continues to contribute to the business throughout its lifetime.

Depreciation is a method of recording the amount of reduction in value of an asset as it gradually decreases over its lifetime. Only physical assets can be depreciated. This accounting principle lets businesses make an expensive investment without showing a big loss in the year that the investment is bought.

Let's say, for example, a restaurant buys a new stove for $5,000. If the cost of the stove couldn't be depreciated, it would have to be recorded as an expense all at once. As a result, the accounting records would show a significant drop in the restaurant's profits for that year, whereas following years might show above normal profits. But since the stove will continue to contribute to the restaurant's sales throughout its life, its dollar value is depreciated, and the expense is spread out over the useful life of the stove.

Depreciation is also an important way that businesses manage the amount of taxes they owe. Taxes are based on a business's profit or loss in any given year. If a restaurant couldn't depreciate a stove purchase over 5 years, its taxes would be low the first year and much higher in the following years. With depreciation, the tax advantage of the stove's expense is spread over 5 years. However, there are guidelines in determining useful life estimates that must be followed. These guidelines are established by the Internal Revenue Service (IRS).

Exhibit 9.13
The value of your operation's mixer will gradually decrease over its lifetime.

There are four basic methods of calculating the depreciation of assets.

1. *Straight-line method*
2. *Declining balance method*
3. *Sum-of-the-years digits method*
4. *Units of production method*

Straight-line method. The simplest way to determine depreciation is to distribute the cost of an asset equally over each year of its estimated useful life. The formula for the straight-line method of depreciation looks like this:

$$\frac{\text{(Cost of asset – Trade-in value)}}{\text{Useful life of asset (in years)}}$$

For example, if a dishwashing machine costs $11,500 and has a trade-in value of $900 after 5 years, depreciation can be calculated as follows:

$$\frac{(\$11{,}500 - \$900)}{5 \text{ years}} = \frac{\$10{,}600}{5} = \$2{,}120$$

Using the straight-line method, the dishwashing machine would depreciate $2,120 per year for each of the five years. In this example, one year's depreciation is 20% of the dishwashing machine's useful life (because the dishwashing machine's useful life is five years).

Declining balance method. Unlike the straight-line method, this method does not consider trade-in value. Instead, you calculate the depreciation rate from the straight-line method (20% in the above example) and double it. Then, you multiply this percentage by the total value of the asset in the first year, and by the remaining value for each following year. Take a look at Exhibit 9.14 to see how our dishwashing machine depreciation would work using the declining balance method.

Since most physical investments like dishwashing machines, trucks, or refrigerators depreciate quickly in their first year, the declining balance method more

Exhibit 9.14
Depreciation using the declining balance method.

Year	Annual Depreciation	Original Cost		Depreciation		Remaining Value
1	$11,500 × 0.40 = $4,600	$11,500	–	$4,600	=	$6,900
2	6,900 × 0.40 = 2,760	6,900	–	2,760	=	4,140
3	4,140 × 0.04 = 1,656	4,140	–	1,656	=	2,484
4	2,484 × 0.04 = 994	2,484	–	994	=	1,490
5	1,490 × 0.04 = 596	1,490	–	596	=	894

accurately reflects the value of the asset in any given year. This method provides major tax advantages in the first years of the investment's lifetime, yet it still provides some tax savings over the entire life of the product.

Sum-of-the-years digits method. This method of depreciation starts by adding up the digits of the years in the estimated life of an asset. Your dishwashing machine, with its five-year life expectancy, would be calculated like this:

$$1 + 2 + 3 + 4 + 5 = 15$$

This sum, 15, becomes the denominator of five fractions that will be used to calculate each year of depreciation. The numerators for each year are the years in descending order (5, 4, 3, 2, 1), with the resulting fractions for each year as follows:

Year 1: $\frac{5}{15}$
Year 2: $\frac{4}{15}$
Year 3: $\frac{3}{15}$
Year 4: $\frac{2}{15}$
Year 5: $\frac{1}{15}$

Finally, each fraction is multiplied by the dishwashing machine's cost ($11,500) minus the trade-in value ($900), as seen in Exhibit 9.15.

Exhibit 9.15
Depreciation using the sum-of-the-years digits method.

Year	Cost minus Trade-in Value				Depreciation
1	$10,600	×	$\frac{5}{15}$	=	$3,533
2	10,600	×	$\frac{4}{15}$	=	2,827
3	10,600	×	$\frac{3}{15}$	=	2,120
4	10,600	×	$\frac{2}{15}$	=	1,413
5	10,600	×	$\frac{1}{15}$	=	707
TOTAL DEPRECIATION:					$10,600

Units of production method. This method determines depreciation values for assets in which you can predict a specific amount of usage. Vehicles are often depreciated through this method, because a business generally knows how many miles it typically puts on a delivery truck before it will buy a replacement. Let's say you buy a delivery truck that you expect to use for 70,000 miles. If the truck costs $23,000 and will have a trade-in value of $6,000 with 70,000 miles on the odometer, the unit of production method would be calculated like this:

$$\frac{\text{(Cost – Trade-in value)}}{\text{Estimated units of production over useful life}}$$

$$\frac{\$23{,}000 - \$6{,}000}{70{,}000 \text{ miles}} = \frac{17{,}000}{70{,}000} = \frac{\$0.2429}{\text{per mile}}$$

If the truck is driven 14,000 miles each year, annual depreciation is $0.2429 × 14,000 miles, or $3,400. This method more closely associates the depreciation expense to the use of an asset over its life.

Review Your Learning 9.1

1. A foodservice manager purchased a new walk-in freezer at a cost of $19,700. The freezer will be worth $600 after 6 years.
   a. How much does the freezer depreciate each year if you use the straight-line method to calculate depreciation?
   b. Using the declining balance method to calculate depreciation, what is the value of the freezer after each year of its useful life?
   c. Using the sum-of-the-years digit method to calculate depreciation, by what amount does the freezer depreciate for each of the six years?

2. Mark each of the following expenses as a direct (D) or indirect (I) cost.
   a. Rent
   b. Advertising
   c. Telephone bills
   d. Servers' wages
   e. Food purchases
   f. General manager's salary
   g. Administrative costs

3. A foodservice manager has purchased a cash-register system for $32,700. On a separate sheet of paper, record this transaction in two T-accounts.

4. An operator wishes to charge indirect costs of $48,650 to three different departments according to each department's percent of revenue. How much will each department be charged based on the following revenue figures?

Department	Revenue	Percent	Indirect Costs
Dining room	$546,100	56	$________
Snack counter	85,600	9	$________
Banquet	344,200	35	$________
		Total	**$48,650**

9.2

SECTION 9.2

The Income Statement

AFTER STUDYING SECTION 9.2, YOU SHOULD BE ABLE TO:

- Read and highlight important concepts on income statements.

An **income statement** shows a business's revenue and expenses over a period of time, as well as the resulting profit or loss. Income statements can be prepared monthly, quarterly (referring to a quarter of a year, or three months), or annually. Income statements give a quick explanation of how a business is doing financially.

KEY TERMS

- Contributory income
- Contributory income percent
- Income statement
- Loss
- Net income
- Profit

Monthly income statements can show managers how one month's sales and expenses compare to other months. They can also let managers know if they're reaching their sales goals. In the foodservice industry, you will also hear income statements sometimes referred to as *profit and loss statements,* or *P&L statements.*

The accounting methods and standards that are used to create income statements are often complicated, and a foodservice manager needs to make sure that his or her accountant produces accurate information. A false income statement can lead to potential lawsuits and serious financial problems with an operation's bank, its investors, and the government.

Taking a Closer Look

In large foodservice operations, each department is often responsible for getting its account information to the accountant, who then prepares the company-wide income statement. After each department's individual income statement has been prepared, the information is combined into a summary income statement, as seen in Exhibit 9.16.

Direct costs (see Section 9.1) and sales are totalled for each department in the operation and recorded at the top of the statement. The middle portion of Exhibit 9.16 is known as *controllable expenses.* These expenses are all systematically subtracted from income to arrive at a final figure, known as the *net income.*

The **net income,** found at the bottom of the statement, reflects the final profit or loss of the business for a given period of time. Profit or loss is determined by subtracting expenses from revenue. **Profit** is the amount left when expenses have been subtracted from revenue; a **loss** occurs when expenses are greater than revenue.

Once the summary income statement has been prepared, the manager will look at financial records for each department to break down the expenses and contributory income for each department. **Contributory income** is the amount of income that a particular department contributes to the foodservice establishment's total income.

This is similar to the concept explained in Section 9.1 where each department contributed a percentage of the establishment's total revenue. Instead of figuring this amount from a percentage, however, the actual income amount is used. Then the contributory income percents can be calculated. **Contributory income percent** is the percentage of a department's revenue that is income.

Did you know?

When someone wants to know the *bottom line,* what they're referring to is the net income, which is found at the bottom of the income statement. Net income gives a quick snapshot of how well or how poorly a business is performing.

For example, the catering department of a restaurant has a total revenue of $35,000 for the year. After subtracting total expenses of $19,250, the department has contributed $15,750 in income to the restaurant. The contributory income percent is then figured by dividing the income from the department by the department's revenue.

$$\frac{\$15,750}{\$35,000} = 0.45 \text{ or } 45\%$$

So the catering department has a contributory income percent of 45%.

Exhibit 9.16
Uniform summary income statement.

Full-Menu, Table-service Restaurant with Food and Beverages Sales
Year Ended December 31, 2001

		AMOUNT	PERCENTAGES
SALES			
Food		$1,017,000	73.75%
Beverage		362,000	26.25
Total Sales		1,379,000	100.00
COST OF SALES			
Food		428,250	31.06
Beverage		92,000	6.67
Total Cost of Sales		520,250	37.73
GROSS PROFIT		858,750	62.27
OTHER INCOME		7,750	0.56
TOTAL INCOME		866,500	62.83
CONTROLLABLE EXPENSES			
Salaries and Wages		354,500	25.72
Employee Benefits		59,750	4.33
Direct Operating Expenses		81,250	5.89
Music and Entertainment		14,250	1.03
Marketing		23,750	1.72
Energy and Utility Services		34,250	2.48
Administrative and General		69,250	5.02
Repairs and Maintenance		23,750	1.72
Total Controllable Expenses		660,750	47.91
INCOME BEFORE OCCUPANCY COSTS, INTEREST, DEPRECIATION, CORPORATE OVERHEAD, AND INCOME TAXES		205,750	14.92
OCCUPANCY COSTS		73,700	5.34
INCOME BEFORE INTEREST, DEPRECIATION, CORPORATE OVERHEAD, AND INCOME TAXES		132,050	9.58
INTEREST EXPENSE		6,000	0.44
DEPRECIATION		34,600	2.51
RESTAURANT PROFIT		91,450	6.63
CORPORATE OVERHEAD		20,685	1.50
NET INCOME BEFORE INCOME TAXES		70,765	5.13
INCOME TAXES		18,920	1.37
NET INCOME		$51,845	3.76%
Retained Earnings, beginning of year	37,200		
Retained Earnings, end of the year	$89,045		

Exhibit 9.17
The dining room's contributory income will be different from other departments'.

Based on these calculations, you could say that $0.45 from every dollar of revenue coming into the catering department is income for the restaurant. This figure, when compared to previous contributory income percents from earlier accounting periods, allows managers to see how a department is performing. The higher the contributory income percent, the better a department is performing.

Let's walk through an entire accounting cycle with Carolyn, a foodservice manager who has opened a new restaurant called The Chef's Delight. During the first several months of operation, Carolyn recorded the transactions listed in Exhibit 9.18.

Exhibit 9.18
Transaction records for The Chef's Delight.

a) Invested $135,000 in cash and used $15,000 of it to purchase equipment
b) Purchased land for $150,000 and a building for $450,000, paying $100,000 in cash and taking out a mortgage with Security Bank for the balance
c) Purchased supplies worth $2,250 on credit
d) Collected $35,000 in revenue
e) Paid $300 cash for advertising
f) Purchased a $1,500 cash register using $500 cash and $1,000 credit
g) Paid $3,500 for wages
h) Paid $2,250 cash on transaction c
i) Collected $2,000 revenue from charge customers
j) Paid $200 cash on transaction f
k) Collected $500 cash from charge customers
l) Paid $3,000 for wages
m) Paid $100 cash for advertising
n) Paid $8,000 cash to Security Bank for mortgage
o) Collected $20,000 in revenue
p) Purchased food with $5,000 cash and $27,000 credit
q) Used food inventory valued at $29,000
r) Paid $25,000 cash on transaction p
s) Used $1,250 worth of supplies

Think about it...

Why do you think the expenses in the middle third of the income statement in Exhibit 9.16 are called *Controllable Expenses?*

Let's look at Exhibit 9.19 to see how Carolyn recorded these transactions in T-accounts. In transaction a, Carolyn entered her initial investment of $135,000 in two

T-accounts. First, she entered it as a debit in the *Cash* account. As we saw in Section 9.1, the *Cash* account is one of the accounts in which the asset is recorded as a debit. Balancing this account is the *Owner's Equity* account, which lists the $135,000 as a credit.

The second part of transaction a, the use of $15,000 to buy equipment, is listed in the *Cash* account as a credit to that account, while the $15,000 is also listed as a debit in the *Equipment* account. Carefully notice how the remaining transactions are each entered in two T-accounts, with one entry on the debit side and the other entry on the credit side. In this way, Carolyn can make sure that all her transactions will balance out.

Since it is the end of the quarter, Carolyn needs to combine her T-account totals into a trial balance statement as shown

Exhibit 9.19
T-accounts for The Chef's Delight.

ACCOUNTS PAYABLE

	Debit	Credit	
h	2,250	2,250	c
j	200	1,000	f
r	25,000	27,000	p
		2,800	

OWNERS' EQUITY

	Debit	Credit	
		135,000	a
		135,000	

EQUIPMENT

	Debit	Credit	
a	15,000		
f	1,500		
	16,500		

BUILDING

	Debit	Credit	
b	$450,000		
	450,000		

CASH

	Debit	Credit	
a	$135,000	$15,000	a
d	35,000	100,000	b
k	500	300	e
o	20,000	500	f
		3,500	g
		2,250	h
		200	j
		3,000	l
		100	m
		8,000	n
		5,000	p
		25,000	r
	27,650		

Exhibit 9.19 (continued)
T-accounts for The Chef's Delight.

	COST OF GOODS SOLD		
q	$29,000		
	29,000		

	ACCOUNTS RECEIVABLE		
i	2,000	500	k
	1,500		

	FOOD INVENTORY		
p	32,000	29,000	q
	3,000		

	LAND		
b	150,000		
	150,000		

	MORTGAGE PAYABLE		
n	8,000	500,000	b
		492,000	

	ADVERTISING		
e	300		
m	100		
	400		

	REVENUE		
		35,000	d
		2,000	i
		20,000	o
		57,000	

	SUPPLIES		
c	$2,250	1,250	s
	1,000		

	SUPPLIES EXPENSE		
s	1,250		
	1,250		

	WAGES		
g	3,500		
l	3,000		
	6,500		

in Exhibit 9.20. First, she totals up each T-account. Notice the *Supplies* T-account on page 400, for example. It had a debit entry of $2,250 and a credit entry of $1,250. Carolyn subtracts the smaller entry from the larger and ends up with the *Supplies* T-account showing a final debit of $1,000.

She then takes the final figures for each account and puts them on either the debit or credit side of the trial balance, as shown in Exhibit 9.20. Each line on the trial balance statement represents a total from one of the T-accounts. Then, Carolyn adds the two columns up and checks to make sure they are equal.

Exhibit 9.20
Trial balance statement.

Cash	27,650	
Accounts receivable	1,500	
Food inventory	3,000	
Supplies	1,000	
Land	150,000	
Building	450,000	
Equipment	16,500	
Accounts payable		2,800
Mortgage payable		492,000
Owners' equity		135,000
Revenue		57,000
Cost of goods sold	29,000	
Supplies expense	1,250	
Wages	6,500	
Advertising	400	
	686,800	686,800

Finally, Carolyn will transfer the revenue and expense information from the trial balance to an income statement as shown in Exhibit 9.21 on the next page. As you can see, Carolyn's expenses are less than her revenue, so her restaurant is profitable. Income statements like this show how well or how poorly a business is doing.

The T-accounts, trial balance statement, and income statement provide a detailed look at the financial activity of a foodservice establishment. Along with the balance sheet (discussed in Section 9.3), the income statement helps managers and stockholders understand important financial aspects of the operation so that they can make informed business decisions.

Exhibit 9.21
Income statement for the Chef's Delight.

Quarterly Income Statement for The Chef's Delight

TOTAL REVENUE		57,000
EXPENSES		
Cost of goods sold	29,000	
Supplies expense	1,250	
Wages	6,500	
Advertising	400	
TOTAL EXPENSES		37,150
INCOME		19,850

Review Your Learning 9.2

1. What are the three main categories of business information that are recorded in an income statement?
   a. Contributory income, cost of sales, taxes
   b. Sales, expenses, income
   c. Overhead, taxes, depreciation
   d. Food sales, interest, profit

2. Businesses that provide inaccurate income statements may have trouble with:
   a. increasing profit margins.
   b. contributory income errors.
   c. trial balance adjustments.
   d. potential lawsuits.

3. What document provides a business with a quick summary of its profits or losses?
   a. Income statement
   b. Trial balance
   c. T-accounts
   d. Double-entry accounting

4. The _____ reflects the final profit or loss of the business for a given period of time.
   a. net balance
   b. contributory income percent
   c. net income
   d. trial balance

5. How is profit or loss determined for a foodservice establishment?

9.3

SECTION 9.3

The Balance Sheet

AFTER STUDYING SECTION 9.3, YOU SHOULD BE ABLE TO:

- Read and highlight important concepts on balance sheets.
- Figure assets, liabilities, and owners' equity using balance sheet equations.

KEY TERMS

- Balance sheet
- Balance sheet equation
- Capital item
- Current asset
- Current liability
- Fixed asset
- Long-term liability
- Owners' equity
- Retained earnings

The **balance sheet** is a basic financial report that provides information about a company's assets, liabilities, and owners' equity at a particular date. The balance sheet includes information transferred from the income statement discussed in Section 9.2. The **balance sheet equation** is a basic formula that shows, at a glance, how much a business owes, what it is worth, and the value of the items it owns. The formula looks like this:

Assets = Liabilities + Owners' equity

For example, if Jack's Deli's liabilities total $63,000, and its owners' equity is $42,000, the value of its assets can be easily determined:

Assets = $63,000 + $42,000

Assets = $105,000

Assets

The assets that appear on a balance sheet are grouped as current, fixed, or other. **Current** (short-term) **assets** are

Exhibit 9.22
Cash taken in during the business day is an example of a current asset.

those that can or will be converted to cash within one year. These include cash on hand (usually the cash taken in during one business day), cash in the bank, accounts receivable (money owed to the operation), and food inventory to be sold in the establishment.

Fixed (long-term) **assets** refer to items like land, buildings, furniture, fixtures, and kitchen equipment that have a life expectancy of at least 3 years. These assets often go by the name of **capital items**. In a foodservice operation, items like linens, uniforms, glasses, and dishware are also considered fixed assets.

Current and fixed assets, combined with other assets (such as deposits, investments, and deferred expenses), make up the operation's total assets. Study Exhibit 9.23 to see how these assets are arranged and calculated.

Liabilities and Owners' Equity

As shown in the equation introduced at the beginning of this section, liabilities and owners' equity must, together, equal the value of all assets in order for a balance sheet to balance.

Apply It Now

The Hamburger Palace has assets worth $164,490, and owners' equity is $97,800. How much are the establishment's liabilities?

Liabilities can be divided into two categories. **Current liabilities** must be paid within one year. These include accounts payable (money owed to suppliers or creditors), accrued expenses (such as unpaid salaries, wages, or rent), income tax payable, deposits and credit balances, the current portion of long-term mortgages that is due, and dividends payable.

Long-term liabilities must be paid beyond one year after the balance sheet date. Some examples of long-term liabilities are mortgages, bonds, debentures

Exhibit 9.23
Balance sheet.

Full-menu, table service restaurant with food and beverage sales.
ASSETS
Year Ended December 31, 2000

CURRENT ASSETS			
House Banks	$3,250		
Cash in Bank	35,500	$38,750	
Accounts Receivable			
Customer-House Accounts		20,750	
Inventories			
Food	15,250		
Beverage	8,500		
Other	6,000	29,750	
Prepaid Expenses		18,500	
Total Current Assets			$107,750
FIXED ASSETS			
Land-Parking Lot		58,750	
Leasehold Improvements	213,000		
Less Accumulated Amortization	64,000	149,000	
Furniture and Fixtures	135,000		
Less Accumulated Depreciation	100,750	34,250	
Operating Equipment and Uniforms		73,750	315,750
OTHER ASSETS			32,500
TOTAL ASSETS			$456,000
LIABILITIES AND STOCKHOLDERS' EQUITY			
CURRENT LIABILITIES			
Accounts Payable		$61,000	
Current Portion of Long-Term Debt		10,500	
Accrued Expenses		25,500	
Other Current Liabilities		14,750	
Total Current Liabilities			$111,750
LONG-TERM DEBT, Less Current Portion			169,250
OTHER NONCURRENT LIABILITIES			31,250
Total Liabilities			312,250
STOCKHOLDERS' EQUITY			
Capital Stock		34,000	
Retained Earnings		109,750	
Total Owners' Equity			$143,750
TOTAL LIABILITIES AND STOCKHOLDERS' EQUITY			**$456,000**

(financing arranged through outside sources), and notes payable.

Finally, **owners' equity** is simply total assets minus total liabilities, and tells the worth of a business.

Owners' equity = Total assets - Total liabilities

Many assets can increase owners' equity. For example, some companies sell stock. Any buyer of the stock becomes a part-owner, or shareholder, in the company. This money, along with any profit that's been earned and put back into the business (known as **retained earnings**), forms the two major sources of owners' equity.

The information contained in the balance sheet helps managers and stockholders see how a foodservice establishment is handling its debts. It also informs them what portion of profits has been reinvested into the company as owners' equity.

Apply It Now

Identify each of the following as an asset (A) or a liability (L). Then, if applicable, note whether the item is short-term (S/T) or long-term (L/T).

	A or L	S/T or L/T
Accounts payable	____	____
Stock in a company	____	____
Tables and chairs	____	____
Food inventory items	____	____
Tablecloths	____	____
Unpaid salaries	____	____
Profits	____	____
Cash on hand	____	____

Exhibit 9.24
Foodservice managers with good computer skills can make accounting easier by using special software.

While managers are not expected to be accountants, their ability to learn basic financial principles and accounting practices will greatly increase their success in the field. In today's technological world, foodservice managers who are comfortable with computers and the financial and accounting software that run on them will find their services to be in high demand.

Review Your Learning 9.3

1. The balance sheet helps investors know all of the following except:
   a. how a foodservice establishment is handling its debts.
   b. portion of profits that have been reinvested.
   c. risk involved in future investment in the company.
   d. how the business will do in the future.

2. On a separate sheet of paper, list each of the following assets as either current (C) or fixed (F).
   Cash
   Dishes
   Uniforms
   Food
   Furniture
   Equipment

3. How do you find owners' equity?
   a. Current liabilities – Current assets = Owners' equity
   b. Fixed assets + Current liabilities = Owners' equity
   c. Long-term liabilities + Retained earnings = Owners' equity
   d. Total assets – Total liabilities = Owners' equity

4. How is an asset different from a liability?

Flashback
CHAPTER 9

SECTION 9.1: THE ABCs OF ACCOUNTING

- Although many foodservice businesses have accountants to take care of financial matters, managers need to know the basics of accounting in order to make a variety of decisions.
- In accounting terms, a **transaction** is when money is exchanged for business reasons and needs to be recorded in the accounting records.
- Careful records must be kept of all transactions that affect a foodservice establishment. These transactions are written in the form of T-accounts.
- **T-accounts** are a type of chart resembling the letter "T" used in double-entry accounting to record debits and credits.
- Since every transaction will affect at least two accounts, the recording system is known as double-entry accounting.
- In **double-entry accounting,** equal debits and credits are recorded for every transaction.
- In T-accounts, **debits** are always recorded on the left side of the account, with **credits** on the right side. Depending on the type of T-account, a debit might increase the account, or it might decrease it. The same is true of credits.
- There are five main types of accounts: liability, owners' equity, revenue, asset, and expenses.
- In liability, owners' equity, and revenue T-accounts, debits (left side) decrease the balance while credits (right side) increase the balance.
- In asset and expenses T-accounts, debits (left side) increase the balance while credits (right side) decrease the balance.
- At the end of the accounting period, a **trial balance** is prepared. A trial balance is a procedure used to make sure that total debits equal total credits.

- After all accounts are balanced and adjustments are made, the information can be transferred to an income statement or a balance sheet.
- **Bank reconciliation** is the process of matching the bank's monthly statement with your business's internal accounting records.
- **Cost of sales** is the food cost for one period, usually a month, and is determined by the following formula:

  Cost of sales = Opening inventory + Purchases – Closing inventory

- Managers must know how to allocate direct and indirect costs. **Cost** is the price paid for goods or services when the goods are received or the services are rendered.
- **Expenses** are costs, like food, supplies, wages, and insurance, that are necessary to run a business.
- A **direct cost** is an expense that is the responsibility of a specific department.
- **Indirect costs** are expenses that are not easily charged to any one specific department; usually distributed according to each department's percent of total revenue.
- **Revenue** is the money that an operation takes in when it sells products or services.
- Most foodservice operations own a large number of physical **assets**, items of value owned by the business, that continue to contribute to the business throughout the item's useful life.
- **Depreciation** is a method of recording the value of an asset as it gradually decreases over its lifetime.
- The straight-line depreciation method distributes the cost of an asset equally over each year of its useful life. The formula for determining annual depreciation is:

  $$\frac{(\text{Cost of asset} - \text{Trade-in value})}{\text{Useful life of asset (in years)}}$$

- In the declining balance method, the depreciation rate is doubled and then multiplied by the remaining value each year.
- With the sum-of-the-years digits method, the sum of the digits of the years becomes the denominator of the fractions that are used to make each year's calculation. The numerators are the yearly digits, arranged from the highest number to the lowest. Each

fraction is then multiplied by the asset's cost minus the trade-in value.

- The units of production method is used to determine depreciation values for only those assets with specific units of production, like vehicles. The following formula is used:

$$\frac{\textit{(Cost – Trade-in value)}}{\textit{Estimated units of production over asset's useful life}}$$

SECTION 9.2: THE INCOME STATEMENT

- An **income statement** shows a business's revenue and expenses over a period of time, as well as the resulting profit or loss. The income statement explains how a business is doing in terms of total sales, shows how one month's sales and expenses compare to other months, and provides other important financial information.
- Providing accurate income statements is important; inaccurate statements could lead to potential lawsuits or legal problems with creditors, investors, and the government.
- Direct expenses are totaled for each department in the operation. **Profit** or loss can then be determined. Profit is money left when expenses have been subtracted from revenue. (A **loss** occurs when expenses are greater than revenue.)
- Other expenses include occupancy cost, interest, depreciation, overhead, and taxes, each of which is systematically subtracted from income to arrive at a final figure.
- Once the summary income statement is ready, the manager can compare the expenses and contributory income for each department. **Contributory income** is the amount of income that a particular department contributes to an operation's total income. Once this figure is known, the **contributory income percent** (the percentage of a department's revenue that is income) can be calculated.
- The income statement, as well as its supporting T-accounts and trial balance, provides a detailed look at the financial activity of a foodservice establishment and helps managers and stockholders understand important financial aspects of the operation.

SECTION 9.3: THE BALANCE SHEET

- The **balance sheet** is a basic financial report that shows a company's assets, liabilities, and owners' equity at a particular date.

- The **balance sheet equation** is a basic formula that shows, at a glance, how much a business owes, what it is worth, and the value of the items it owns. The formula looks like this:

  Liabilities + Owners' equity = Assets

- The assets that appear on a balance sheet can be grouped as current, fixed, or other. **Current** (short-term) **assets** are those that can or will be converted to cash within one year. **Fixed** (long-term) **assets** are items, such as land, buildings, and equipment that have a life expectancy of at least three years. Other assets include deposits, investments, and deferred expenses.
- Liabilities can be divided into two categories. **Current liabilities** must be paid within one year. **Long-term liabilities** must be paid beyond one year after the balance sheet date.
- **Owners' equity** is total assets minus total liabilities, and tells the worth of a business.

  Total assets - Total liabilities = Owners' equity

- Stock and **retained earnings** (money put back into the business) are two major owners' equity sources.
- The information contained in the balance sheet helps managers and stockholders know about a foodservice establishment's ability to pay its debts, what portion of profits has been retained, and whether any risk is involved in future operations.

Congratulations! After this unit, you will be ready to continue your foodservice career path. This unit completes your study of the culinary basics, promotes additional career opportunities, and develops your communication skills.

UNIT 4

CHAPTER 10	**Stocks, Soups, and Sauces** Wraps up basic culinary training with the sophisticated techniques that will showcase your culinary talent
CHAPTER 11	**Tourism and the Retail Industry** Expands your knowledge about opportunities in the hospitality industry
CHAPTER 12	**Communicating with Customers** Recaps important communication techniques to help you interact with customers

John Silvia

Food and Beverage Director
Chicago-O'Hare Hilton

I started my foodservice career during high school. Soon after I started my job, I realized that I loved the foodservice industry. After high school, I attended Johnson and Wales University to study culinary arts. When I graduated, I spent ten years working for the Sheraton Corporation. Now I work for the Hilton Corporation. Working for large hotel companies has given me the opportunity to travel and work throughout the world and meet many different kinds of people. I have had many unique experiences that I don't think I would have had working in any other industry.

Working as the food and beverage director at the only hotel in the world's busiest airport (Chicago-O'Hare Hilton) is very exciting. I oversee six different departments, including catering (banquets)/room service, the culinary department, restaurants, beverage service, conference services (setting up meeting rooms and the banquet facilities), and stewarding (cleaning and the supply of non-food items).

Here at the Chicago-O'Hare Hilton, we serve almost 3,000 people every day! It's really important that the presentation of food is perfect. We serve everything from simple foods, like sandwiches and hamburgers, to more upscale foods that require special presentation techniques. Often, a sauce added to a meal really enhances the appearance, taste, and texture of the dish. It can be a simple sauce that complements a single item, or it can be very elaborate and the focus of the course. A sauce should never hide or cover the main ingredient, but should be prepared to accent the main item. A sauce can turn an average meal into a true fine-dining experience. Sauces often add to a chef's reputation for creativity and detail.

To be successful in the hospitality industry you need to be committed. It may take time to progress in your career, but if you stick with it you will have a career that is both financially and personally rewarding.

CHAPTER 10

Stocks, Soups, and Sauces

SECTION 10.1

Preparing Stocks

AFTER STUDYING SECTION 10.1, YOU SHOULD BE ABLE TO:

- Identify the four essential parts of stock and the proper ingredients for each.
- List and explain the various types of stock and their ingredients.
- Demonstrate three methods for preparing bones for stock.
- Prepare the ingredients for, and cook several kinds of stock.
- List the ways to cool stock properly.

Stocks are often called the chef's building blocks because they form the base for many soups and sauces. A **stock** is a flavorful liquid made by gently simmering bones and/or vegetables in a liquid to extract their flavor, aroma, color, body, and nutrients. While stocks are almost never served by themselves, they are a part of many other preparations. Some stocks may take up to

KEY TERMS

- Aromatics
- Bouillon (boo-YON)
- Bouquet garni (boo-KAY gahr-NEE)
- Brown
- Brown stock
- Court bouillon (cort boo-YON)
- Degrease
- Fumet (foo-MAY)
- Glace (glahss)
- Mirepoix (meer-PWAH)
- Remouillage (RAY-moo-LAJ)
- Sachet d'épices (sah-SHAY day-PEESE)
- Stock
- Sweat
- White stock

24 hours to properly cook, but it's worth the time. Preparing stock is the most cost-effective, flavorful way to use valuable vegetable, meat, and fish trimmings.

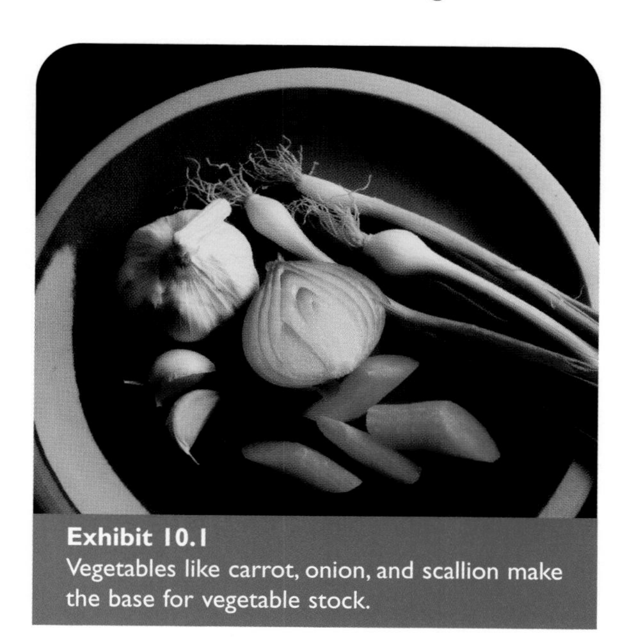

Exhibit 10.1
Vegetables like carrot, onion, and scallion make the base for vegetable stock.

The following are several types of stock:

- **White stock** is a clear, pale liquid made by simmering poultry, beef, or fish bones.
- **Brown stock** is an amber liquid made by first browning poultry, beef, veal, or game bones.
- **Fumet** (foo-MAY) is a highly flavored stock made with fish bones.
- **Court bouillon** (court boo-YON) is an aromatic vegetable broth, and is used for poaching fish or vegetables.
- **Glace** (glahss), sometimes called glaze, is a reduced stock with a jelly-like consistency. Glace can be made from brown stock, chicken stock, or fish stock.
- **Remouillage** (RAY-moo-LAJ) is a stock made from bones that have already been used in another preparation. It can replace water as the liquid used in a stock.
- **Bouillon** (BOO-yon) or broth is the liquid that results from simmering meats or vegetables.

Essential Parts of Stock

Mirepoix

All stocks contain four essential parts: a major flavoring ingredient, liquid, aromatics, and mirepoix. Exhibit 10.2 shows the steps to make stock. **Mirepoix** (meer-PWAH) is a mixture of coarsely chopped onions, carrots, and celery that is used to flavor stocks, soups, and stews. The mixture is usually 50% onions, 25% carrots, and 25% celery. White mirepoix substitutes parsnips, additional onions, leeks, and even chopped mushrooms instead of carrots, and is used for pale or white sauces and stocks, such as fish fumet.

Exhibit 10.2
Preparing stock.

- Combine the major flavoring ingredient and the cold liquid.
- Bring to a simmer.
- Skim as necessary throughout the cooking time.
- Add the mirepoix and aromatics at the appropriate time.
- Simmer until the stock develops flavor, body, and color.
- Strain, use immediately, or cool and store.

Mirepoix should be trimmed and cut into a size appropriate for the type of stock. For preparations with short cooking times, like fish stock, the mirepoix should be sliced or chopped in small pieces; for preparations with cooking times of longer than one hour, as with beef stock, the vegetables may be cut into larger pieces, about 1 to 2 inches long, or even left whole.

Aromatics

Aromatics are herbs, spices, and flavorings that create a savory smell and include bouquet garni and sachet d'épices. **Bouquet garni** (boo-KAY gahr-NEE), French for "bag of herbs," is a combination of fresh vegetables and herbs like fresh thyme, parsley stems, celery, and a bay leaf tied together. Bouquet garni is added to simmering stock. As the stock cooks, the bouquet garni releases the aromatics.

Exhibit 10.3
Fresh herbs can be used to make bouquet garni.

Sachet d'épices (sah-SHAY day-PEESE) is similar to bouquet garni, except it is really a bag of spices. The spices commonly used in sachet d'épices are parsley stems, dried thyme, bay leaf, and cracked peppercorns placed together in a cheesecloth bag. Both bouquet garni and sachet d'épices should be removed once the stock has been sufficiently flavored.

Major Flavoring Ingredient

Often, the *major flavoring ingredient* consists of bones and trimmings for meat and fish stocks, and vegetables for vegetable stocks and court bouillons. When using bones for stock, they must be cut to the right size and prepared by blanching, browning, or sweating.

Blanching the bones rids them of some of the impurities that can cause cloudiness in stock. In a stockpot, bones are covered with cold water and brought to a slow boil. When a full boil is reached, the excess water debris or scum is removed. Exhibit 10.4 shows how to blanch bones.

Exhibit 10.4
Blanching bones.

- Place bones in a stockpot and cover with cold water.
- Bring the water to a slow boil. Skim the surface if necessary.
- Once a full boil has been reached, drain the bones through a sieve or allow the water to drain away through a spigot. Discard the water.
- Rinse the bones thoroughly to remove any debris or scum.
- Proceed with the recipe.

Bones used for making fish fumet must be sweated with vegetables before adding the cooking liquid and seasoning. In the **sweating** process, the bones are cooked in a small amount of fat over low heat until the bones soften and release moisture. Sweating causes mirepoix and bones to release flavor more quickly when the liquid is added.

As with blanching and sweating bones, **browning** (roasting) bones for brown stock does much to enhance the flavor and color of the finished stock. The unwashed bones should be placed in a roasting pan and roasted for one hour. Once they are browned evenly, they are simmered in cold water. This allows for a full robust flavor and color of the stock.

Liquid

Water is the liquid most frequently used when making stock. The ratio of liquid to flavoring ingredients is standard.

- Chicken, beef, veal, and game stock: 8 lb of bones to 6 qt of water yield 1 gal of stock; 1 lb of mirepoix is needed.
- Fish/shellfish stock or fumet: 11 lb of bones or shells to 5 qt of water and 1 lb of mirepoix yield 1 gal.
- Vegetable stock: 1 lb of vegetables to 1 qt of water yields 1 qt of stock.

The taste of a stock should be very flavorful, but not so strong that it overpowers the other ingredients used in the finished dish. Fish, chicken, and beef stock have the strongest flavors; white veal stock is considered neutral.

Depending on what ingredients are used to make stocks, they can be very nutritious and a great way to reduce the overall fat and calorie content of soup. Homemade soups made with vegetable-based broth will be low in fat and calories, while adding many vitamins and other essential nutrients.

The quality of stock is evaluated on the basis of its flavor, color, body, and clarity. The major flavoring ingredient should dominate, and the stock should taste fresh. With the exception of fumet, stocks should be almost crystal clear when they are hot.

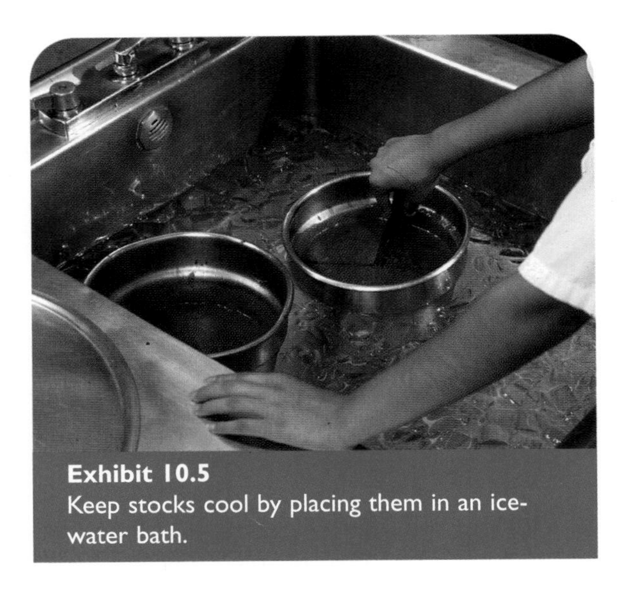

Exhibit 10.5
Keep stocks cool by placing them in an ice-water bath.

Cooling and Storing Stock

To cool stock, it should be put in a stockpot and placed in an ice-water bath, and stirred often. When it has cooled, place it in the refrigerator. Another method of cooling stock is to break down the large amount of stock into smaller amounts and place them in small containers in the refrigerated unit. These should be stirred occasionally so the entire contents in each container cools at the same rate. Always observe sanitation rules and time in the temperature danger zone when cooling stocks.

After the stock has been stored, it must be degreased before it can be used. **Degreasing** is the process of removing fat that has cooled and then hardened from the surface of the stock. Fat can then be lifted or scraped away before the stock is reheated. Not only does degreasing give the stock a more clear and pure color, it also makes the stock more nutritious. Note that this is not a substitute for skimming the fat and impurities that rise to the top of the pot during the cooking process.

Making stocks in the professional kitchen is time-consuming. For this reason, some foodservice operations use pre-packaged, commercially prepared stock bases. These are powdered or dried flavorings added to water to create stocks, or sometimes to enhance the flavor of soups or sauces. The flavor of these ready-made mixes can be improved by adding a mirepoix, standard sachet d'épices, and a few appropriate bones to the mixture. While there is no substitute for a homemade stock, a good prepared mix is appropriate when the tools, time, and skilled kitchen staff are not available.

Review Your Learning 10.1

Match each item on the left with its definition on the right.

1. Sachet d'épices
2. Mirepoix
3. Fumet
4. Bouquet garni
5. Glace

a. Mixture of coarsely chopped onions, carrots, and celery
b. Reduced stock that develops a jelly-like consistency
c. Bag of herbs used to flavor stocks
d. Highly flavored stock made with fish bones
e. Bag of spices used to flavor stock

6. Explain in your own words why stock is important.

7. You are responsible for cooling a large amount of chicken stock. Describe how you will cool the stock.

8. Describe how and why bones, shells, and vegetables are:
   a. sweated.
   b. browned.
   c. blanched.

Preparing Soups

AFTER STUDYING SECTION 10.2, YOU SHOULD BE ABLE TO:

- Identify the two basic kinds of soups and give an example of each.
- Explain the preparation of the basic ingredients for broth, consommé, pureé, clear, and cream soups.
- State in your own words the steps in the prepreparation of several kinds of soups.

Any good soup is made with the best ingredients available. There are two basic kinds of soups: clear soups and thick soups. Flavored stocks, broths, and consommés are considered clear soups; cream soups and purée soups are considered thick soups. To make excellent soups, major flavoring components must be carefully selected. When preparing

KEY TERMS

- Bisque (bisk)
- Borscht (borsht)
- Broth
- Chowder
- Clarify
- Clear soup
- Consommé (con-soh-MAY)
- Cream soup
- Filé (fee-LAY)
- Gazpacho (gahz-PAH-cho)
- Gumbo
- Minestrone
- Oignon brûlé (oy-NYON broo-LAY)
- Purée soup
- Raft
- Vichyssoise (vee-shee-SWAH)

Exhibit 10.6
As an appetizer or main course, soup makes a nutritious and hearty meal.

soups of any kind, always follow sanitation guidelines for preparing safe foods. These guidelines are discussed in detail in *Chapter 3: Preparing and Serving Safe Food* of *Becoming a Foodservice Professional, Year 1.*

FUN FOOD FACT

Soups were the early American colonists' first convenience foods. Soups would be left simmering over the fire and leftover vegetables and meat would be added each day. In colder climates, the soup kettle was hung in an outdoor shed. The French called this a "pot au feu" or "pot of fire." The French have made this for hundreds of years, and it is still made and enjoyed today.

Preparing Clear Soups

Clear soups include stocks, broth, and consommés. Basic stock or broth is an essential base in creating clear soups. **Broth** is made from a combination of water, vegetable, or meat (beef, veal, chicken, fish), mirepoix, and bouquet garni. As the mixture simmers, the flavors combine giving the broth a unique taste. A good broth should be clear to pale amber, with the distinct flavor of the major ingredient. Exhibit 10.7 shows steps for making broth.

Exhibit 10.7
Basic broth.

- Combine the meat and water.
- Bring to an even simmer.
- Add the mirepoix and bouquet garni.
- Simmer to the appropriate cooking times depending on the main ingredient in the broth.
  - Beef, veal, game, chicken: 2-3 hours
  - Fish: 30-40 minutes
  - Vegetables: 30 minutes-1 hour
- Skim and strain. Cool, store, or finish and garnish for service.
- A good broth should be clear, pale amber, with the distinct flavor of the major ingredient.

Consommé is a kind of clear soup, and is sometimes considered one of the greatest of all soups. **Consommé** (con-soh-MAY) is actually a rich, flavorful broth or stock that has been clarified. To **clarify** a

Exhibit 10.8
Chicken noodle soup is just one example of a clear soup.

stock or broth means to make it absolutely clear. Basic consommé, like broth, consists of mirepoix, seasonings, and meat. It also includes a tomato product, egg white, and **oignon brûlé** (oy-NYON broo-LAY), a burned onion that has been grilled over very high heat to brown the outside.

As the ingredients simmer, the **raft,** or meat and egg white proteins, will form on the surface of the consommé. The raft traps any impurities in the mixture that can cloud the consommé. Good consommé should be clear, aromatic, and emphasize the flavor of the major ingredient. To bolster the flavor of a weak consommé, a meat or poultry glaze may be added. Exhibit 10.9 shows steps to make consommé.

Exhibit 10.9
Basic consommé.

- Combine the ground meat, mirepoix, seasonings, tomato product, oignon brûlé, and egg white.
- Blend in the stock.
- Bring to a boil and stir frequently.
- Simmer.
- Do not stir after the raft has formed.
- Break a hole in the raft and simmer.
- Strain, cool and store, or finish and garnish for service.
- Good consommé should be crystal clear, aromatic, and emphasize the flavor of the major ingredient.

Preparing Thick Soups

Cream Soups

There are two kinds of thick soups: cream soups and purée soups. Unlike consommés and broth, **cream soups** are made with a thickener, like roux (a mixture of fat, usually butter, chicken fat, or vegetable oil, and flour). Roux will be discussed in greater detail in Section 10.3.

To make a cream soup, the major flavoring ingredient of the soup is first sautéed in a small amount of butter or oil. Flour is then added and the roux is cooked for a short time to eliminate the starchy taste. The stock is then added along with any remaining vegetables and simmered until tender. The mixture is puréed, strained, and its consistency is adjusted with more stock. The soup is finished with cream and garnished for service.

The major ingredient in cream soups should be the dominant flavor. For example, in cream of mushroom soup, the dominant flavor should be mushroom, not cream. The thickness of soup must be of heavy cream, and its texture should be smooth. Often, cream soups are garnished with a bit of the soup's main ingredient (i.e., several small blanched broccoli florets on a cream of broccoli soup). Exhibit 10.11 shows steps to make cream soups.

Exhibit 10.10
Thick soup includes cream and a thickener, like roux.

Exhibit 10.11
Cream soup.

- Sweat the vegetables in a small amount of fat.
- Add the flour and cook the roux.
- Add the liquid.
- Bring to a boil.
- Lower to a simmer.
- Add the bouquet garni or sachet d'épices.
- Skim, and discard the bouquet garni or sachet d'épices as necessary.
- Purée, then strain.
- Add more stock to adjust the soup to the proper consistency.
- Finish with cream and garnish for service.
- The major ingredient in cream soups should be the dominant flavor. The soup should not taste like cream.
- Garnish with a bit of the soup's main ingredient.

Purée Soups

Cream and purée soups are similar because they both use a puréed main ingredient that is then blended into the rest of the soup. The main difference between a purée and cream soup is that cream soups are thickened with an added starch, while **purée soups** are thickened by the starch found in the puréed main ingredient. Like cream soups, purée soups are also made with sachet d' épices or bouquet garni, and a liquid.

Purée soups are more coarse than cream soups. As with a cream soup, the flavor of the main ingredient should be dominant. Purée soups should be liquid enough to pour easily from a ladle. Exhibit 10.12 lists some suggestions for preparing cream and purée soups.

Exhibit 10.12
Helpful hints for cream and purée soups.

- If a cream soup becomes too thick, use water or stock until the correct consistency is achieved. Never use heavy cream—it can hide the flavor of the main ingredient.
- If the soup has a sour or "off" flavor, or has curdled, discard it. Cream soups have a brief storage time once the cream has been added. To store cream soups longer, be sure that the base is properly chilled and stored. Finish only the amount needed for a single service period.
- If the soup has a scorched taste, transfer it immediately to a cool, clean pot and check the flavor. If it doesn't taste scorched in the clean pan, it is safe to continue cooking.

Bisques, Chowders, and Specialty Soups

Bisques are another kind of thick soup. **Bisque** (bisk) is a cream soup made from puréed shellfish shells. The base for bisque is made from shellfish, like lobster, shrimp, or crab. The shells are puréed along with vegetables to enhance the flavor of the major ingredient, making the texture slightly grainy. A properly prepared bisque should have the flavor of the shellfish and have a pale pink or red color. Exhibit 10.13 shows steps to make bisque.

Exhibit 10.13
Making bisque.

- Sear the crustacean shells in a fat or stock.
- Add the mirepoix and sweat.
- Add the tomato product.
- Reduce until it is au sec (reduced until it is very dry).
- Add the stock and sachet d'épices or bouquet garni.
- Mix in the roux.
- Simmer, and skim.
- Discard the sachet d'épices or bouquet garni when the desired flavor has been achieved.
- Strain, then purée the solids.
- Remix the liquid to the proper consistency.
- Strain, then cool and store, or finish and garnish with the cooked, reserved meat from the crustacean.
- A properly prepared bisque should have the flavor of the crustacean and a pale pink or red color.

Chowders are hearty soups made in much the same way as cream soups, except chowders are not puréed before the cream or milk is added. Chowders typically include large pieces of the main ingredients (usually potatoes) and garnishes. Chowders almost always include milk or cream, and are usually thickened with roux.

Of the three types of soups mentioned in this chapter, cream soups most often include high portions of fat and sodium. Butter, cream, and salt are generally used as main ingredients. To lower your fat and sodium intake, stick to low-fat, clear soups like consommé or flavored stocks or broths.

Specialty or national soups include **minestrone,** a tomato-based vegetable soup from Italy; **gumbo,** a thick Creole soup from Louisiana made with okra, **filé** (fee-LAY) powder, a thickening agent and seasoning made from ground sassafras leaves; **vichyssoise** (vee-shee-SWAH), a cold potato and leek soup from France; **gazpacho** (gahz-PAH-cho), a cold, tomato-based soup made with cucumbers, onions, green peppers, and garlic from Spain; and **borscht** (borsht), a Russian cold beet soup.

Cooking Soups

Soups must be cooked properly. Most soups are cooked at a gentle simmer and stirred occasionally. Cream soups should never be boiled because boiling can cause the milk fat to break down, making the soup too thin and watery. Any scum or foam should be removed with a skimmer. It's a mistake to cook soup too long—not only does the flavor become flat, but all the nutrients are lost in the cooking process. Adding chopped fresh herbs, lemon juice, or a dash of hot pepper sauce to soup can brighten its flavor.

Finishing Soups

Finishing techniques are essential in preparing soup for service. It is important to remove the surface fat on the soup before service. Blot soups with strips of unwaxed brown butcher paper to eliminate unwanted fat. Soups should be garnished just before service. Sometimes a light sprinkling of chopped parsley is all that is required to make the presentation attractive and pleasing to the guest.

Soups are a very versatile meal. They can be reheated very easily. Only the amount of soup that is to be used for the service should be reheated. Clear soups should be brought to a full boil, while thick soups should be reheated gently. Soups can be heated in a microwave oven if they are placed in microwave-safe bowls, stirred, and returned to the microwave before serving.

Exhibit 10.14
Squash soup is finished with a dollop of sour cream.

Review Your Learning 10.2

Match each soup on the left with its lettered description on the right.

1. Bisque
2. Gumbo
3. Borscht
4. Minestrone
5. Gazpacho

a. Tomato-broth vegetable soup
b. Cream soup made with shellfish
c. Cold soup made with tomatoes, cucumbers, onions, green peppers, and garlic
d. Beet soup
e. Thick Creole soup made with okra and other ingredients

6. Explain in your own words how you would remove surface fat on clear soup before serving.
7. What is the main difference between cream and purée soups?
8. Why is it important to clarify consommé?

Preparing Sauces

AFTER STUDYING SECTION 10.3, YOU SHOULD BE ABLE TO:

- Identify the grand sauces and describe other sauces made from them.
- List the proper ingredients for sauces.
- Prepare several kinds of sauces.
- Match sauces to appropriate foods.

The use of all types of sauces is very important in cooking. While adding moisture and richness to food, they also introduce complementary and contrasting flavors, enhance the appearance of food, and add texture to the dish.

There are five base sauces upon which most other sauces are made. These five sauces are called **grand sauces.** They are sometimes referred to as *mother sauces*

KEY TERMS

- Au jus (ow ZHEW)
- Béchamel (BAY-shah-MELL)
- Beurre manié (byurr man-YAY)
- Brown sauce
- Compound butter
- Coulis
- Demi-glace (DEH-mee glahs)
- Espagnole sauce (ess-spah-NYOL)
- Grand sauce
- Hollandaise (HALL-en-daze)
- Jus (zhew)
- Liaison (lee-AY-zohn)
- Maître d'hôtel butter (MAY-tra doh-TEL)
- Roux (roo)
- Salsa
- Slurry
- Tomato sauce
- Velouté (veh-loo-TAY)
- Wringing method

because they are the bases for so many other sauces. The five grand sauces are:

- **Béchamel** (BAY-shah-MELL), which is made from milk and white roux.
- **Velouté** (veh-loo-TAY), which is made from veal, chicken, or fish stock and a white or blond roux.
- **Brown** or **espagnole sauce** (ess-spah-NYOL), which is made from brown stock and brown roux.
- **Tomato sauce,** which is made from a stock and tomatoes. Roux is optional.
- **Hollandaise** (HALL-en-daze),which is a rich, emulsified sauce made from butter, egg yolks, lemon juice, and cayenne pepper.

Exhibit 10.15
Hollandaise sauce traditionally tops eggs benedict.

Grand sauces are rarely used by themselves and often form the bases of derivative sauces. *Derivative* sauces are sauces made using one of the five grand sauces as a base. For example, **demi-glace** (DEH-mee glahs) is a very rich sauce that is a derivative of the grand sauce known as brown sauce, or espagnole. Demi-glace is made by mixing the brown sauce with beef stock and Madeira wine or sherry. Demi-glace can then be used as a base for other, smaller sauces in the espagnole family. Exhibit 10.16 lists grand sauces and their derivatives.

Not all sauces are classified as grand sauces or as a derivative of a grand sauce. Other types of sauces include compound butters and other miscellaneous sauces, like salsa and coulis.

Compound butter is a mixture of raw butter and various flavoring ingredients. Compound butters are used to finish grilled or broiled meats, fish, poultry, game, pastas, and sauces. Some ingredients used in compound butters are herbs, nuts, citrus zest, shallots, ginger, and vegetables. The butter is rolled into a long tube shape, then thoroughly chilled and sliced for use as needed. One example is **maître d'hôtel butter** (MAY-tra doh-TEL), which is softened butter flavored with lemon juice and chopped parsley.

Exhibit 10.16
Grand sauces and their derivatives.

Grand Sauce	Derivative Sauce	Additional Ingredients
Béchamel	Cream	Cream (instead of milk)
	Cheddar cheese	Cheddar cheese
	Soubise	Puréed cooked onions
Veal velouté	Allemande	Egg yolks
	Hungarian	Egg yolks, Hungarian paprika
	Curry	Egg yolks, curry spices
Chicken velouté	Mushroom	Cream, mushrooms
	Albufera (Ivory)	Cream, meat glaze, pimiento butter
	Hungarian	Cream, Hungarian paprika
Fish velouté	White wine	White wine
	Percy	White wine, shallots, butter, parsley
	Herb	White wine, herbs
Brown (espagnole)	Bordelaise	Red wine, parsley
	Diable	White wine or vinegar, cayenne pepper
	Lyonnaise	Sautéed onions, butter, white wine, vinegar
	Piquante	Shallots, white wine, vinegar, chopped gherkins, parsley, chervil, tarragon
Tomato	Creole	Sweet peppers, onions, chopped tomatoes
	Portuguese	Onions, chopped tomatoes, garlic, parsley
Hollandaise	Béarnaise	Tarragon, white wine, vinegar, shallots
	Maltaise	Grated orange zest, orange juice

Other miscellaneous sauces include salsa and coulis. **Coulis** is a thick puréed sauce, such as tomato coulis. **Salsa** is a cold mixture of fresh herbs, spices, fruits, and/or vegetables, used as a sauce for meat, poultry, fish, or shellfish. Though these are not traditional grand or derivative sauces, they do function in much the same way that those sauces do. For example, they do add flavor, moisture, texture, and color to the dish. They also allow chefs to change the menu item by providing a lower-fat alternative to the usually heavy grand or derivative sauces.

Sauces are sometimes made with the natural juices from meat. As you remember from *Chapter 8: Meat, Poultry, and Seafood*, **jus** (zhew) is sauce made from the juices from cooked meat and brown stock; meats served with their own juice are called **au jus** (ow ZHEW).

Exhibit 10.17
Salsa decorates Mexican chimichangas.

Thickeners

Thickeners are also important in preparing sauces. They are added to sauces to give them additional richness and body. Some examples of thickeners are roux, beurre manié, slurry, and liaison.

Roux

Roux, as mentioned in Section 10.2, is a thickener made of equal parts cooked flour and a fat like clarified butter, oil, or shortening. Butter that is clarified has been heated to remove the water and milk solids, leaving only the butterfat. It is important to clarify butter for use in many cooking procedures because the milk solids cause the butter to burn.

There are three types of roux most often used. They are:

- *white roux*—cooked for a very short period of time, and used in sauces where little color is needed, like béchamel;
- *blond roux*—cooked longer than white roux until the flour turns light brown and has a nutty aroma. Blond roux is used in ivory-colored sauces like velouté;
- *brown roux*—cooked until it develops a dark brown color. Brown roux is used in dishes that require a dark brown color.

It doesn't matter if the roux is white, blond, or brown—the procedure for making any kind of roux is the same. Exhibit 10.18 shows the proper procedure for making roux.

It is important to observe sanitation guidelines when preparing sauces that use eggs, milk, or other dairy products. Emulsified butter sauces, like Hollandaise, should not be held between 40° to 140°F to prevent foodborne illness and to maintain the quality of the sauce. As always, make sure all utensils are clean and sanitized!

Exhibit 10.18
Making roux.

1. Heat the clarified butter or other fat in a heavy saucepan.
2. Add the flour and stir together with the fat to form a paste.
3. Cook the paste over medium heat until the desired color is reached.
4. Stir the roux continually to avoid burning.

Beurre Manié

Beurre manié (byurr man-YAY) is a thickener made of equal parts flour and soft, whole butter. The flour and butter are mixed together, and then shaped into small pea-sized balls that are added to the cooking sauce. Beurre manié is used to thicken a sauce quickly at the end of the cooking process.

Slurry

Sometimes cornstarch is added to sauce as a thickener. To properly incorporate cornstarch into a sauce, it must first be mixed with a cold liquid before it is introduced to the sauce. This is done to prevent the cornstarch from becoming too lumpy once it is mixed with the sauce. The mixture of cornstarch and cold liquid is known as a **slurry.** Sauces thickened with cornstarch must be cooked until the liquid turns clear and the starch flavor disappears. However, the sauce must not be boiled too long or the starch will break down, creating a watery sauce.

Liaison

Another type of thickener used for sauces is called a liaison. A **liaison** (lee-AY-zohn) is a mixture of egg yolks and heavy cream that adds a rich flavor and velvety smoothness to the sauce without making it too thick. Therefore, it is often used as a finishing technique. It is important to temper the liaison very carefully into the sauce to prevent the egg yolks from curdling. Tempering is when you slowly mix a little bit of the hot sauce with the eggs before adding the rest of the egg mixture back into the sauce.

Finishing Sauces

A key to finishing sauces is to adjust their consistency. For example, it may be necessary to add stock to a sauce to thin out the consistency. The added stock will also help flavor the sauce. Sometimes a red or white wine can be added to thicken a sauce, providing a very distinctive taste.

Straining is another finishing technique that is done once the consistency and flavor of the sauce has been adjusted. One method

Exhibit 10.19
Salmon steak served with sauce thickened with roux.

most often used when straining sauces in the wringing method. In the **wringing method,** a clean cheesecloth is draped over a bowl, and the sauce is poured into the bowl and through the cheesecloth. The cloth is then twisted at either end to squeeze out the strained sauce. The cheesecloth catches the unwanted lumps of roux, or herbs, spices, and other seasonings that may have been added for flavor. Sauces may also be strained through a china cap lined with cheesecloth, or a fine meshed strainer, or chinois (chee-no-AH). Straining helps ensure the sauce will have a smooth consistency.

The final step before serving anything is always to adjust the seasoning: the same is true for sauces. Both salt and lemon juice, when added as seasonings, emphasize the flavors in the sauce. Cayenne and white pepper are also very flavorful seasonings use when finishing sauces.

There are various factors to consider when selecting the correct sauce to serve with a meal. The sauce should be suitable for the style of service; the sauce should be suitable for the main ingredient's cooking technique; and the sauce's flavor must be appropriate for the flavor of the food it is accompanying.

Review Your Learning 10.3

Match each grand sauce on the left with its primary ingredients on the right.

1. Béchamel
2. Velouté
3. Espagnole
4. Tomato
5. Hollandaise

a. Stock and tomatoes
b. White or blonde roux and veal, chicken, or fish stock
c. Brown stock and brown roux
d. Butter, egg yolks, lemon juice, cayenne pepper
e. Milk and white roux

6. Name some sauces that are not classified as grand sauces.
7. What is the most important factor to consider when matching a sauce with a meal?
8. How are thickeners important in preparing sauces? List some examples.

Flashback

CHAPTER 10

SECTION 10.1: PREPARING STOCKS

- A **stock** is a concentrated, flavorful liquid made by gently simmering bones and/or vegetables in a liquid to extract their flavor, aroma, color, body, and nutrients. Stocks form the base for many soups and sauces.
- There are many different types of stock.
- **White stock:** clear, pale liquid made by simmering poultry, beef, or fish bones.
- **Brown stock:** amber liquid made by first browning (roasting) poultry, beef, veal, or game bones.
- **Fumet:** highly flavored stock made with fish bones.
- **Court bouillon:** aromatic vegetable broth.
- **Glace:** reduced stock that develops a jelly-like consistency. Glace can be made from brown stock, chicken stock, or fish stock.
- **Remouillage:** stock made from bones that have already been used in another preparation. It can replace water as the liquid requirement in stock.
- **Bouillon** or broth: liquid that results from simmering meats or vegetables.
- Stocks contain a major flavoring ingredient, liquid, aromatics, and mirepoix.
- **Mirepoix** is a mixture of coarsely chopped onions, carrots, and celery that is used to flavor stocks, soups, and stews.
- **Aromatics** are herbs, spices, and flavorings that create a savory smell and include **sachet d'épices** (bag of spices) or **bouquet garni** (bag of herbs).
- The *major flavoring ingredient* consists of bones and trimmings for meat and fish stocks, and vegetables for vegetable stocks and court bouillons.
- Bones used for meat and fish stocks must be cut into the right size and prepared by blanching, browning, or sweating.
- When blanching bones, they are boiled in water to rid them of debris and scum.

- Bones that are **browned** are roasted and then simmered in water to enhance the flavor of the stock.
- Bones or shells used in fumets must be **sweated,** a process in which bones and mirepoix are gently cooked before the liquid is added.
- The *liquid* most often used when making stock is water.
- The taste of a stock should be very flavorful and shouldn't overpower the other ingredients used in the finished dish. Fish, chicken, and beef stock have the strongest flavors; white veal stock is considered neutral.
- Stocks are evaluated based on flavor, color, aroma, and clarity. The major flavoring ingredient should dominate and taste fresh.
- Stock should be placed in a stockpot in an ice-water bath, and stirred often to cool. Stock can also be broken down into smaller containers and then refrigerated. Always observe sanitation rules when cooling stocks.
- Stock must be **degreased,** or removed of hardened fat that rises to the surface during the cooling process.

SECTION 10.2: PREPARING SOUPS

- There are two kinds of soup: clear soups and thick soups. Quality stock forms the best soup base.
- Flavored stocks, broths, and consommés are considered **clear soups. Thick soups** are cream soups and purée soups.
- Basic **broth** is an essential base in creating other soups. It is made from a combination of stock, vegetable or meat (beef, veal, chicken, or fish), mirepoix, and bouquet garni.
- **Consommé** is actually a rich, flavorful broth or stock that has been clarified. It consists of mirepoix, seasonings, meat, and egg whites.
- To **clarify** a stock or broth means to make it absolutely clear.
- Sometimes a tomato product, egg white, and **oignon brûlé** are included to clarify the stock. As the ingredients simmer, **raft** will form on the surface of the consommé trapping impurities that can cloud the consommé.
- Consommé should be clear, aromatic, and emphasize the major ingredient.

- **Cream soups** use more ingredients, like cream and roux. The major ingredient should be the dominant flavor.
- Both cream and purée soups use a puréed main ingredient that is then blended into the rest of the soup. The main difference between the two is that while cream soups are thickened with a starch like roux, **purée soups** are thickened by the natural starch found in the puréed main ingredient, not by an added starch.
- **Bisques** have a base of puréed shellfish, like shrimp, lobster, or crab. The shells are puréed with the vegetables. A properly prepared bisque should have a pale pink color and the flavor of the shellfish.
- **Chowders** typically include large pieces of the main ingredients (usually potatoes) and garnishes. Chowders almost always include milk or cream, and are thickened with roux.
- Specialty or national soups include **minestrone, gumbo, vichyssoise, gazpacho,** and **borscht.**
- Soups must be cooked properly. They should be cooked at a gentle simmer and stirred occasionally.
- Cream soups should never be boiled because boiling can cause the milk fat to break down making the soup too watery. Scum or foam that rises to the surface should be removed.
- Cooling and finishing techniques are essential in preparing soup for service. Blot soups with strips of unwaxed brown butcher paper to eliminate unwanted fat.
- Soups should be garnished just before service.

SECTION 10.3: PREPARING SAUCES

- Sauces add moisture and richness to food, introduce complementary and contrasting flavors, enhance the appearance of food, and add texture to the dish.
- **Grand sauces** include:

  —**Brown** or **espagnole**—brown stock and brown roux.

  —**Velouté**—veal, chicken, or fish stock and white or blonde roux.

  —**Béchamel**—milk and white roux.

  —**Tomato**—stock and tomatoes; roux is optional.

—**Hollandaise**—rich, emulsified sauce made from butter, egg yolks, lemon juice, and cayenne pepper.

- Grand sauces are rarely used by themselves and often form the base for derivative sauces. Derivative sauces are made using one of the five grand sauces as a base.
- Not all sauces are classified as grand sauces or as a derivative of a grand sauce. Other types of sauces include compound butters and other miscellaneous sauces, like salsa and coulis.
- **Compound butter** is a mixture of raw butter and flavoring ingredients. **Maître d'hôtel butter,** butter flavored with lemon juice and chopped parsley, is one example of a compound butter.
- Miscellaneous sauces include salsa and coulis. **Salsa** is a cold mixture of fresh herbs, spices, fruits and/or vegetables often used as a sauce for meat, poultry, fish, or shellfish. **Coulis** is a thick puréed sauce, such as tomato coulis.
- **Jus** is a sauce made with the juices from cooked meat; meats served with their own juices are called **au jus.**
- Thickeners are important when preparing sauces. They are added to sauces to give them additional richness and body. Some commonly used thickeners are roux, beurre manié, slurry, and liaison.
- **Roux** is made of equal parts flour and fat. There are three types of roux: **white roux, blond roux,** and **brown roux.**
- **Beurre manié** is a thickener made of equal parts flour and soft whole butter that is mixed together, shaped into small pea-sized balls, and added to the sauce.
- A **slurry** is a mixture of cornstarch and a cool liquid.
- A **liaison** is a mixture of egg yolks and heavy cream that adds a rich flavor to the sauce without making it too thick.
- A key to finishing sauces is to adjust its consistency and flavor if necessary.
- Straining is also important in finishing sauces. A common form of straining is the **wringing method.** Straining helps the sauce have a smooth consistency by preventing unwanted clumps of roux, or herbs, spices, and other sea-

sonings from ending up in the finished product.

- Adjusting the seasoning of a sauce is part of the finishing process. Adding salt, lemon juice, cayenne, or white pepper is common.
- When selecting the correct sauce to serve with a meal, a few factors should be considered: the sauce should be suitable for the style of service; the sauce should be suitable for the main ingredient's cooking technique; and the sauce's flavor must be appropriate for the flavor of the food it is accompanying.

PROFILE

Ernest P. Boger

Professor
Director of Hospitality Management Program
Bethune-Cookman College
Daytona Beach, Florida

I worked as a waiter and dishwasher while attending the University of Southern Florida, where I became the first African-American graduate in 1965. Since then, I've managed hotels, inns, and apartment buildings in Jamaica and Texas, and taught hospitality management in Florida, South Carolina, and the Bahamas. I now head the entire hospitality management program at Bethune-Cookman College.

I love teaching because I'm helping a new generation of people succeed in the foodservice, hotel, and travel industries by equipping them with not only academic theory, but real skills that managers need.

I'm excited about the present and future of the travel industry. The world is shrinking. Our ability to travel anywhere in the world quickly allows us to be face-to-face with our global neighbors. It's a new and exciting time we're living in.

The complexity of our world means that much is expected of people who work in the travel industry. They must be well-educated, and have the skills to give accurate and complete service.

To be a true professional, you must have not only the personality and attitude to give good personal service, but the technical skills to help people travel; people need itineraries, tickets, passports, visas, and all sorts of other details when they travel, and the travel professional must know how all that works. Having an education helps you give that kind of service and have a successful travel career. There's no substitute for that.

CHAPTER 11

Tourism and the Retail Industry

Understanding Tourism

AFTER STUDYING SECTION 11.1, YOU SHOULD BE ABLE TO:

- Explain the role of tourism in the hospitality industry.
- Categorize the types of businesses that make up the tourism industry.
- List and discuss reasons why people travel.

You have probably been a tourist at some time in your life. If you've ever visited a museum, flown on an airplane, or stayed overnight in a motel, you've experienced the travel and tourism industry firsthand. People travel for many reasons and need a variety of services while they are away from home. Crossing over the entire hospitality industry, tourism provides these services to travelers on-the-go.

What Is Tourism?

Tourism is a combination of all of the services that people need and will pay for when they are away from home. Tourism includes

KEY TERMS

- Accommodations
- Business tourism
- Cultural and historic tourism
- Eating establishment
- Entertainment
- Environmental tourism
- Recreational tourism
- Shop
- Tourism
- Transportation

all of the businesses that benefit from people traveling and spending their money:

- **Transportation**—cars, airlines, railways, cruise ships, bus lines
- **Accommodations**—hotels, motels, resorts, inns, convention centers
- **Eating establishments**—full-service restaurants, quick-service restaurants, vending services, catering and banquet facilities at convention centers, highway rest stops
- **Shops**—malls, gift shops, convenience stores
- **Entertainment**—theater, concerts, sightseeing attractions, museums, historical landmarks, sports events

As you can see, the tourism industry includes many different types of businesses. The people who work in these businesses and serve travelers need to know what's happening in town, where to stay and where to eat, and how to get from one place to another.

Apply It Now

Travelers are visiting your city and want to know what's happening in town, where to stay and where to eat, and how to get from one place to another. What information can you provide them?

The Growth of Tourism

While the travel industry hasn't always been as complex as it is today, it has existed for thousands of years. As you'll recall from *Chapter 1: The History of Food Service,* people traveled in ancient times mainly to trade goods with others. As travel increased along trade routes between Europe, Asia, the Middle East, and Africa, people opened inns along the way to offer travelers meals and places to stay.

It wasn't until the 1700s that the idea of travel as a form of entertainment really caught on. Wealthy Europeans began to spend several months a year traveling to major cities in Europe, Turkey, and North Africa to see famous art, visit historic buildings, and eat local foods. In the

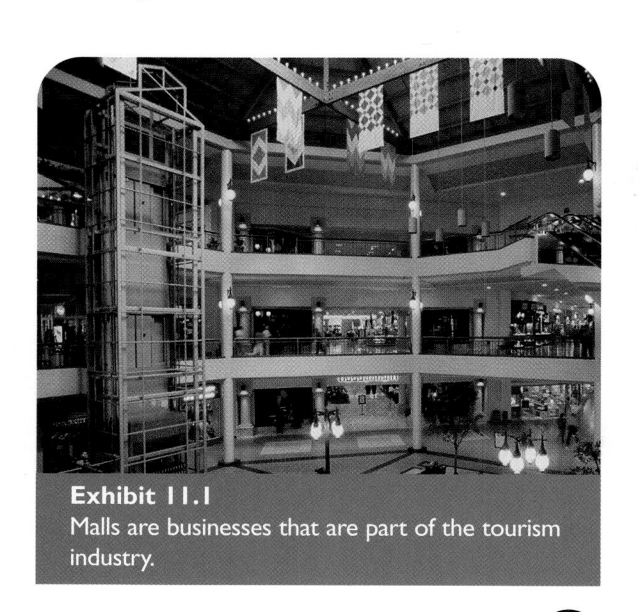

Exhibit 11.1
Malls are businesses that are part of the tourism industry.

1800s, an increasing number of people, especially Americans and Europeans, had money to spend on traveling for pleasure. As a result, more and more hotels and restaurants were built, and a variety of events were offered to attract tourists.

As you learned in *Chapter 3: The Lodging Industry,* the development of the railroad in the 1800s helped people travel faster—and to more places. In the 1920s, travelers began to journey by car. And as Henry Ford and other industrialists began mass-producing cars, making them more affordable, people traveled more than ever before. In addition to the creation of major highway systems, the 1950s saw the growth of commercial airlines, with faster and bigger airplanes being developed after World War II.

Tourism is big business. The United States has become the world's top international tourism earner, taking in about $56.5 billion from tourists in 1993 alone. In addition to the United States, Italy, Spain, France, and Austria take in the most money from tourism.

Types of Tourism: An Overview

As you should recall from *Chapter 3: The Lodging Industry,* there are two broad categories of travelers—leisure travelers and business travelers. *Leisure travelers* often visit friends or relatives, sightsee, or vacation just to get away and relax. *Business travelers* meet with associates, attend conventions, and generally stay at properties close to business complexes.

To meet the needs of both leisure and business travelers, marketers classify tourism according to the type of travel experience that people are looking for.

- **Cultural and historic tourism**—In addition to visiting places of historical interest and importance, cultural travelers visit to other lands to observe, learn about, and live among people whose cultures are different from their own. Cultural and historic tours are often organized for groups of travelers, although many people plan their own trips. Examples include visiting Paris to learn how the French live; going to Washington, D.C., to see famous monuments; traveling to Williamsburg, Virginia, to walk along colonial streets; and traveling to Beijing to meet Chinese people and see the Great Wall.
- **Environmental tourism**—Some travelers visit places in order to enjoy their natural beauty. These tourists

Exhibit 11.2
Traveling to Paris, France, to see the Eiffel Tower is an example of cultural and historical tourism.

Exhibit 11.3
Southern Utah provides travelers with some spectacular scenery and outdoor recreation opportunities.

often enjoy photography, hiking, biking, mountain climbing, camping, and canoeing. Examples of environmental destinations include the Grand Canyon and Niagara Falls.

- **Recreational tourism**—Travelers on recreational vacations usually look for places where they can swim, lie in the sun, ski, play golf and tennis, see shows, or gamble. Examples include Vail, Colorado; Las Vegas, Nevada; and Ft. Lauderdale, Florida.
- **Business tourism**—Conventions, meetings, and seminars provide their host cities with big business. It's not surprising then that cities compete with each other for such business. The more a city can offer in terms of hotels, restaurants, attractions, and entertainment, the more business tourists it will attract.

Exhibit 11.4
The National Restaurant Association's annual Restaurant Hotel-Motel Show means big business for its host city, Chicago.

Review Your Learning 11.1

Match the travelers described below with the type of tourism their trip involves. Some letters will be used more than once.

1. Jaime, who is traveling to New York City to meet with his book publisher
2. The Kincaid family, who are traveling to Washington, D.C., to see the White House
3. Letisha and Mark, who are going on their honeymoon to Mexico
4. College students in a culinary arts program who are traveling through Italy to sample and learn about Italian cuisine
5. Three college friends traveling to Colorado to go skiing over spring break
6. A youth group going on a bike trip to see the Great Redwoods in northern California

a. Cultural/historic tourism
b. Environmental tourism
c. Recreational tourism
d. Business tourism

7. Which of the following happened in the 1800s that helped people travel faster and to more places?
   a. Trade routes were established.
   b. Railroads were built.
   c. The idea of travel as a form of entertainment caught on.
   d. Major highway systems were created.

8. List the types of businesses that make up the tourism industry and provide three examples for each category.

11.2

SECTION 11.2

Why People Travel

AFTER STUDYING SECTION 11.2, YOU SHOULD BE ABLE TO:

- Identify and list area events and explain why they have a positive economic impact.
- List services of state and national parks.
- Describe the differences among primitive, transient, and vacation camping.
- List the reasons why theme parks are important to the hospitality and travel industries.
- Outline the processes and special circumstances involved in international travel.

KEY TERMS

- Convention
- Currency
- Currency exchange
- Discount outlet center
- Exposition
- Jet lag
- Mall
- Passport
- Primitive camping
- Recreation
- Theme park
- Time zones
- Trade show
- Transient camping
- Traveler's check
- Vacation camping
- Visa
- World Health Organization

As you saw in the last section, people travel for many reasons. Businesspeople travel to meet with clients, associates, and vendors, as well as to attend trade shows, conventions, and other professional functions. Leisure travelers, on the other hand, vacation in search of both recreation and entertainment.

Recreation refers to any activity that refreshes the body or mind. Many travel destinations offer opportunities for recreation. These include national and state parks, camp sites, and shopping areas. In contrast, events that we watch or listen to usually fall under the category of entertainment. People seeking entertainment can choose from among a huge assortment of events and places, including theme parks, theatrical performances, and sports events.

For those in search of exotic or more remote destinations—as well as recreation and entertainment—international travel is often the answer. Traveling to other countries frequently exposes travelers to different cultures and languages and provides people with unique sightseeing experiences.

Conventions, Expositions, and Trade Shows

Every day of the year, special events attract huge numbers of business travelers—as well as vacationers—to many different areas across the country. Many cities have built facilities specifically to house such large-scale special events, which include conventions, expositions, and trade shows.

A **convention** is a gathering of people, all of whom have something in common. They are often all members of a particular organization, or they may simply be individuals who share a hobby. Although

Exhibit 11.5
Conventions attract people with common interests.

many conventions are held annually, the convention sites can change from year to year for the convenience of attendees.

Expositions are large shows, open to the public, that highlight a particular type of product or service. Such shows give manufacturers and service providers a chance to display their offerings to many people at a single event. Examples of expositions include auto shows, garden shows, and computer product shows.

While expositions are open to the general public, **trade shows** are restricted to those involved in the industry being featured. Producers or manufacturers rent space at trade shows to exhibit, advertise, and demonstrate their products or services to people specifically interested in those fields. Trade shows may also feature presentations, seminars, and other educational programs relating to current industry issues.

Depending on the size of the event, a convention, exposition, or trade show can have a major impact on the local economy of its host city. Guests will eat in the city's restaurants, shop in its stores, and use its hotels for lodging. The events are also good sources of jobs in catering, customer service, and contract food service.

Every year, the National Restaurant Association holds its annual Restaurant Hotel-Motel show at Chicago's McCormick Place, one of the largest convention centers in the country. For the spring 1998 show, there were over 97,000 attendees representing all 50 states and 94 countries. And 2,900 foodservice-related businesses and industries came to show and sell their goods, occupying a total of 600,852 square feet.

National and State Parks

Many people make national or state parks their travel destinations. The national park system is operated by the National Park Service, which is part of the U.S. Department of the Interior. Some of the best-known national parks include Yellowstone, Glacier, Sequoia, the Everglades, Yosemite, and the Grand Canyon. In addition to parks, the system includes recreation areas, former battlefields and other historic sights, monuments, and memorials.

National and state parks offer a variety of attractions. Some people come mainly to see natural wonders like the Grand Canyon; others are more interested in

Exhibit 11.6
Old Faithful geyser attracts thousands of people to Yellowstone National Park every year.

studying plant and animal life. Still others visit parks to camp, ski, hike, boat, fish, and swim. Many parks offer high-quality accommodations, ranging from campgrounds to hotels, as well as a wide variety of restaurants.

Camping has become especially popular among American vacationers in recent years, partly because it is one of the least expensive recreational activities available. The national and state park systems offer many opportunities for three different kinds of camping: primitive, transient, and vacation.

Done mainly in unimproved areas of public lands, **primitive camping** is ideal for backpackers willing to "rough it" without amenities like running water and electricity.

Transient camping is done in areas that have incorporated electricity and built bathroom facilities. These campgrounds, many of which are privately run, cater to people staying for a few nights who prefer some comforts that primitive camping does not offer.

Exhibit 11.7
Camping in the mountain wilderness is an example of primitive camping.

Finally, **vacation camping** is intended for people who are staying for longer periods of time. These facilities often include stores for buying supplies and offer recreational activities, such as swimming and boating.

Unique among all of the parks in the national park system, Florida's John Pennekamp Coral Reef State Park is completely under water! Among the park's features is Jules' Undersea Lodge, a small facility with two suites available for visitor accommodations. The lodge can be reached only by diving and then passing through an airlock.

Shopping

In recent years, shopping areas have become major destinations for travelers in the United States and other countries. With the growth of automobile travel over the last half-century, the traditional downtown shopping areas have been replaced by big shopping centers located outside larger cities. The rise of large retail chains has helped to continue this trend.

Malls and discount outlet centers attract millions of tourists who choose shopping as one of their main recreational activities. While many people flock to shopping centers simply to look for bargains, others find shopping enjoyable in itself. They value the socializing and relaxation as much as the act of buying.

Exhibit 11.8
Shopping is a popular activity for travlers.

Malls are enclosed structures de- signed to accommodate many stores under one roof. Since shoppers never have to go outside once they enter a mall, weather is never a concern. Some malls are very large, with hundreds of stores on several levels. Most include a handful of major department stores and a wide assortment of other retailers (including restaurants), as well as free parking. Many malls also contain movie theaters, banks, and video arcades. The largest fully enclosed retail and family entertainment complex in the U.S., the Mall of America in Bloomington, Minnesota, employs about 12,000 people. In its first year of operation, the mall drew about 35 million visitors, about a third of whom were tourists from outside the Minneapolis area.

Discount outlet centers have become major destinations for travelers over the last several years. These centers offer retail stores that specialize in selling name-brand merchandise at discounted prices. Much of the merchandise is the result of factory overruns; other items come in irregular sizes or discontinued styles.

Discount outlets have become regular stops on bus tours and are especially popular among retired people. Big outlet centers attract travelers from hundreds or even thousands of miles away—particularly from areas where desirable name-brand merchandise is hard to come by—thereby generating income for the restaurants, hotels, and other businesses in the surrounding community.

Theme Parks

While national and state parks are natural attractions, theme parks are created by people. This form of entertainment began as the amusement park, which featured rides, fun houses, and snack foods. The Chicago World's Columbian Exposition of 1893, for example, offered people rides on a large, rotating wheel designed by George W. Ferris—the first Ferris wheel. From then on, amusement parks spread to most major cities, and their popularity grew throughout the 20th century. Many larger parks were eventually built by private companies.

By the 1970s, however, many amusement parks had become old and run-down, and most closed their gates for good. In their places emerged a new type of entertainment called the theme park. Theme parks evolved to meet the needs of a more modern generation of customers; whose expectations had grown with advances in other forms of entertainment, such as television and movies. The first theme parks were developed around 1960.

Modern theme parks offer a full array of entertainment features that create an overall atmosphere of fun. A typical **theme park** includes exhibits, rides, and other attractions focusing on one unifying idea, such as jungle animal, or the Old West. The growing popularity of theme parks as tourist destinations has had a major impact on all hospitality industries, including food service, lodging, and transportation, as well as on the local economies and job markets of the areas in which the parks are located.

Some well-known theme parks in the United States include:

- Sea World in Orlando, Florida, and San Diego, California, which offers a unique variety of sea life exhibits.
- Universal Studios in Los Angeles, California, and Orlando, Florida, where visitors will find thrill rides based on famous movies.
- Disney World in Orlando, Florida, the largest and most famous theme park in the world, which includes the Magic Kingdom, EPCOT, Disney-MGM Studios, and Animal Kingdom.
- Busch Gardens in Tampa, Florida, featuring the 300-acre "Dark Continent," which is home to actual African big game.

Many trends and issues currently face the theme park industry. In the coming years, international competition is likely

Exhibit 11.9
Sea World is a well-known theme park.

to grow as new parks are built in Europe and Asia. Also, the types of entertainment offered at theme parks is expected to become more diverse. Finally, a growing number of theme parks may eventually be linked directly to shopping malls or other related facilities.

International Travel

To experience other cultures and really "get away from it all," many people enjoy traveling to other countries. International travel can be exciting, glamorous, and fun. However, traveling to foreign countries usually requires some special preparations.

Exhibit 11.10
Big waves off the coast of Australia attract many tourists every year.

Unlike a domestic traveler, or someone traveling within their own country, a person leaving his or her home country to travel needs more than just a plane or cruise ship ticket. Most countries, including the United States, require that anyone crossing their borders has a valid **passport,** a document that contains the traveler's name, a photo, date and place of birth, and country citizenship.

Some countries also require visitors to have visas. A **visa** is a foreign government's written permission for a traveler to enter that country for a specific reason and length of time. A visa might be a separate document or simply a stamp on one of the pages of a traveler's passport.

It's always important to be aware of political and social circumstances before planning a trip abroad. The U.S. State Department helps people stay informed of world events by publishing reports on the status of travel to most countries in the world. When safety is a concern in certain countries, the State Department issues warnings to the public.

People traveling to some countries, primarily in Central and South America, Africa, and Asia often need to receive vaccinations (shots that build the body's immune system) to prevent the threat of diseases. The **World Health Organization** (WHO) determines whether vaccinations are required for travelers going to specific countries and, if so, for which diseases. Common diseases for which vaccinations are sometimes required are yellow fever and cholera.

International travel often takes people across one or more time zones. A **time zone** is a geographical area in which the same standard time is used. Long flights that span several time zones can cause travelers to get something called **jet lag,** or feelings of extreme tiredness, and as a result, people have trouble sleeping and waking at regular times.

Travelers going east tend to experience jet lag more often than those heading west because they gain several extra hours, making their day longer than it would ordinarily be. For example, if someone left Chicago at 8:00 a.m., for Honolulu, Hawaii the plane would land at 8:30 a.m. in Honolulu. Although the flight would have actually lasted $6\frac{1}{2}$ hours, Honolulu is six hours behind Chicago's time zone. The traveler would feel as if it were already 2:30 p.m., even though everyone in Honolulu would be just starting their day!

In addition to preparing for a trip, international travelers must become familiar with a new system of money. Every country in the world has its own **currency**, or money. Most countries will exchange American dollars for the currency of the country easily, and many foreign businesses will accept traveler's checks as if they were cash. **Traveler's checks** are checks that have already been paid for at a bank and that require only the buyer's signature to be cashed. It is also becoming increasingly easier to use credit cards and ATM cards in other countries.

Most countries have **currency exchanges** for changing money, and many hotels will change money for their guests. Exhibit 11.11 lists the names of the currencies used in a variety of countries.

Exhibit 11.11
Foreign currencies.

COUNTRY	CURRENCY
Argentina	Argentine peso
Australia	Australian dollar
Austria	Schilling
Belgium	Belgian franc
Brazil	Cruzeiro
Canada	Canadian dollar
China	Yuan
France	Franc
Germany	Mark
Greece	Drachma
Hungary	Forint
Ireland	Irish pound
Italy	Lira
Japan	Yen
Mexico	Mexican peso
Morocco	Dirham
Nigeria	Naira
Poland	Zloty
Russia	Ruble
Spain	Peseta
Sweden	Krona
Switzerland	Swiss franc
United Kingdom	Pound
United States	American dollar

Apply It Now

Visit a bank in your neighborhood and ask for information on currency exchange rates. Then find the exchange rates for the following currencies.

a. $1 = _____ Greek drachmas

b. $1 = _____ Spanish pesetas

c. $1 = _____ Japanese yen

d. 1 French franc = $_____

e. 1 Mexican peso = $_____

Review Your Learning 11.2

1. The purpose of recreation is to:
   a. prepare a person for a new job.
   b. refresh the mind or body.
   c. divert a person's attention through art.
   d. help businesspeople make connections.

2. Explain the difference between the following.
   a. An exposition and a trade show
   b. A mall and a discount outlet center
   c. A theme park and an amusement park
   d. A visa and a passport

3. Identify each of the following as a convention (C), an exposition (E), or a trade show (T).
   a. An annual gathering of toy train hobbyists
   b. An electronics show for computer professionals
   c. Boat show
   d. The North American Food Equipment Manufacturers Association show
   e. The Annual Flyers show for anyone interesting in flying, making, or selling kites

4. Indicate whether each of the following describes primitive (P), transient (T), or vacation (V) camping.
   a. Campers stay in a cabin and boat across the lake for groceries, water sports, and restaurants
   b. Backpackers must bring all of their own supplies, including food and a tent
   c. This campground, located off a toll road, offers families electricity and bathroom facilities

5. Which of the following travelers would most likely suffer from jet lag?
   a. A person flying from Chicago, Illinois, to Los Angeles, California
   b. A person flying from Seattle, Washington, to San Diego, California
   c. A person flying from New York, New York to Phoenix, Arizona
   d. A person flying from Miami, Florida to Honolulu, Hawaii

SECTION 11.3

How People Travel

AFTER STUDYING SECTION 11.3, YOU SHOULD BE ABLE TO:

- List the advantages and disadvantages of travel by airplane, car, train, bus and cruise ship.

KEY TERMS

- Charter
- Coach
- Commuter

Once people decide that they want—or need—to travel, they have many options as to how to get to their destinations. They can travel by car, plane, train, bus, or ship. Each kind of transportation is suited to different tastes and different reasons for traveling.

Car Travel

Cars are by far the most popular form of transportation in the United States, accounting for about 80 percent of all travel miles. The U.S.'s system of highways has made just about every place on the map accessible by car.

People travel by car for convenience: they can leave at any time, stop along the way, and arrive whenever they want. They can also talk, sing, sleep, and stretch out without bothering strangers. In addition, the more people who ride in a car, the less expensive it is for each person. That's not true for any other type of transportation, where each person pays the full price. On the other hand, travel by car takes longer than travel by other kinds of transportation, such as airplanes.

An important part of car travel is the rental car industry. Both business and leisure travelers rent cars, especially when

Exhibit 11.12
Cars are the most popular mode of transportation in the United States.

they fly into a city. *Hertz, Avis, National, Enterprise,* and *Budget* dominate the rental car industry, and their counters are a familiar sight in airports and at other locations around the world.

Another significant member of the car travel segment is the American Automobile Association (AAA), which provides road service, car insurance, and travel services to its members. AAA can also furnish information to its members about the places they're planning to visit.

The Airline Industry

The airline industry is the youngest mode of transportation. In only 50 years, it has grown from being only a part of the military industry into a multi-billion-dollar commercial operation.

The main benefit of air travel over all other modes of transportation is speed. Nothing is faster, or even nearly as fast, as flying from one city to another. Flying is also easy for travelers, since the airline takes care of everything. All that passengers need to do is get to the airport, check their baggage, and go to the right gate.

Air travel has a few disadvantages too. Many small towns and remote areas, for example, don't have airports, so even if travelers fly to or from a nearby city, they still often have to drive, take a train, or ride a bus to the airport or to their final destination. Airfare can also be expensive, depending on when travelers fly and when they purchase their tickets. Finally, some people, for a variety of reasons, are simply afraid to fly.

Exhibit 11.13
The primary benefit of air travel over all other modes of transportation is speed.

There are about a dozen airlines that dominate the industry, including *United, Delta, American,* and *Southwest.* Smaller airlines, however, such as *Mesaba Airlines* and *Hawaiian Airlines,* have also had success by serving specific geographic regions.

Traveling by Rail

As you read in *Chapter 1: The History of Food Service,* railroads were first built in the United States in the mid-1800s to link cities and to carry goods from one part of the country to others. From the 1850s until the 1920s, trains were the most popular way to travel in the United States.

Today, trains carry cargo—such as fruits and vegetables, timber, and electrical appliances—more often than they carry passengers. However, one company, *Amtrak,* has continued to offer train service to travelers. In addition to **coach** travel (standard passenger seating), some of Amtrak's lines also include foodservice cars with servers, covered tables, and full meal service, as well as sleeping cars for longer trips.

For people who have time to get from one place to another, train travel is a great way to see the scenery along the way. On the down side, train travel takes longer than travel by plane, and most people don't have much time to travel. The time they do have they prefer to spend at their aren't travelers but **commuters,** going from their homes in the suburbs and rural communities to work in the city.

Train travel is much more popular in other parts of the world than it is in the United States. While European countries, for example, don't have nearly as many highways as the United States does, they have more miles of train track. *Eurail, Interail,* and other types of passes allow tourists to travel easily and economically by train from city to city and from country to country.

Exhibit 11.14
Traveling by train.

Buses

Led by *Greyhound* and *Trailways,* the bus industry is also made up of many small, family-owned bus companies. One major advantage of bus travel over other kinds of transportation is that the thousands of communities in the United States that cannot be reached by airlines and trains are accessible by commercial bus. Bus travel is also economical, but, like trains and cars, it is slower than air travel.

A growing part of the bus industry is the charter and tour segment. A **charter** company offers organized tours for travel groups. These charter companies usually rent buses that take passengers from one destination on their tour to another. Today, many companies have improved their buses by installing restrooms, air conditioning and heat, reclining seats, and tinted glass windows.

The Cruise Industry

In the early part of the 20th century, ocean liners provided a glamorous way for wealthy people to travel. Today, people no longer travel by ship simply as a way to cross the ocean. Instead, people take leisurely cruises for vacation. The cruise industry has emerged to pamper travelers who want to get away from their busy lives, allowing guests to play all day in the sun and dine and dance into the night.

Some of the larger cruise lines include *Carnival, Holland America, Cunard, Royal Caribbean,* and *Princess.* While people take cruises to a variety of vacation spots, some of the more popular destinations include the Caribbean, the Mediterranean, and Scandinavia.

Apply It Now

Identify each mode of transportation described below.

Key:
C—Car
A—Airplane
T—Train
B—Bus
CR—Cruise ship

1. **Began as a military industry.**
2. **The more people who ride, the less expensive it is per person.**
3. **First built in the U.S. in the mid-1800s.**
4. **The Caribbean is a popular destination for this mode of transportation.**
5. **Most popular mode of transportation in the U.S.**
6. **Accommodates both travelers and commuters.**
7. **Includes the charter and tour segment.**
8. **The youngest of the five primary modes of transportation.**

Review Your Learning 11.3

1. What is one advantage and one disadvantage of each of the following modes of transportation?
   a. Buses
   b. Airplanes
   c. Cruise ships
   d. Trains

2. What's the difference between a traveler and a commuter?

3. Angela wants to travel round-trip between Phoenix and Santa Fe. The trip is approximately 400 miles one way. By air, Angela would have to fly first to Albuquerque for $69 and then to Santa Fe for $49. (She'd have to do the same thing going back.) A one-way train ticket from Phoenix to Santa Fe costs $105. A one-way bus ticket between the two cities is $44. A car trip would cost approximately $0.28 per mile.
   a. How much would Angela have to pay for each of the following methods of transportation?
      Air:
      Train:
      Bus:
      Car:
   b. Which mode of transportation is the most expensive?
   c. Which is the least expensive?
   d. Which would you advise Angela to choose and why? (Remember, there's more to consider than just cost.)

11.4

SECTION 11.4

Careers in Travel and Tourism

AFTER STUDYING SECTION 11.4, YOU SHOULD BE ABLE TO:

- Identify career opportunities offered by travel and tourism.
- Compare the roles of a travel agent and a tour guide.
- Outline the work done by concierges, state and local tourism offices, corporate travel offices, and convention and meeting planners.
- List and describe required customer service skills in the travel industry.

According to the Travel Industry Association of America, Americans took almost 1.2 billion trips in 1996, and domestic travel was up more than 5 percent through the first half of 1997. In addition, the U.S. Department of Commerce reports that a record 48.9 million international travelers visited the United States in 1997.

What does all of this mean to job seekers in the hospitality industry? In addition to having a large impact on our

KEY TERMS

- Concierge (kahn-see-AIRJE)
- Corporate travel office
- Empathize
- Itinerary
- Niche market
- Tour guide
- Tourism office
- Travel agent
- Travel package

economy, tourism supports many hospitality industry jobs. For example, more than 29 percent of all salaried jobs in Columbia Falls, Montana, near Glacier National Park, are supported by the travelers who come to the winter sports-oriented city.

Types of Opportunities

Travel and tourism offer many options for those seeking careers in the hospitality industry, including jobs in food service, lodging, human resources, accounting, marketing, and many other areas. Whether you're interested in corporate travel or theme parks, travel writing or conventions, the hospitality industry has many career opportunities.

- **Travel agent**—Helping travelers with just about all of their arrangements, travel agents must know how to make airline reservations, plan trips and set **itineraries,** which are travel plans. They also rent cars, purchase tickets for shows and events, book cruises and train travel, make hotel reservations, and put together tours and travel packages. **Travel packages** combine several travel services for one set price. Travel agents are often sent on trips so they can

Exhibit 11.15
Eating-and-drinking-place employment as a percentage of total employment in metropolitan areas.

City	Employment level (1996)	Percent of total employment
Daytona Beach	13,900	9.4
Honolulu	35,300	8.7
Santa Barbara	12,300	8.4
Knoxville	24,600	7.8
San Diego	76,300	7.6
San Antonio	48,300	7.6
New Orleans	45,700	7.6
Orlando	56,500	7.5
Indianapolis	61,200	7.5
Ft. Worth-Arlington	48,500	7.1
Sacramento	43,000	7.1
Austin	37,900	7.0
Denver	70,200	7.0
St. Louis	87,700	6.9
Phoenix	90,500	6.9

Source: U.S. Bureau of Labor Statistics.

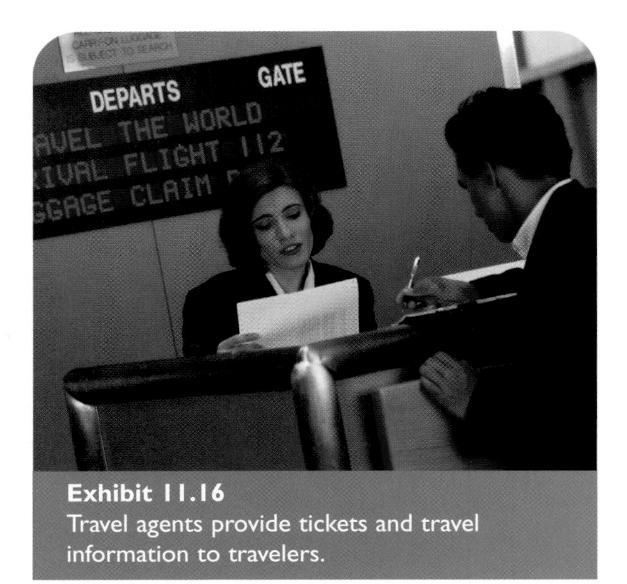

Exhibit 11.16
Travel agents provide tickets and travel information to travelers.

describe the hotels at which they've stayed and the places they've visited.

- **Tour guide**—Some travelers choose to be part of an organized group with a leader who knows all about where the group is, where it's going, and how to get from one place to another. That leader is the tour guide. Many tour guides lead trips that appeal to **niche markets,** or groups of people having similar interests, ages, or skills who have common travel objectives.
- *Airline careers*—The airline industry offers a number of jobs, including flight attendant, reservations agent, ticket agent, pilot, mechanic, and baggage handler. Airports themselves also employ many people, such as baggage porters (skycaps), foodservice workers, and taxi coordinators.
- **Concierge**—Employed by hotels, motels, and resorts, the concierge (kahn-see-AIRJE) serves guests by helping them buy tickets to shows and events, answering questions, booking restaurant reservations, and more. Providing a wide range of information services, the concierge has done much to further the tourism industry by giving travelers suggestions about how to spend their time while in town.

Exhibit 11.17
The concierge provides travelers with a wide range of information services.

- *Tourism office employees*—**Tourism offices** are established by state and local governments and provide information to people who are visiting or who would like to visit an area. Many people work in and for these offices by answering questions, creating marketing and advertising campaigns, and collecting statistics on travelers.
- *Corporate travel office employees*—Many companies are large enough to employ their own in-house travel services. Employees of these **corporate travel offices** take care of the arrangements for the company's employees, officers, and representatives, much like travel agents do for the public.
- *Convention* and *meeting planners*—Planners are needed to see to the countless arrangements and details that go into large meetings and conventions. Planners do everything from inviting speakers and arranging meeting rooms to hiring video producers and selecting banquet centerpieces.
- *Travel writers* and *photographers*—Most newspapers and many magazines and journals carry travel-related stories. Journalists and professional photographers provide the words and pictures for these stories. Many travel firms and tour companies also employ writers and photographers to create promotional materials.
- *Theme park* and *amusement park employees*—Large theme parks can employ hundreds or sometimes thousands of people. The Disney Company, for example, has become one of the largest employers in the world, with Disney World alone employing thousands of people in management, accounting, administrative, and entertainment positions.

In addition to the opportunities discussed here, there are many other hospitality employers as well, including bus companies, cruise operations, passenger rail service establishments, and rental car companies. All of these companies must employ drivers, ticket agents, mechanics, engineers, managers, and other administrators.

Customer Service in Travel Careers

Customer service skills are crucial for anyone working in the hospitality industry. When people eat out, buy airplane tickets, stay in hotels, or spend their money in any other way, they expect to be treated with courtesy and respect.

Apply It Now

On a separate sheet of paper, match the job on the left with its description or related duty on the right.

1. Journalist
2. Travel agent
3. Convention and meeting planner
4. Corporate travel employee
5. Concierge
6. Tour guide

a. Provides a range of information services.
b. Invites speakers to talk at meetings.
c. Leads organized groups of travelers.
d. Provides the words for travel-related stories.
e. Handles the travel arrangements for a company's employees.
f. Plans trips and sets itineraries.

As you recall from reading *Chapter 8: Working with People* in *Becoming A Foodservice Professional, Year 1,* customers deserve to be treated well. They want to feel that they're important; they want information; they want to be treated fairly, especially if they experience trouble or have a problem; they want to know that a company—and its employees—value them as customers; and they want service from people who don't act as though they're being put out or inconvenienced.

The best way for you to find out *exactly* what customers want or need is to ask them. Asking how you can help and listening carefully and attentively to what they have to say makes people feel good—especially about spending their money.

Any professional coming in contact with travelers should try to be friendly, tactful, sincere, and well-informed. In addition, those working in the travel industry will have an edge if they are courteous, considerate, and honest. Most customers appreciate service personnel who have a sense of humor, as well as those who put customers first. No matter what customer service approach is used, the outcome should always be the same: the customer leaves happy and anxious to return.

Helping people with their travel plans also requires patience and sensitivity to customers' needs and concerns. People making travel arrangements want everything to go as planned. If they can't leave or return when they want, if prices are higher than they expected, or if flights are canceled or delayed, travelers are likely to be impatient and even angry.

Service employees are often the ones responsible for handling customers' complaints. What should you do when a customer complains or comes to you with a problem?

- *Listen to the customer.* Sometimes customers don't really want *anything* except for someone to listen to them blow off steam. If they do want something, listening is the only way for an employee to find out what that is.
- *Empathize with the customer.* To **empathize** means to see a situation from another person's perspective. Telling a customer that you understand or that it must be very frustrating to wait often goes a long way toward making customers calmer.
- *Offer a solution.* If a customer has a problem, find out what the problem is—and what the customer would like done about it. If you can accommodate the customer in the way suggested, then the problem is solved. If you can't, explain why you can't and then suggest another solution.

Remember, it's never okay to ignore customers, make fun of them, or shout back at them—even if they shout at you. You can usually help angry people settle down by remaining calm. If things get out of hand, you should always call a manager to help.

Review Your Learning 11.4

1. Give two examples of each of the following:
   a. Niche markets
   b. Career opportunities at theme parks
   c. Duties of travel agents
   d. Ways to handle customer complaints
2. What does a concierge do, and who usually employs him or her?
3. To empathize means to:
   a. be honest.
   b. see a situation from another person's perspective.
   c. resolve problems and complaints.
   d. remain calm.
4. You work as a travel agent. You pick up your phone, and a customer tells you that she's been on hold for 10 minutes. You know that you didn't put the customer on hold, and you think it was probably David, your co-worker. What should you do? What should you say to the customer?

SECTION 11.5

The Retail Industry

AFTER STUDYING SECTION 11.5, YOU SHOULD BE ABLE TO:

- Describe the differences among specialty stores, department stores, and other types of stores.

KEY TERMS

- **Home meal replacement**
- **Retail**

The term **retail** refers to the sale of products directly to consumers. In the life of a product, placement in a retail store is usually the last stop before the product is purchased by customers.

Merchandise Stores

Retailing is closely related to the hospitality industry. As you saw in Section 11.2, shopping areas have become major destinations for travelers in recent years. In addition, many of the skills needed for working in the hospitality industry, such as providing good service and managing people and products, are also useful in retail.

Department stores make up one major segment of the retail industry. The biggest advantage to shopping at a department store is that the shopper can purchase all sorts of items during a single visit to just one store. Examples of department stores include *JC Penney, Marshall Field's,* and *Bloomingdale's.* While some department stores are part of large national chains, others are independent.

Specialty stores, such as shoe stores, pet shops, and appliance stores, represent another retail segment. Unlike department stores, specialty stores sell only a small range of goods. Within that range the shopper can usually find a much wider selection of brands, styles, and products. A serious tennis player, for example, would probably shop for a racket at a sporting goods store rather than at a department store.

A third segment of the retail industry consists of large discount chains, such as *Wal-Mart, Kmart,* and *Target.* Discount chains make up for their lack of upscale name-brand products with lower prices. Discount chains often have an edge over department stores because of national advertising campaigns, larger-volume purchasing, and sophisticated ordering and distribution networks.

Exhibit 11.18
Target competes with department stores for customers by offering lower prices.

Apply It Now

On a separate sheet of paper, indicate whether shoppers would probably buy the following at a department store (D), a specialty store (S), or a large discount chain (C):

1. **In-line skates**
2. **Plastic dishware**
3. **A guitar**
4. **No-brand-name, low-priced clothing**
5. **A pedigree poodle**
6. **A crib, a bathing suit, tires, and a television, all at one store**

In recent years, research has been done on the behavior of department store customers. Studies have shown that most people turn to their right after entering the store. There is also evidence that the further into a store a person can be drawn, the more likely he or she is to make a purchase. Retailers use this sort of information in the design and layout of their stores to increase sales.

FOOD RETAIL

The food segment of the retail industry is composed of both large supermarket chains and small specialty grocery stores. When purchasing food for the week, many shoppers look for low prices and go to large supermarkets. When the same shoppers want to prepare something special, however, many often go to specialty gourmet food stores that have reputations for selling high-quality, hard-to-find items.

Another part of the food segment is home meal replacement. **Home meal replacement** refers to meals that are eaten at home but prepared somewhere else. A common example is carry-out food from a restaurant. Food that is purchased ready-to-eat from a grocery store deli counter is another example. "Meals-on-wheels" services that deliver prepared food to those unable to cook for themselves also fall into the home meal replacement category.

Exhibit 11.19
Large supermarkets offer lower prices than specialty gourmet food stores.

JOB OPPORTUNITIES IN RETAIL

The retail industry is a major source of employment in the United States. In the merchandise arena, job opportunities include:

- ***Sales clerk***—A job that appeals to people who enjoy interacting with others.
- ***Buyer***—Responsible for choosing which merchandise a store will stock and finding the right supplier or manufacturer.
- ***Public relations/marketing employee***—Works to enhance the image of the store for its potential customers.
- ***Design and display professional***—Responsible for deciding how to decorate the store and present merchandise to customers.
- ***Security person/guard***—Responsible for protecting the establishment against theft, as well as customers and employees from injuries.

Many of the jobs associated with the retail food business are the same as those found in the rest of the merchandise segment. In addition, food retail provides job opportunities in catering, baking, meat cutting, and preparation of ready-to-eat deli items.

Apply It Now

What type of store is each of the following?

1. **Macy's**
2. **Mike's Kosher Meat Market**
3. **Toko's Takeout Sushi Hut**
4. **Kinder Toy Store**
5. **Wal-Mart**

Review Your Learning 11.5

1. The sale of products directly to consumers is called:
   a. merchandise. b. direct sale. c. wholesale. d. retail.

2. Which of the following businesses are considered retail operations?
   Sock factory, Cheese shop, Children's clothing store, Pharmacy, Dairy farm, Furniture store, Supermarket

3. How is a large discount chain different from a department store?

4. Match the job on the left with its duty on the right.

1. Sercurity person	a. Makes decisions about merchnadise presentations
2. Design and display professional	b. Prepares foods for meetings and events
3. Caterer	c. Finds suppliers and manufactirers from whom to obtain merchandise
4. Public relations employee	d. Enhances the image of the store in the eyes of potential customers
5. Buyer	e. Protects customers and employees against injuries

5. Are there any areas of the city in which you live that are well-known as shopping districts even to nonresidents? What are some of the well-known shopping areas in cities you have visited?

Flashback

CHAPTER 11

SECTION 11.1: UNDERSTANDING TOURISM

- **Tourism** is a combination of all of the services that people require and will pay for when they are away from home for any period of time. Tourism includes all of the businesses that benefit from people traveling and spending their money, including transportation, accommodations, eating establishments, shops, and entertainment.
- In ancient times, people traveled mainly to trade goods with others. As travel increased along trade routes, people opened inns along the way.
- By the 1700s, the idea of travel as a form of entertainment caught on. In the 1800s, an increasing number of people had money to spend on traveling for pleasure. As a result, more and more hotels and restaurants were built.
- The development of the railroad in the 1800s helped people travel faster—and to more places. In the 1920s, travelers began to journey by car. In addition to the creation of major highway systems, the 1950s saw the growth of commercial airlines.
- Marketing experts tend to look at two broad categories of travelers—leisure travelers and business travelers. Leisure travelers often visit friends or relatives, sightsee, or vacation just to get away and relax. Business travelers meet with associates, attend conventions, and generally stay at properties close to business complexes.
- Marketers classify tourism according to the type of travel experience that people are looking for. **Cultural** and **historic tourists** travel to other countries to observe, learn about, and live among people whose cultures are different from their own. **Environmental tourists** visit places in order to enjoy their natural beauty. **Recreational tourists** usually look for places where they can swim, lie in the sun, ski, play golf and tennis, see shows, or gamble. **Business tourism** includes conventions, meetings, and seminars.

SECTION 11.2: WHY PEOPLE TRAVEL

- **Recreation** refers to any activity that refreshes the body or mind. Events that we watch or listen to usually fall under the category of **entertainment.**
- A **convention** is a gathering of people, all of whom have something in common. **Expositions** are large shows, open to the public, that highlight a particular type of product or service. **Trade shows** are restricted to those involved in the industry being featured.
- Many people make national or state parks their travel destinations of choice. Some visitors come mainly to see natural wonders; others are more interested in studying plant and animal life. Still others visit parks to camp, ski, hike, boat, fish, and swim.
- The park systems offer a variety of opportunities for three different kinds of camping: **Primitive camping** is ideal for backpackers willing to "rough it" with few amenities. **Transient camping** is done in areas that have incorporated electricity and built bathroom facilities. **Vacation camping** is intended for people staying for longer periods of time who are looking for more amenities than the other two kinds of camping provide.
- In recent years, shopping areas have become major destinations for travelers in the United States and other countries. Malls and discount outlet centers attract millions of tourists who choose shopping as one of their main recreational activities.
- **Malls** are enclosed structures designed to accommodate many stores under one roof.
- **Discount outlet centers** offer retail stores that specialize in selling name-brand merchandise at discounted prices.
- **Theme parks** evolved to meet the needs of a more modern generation of customers, whose expectations had grown with advances in other forms of entertainment. A typical theme park includes exhibits, rides, and other attractions focusing on one unifying idea.
- Most countries require that anyone crossing their borders have a valid **passport.** Some countries also require visitors to have a **visa.**
- It's important to be aware of political and social circumstances before planning a trip abroad. Travelers to some countries must also often

receive vaccinations to thwart the threat of diseases.

- International travel often takes people across one or more **time zones.** Long flights that span several time zones can cause travelers to get **jet lag.** Travelers going east tend to experience jet lag more often than those heading west because they gain several extra hours.
- Every country in the world has its own currency. Most countries will exchange American dollars easily and willingly, and many foreign businesses will accept **traveler's checks** as if they were cash. Credit cards and ATM cards are also used.
- As powerful as American dollars might seem, they still must be exchanged for local money. Most countries have **currency exchanges** for changing money.

SECTION 11.3: HOW PEOPLE TRAVEL

- Cars are the most popular mode of transportation in the United States.
- People travel by car for convenience. The more people who ride in a car, the less expensive it is for each person. On the down side, travel by car takes longer than travel by other modes of transportation, such as airplanes.
- An important part of the car travel segment is the rental car industry. Another significant member of the car travel segment is the American Automobile Association (AAA), which provides road service, car insurance, and travel services to its members.
- The primary benefit of air travel over all other modes of transportation is speed. Flying is also easy for travelers, since the airline takes care of everything.
- Air travel has a few disadvantages too. Many small towns and remote areas don't have airports, airfare can be costly, and some people are simply afraid to fly.
- Railroads were first built in the United States in the mid-1800s to link cities and to carry goods from one part of the country to others. Today, trains carry cargo more often than they carry passengers.
- Amtrak has continued to offer train service to travelers. In addition to **coach** travel, some of Amtrak's lines include foodservice cars with servers, covered tables, and full meal service, as well as sleeping cars for longer trips.

- For people who have time to get from one place to another, train travel is a great way to see the scenery along the way. Train travel is less harmful to the environment than cars. On the down side, most people don't have much time to travel, and the time they do have they prefer to spend at their destinations.
- Many train passengers aren't travelers but **commuters.**
- One major advantage of bus travel over other methods of transportation is that thousands of communities in the United States that are not serviced by airlines and trains are accessible by commercial bus. Bus travel is also economical, although it is slower than air travel.
- A growing part of the bus industry is the **charter** and tour segment. Chartered buses are often rented by companies that offer organized tours for travel groups.
- The cruise industry has emerged to pamper travelers who want to get away from their busy lives, allowing guests to play all day in the sun and dine and dance into the night.

SECTION 11.4: CAREERS IN TRAVEL AND TOURISM

- Travel and tourism offer many options for those seeking careers in the hospitality industry.
- **Travel agents** help people with just about all of their travel arrangements.
- Some travelers choose to be part of an organized group with a leader who knows all about where the group is, where it's going, and how to get from one place to another. That leader is the **tour guide.**
- The airline industry offers a number of jobs, including flight attendant, reservations agent, ticket agent, pilot, mechanic, and baggage handler.
- Employed by hotels, motels, and resorts, the **concierge** (kahn-see-AIRJE) serves guests by providing a wide range of information services.
- Established by state and local governments, **tourism offices** provide information to people who are visiting or would like to visit their area.
- Employees of **corporate travel offices** take care of the arrangements for a company's employees, officers, and representatives.

- **Convention and meeting planners** see to the countless arrangements and details that go into large meetings and conventions.
- **Travel writers and photographers** provide the words and pictures for travel-related stories in newspapers and magazines.
- Large theme parks can employ hundreds to thousands of people.
- Customer service skills are crucial for anyone working in hospitality.
- Customers want to feel that they're important. They want information. They want to be treated fairly and to know that a company—and its employees—value them as customers. They also want service from people who don't act as though they're being put out or inconvenienced.
- Any professional coming in contact with travelers should try to be friendly, tactful, sincere, and well-informed. In addition, those working in the travel industry will have an edge if they are courteous, considerate, and honest. Helping people with their travel plans also requires patience and sensitivity to customers' needs and concerns.
- When a customer comes to you with a problem or a complaint, you should listen to the customer, **empathize** with him or her, and offer a solution.

SECTION 11.5: THE RETAIL INDUSTRY

- The term **retail** refers to the sale of products directly to consumers. In the life of a product, placement in a retail store is usually the last stop before the product is purchased by customers.
- Retailing is closely related to the hospitality industry. Many of the skills needed for working in the hospitality industry are also useful in retail.
- Department stores make up one major segment of the retail industry. The main advantage to shopping at a department store is that the shopper can purchase all sorts of items during a single visit to just one store.
- Specialty stores sell a narrow range of goods. Within that range, however, the shopper will usually find a much wider selection of brands, styles, and products.
- A third retail segment consists of large discount chains that make up for their lack of upscale name-brand products with lower prices.

- The food segment of the retail industry is composed of both large supermarket chains and small specialty grocery stores.
- Another part of the food segment is home meal replacement. **Home meal replacement** refers to meals that are eaten at home but prepared somwhere else.
- The retail industry is a major source of employment in the United States. In the merchandise arena, job opportunities include sales clerk, buyer, public relations employee, design and display professional, and security person/guard.
- Food retail also provides job opportunities in catering, baking, meat cutting, and preparation of ready-to-eat deli items.

Damon Skinner

Department Coordinator of
Restaurant Management
CHIC
(Cooking and Hospitality Institute of Chicago)
Chicago, Illinois

The hospitality industry has been a part of my life since I was 14, when I began my career as a dishwasher at a local bed and breakfast. I instantly loved the environment and have continued on in the industry. I've pretty much done it all—server, restaurant manager, chef, maître d', food and beverage director, entrepreneur, and business owner—and in every part of this industry, the customer is the most important part of the business.

If there is one thing I have learned about this industry, it's that our customers make it possible for us to come to work every day. This industry cannot afford to have customers walk away unhappy—so I do my part to make sure that every student I teach and every employee I train have the skills to be effective and successful communicators.

Throughout my career in this industry, I have seen how important it is to have good customer relations. As an instructor at CHIC (Cooking and Hospitality Institute of Chicago), I teach my students that every conflict with a customer is a win-win situation—all it takes is the ability to listen well and to understand where the customer is coming from.

I also have my own consulting business, Creative Hospitality Network. Through Creative Hospitality Network, restaurants hire me to help them improve their business. One way I do this is to train their employees. I always make sure employees learn how to read customers' verbal and nonverbal cues—their language, tone of voice, and hand gestures—as a way to react honestly and positively to the customer. These clues really tell a lot about how a customer is feeling. If the employee can read them well, then that employee can adjust their service based on what the customer needs.

I love the excitement that the hospitality industry offers. It's great to go to work every day and make people happy—that's why we're in business. If a restaurant offers so-so service but great food, customers will not return. But, if the service is excellent, they'll come back again and again.

CHAPTER 12

Communicating with Customers

12.1

SECTION 12.1

Handling Customer Complaints

AFTER STUDYING SECTION 12.1, YOU SHOULD BE ABLE TO:

- Give examples of ways to respond to and resolve customer complaints.

KEY TERMS

- **Rule of 10**

When customers do not receive a basic level of service, they become disappointed, irritated, upset, and even angry. The foodservice industry has become very competitive and customers can afford to be choosy. The challenge for you as a foodservice manager is to distinguish your operation from your competitors'. Creating a work environment in which all of your employees are encouraged to work hard to satisfy and please customers is a great way to set your operation apart from others.

In *Chapter 1: Successful Customer Relations* of *Becoming a Foodservice Professional, Year 1,* you learned that first impressions are extremely important. But first impressions are only the beginning. If you don't have a professional attitude, your first impression will be replaced with disappointment from your customers. The best way to prevent most complaints and maintain a high level of service from your employees is to ensure that all jobs are done with care. Exhibit 12.1 lists some of the things that you should *never* do to avoid angering customers.

Overcoming the Rule of 10

In spite of your best efforts, there will be times when things go wrong and a customer becomes dissatisfied. What

Exhibit 12.1
Things to avoid when working with customers.

- ***Never*** ignore customers—let them know you will help them soon.
- ***Never*** rush customers who want to take their time finishing a meal.
- ***Never*** serve substandard food.
- ***Never*** allow customers to sit at sloppy or dirty tables.
- ***Never*** allow unsanitary conditions anywhere in your operation.
- ***Never*** behave indifferently or rudely to a customer.
- ***Never*** eat or chew gum in front of customers.
- ***Never*** discuss personal business in front of customers.
- ***Never*** speak poorly of another employee in front of customers.

should you do if a guest complains? Remember the **rule of 10:** one dissatisfied customer tells an average of 10 people about their bad experience. What's worse, only 4% of unhappy customers actually let management know they are unhappy; the other 96% tell 10 of their friends or family. When you think about it this way, a customer who complains is actually helping you save at least 10 potential customers!

It's easy to see why resolving one customer's problem is worth the effort. Studies have shown that if you quickly determine the customer's problem and fix it before he or she leaves, you can often win that person back. In fact, a customer whose complaint is handled well will come back—again and again. In the end, a complaint can often be one of the best opportunities managers have to improve their business.

Some customer service problems are easy to recognize, especially when a guest is loudly demanding that something be done. However, many problems are more difficult to spot because most customers will not complain.

Identifying Customer Complaints

All employees should be trained to ask customers how they enjoyed their visit. In fact, most people want to share their opinions. Employees can gather valuable insight by asking questions in a way that helps the customer answer with specific information. Rather than asking, "Was everything okay?" servers should ask, "Did you enjoy your pizza?" or "Was my staff helpful?" If the guest's manner suggests something is lacking in service or the meal, encourage him or her to tell you the problem. Exhibit 12.2 lists some subtle signs of a dissatisfied guest.

Usually, a few specific questions on your part will result in an honest answer. In all cases, it's important for employees to maintain a positive, friendly attitude toward all customers.

Exhibit 12.2
Subtle signs of a dissatisfied guest.

- Looking irritated or annoyed
- Not finishing a meal
- Avoiding eye contact with employees
- Saying unconvincingly that everything was "okay"

Think About It

Can you remember the worst service you ever received in a restaurant? How did you react? Why were you upset? What did you expect from the server that he or she didn't do? What should the server have said or done differently to make the situation better?

Everyone has heard the phrase, "The customer is always right." A more practical saying might be that even when the customer is wrong, the customer is still a valuable customer. Customers are the only reason you are in business. They deserve to be treated respectfully and professionally, even when their demands may seem unreasonable to you. In most cases, customer complaints are valid and should be corrected.

Resolving Customer Complaints

As you learned in *Chapter 4: The Art of Service,* knowing how to resolve customer complaints is critical to providing good customer service.

Let's review the steps necessary to solve customer complaints:

1. *Stay calm.*
2. *Listen carefully.*
3. *Empathize.*
4. *Don't be defensive.*
5. *Never ignore a dissatisfied guest.*
6. *Don't say it's not your job to help the customer.*
7. *Never blame the customer.*
8. *Don't try to prove that you're right and the customer is wrong.*
9. *Never pass the buck or blame other employees.*
10. *Accept responsibility.*
11. *Find a solution.*
12. *Follow up.*

Always refer difficult complaints to your manager. Most foodservice organizations have strict guidelines for resolving customer complaints and they must be followed. Servers should remember that giving away food is not always the best answer to the problem. Increasing portion sizes and comping meals without approval from the management might be seen as stealing by many companies.

Even if you handled the problem yourself, you should immediately notify your manager of any complaints. This helps the manager understand the cause of the problem and allows changes to be made so that the problem won't occur again. As a manager, you should try to apologize personally to customers and make sure the problem was handled well. Customers appreciate a manager who is concerned about the service they receive. Remember to apologize for the customer's inconvenience and never criticize a member of your staff. For many customer-service problems, a follow-up letter of apology is often a good idea.

Exhibit 12.3
When guests share a complaint with you, they're giving you a great opportunity to improve your business.

Review Your Learning 12.1

1. Which of the following statements best describes the rule of 10?
   a. Ten customers know of one person who's had a bad food service experience.
   b. Always count to 10 before replying to a customer's complaint.
   c. One dissatisfied customer tells an average of 10 people about their bad experience.
   d. Apologize to one out of 10 customers who complain.

2. What do customers typically do when they are dissatisfied with a restaurant's food or service?
   a. Call 911
   b. Tell their friends about their unsatisfactory experience
   c. Return despite their discontent
   d. Refuse to pay the bill

Continued on next page

3. Which of the following customer complaints does a manager need to hear about?
   a. "My pasta is cold."
   b. "This table is kind of close to the smoking section."
   c. "It's about time you showed up—I thought I might have to get my own water."
   d. All of the above—every complaint is an opportunity to improve the quality of your operation.

4. A customer in a quick-service restaurant orders a sandwich and a large order of fries. When the server places the order on his tray, the customer looks upset and asks if this is the normal large fries portion, and the server tells him it is. The customer asks for his money back. What can and should the server do to best handle this situation?
   a. Tell the customer this is the correct size and offer to sell him a larger order of fries.
   b. Tell the customer that this restaurant is really cheap.
   c. Agree with the customer that the fries are skimpy and add more fries.
   d. Tell the customer to leave if he's not happy with the portion sizes.

5. You are the manager and a customer complains that his table has been waiting over an hour for a pizza that normally takes 15 minutes; Which of the following is the best response?
   a. "Well, I'm sorry, but our pizzas never take 15 minutes; 20-30 minutes maybe, but never 15."
   b. "What can I do? We're short a cook tonight; they're getting the food out as fast as they can.
   c. "Who is your server?! Let me see if that idiot turned in your order. Wait right here."
   d. "That sure is a long time; I'll go check on that pizza right away and be right back."

12.2

SECTION 12.2

Written Communication Skills

AFTER STUDYING SECTION 12.2, YOU SHOULD BE ABLE TO:

- List and demonstrate the skills of effective writing.

No matter what jobs you hold during your lifetime, you will have to know how to write well. Your writing will need to express your ideas clearly, intelligently, and persuasively. Every memo, financial report, invoice, or letter you write is a reflection of both you and your operation. Poorly worded instructions in a memo can result in unnecessary explanations and errors; unclear writing can cause confusion in the monthly report; a poorly worded job description could lead to a lawsuit. While most professionals rank their fear of writing as one of their biggest on-the-job obstacles, eliminating this anxiety can be as easy as ABC.

The ABCs of Business Writing

The next time you write something, try using the ABCs of business writing.

Audience—Who will read your report, memo, or letter? What do you know about your audience? What's in it for the reader? How do you meet the reader's needs? What do you expect the reader(s) to do with the information? Why should the reader take action or want the information? Are you telling your readers more than they need to know?

The monthly financial update to the vice president of sales has a different audience than a training manual written for new servers. A memo to the kitchen staff summarizing new sanitation procedures has a different audience than a memo on the same subject sent to management. Some readers need thoroughness and detail. Others just want the bottom line, while some expect the written word to be a personal transaction between two people. The words and the sense these words convey are different in each case. Each piece of writing should be adapted to your particular audience. Write to them in a style they accept and expect.

Exhibit 12.4
The ABCs of business writing.

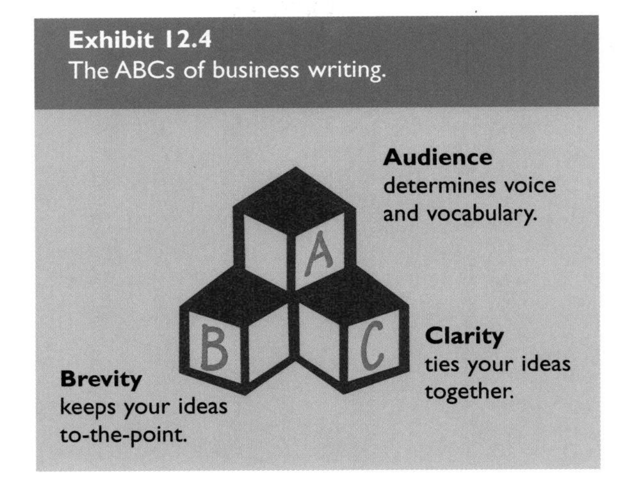

Brevity—Why not just say what you mean? Write as you speak—simple and to-the-point. Long sentences can become a tangled maze for your readers. Eliminate long words when short ones work just as well. Don't use adverbs when the verb has already described the action. Avoid stuffy sentences—they rarely impress a reader.

Clarity—The reason you put a message down on paper is to make it clear to your audience. One sentence should lead logically into the next sentence. It is

Give It A Try...

Weeding Out Wordiness

Cutting out the wordiness from your writing takes practice. Look at the following memo that a manager has sent to her staff. Now try rewriting it to make it more clear and to the point.

Attached herewith is management's previously discussed recommendation for our foodservice establishment's newly revised schedule of dining hours.

your responsibility as a business writer to communicate your ideas clearly. In most cases you will be writing to confirm oral agreements made over the phone with your suppliers. In some cases, however, you will have an idea that differs from the person you are writing to. It will then be necessary to carefully choose words and phrases that convey your opinion and can persuade the reader to accept your idea. At all times your writing is a reflection of you and your organization and must be free of errors to show a positive image.

To guarantee clarity in your writing, always keep your overall purpose for writing in mind. One way to do this is to write the purpose of your letter, report, or memo on a separate sheet of paper and keep it in front of you as you write. One of the most important points to remember is that you should write to express, not to impress.

Here are a few more tips to polish your writing once you've finished a first draft:

- *Take a time-out.* After you've written something, set it down, even if it's only for a few hours. When you come back, you'll be amazed how easy it is to spot and correct errors and awkward phrases. You'll be glad you didn't send your first draft the way it was.
- *Reread carefully for spelling.* A computer spell-checker only spots misspelled words. If your mistake spells a correct word, the spell-checker will let it slip by. (Check out Exhibit 12.5 to see what we mean.)
- *Read out loud to check grammar and punctuation.* If a phrase or sentence is difficult to say, chances are there's a grammar or punctuation problem.
- *Avoid slang and jargon.* Slang are words you may use in everyday speech, but are inappropriate for writing: *ain't, yous,* and *y'all* fall into this category. Jargon are words that are known only to a particular group of people. In the restaurant world, a phrase like "front-of-the-house" has a meaning that might not be understood by a customer.

Exhibit 12.5
Check your spell-checker at the door.

Think spell-checking a document on your computer is all the proofreading you need to do? Read the following poem to discover why it pays to personally review your writing.

Eye have a spelling checker,
It came with my pea see,
It kindly marks four my review
Mistakes eye cannot sea.
I've putt this silly verse threw it,
And know mistakes where found.
Who wood halve thought eyed be so good
At righting stuff sew profound?

August 1, 2003

Emerald Grove Restaurant
Maya Samuels, Manager
26113 SE Western Dr.
Clackamas, OR 97235

Ms. Deena Smith
314 Partridge Ln.
Albany, OR 97415

Dear Ms. Smith:

I am very sorry for the misunderstanding regarding your dinner reservation last Saturday evening. I understand your frustration at making reservations and arriving on time, only to discover that the host could not find your name.

The staff and I appreciate your business, especially when you feel comfortable bringing your friends here for dinner. We apologize for the inconvenience. I understand that your party was detained for about 20 minutes.

We hope you and your friends will join us again. Enclosed is a gift certificate for dinner for two people. We appreciate loyal customers and their understanding when mix-ups occasionally occur.

Once again, we apologize for any inconvenience. We look forward to serving you and your guests in the near future.

Sincerely,

Maya Samuels

Maya Samuels, Manager

Exhibit 12.6
A sincere note of apology can restore a customer's loyalty.

When you respond to a customer's complaint with a letter, be honest. Let the customer know that you are sorry for the inconvenience, the poor service, or the misunderstanding. In the opening paragraph, put yourself in the reader's place and talk about the reader, not about yourself.

Next, focus on the positive steps you have taken to solve this problem, explain how the misunderstanding happened, tell your customers that you appreciate their business, and assure them that you will guard against future misunderstandings. Offer them an incentive to return to your business if it seems appropriate. As shown in Exhibit 12.6, always end your letter on a positive note. Most importantly, always proofread spelling, grammar, and punctuation at least twice. Even the most carefully crafted letter will reflect poorly on your restaurant if it has any spelling errors.

Review Your Learning 12.2

1. Which of the following is *not* one of the three ABCs of good business writing?
   a. Action
   b. Brevity
   c. Clarity
   d. Necessity

2. You need to report on your efforts to improve customer service at your hospital cafeteria. Which of the following opening sentences would make your boss want to read on?
   a. The impact of my very timely training interventions, while appearing to be positively received, have yet to reap the major benefits hoped for in this quarter, and premature conclusions would most likely be deemed inappropriate at this juncture.
   b. While my staff enjoyed participating in the customer service training, it's too early to tell whether it will increase our profits as hoped.

3. Write a short letter of apology to a customer who ordered a white cake for a party and got a chocolate cake instead.

12.3

SECTION 12.3

Telephone Skills and Communicating in a Crisis

AFTER STUDYING SECTION 12.3, YOU SHOULD BE ABLE TO:

- Model proper and courteous telephone skills through demonstration.
- State guidelines for communicating effectively during and after a crisis.

KEY TERMS

- **Crisis**
- **Media**

A phone call is often a customer's first impression of your establishment. There is an art to telephone manners that everyone should practice. Good telephone skills start with identifying yourself and your establishment: "Hello, thank you for calling Isaac's Delicatessen, this is Laurie. How may I help you?"

Taking Reservations Over the Phone

Hosts who handle telephone reservations are often busy, but it's important for them to sound in control of the situation, not rushed or confused. Here are some tips for taking reservations by phone. When taking reservations (in phone or in person), be sure to ask for the information listed in Exhibit 12.7.

For large parties or banquets, include additional questions such as type of event, rooms available on the requested date, time and hours requested, deposit required, etc. Many establishments have a banquet or catering manager who handles these details. Have the banquet manager's name and extension posted for

Exhibit 12.7
Taking reservations by phone.

- Party's name (spelled correctly)
- Date and time of arrival
- Number of guests in the party
- Smoking or nonsmoking preference
- Birthday cake or other special items
- Other special requests, such as help with a person's disability or preference for a particular table. Remember to always write down any special requests or orders.
- Phone numbers (day and evening if necessary) where the person can be reached

easy reference. Assure the customer that the banquet manager will call back if he or she cannot take the call at this time.

Basic Telephone Skills

If you become the manager of a foodservice establishment, you'll want to make sure that your employees have excellent telephone skills. Telephone training is necessary for anyone who answers the phone. Besides being pleasant and helpful, each employee needs to know what questions to ask and what information to write down. Here are a few helpful hints to improve your performance on the phone.

- *Be an effective speaker.* Speak loud enough, but don't shout. Don't talk too fast, and don't slur your words. Remember that some people have a difficult time hearing.
- *Be enthusiastic.* Remember that the person on the other end is hearing the information for the first time. This is your one chance to make a good first impression. Even if you are tired of answering the same questions all day long, never let it show.
- *Effective listening is just as important as effective speaking.* Really listen to the customer. Make sure you understand their needs and requests.
- *Don't be afraid to ask the customer to repeat important information.* It's better to be sure of the order or reservation than to make serious mistakes, such as booking the banquet on the wrong day, or ordering the wrong type of wedding cake.
- *Smile.* This may seem like a strange thing to do for a phone conversation, but our voices actually sound more pleasant when we smile. Smiling realigns the throat muscles, causing the mouth to be more open and the jaws to be less tense and produces a better tone. As a result, customers have a positive impression of your business before they even walk through the door.

Exhibit 12.8
Our voices actually sound more pleasant when we smile.

- *Know your business.* The more you know about your business' products or services, the easier it is to answer questions without having to call back the customer.
- *Know the answers to frequently asked questions.* Tape a list of important facts and figures to the desk or to the phone itself so every employee can provide quick answers. This list simplifies things for other employees and controls the information they give out.
- *List the extensions of frequently called people on your phone list.*
- *Write messages down on a pre-printed message form.* Clearly note who called and the date and time they called. Sign your name on the memo in case the person who receives it has any further questions about the message itself.
- *Never make a guess.* If you don't have the requested information, refer the person to the correct source or offer to find out and call back.
- *Always end the conversation on a positive note.* Thank them for choosing your restaurant and let them know that you look forward to their visit.

Try This!

Getting the Message

You are the manager of a large catering company. You get a call from one of your main beverage distributors. As you place your weekly soft drink order, she mentions that it's a shame you didn't get back to her earlier in the week, when the soda you just ordered was discounted 20%. But you never got her first message. You realize that it's time for your staff to have a phone skills refresher course. Write down a few of the major phone skills you want to see improved.

Putting Customers on Hold

Many hospitality establishments have installed special telephone systems that provide useful messages to callers who are put on hold. Often these pre-recorded messages inform customers of information they'll need once their call is picked up—such as account numbers, order numbers, etc. Other messages alert callers to an establishment's latest promotion or new business hours. While these message systems help callers stay patient, don't expect your customers to hold forever. Thirty seconds on hold seems like an eternity to many people.

You might want to "hold" on to these helpful guidelines.

- If you've put a caller on hold, get back to him or her as quickly as possible.
- If the person who the caller is trying to reach is still unavailable, ask the caller if he or she wishes to continue to hold, and thank them for being patient.
- If a caller has waited longer than a minute, offer again to take a message.
- If possible, let the person who the caller is holding for know that there is another call waiting. Try to find out how long the caller will have to hold.

Finally, be careful about side conversations with coworkers while you are talking to a customer on the phone. Putting your hand over the receiver doesn't completely block out the sound, and callers often hear what's being said in the background.

Resolving Complaints on the Phone

When you receive complaints from customers over the phone, you are often trying to understand a situation in which you were not personally involved. Follow the same steps for resolving a customer complaint that you would if you were talking to the customer in person. Remember, the caller is probably not angry at you personally, but at the situation.

It's a good idea to take notes while you're hearing a guest's complaint over the phone. You will need the facts to work out a solution or pass along the information. Follow up on details that are unclear to you. This lets the caller know that you are really listening to the complaint. Apologize for the problem even if you can't take responsibility for it, so the caller knows you understand and sympathize. If the caller needs to be referred to someone else, be sure to give the customer the name of the person who will be handling the complaint. Most importantly, be sure the person who is responsible for dealing with the customer receives the message.

Communicating in a Crisis

A **crisis** is a situation which has or threatens to have a significant negative effect on your operation. Crises can range from a serious accident involving a single employee or customer, to crime-related violence, a death, an outbreak of food poisoning, or an earthquake. Most importantly, crises can and do happen to any operation.

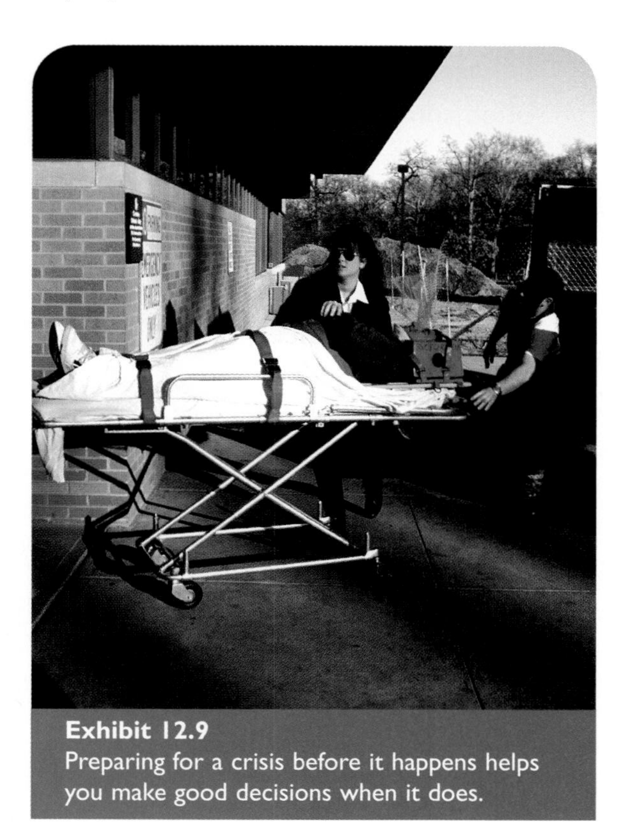

Exhibit 12.9
Preparing for a crisis before it happens helps you make good decisions when it does.

During a crisis, customers may be victims, witnesses, or simply concerned bystanders. They may also be angry, fearful, or threatening legal action. Management and staff need to keep their customers safe, try to regain their goodwill, and, in the worst cases, avoid a lawsuit.

When a crisis develops, employees need to involve their manager right away. The manager should act as the main representative for the establishment, handling all major questions and concerns. During a crisis, a manager should:

1. *Listen to the customer.* Show concern and let customers express their observations or feelings. Never argue or laugh at them.

2. *Discuss facts.* When appropriate, use a standard form to record each complaint. It's important to record the sequence of alleged events according to the customer's point of view.

3. *Never pressure the customer.* Just ask for details. Let the customer tell the story in his or her own words.

4. *Offer help immediately, but carefully.* Always offer first aid or call the police or rescue unit as needed. For less serious complaints or requests,

reassure the customer that his or her complaint will be taken seriously. If you have already started to work on the problem, tell the customer. When appropriate, offer food, beverages, or gift certificates in appreciation of the customer's patience and goodwill.

5. *Limit what you say.* Managers should avoid admitting guilt or responsibility, since the complete situation may not yet be clear. Do not offer insurance, medical, or legal opinions on injuries or complaints, since you are not an expert. You should express concern for the customers' well-being, and emphasize that help has been contacted.
6. *Follow up and inform the customer of the outcome.* Tell the customer how you will deal with his or her problem. Act quickly, and contact the customer afterward to relate your progress. Whenever possible, build a positive relationship that will survive the crisis.

Media Relations During a Crisis

As a foodservice manager, you will most likely represent your operation or company to the media during a crisis. **Media** are organizations that provide news and information to the public. Newspapers, radio stations, magazines, and television stations are all members of the media.

When you talk to reporters from the media about a crisis at your establishment, remember the following:

- *Accept and return reporters' calls.* If you don't, you risk developing a poor relationship with reporters. Without your side of the story, a reporter is much more likely to write a piece that makes your establishment look bad. Also, if you don't talk to reporters, someone else will, often someone with a completely different set of facts than those you would like to share with the public. Talking to reporters helps you control the flow of information.
- *Make sure your employees refer all media questions to you.* Your employees must know and understand that you are the company's spokesperson and that their comments can legally hurt the organization. If you are part of a larger chain, make certain that you follow your organization's policy regarding talking to reporters.

- *Ask reporters:*
  —What is the subject and scope of the story?
  —Has the reporter seen official evidence or documents?
  —Has the reporter spoken to anyone else?
  —What information does the reporter want from you?
- *Set a time for you or a company spokesperson to get back to the reporter.* This allows your operation to better prepare for the interview.
- *Gather information and write it down before talking with a reporter.*
- *Try to anticipate questions.*
- *Give some key points to develop your perspective.*
- *Prepare a few meaningful quotes to be used in the story.*
- *If you do not know the answer to a question, admit it.* Avoid saying, "No comment." If you cannot answer due to legal or other considerations, explain this to the reporter. Under no circumstance should you speculate on the situation in front of the reporter.
- *Never lie to a reporter.* You will only make your operation look bad, and ruin your credibility with the public.
- *Do not make remarks "off the record."* Expect reporters to print or mention everything you tell them.
- *Do not expect to review or edit the story before it becomes public.*
- *If you like the story, tell the reporter or writer.*
- *Discuss any discrepancies in a story's facts with the reporter.* If the errors put your company in a bad light, request a public correction.
- *If this approach is not successful, call the editor or write a letter to the editor to set the facts straight.*

Review Your Learning 12.3

1. Nick calls three restaurants to make reservations for dinner. He gets three very different telephone greetings. Which restaurant is most likely to get Nick's business?
   a. "Rocco here! Whad'ya want?!"
   b. "Thank you for calling Succi's Bistro. Our hours are from 11 to 10, Tuesday through Saturday. We accept all major credit cards. Please push one if you'd like to use our automated reservation system. Then press the star symbol..."
   c. "Hello, thank you for calling The Little Garden. This is Sam. How may I help you?"
   d. "We're not open yet. Call back later."

2. When handling customer complaints on the phone, it's a good idea to _______ so that you can develop a complete picture of the caller's problem.
   a. smile
   b. speak effectively
   c. hang up
   d. take notes

3. Diana, the manager of a restaurant, wants to develop a training program that will help her employees answer the phones professionally. Which topic would you expect to see on her training outline?
   a. "How to Get Rid of Rude Callers"
   b. "They Can Hear You Smile"
   c. "Speaking Quickly Saves Time and Money"
   d. "Tips for Suggestive Selling"

4. Which of the following is not a crisis situation?
   a. A tornado touches down near the restaurant where you are a manager
   b. A customer is accidentally burned by a fajita tray
   c. A drunken guest becomes abusive to one of your waitresses
   d. The men's bathroom needs more paper towels

12.4

SECTION 12.4

Effective Listening and Speaking

AFTER STUDYING SECTION 12.4, YOU SHOULD BE ABLE TO:

- List and demonstrate effective listening and speaking skills.

KEY TERM

- **Nonverbal communication**

In the foodservice industry, almost every employee has regular contact with customers. No matter what job you hold, your ability to listen and speak clearly to customers will set you apart as a valuable employee or manager. Since we spend nearly 80% of each day communicating with other people, developing effective speaking and listening skills is important to both your career and your life.

Effective Listening

It may sound strange, but good speaking starts with what you hear, not with what you say. Studies show that 60% of all business misunderstandings are due to poor listening skills. Maybe that's because on any given day, we take in only about 25% of what is said to us. Why are we so poor at something we do so often?

First, we selectively listen to other people, paying more attention to someone when he or she says something that agrees with our own opinions. Second, we become easily distracted when we are tired, cold, or hungry. When any noise interrupts a conversation, the last few seconds of the conversation are lost unless repeated. Finally, we often are busy thinking about what we are going to say while the other person is still speaking.

Exhibit 12.10
Knowing how to listen between the lines will help you become a better listener.

Do you want to improve your brain-to-ear coordination? Listen in on these helpful hints:

- *Don't finish the other person's sentence*—in your mind or aloud. Listening to only the first few words of someone's sentence, then assuming you know the rest, is a common mistake of poor listeners. Let the other person finish their ideas. That way, your reply addresses what the person actually said, not what you think he or she said.
- *Stay focused on what the person is saying, not on the way they're saying it.* This technique helps prevent your mind from wandering.
- *It's okay to repeat.* Ask your speaker to repeat something you didn't quite catch. Or check your listening by saying, "Here's what I think I hear you saying..." then repeat their main message.
- *Ask questions to clarify your speaker's ideas.*
- *Don't overreact.* When someone says something that you strongly disagree with, don't interrupt, become emotional, or answer rudely. Such reactions send out a strong signal that you've stopped listening and you only want to be heard. Would you listen to someone who doesn't want to listen to you?
- *Listen between the lines.* Often, it's not what someone says but how the person says it. Learn to read a person's body language. It will give you important clues to his or her true feelings on a subject.
- *Record key ideas and phrases.* While you probably don't need to take notes when talking to friends, note-taking is a valuable way to improve your listening

skills in the classroom or workplace. Notes allow you to remember important points that you might otherwise forget.

- *Listen more.* A good conversation involves 50% listening and 50% speaking. Check out your next conversation—do the numbers add up?

Effective Speaking

Becoming a foodservice manager calls for many things, and communication skills may very well top the list. Your ability to speak clearly and effectively can be developed over time. The next time you speak to someone, whether it's a coworker or a customer, try to use some of these important techniques.

You can communicate a pleasant attitude through positive nonverbal communication. Also known as body language, **nonverbal communication** includes things such as facial expressions, tone of voice, gestures, and overall posture. Even though nonverbal communication is unspoken, it lets people know how you feel about yourself, your job, your feelings for the operation, and your customers before you even open your mouth.

It is also very important to use complete sentences when speaking to customers. This shows your professional attitude and will immediately improve the level of service you offer. By saying, "What would you like to order this evening?"

What do the facial expressions of these people tell you about how they are feeling?

Exhibit 12.11
Cluing in to nonverbal communication.

instead of "What'll it be?" you exhibit a more educated and professional appearance. Another common error is to use slang such as *nope, ya-know* and *whatever.*

It is best to remember that you're a representative of the restaurant and are being paid to show it off to the best of your ability. By describing menu items in concise, appetizing, and accurate terms you improve the imaginary appearance of the food on the menu before it is brought to the table. Remember that your customers are constantly evaluating everything you say. If you use tired phrases like, "Have a nice day", or "Hope to see ya' again real soon", your customers may not be listening to your words, but be hearing instead your lack of interest. Try to be more creative. "It's been a pleasure waiting on you this evening" has a much better ring to it than "Hope you liked everything."

Review Your Learning 12.4

1. A customer begins to ask you for something, and you say, "Oh that's right—you needed some water. I'll get it right away," and you run off for the water pitcher. This is an example of poor listening skills because:
   a. you never should have forgotten her request in the first place.
   b. you should have asked the customer to repeat her request the first time.
   c. you should not have mentioned that you forgot to bring the water.
   d. you should have allowed the customer to fully ask her question, in case she wanted something other than water.

2. A customer asks you if a dish can be made with olive oil instead of butter. Which of the following replies is the best example of effective speaking?
   a. "Nope, our cook doesn't like too many curve-balls."
   b. "Beats me, but I'll go find out."
   c. "Maybe you should choose one of our low-fat entrées."
   d. "I think our cook would be happy to do that. Let me go ask."

Continued on next page

3. Your boss begins talking about improving communication between the front-of-the-house and the back-of-the-house. Then you start to notice a tomato stain on his tie. Your boss asks you a question. You have no idea what he's just asked. Which effective listening tip have you forgotten to use?
   a. Stay focused on what the person is saying
   b. Read between the lines
   c. Don't overreact
   d. Don't finish the other person's sentence

4. When one of your customers asks what types of salad dressings you have, you should:
   a. point to the list on the menu.
   b. go back to the kitchen to ask the chef.
   c. look up at the ceiling and quickly run through the list.
   d. carefully list each one of the salad dressings available.

5. You are having trouble hearing your customer's order. To avoid any mistakes, you should:
   a. bend down closer to the table.
   b. ask them to point to the items on the menu.
   c. repeat back what they have ordered.
   d. try to read their lips.

12.5

SECTION 12.5

Communicating Promotional Information

AFTER STUDYING SECTION 12.5, YOU SHOULD BE ABLE TO:

- List and give examples of innovative ways to attract and keep customers.
- Point out menu items and demonstrate suggestive selling techniques.

For restaurant and other foodservice operations to be successful, they need to find ways to constantly attract and keep customers. Satisfied customers often tell their friends and family about good restaurants and hotels. This traditionally important way of building business is called **word-of-mouth.** Unfortunately, it is a very slow and indirect method of promoting your business. Also, an increase in customers from good word-of-mouth can be just as easily erased by the rule of 10.

KEY TERMS

- Contests
- Coupons
- Games
- Intermediaries
- Point-of-sale (POS)
- Premium
- Promotional campaign
- Sampling
- Signature item
- Special offer
- Specialty item
- Suggestive selling
- Sweepstakes
- Trade promotion
- Trial and usage promotion
- Word-of-mouth

Promotional campaigns are a more direct way for managers to build and maintain their businesses. As you learned in *Chapter 6: Marketing and the Menu,* a **promotional campaign** refers to the various methods and strategies that create customer interest and loyalty. While national chains spend time and energy creating nationwide promotional campaigns, local owners and managers often have a lot of freedom to develop campaigns on their own. A promotional campaign might include one or more of the following methods and strategies.

- Trade promotions
- Trial and usage promotions
- Special offers
- Specialty items
- Premiums
- Games, contests, and sweepstakes
- Point-of-sale displays
- Suggestive selling techniques

Types of Promotions

Trade promotions involve promoting your business to other businesses whose customers might in turn visit your establishment. These other businesses are known as **intermediaries.** As a manager of a restaurant near a convention center, for example, you might launch a trade promotion that targets hotels in your area.

In **trial and usage promotions,** managers get new customers to try a service or product. Sampling of products and coupons are the most important types of trial and usage promotions. **Sampling** involves giving away free samples of items to encourage sales, or arranging in some way for people to try all or part of a service free of charge. Restaurants often offer customers free samples of new menu or beverage items such as appetizers or desserts. They also use sampling to promote new meal periods such as breakfast or an early bird buffet.

Coupons are printed certificates that entitle customers to a reduced price on food items or services. Coupons have both advantages and disadvantages, and their popularity as a sales promotion method has decreased over the years (see Exhibit 12.12). Coupons are often delivered to your customer through the mail, newspapers, or magazines. Other coupons are put in places where customers are likely to see them, such as on bulletin boards or pizza boxes.

Special offers usually require customers to make a purchase or reservation

Exhibit 12.12
The pros and cons of coupons.

Coupons can help:

- encourage people to try a product or service for the first time.
- generate temporary increase in sales.
- introduce new products and services effectively.
- increase use of products and services by repeat customers.
- encourage customers to "trade up" to larger portions, complete meals, and more expensive items.
- generate a relatively quick response to advertising.
- add appeal and recall to an advertising campaign.

Coupons can hurt:

- sales during off-seasons.
- service when employees are confused by the coupon offer.
- sales since they create an unpredictable customer response and are expensive to redeem.
- when they promote new products or services that are completely unknown.
- when frequent "full-price" customers use them and sales are lost.

within a certain time period. Two-for-one deals used by restaurants and airlines are good examples of special offers. Some offers require customers to take some definite action, such as filling out and mailing back a completed sweepstakes entry. Others use price reductions, gifts, and free meals as incentives.

Specialty items help reinforce a company's product or service. Businesses print their name, logo, or ad message on such things as sweatshirts, coffee mugs, and baseball caps. Specialty items are then sold (often at a discounted price) or given away to customers.

Premiums are merchandise items offered at a reduced price or free with a purchase of other services or products. A free order of fries with the purchase of a hamburger is one example of a premium. Specialty items are often used as premiums. Take, for example, the plastic action figures that many fast-food restaurants give away with children's meals. While these novelties may not seem like much in themselves, the customer interest, goodwill, and loyalty can often make them worth the cost.

In **games,** customers win prizes based on luck. **Contests** require customers to demonstrate some sort of skill. **Sweepstakes** are sales promotions that require entrants to submit their names and

Give It a Try...

Lots of restaurants provide promotional materials to increase their business. Think about some of the restaurants you've been to. What are some of the promotions they have done to promote business?

addresses, and winners are chosen randomly. The personal information gathered through a sweepstakes is often used in a later promotion of products and services.

Point-of-sale, or **POS,** is promotional material that is displayed in the restaurant to promote various products or services. Once a customer is in the establishment and ready to spend money, a well-placed POS can greatly influence their buying decision. POSs come in a variety of shapes and sizes. Large soft-drink manufacturers often send restaurants extensive POS kits, complete with colorful posters, cards for counters and tables, and mobiles.

Exhibit 12.13
Signature items are dishes that are unique to an operation.

Having your servers recommend and suggest menu items is one of the most important ways you can help your operation increase its sales. As you have learned, servers must always know the soup of the day, specials, prices, and other daily information before the start of their shift. They must also be trained in the art of suggestive selling, which is similar to POS in that they both take advantage of a customer's willingness to spend money once he or she has entered your establishment.

Suggestive selling, as discussed in *Chapter 6: Marketing and the Menu,* is a cost-effective way to promote an operation's products and services. It is a low-cost promotional method managers use in order to increase profits. It is not pushing expensive food items on people who don't want it. Actually, the more your guests know about each menu item, how it is prepared, and why your operation is pleased to offer it, the more likely they are to enjoy every aspect of their meal.

To answer guests' questions thoroughly and to suggest products effectively, employees first must learn their restaurant's menu very well. All servers should be enthusiastic about **signature items,** dishes that are unique or well-known to your operation.

They must also know the meaning of specialized cooking terms that appear on the menu, such as *flambé* and *au gratin* and be able to explain preparation terms and methods, such as *grilled* and *sautéed.*

Once servers are comfortable with the basics, they should begin to describe menu items more creatively by using words that communicate the quality of the food in a dish. Or they can incorporate words that suggest the chef's enthusiasm in preparing a dish (see Exhibit 12.14). Rice becomes "multi-grained rice seasoned with mushroom and almonds;" a cheeseburger becomes "char-broiled, 100-percent pure beef hamburgers with melted Monterey Jack cheese."

As a server, it's important to ask for the sale after you've made a suggestion. Sometimes this can be as easy as returning to a table and saying, "Well, have you decided which appetizer I can bring for you today?" Other times it helps to observe your guests as they think over or discuss their options. If, for example, one person at a table for two says that he or she isn't very hungry, you might suggest something like, "You could easily split the potato skins." Once your guests have made a choice, compliment them by saying, "I'm sure you'll like that," or "Excellent choice."

Exhibit 12.14
The art of suggestive selling makes a dish sound as good as it tastes!

The power of suggestive selling.

Server #1: "Umm, for appetizers, we got some nachos, mushrooms, and a few other things on your menu there."

Server #2: "Can I interest you in some appetizers to start things off? I'm a big fan of our nachos. They're made with Iowa corn tortilla chips, refried pinto beans, and our marinated fajita steak, then topped with melted, aged Wisconsin cheddar cheese."

Will foodservice managers still be handling customer complaints 20 years from now? Yes, without a doubt. In fact, foodservice experts at the National Restaurant Association predict that direct customer relations will make up the majority of a manager's work day in the 21st century. As a result, expect more managers to start linking employee pay raises to improvements in customer service. Extensive customer-service training—for both managers and their employees—will be a crucial ingredient for the successful hospitality business of tomorrow.

Review Your Learning 12.5

1. Which of the following best describes the suggestive selling concept?
   a. Persuade your customer to always order the most expensive item.
   b. Push food on people even if they're not particularly hungry.
   c. Make sure your latest POS promotion from your soda distributor is in full view.
   d. Use your knowledge of the menu to help guests select a meal they'll enjoy.

2. Luigi talks to his friend, Ernesto, the owner of a health club around the corner from Luigi's Pizza. Luigi has created some flyers to promote his new low-fat pizzas, and Ernesto agrees to put them up on his club's bulletin board. This is an example of a _________ promotion. In this type of a promotion Ernesto's health club serves as the _________ for Luigi's promotional efforts.
   a. coupon; source
   b. point-of-purchase; distributor
   c. trade; intermediary
   d. word-of-mouth; conduit

3. Why might coupons be a good way for Luigi to promote his new products?

4. CJ is watching TV when an ad for King Big Burger comes on: "For a limited time," it says "this glow-in-the-dark 'King Kup' can be yours with the purchase of a sandwich and fries." This is a good example of a ____ promotional campaign.
   a. specialty item
   b. premium
   c. point of purchase
   d. trial and usage

5. Write a description for macaroni and cheese that uses suggestive selling techniques.

Flashback

CHAPTER 12

SECTION 12.1: HANDLING CUSTOMER COMPLAINTS

- When customers do not receive a basic level of service, they become disappointed, irritated, annoyed, even angry.
- The best way to prevent most complaints is to ensure that all jobs are done with care.
- Remember the **rule of 10:** one dissatisfied customer tells an average of 10 people about their bad experience.
- Complaints are actually a valuable key that helps you learn what customers expect.
- Statistics show that a customer whose complaint is handled well often becomes a repeat customer.
- Employees should notice subtle clues that guests give to show they are dissatisfied with their meal.
- Employees should handle customer complaints with a positive, friendly attitude. They should remain calm, listen carefully, show empathy, and accept responsibility.
- Employees should notify managers of all complaints, even if they can handle the problems themselves.
- Managers should try to apologize personally to customers and make sure the problem was handled satisfactorily.

SECTION 12.2: WRITTEN COMMUNICATION SKILLS

- Written communication skills are essential for the many memos, letters, and reports that foodservice managers create daily.
- Learn the ABCs of business writing in order to express your ideas clearly, intelligently, and persuasively.

—Write to your audience in a style they accept and expect.

—Brevity comes from short, to-the-point sentences.

—Clarity demonstrates your ability to logically put ideas together.

- Better writing happens when you:

—Take a time-out before proofreading.

—Review spelling carefully—even after using a computer's spell-checker.

—Read out loud to check grammar and punctuation.

—Avoid slang and jargon.

- Written letters of apology should apologize to the customer for the inconvenience, explain the steps taken to solve problem, and offer some incentive to have the customer return.

SECTION 12.3: TELEPHONE SKILLS AND COMMUNICATING IN A CRISIS

- A phone call is often a customer's first impression of your establishment.
- Answer the phone by identifying your establishment, yourself, and your desire to help the customer.
- When you take reservations (in phone or in person), be sure to get the caller's:

—Name

—Date and time of arrival

—Number of guests

—Smoking/nonsmoking preference

—Other special requests

- Helping angry callers requires the same calm approach used in person.
- Take notes to help understand the customer's complaint.
- If you can't help, make sure you give the name and phone number of the individual who can.
- Be sure that the person who is responsible for dealing with the customer receives the message.
- A **crisis** is a situation like a natural disaster, violent crime, or food poisoning that may have a significant negative effect on your operation.
- During a crisis, keep customers safe, try to regain their goodwill, and, in the worst case, avoid a lawsuit.
- Managers should handle all major questions and concerns during a crisis. They should:

—Listen to the concerns of the customer.

—Offer to provide medical help if necessary.

—Follow up to make sure the customer is safe and satisfied.

- **Media** are organizations that provide news and information to the public.
- Speaking to the media is an opportunity to positively portray your

operation to the public. This is true even during a crisis—if your spokesperson is knowledgeable and concerned.

- To avoid bad press, return all calls from reporters.

SECTION 12.4: EFFECTIVE LISTENING AND SPEAKING

- All employees, including managers, need to develop effective listening and speaking skills.
- Poor listening skills are common in the working world. Most of us take in only 25% of what is said to us.
- Key steps to better listening include:

—Avoiding finishing other people's sentences.

—Asking questions to improve understanding.

—Staying focused on what the person is saying.

- You can become a more effective speaker by:

—Being aware of your **nonverbal communication,** or body language.

—Speaking courteously.

—Using complete sentences.

—Keeping a pace that is not too fast or too slow.

SECTION 12.5: COMMUNICATING PROMOTIONAL INFORMATION

- Successful foodservice operations are constantly looking for new ways to attract and keep customers.
- **Word-of-mouth** from satisfied c ustomers is a very effective but very indirect method of promotion.
- A **promotional campaign** refers to the more direct methods and strategies that create customer interest and loyalty, such as:

—Trade promotions

—Trial and usage promotions

—Special offers

—Premiums

—Games and contests

—Point-of-sale (POS)

—Suggestive selling

- **Trade promotions** involve promoting your business to other hospitality businesses, which are known as **intermediaries.**

- **Trial and usage promotions** are used to get new customers to try a service or product. **Sampling** and **coupons** are two types of trial and usage promotions.
- **Special offers** usually require customers to make a purchase or reservation within a certain time period.
- **Premiums** are merchandise items offered at a reduced price or free with a purchase of other services or products.
- In **games** and **contests,** customers win prizes based on luck or some skill they must demonstrate.
- **Point-of-sale,** or **POS,** promotional materials are displayed inside the restaurant to promote various products or services.
- **Suggestive selling** is a cost-effective way to promote an operation's products and services.

Glossary
OF KEY TERMS

#

3-2-1 dough
Pie dough made of three parts flour, two parts fat, and one part water

A

À la carte (AH le CART) menu
Menu that offers items separately at separate prices

Á point
Food is cooked through, but not overcooked

ABCs of business writing
Set of guidelines that help writers remember the importance of audience, brevity, and clarity in their writing

Accommodations
Any place that travelers stay overnight, including hotels, motels, resorts, inns, and convention centers

Accounts payable
All the money that a business owes to other businesses

Accounts receivable
All the money that is owed to a business

Administrative department
Department that manages the business responsibilities, such as accounting, human resources and training, and marketing and sales

Aging
Process that allows muscles to relax. Longer aging gives meat a darker color, more tender texture, and fuller flavor

Air
Physical leavener used in baking

Al dente (ahl DAN-tay)
Pasta that is cooked, but still chewy; literally means 'to the tooth'

All-purpose flour
Type of wheat flour used in baking cookies and biscuits and general production work

All-purpose potato
Irregularly shaped potato that is usually less expensive; also called chef's potato

All-suite property
Establishment providing apartment-style facilities

Amenity (a-MEN-i-TEE)
Services or facilities located inside the lodging operation that guests may use or enjoy without having to leave the hotel; adds value to the guest's stay

American service
Service style in which food is portioned onto plates in the kitchen by employees and brought directly to guests' tables

Application form
Form that asks basic information about you and your background; must be completed in order to apply to colleges, trade schools, or for a job

Apprentice
Server in training

Aquaculture
Farm-raising fish and seafood

Arborio (ahr-BORE-ee-oh)
Special short grain rice used in the risotto method

Aromatics
Herbs, spices, and flavorings that create a savory smell and flavor in stocks

As purchased price (AP price)
Price of food purchased before trimming and preparing

Asset
Item of value that's owned by a business

Assistant general manager
Manager who implements the GM's plans and serves as a liaison between management and the staff

Au jus (oh ZHEW)
Meat served with a sauce made from the meat's own juices

Average contribution margin achievement rate
Menu contribution margin divided by total number of items sold

B

Back-of-the-house
Positions in all areas outside of public space; the team of individuals who perform all the food production tasks for an operation; support areas or departments that operate behind the scenes

Baker's percentage
System used in baking in which flour is always given a percentage of 100%, and all other ingredients are given a percentage in relation to the flour

Baking blind
Procedure for preparing a pre-baked pie shell

Baking powder
Chemical leavener made from baking soda, an acid, and an inactive material, like starch

Baking soda
Chemical leavener that releases carbon dioxide gas when combined with a liquid and an acid

Balance sheet
Financial report showing a company's assets, liabilities, and owners' equity at a particular date

Balance sheet equation
Formula that shows what a business owes, what it is worth, and the items it owns; Assets = Liabilities + Owners' equity

Bank reconciliation
Process of matching the bank's monthly statement with a business's internal accounting records

Bard
Tying thin slices of fat (bacon or pork fatback) over meats or poultry that have little or no natural fat covering in order to protect and moisten them during roasting

Bavarian cream
Custard made from combining vanilla sauce, gelatin, and whipped cream

Béchamel (BAY-shah-MELL)
Grand sauce made from milk and white roux

Bed and breakfast
Privately owned homes converted to have several guest rooms

Bell captain
Person who oversees bellhops, door attendants, and valet parking crew members at a full-service lodging operation

Beurre manié (byurr man-YAY)
Thickener used to thicken stocks or other sauces; a mixture of equal parts flour and whole butter

Bids
Specialized, written price lists created for an organization by a supplier

Bisque (bisk)
Thick soup made from puréed shellfish

Block
To reserve a room on a specific day

Block-out
Yield management strategy that forces guests to commit to a minimum number of nights

Bloom
White coating that appears on the surface of chocolate when the cocoa butter has melted and recrystallized

Boning
Separating meat from the bone

Borscht (borsht)
Russian cold beet soup

Bouillabaisse (BOO-ya-base)
French seafood stew made with assorted fish and shellfish, onions, white wine, olive oil, garlic, saffron, and herbs

Bouillon (BOO-yon)
Also called broth; the liquid that results from simmering meats or vegetables

Bouquet garni (boo-KAY gahr-NEE)
Fresh vegetables and herbs tied together and used to flavor stocks

Bran
Outer layer of a grain and the part highest in fiber

Bread flour
Strong flour used for making breads, hard rolls, and any product that needs a high gluten content for strong texture

Broth
Liquid that results from simmering meats; also called bouillon

Brown
Process of roasting bones in an oven and then simmering them in water to enhance their flavor in stock

Brown sauce
Sauce made from brown stock and brown roux; also called espagnole sauce

Brown stock
Brown liquid made by first browning the bones of poultry, beef, veal, or game

Business tourism
Visiting places for business purposes, such as conventions, meetings, and seminars

Business traveler
Anyone who travels primarily for the purpose of business

Butterfly
Cutting a piece of meat lengthwise nearly in half so it spreads out flat

Buyers
People who order all of the food, beverages, supplies, and equipment for a foodservice operation

C

Cafeteria
Assembly-line system of serving food

Café
Coffeehouses where people gathered for coffee and conversation with friends and neighbors

Cajun
Spicy and rustic cuisine from the Louisiana bayou based on a combination of French, American Indian, African, and Spanish cooking

Cake flour
Flour that has a low gluten content, with a smooth texture and pure white color; used for making cakes and other baked goods

California menu
Menu that has a varied number of items that are offered at any time of the day

Capital item
Fixed asset (furniture, fixtures, or equipment) that has a life expectancy of at least three years

Captain
Employee responsible for a server area of usually 15-25 guests

Caramelization
Browning of sugar in foods in the presence of heat

Career
Profession or work in a certain field

Career ladder
Series of jobs through which a person can advance in a career

Carryover cooking
Heat retained in cooked foods that allows them to continue cooking even after removal from the oven

Central reservation system (CRS)
Service that allows guests to reserve a room at any branch property by calling one telephone number

Chain
Group of restaurants owned by the same business organization

Channel of distribution
The particular businesses that buy and sell a product as it makes its way from its original source to a retailer

Charcuterie
Specially prepared pork products, including sausages, smoked hams, pâtés, bacon, and terrines.

Charter
Arrangement by which a bus is rented by a tour company for a travel group

Ché (Kay)
Clarified butter used in Indian cuisine

Chef's potato
Irregularly shaped potato that is usually less expensive; also called all-purpose potato

Chief engineer
Head person for the engineering and facility maintenance department; oversees ongoing maintenance of lodging equipment and physical building

Chocolate liquor
Cocoa beans that have been crushed into a paste and left unsweetened

Chowder
Hearty soup made with milk or cream that is not puréed

Chutney
Relish made of fruits, spices, and herbs

Clambake
Method of cooking where fish and corn are cooked in a pit dug in wet sand

Clarify
To make stock or broth perfectly clear

Clear soup
Soups including stocks, broth, and consommés; made from a base of basic broth

Clip-on
Advertising material attached to a menu that announces special items

Coach
Standard passenger seating

Cocoa butter
Chocolate liquor that has been pressed with a sweetener added

Cocoa powder
Ground cocoa solids

Collagen
Type of connective tissue that breaks down during long, slow, moist heat cooking

College application
Form designed by colleges that asks basic personal information about background and education

Commercial
Includes any type of operation that sells food and beverages for profit, such as full-service restaurants, quick-service chains, recreational and sports centers, hotel restaurants, and others

Commercial segment
Segment of the foodservice industry that includes restaurants, bars, supermarket delis, convenience stores, lodging facilities; any location that prepares and serves food for profit

Commissary
Distribution warehouse that provides goods to individual locations of a multi-unit company

Communication mix
Combination of all the ways in which an operation communicates to its customers

Commuter
Person who travels from home in the suburbs or a rural community to work in the city

Compound butter
Mixture of raw butter and various flavoring ingredients, used to finish grilled or broiled meats, pastas, and sauces

Concierge (con-see-AIRJ)
Front office employee who provides guests with information services and responds to special requests

Connective tissue
Surrounds bundles of muscle fibers; breaks down through cooking or trimming

Consommé (con-soh-MAY)
Broth or stock that has been clarified

Consulting services
Service in which the supplier provides helpful handling and safety instructions for products sold to buyer

Contemporary marketing mix
Combination of an operation's product-service mix, presentation mix, and communication mix

Contests
Promotional method in which customers compete to win prizes by demonstrating some skill

Contribution margin
Found by subtracting a food item's standard food cost from its selling price

Contribution margin proportion
Item's contribution margin divided by menu contribution margin

Contributory income
Amount of income that a particular department contributes to a foodservice establishment's total income

Contributory income percent
Percentage of a department's revenue that is income

Controller
Manages the accounting department, participates in long-term financial planning, and provides daily financial reports to management

Convenience foods
Items that have been processed to make them easier to use and prepare

Convention
Gathering of people, all of whom have something in common

Convention manager
Plans meetings, determines rates for convention guests, and sells the facility's banquet services

Convention sales manager
Brings in new convention business by promoting the establishment as a site for conferences, seminars, and meetings

Cooperative (co-op) buying
System in which buyers combine their purchase orders to receive lower prices from suppliers

Corporate travel office
In-house travel service for a large company

Cost
Price paid for goods or services when the goods are received or the services are rendered

Cost of sales
Food cost for one period, usually a month; Cost of sales = Opening inventory + Purchases – Closing inventory

Cost-plus buying
Supplier service in which the buyer is charged the supplier's costs plus a predetermined markup

Coulis
Contemporary sauce made of a purée of a single vegetable

Country-style forcemeat
Forcemeat with a slightly course texture, with the cured meat as the main ingredient

Coupons
Printed certificates that entitle customers to a reduced price on a product or service

Court bouillon (cort boo-YON)
Stock made with vegetables and an acid such as wine or vinegar; aromatic vegetable broth

Cover letter
Letter sent with a résumé to a potential employer, introducing yourself to them

Cover stock
Heavy cover paper

Cream soup
Soup that uses a thickener, like roux

Creaming method
Fat and sugar beaten together for an exceptionally fine crumb and dense, rich texture

Credit
Amount entered on the right side of a double-entry account (T-account)

Crème anglaise (krem an-GLAY)
Light, vanilla-flavored sauce made from milk, egg yolks, and sugar

Creole (KREE-ole)
Cooking style from New Orleans similar to Cajun, but more refined

Crisis
Situation that has, or threatens to have, a significant negative effect on people's lives

Crustacean
Shellfish that have segmented shells and jointed legs, including lobster and shrimp

Cultural and historic tourism
Visiting places in order to observe, learn about, and live among people whose culture is different; to visit places of historical interest and importance

Curdle
Separation of milk or egg mixtures into solid and liquid parts caused by overcooking, high heat, or the presence of an acid

Currency
Money

Currency exchange
Business set up to exchange foreign money for local currency

Current asset
Asset that can or will be converted to cash within one year

Current liability
Liability that must be paid within one year

Curry
Popular blend of spices native to India

Customer service
Making customers feel comfortable and satisfied with the choices they have made

Cyclical menu
Menu that is made up for a certain time period and is then repeated; a cycle usually varies from three to seven or more days

D

Daily food cost sheet
Ongoing record of daily and monthly food costs for an operation

Debit
Amount entered on the left side of a double-entry account (T-account)

Deglazing
To swirl a liquid in a pan to dissolve cooked particles of food remaining on the bottom

Degrease
Process of removing fat that has cooled and then hardened from the surface of stock

Delivery schedule
Supplier service in which the buyer specifies day and time of delivery

Demi-glace (DEH-mee glahs)
Rich, reduced brown sauce mixed with beef stock and Madeira wine or sherry

Demographics
Information about people, such as their ages, sex, incomes, occupations, home or office locations, lifestyles, business patterns, and tastes

Depreciation
Method of recording the value of an asset as it gradually decreases over its lifetime

Desk clerk
Lodging employee who greets and registers guests, and performs all check-in functions

Deveining
Process of removing a shrimp's digestive tract

Diner
Originally, a mobile kitchen that served food to factory employees

Direct cost
Expenses that are the responsibility of a specific department

Discount outlet center
Shopping center that offers retail stores that sell name-brand merchandise at discounted prices

Distribution
Act of moving goods and services from where they are raised or made to where they are bought by customers

Dog
Menu item with low menu mix percent and low contribution margin

Double-entry accounting
System for recording equal debits and credits for every business transaction

Du jour menu
Menu that changes daily

Dumpling
Small dough or batter item that can be steamed, poached, or simmered

Durum wheat
Type of wheat, good for making pasta

E

Eating establishment
Place where people buy and eat food away from home, including full-service restaurants, fast-food restaurants, vending

services, catering and banquet facilities at convention centers, and highway rest stops

Economies of scale
The savings that a multi-unit business creates for itself by sharing the cost of operating expenses

Economy lodging
Lodging properties that offer clean, low-priced accommodations with limited amenities

Edible portion (EP)
Food quantity after trimming and preparing

Elastin
Type of connective tissue that does not break down duing the cooking process and needs to be trimmed by hand

Empathize
To see a situation from another person's point of view

Employee manual
Written booklet containing general information about employment, including company policies, rules and procedures, employee benefits, and other topics related to the company

Emulsified
Two foods that are forced to combine in a food grinder and then pushed through a sieve to create a very smooth paste

En casserole
Potato dish in which peeled, raw potatoes are combined with heavy cream, sauce, or uncooked custard and then slowly baked

En papillote (on paw-pee-YOTE)
Moist-heat cooking method in which fish, herbs, vegetables and/or sauce are encased in parchment paper and steamed in a hot oven

Endosperm
Largest part of the whole grain, and a good source of protein and carbohydrate

English service
Service style in which bowls and platters of food are placed on the table and a seated host or hostess portions food onto plates for the guests

Entertainment
Diversions, including theater, concerts, sightseeing attractions, museums, and sports events; events that people watch or listen to

Entrepreneur (ON- trah -prah -NOOR)
Person who owns and runs his or her own business

Entry-level job
Job that requires very little or no previous experience

Environmental tourism
Visiting places for their natural beauty

Epicurean (ep-ih-KUR-ee-an)
Person with a refined taste for food and wine

Espagnole sauce (ess-spah-NYOL)
Grand sauce made from brown stock and brown roux

Etiquette (EH-tah-kit)
Proper behavior; good manners

Executive assistant manager
Head person who is responsible for all room rentals

Executive housekeeper
Head of housekeeping department who hires, trains, schedules, and directs staff; purchases and maintains cleaning supplies and equipment; and sets cleaning priorities; may also supervise the lost and found, laundry services, and maintenance functions

Expenses
Cost of items like food, supplies, wages, and insurance that are necessary to run a business

Experimental method
Conducting market research by trying out different services or products to groups of people

Exposition
Large show, open to the public, that highlights a particular type of product or service

Extract
Flavorful oil or other substance taken from such foods as vanilla, lemon, and almond

F

Fabricate
Process of cutting primal cuts of meat into usable portions

Fast-food operation
Restaurant where food is prepared and eaten quickly, or on-the-go

Ferment
Produce carbon dioxide gas and alcohol when yeast and a carbohydrate, such as sugar or flour, are combined

Filé (fee-LAY)
Ground sassafras leaves; used as a thickening agent in gumbo

Filleting
Separates the flesh of the fish from the bones

First in, first out (FIFO)
Inventory rotation system in which oldest stock is placed in front of or on top of the newer stock

Fixed asset
Items such as land, buildings, and equipment that have a life expectancy of at least three years

Flambé (flahm-BAY)
Method of preparing food at the table by pouring alcohol on it and lighting it on fire

Flavoring
Spices, salt, and extracts that affect a baked item's taste and color; usually bones, trimmings from meat, or vegetables that are used to flavor stock; one of the four essential parts of stock

Foaming method
Foam of whole eggs, yolks, or whites that provides the structure for cakes with the lightest texture, such as angel food and chiffon cakes

Focus group
Group of people who react to ideas, concepts, or services before these are communicated to the market at large

Fonts
Different styles of type

Food and beverage director
Head of food and beverage department in a full-service lodging operation; manages the formal dining room, coffee shop, lounge, banquet, catering, and room service

Food cost percentage
Daily food cost divided by daily sales figures

Foodservice management
Coordination of people, resources, products, and facilities related to the design, preparation, and presentation of food outside the home

Forcemeat
Mixture of lean ground meat and fat forced through a sieve; used as a base for pâté

Forecasting
Estimating ahead of time what sales will be while considering other conditions that will affect planning and food production; method of predicting future purchasing needs by looking at a foodservice operation's production records

Form value
Price savings created when a buyer purchases bulk quantities of food rather than individually portioned servings

Formal purchasing method
Purchasing method in which businesses use suppliers' bids to find the lowest price for their purchases

Formula
Standardized recipe; a term most often used in the bakeshop

Franchise
Legal business relationship in which an independent owner buys the right to use a company's name, products, and logo

Free-range
Poultry that is raised in large yards and given a lot of space to roam and exercise their muscles

French service
Service style in which food is served from a tableside cart

Front desk manager
Head of front desk operations; prepares budgets, maintains cost-control systems, forecasts room sales, and supervises the front desk team

Front waiter
Server with only 1-2 years serving experience; usually assists the captain

Front-of-the-house
Positions involved with guest service, including host/hostess, cashier, bar staff, wait staff, and bus persons; all areas or departments that come into direct contact with guests

Full-service property
Establishment that has a complete line of departments and services

Fumet (foo-MAY)
Highly flavored stock made with wine and fish bones

G

Galantine (gal-en-TEEN)
Forcemeat placed in a chicken skin and poached

Game meats
Meats from animals that are not raised domestically

Games
Promotional method in which customers play to win prizes based on luck

Garde-manger (gard mawn-ZHAY)
Kitchen's pantry section, where cold-meat items are prepared and stored

Gazpacho (gaz-PAH-cho)
Cold, Spanish tomato-based soup

General manager
Responsible for the overall performance of the establishment and its employees

Genetic engineering
Improving meats and produce through genetic alteration

Genoise (zhen-WAAHZ)
French sponge cake used to make a torte

Germ
Smallest part of the whole grain

Glace (glahss)
Reduced stock with a jelly-like consistency; also called glaze

Gluten (GLOO-ten)
Protein found in flour that develops into long, elastic strands during the mixing and kneading process; it produces a light, even texture in the finished bread product

Gnocchi (nee-YO-key)
Small potato dumplings served in Italian cuisine

Goujonette (goo-sha-NET)
Fish fillet cut in small strips

Grades
Labels that foods like meat, eggs, and dairy are given to help buyers know what level of quality they are receiving

Grain
Grass that grows edible seeds

Grand sauce
One of five base sauces that are used in the preparation of many other sauces; also called mother sauces

Guéridon (gay-ree-DAHN)
Tableside cart used in French service

Guest folio (FOE-lee-oh)
Record of guest charges and payments

Guild
Associations of people with similar interest or professions formed during the Middle Ages to organize the growing number of merchants and craftsmen

Gumbo
Thick soup from Louisiana made with filé powder and okra

Gutting
Pull out the guts of a fish

H

Haute cuisine (hote kwee-ZEEN)
High food preparation introduced to France by Catherine de Medici

Headwaiter
Oversees service in a dining room or banquet area

Herbs
Aromatic plants used for seasoning, such as thyme, rosemary, and sage

High-ratio
Cakes that contain a higher ratio of sugar and liquid to flour

Hollandaise (HALL-en-daze)
Grand sauce made from butter, lemon juice, egg yolks, and cayenne pepper

Home meal replacement
Meals eaten at home but prepared somewhere else

Hospitality
Being kind and respectful to those that visit the foodservice operation

Hotelier (OH-tell-YAY)
Owner or manager of a lodging property

Hubbart formula
Formula used to set room rates

Hull
Protective coating, or husk, that surrounds a whole grain

Human resources (HR) director
Person in charge of hiring and keeping quality employees for a lodging operation

Humidity
Amount of water moisture in the air or in a contained space

Hydroponic (hi-droh-PON-ick) farming
Growing food in nutrient-enriched water rather than soil

I

Icing
Sweet coating for cakes, cookies, and other baked goods

Idaho potato
Standard white baking potato; excellent for baking and frying

Income statement
Financial statement showing revenue and expenses over a period of time, as well as the resulting profit or loss

Indirect cost
Expenses that are not easily charged to any one specific department; usually distributed according to each department's percent of total revenue

Informal purchasing method
System in which a business gets several verbal price quotes from suppliers before selecting one of them

Intangible (in-TAN-je-BUL)
Something that cannot be touched or held

Intermediaries
Businesses that are targeted by another company's trade promotion

Intermediary sources
Businesses that buy products from primary sources and sell them to retailers

Internet
Worldwide computer network that brings information to anyone with access to an Internet connection

Inventory
Record of all goods that a restaurant has on hand both in storage and in the kitchen prep area

Invoice
Supplier's bill that lists all items delivered and their prices

Issuing
Official procedures employees use when taking an item out of the storeroom and putting it into production

Itinerary
Travel plan

J

Jambalaya (jam-bo-LIE-ah)
Creole stew made with rice, shellfish, and vegetables

Jet lag
Feeling of extreme tiredness that airplane passengers often get from long flights that span several time zones

Job application
Form designed for employers that asks for basic personal information and employment background

Job interview
Meeting with a potential employer in which qualifications for a job are discussed

Jus (zhew)
Sauce made from the unthickened juices of cooked meat

Jus lié (zhew lee-AY)
Jus that has been thickened with cornstarch

K

Kitchen brigade system
System of assigning certain responsibilities to kitchen staff; created by Escoffier

Knead (need)
Working and handling yeast dough to develop the gluten in the dough, and give the dough the "stretch" and "give" it needs to develop the proper texture

Kosher
Method of slaughtering meat to comply with Jewish dietary laws

L

Laminated
Protected with a plastic coating

Latke (LAHT-key)
Potato pancake common in Eastern Europe, often served with apple sauce and sour cream

Lead time
The gap between placing an order and its delivery; shorter lead times are more convenient for the buyer

Lean dough
Dough made with flour, yeast, and water

Leavener
Any ingredient or process that produces air bubbles and causes the rising of baked goods

Legume (LEG-yoom)
Seeds from pod-producing plants, including beans and peas, with high nutritional value

Leisure traveler
Anyone who travels primarily for pleasure

Liability
Debt, obligation, or claim owed by a business

Liaison (lee-AY-zohn)
Mixture of egg yolks and heavy cream used to thicken and finish sauces

Limited menu
Menu offering only a few specialized items

Liquid
Usually water, milk, cream, molasses, honey, or butter used in baking to provide moisture and allow the gluten to develop in the baked product; one of the four essential parts when preparing stocks, usually water

Lodging property
Establishment that provides temporary housing to overnight guests for a price

Long-term liability
Liability that must be paid a year or more after the balance sheet date

Loss
When a business's expenses are greater than its revenue

Luxury property
Establishment offering the ultimate in comfort and elegance

Lyonnaise (LEE-on-AZE)
Potatoes prepared using a multiple-stage technique; the potatoes are precooked, sliced, and then fried with onions

M

Maître d'hôtel (MAY-tra doe-TELL)
Responsible for the overall management of service in a restaurant

Maître d'hôtel (MAY-tra doh-TEL) butter
Softened butter flavored with lemon juice and chopped parsley

Make-or-buy analysis
Comparison of costs involved in preparing menu items from scratch or purchasing them pre-prepared

Mall
Enclosed structure designed to accommodate many stores under one roof

Management information systems (MIS) supervisor
Computer specialist responsible for solving computer-related problems and making sure computer systems are running efficiently as possible

Marbling
Fat that builds up between muscle fibers

Marinade
Liquid used to marinate foods; generally containing herbs, spices, and other flavoring ingredients, as well as an oil, and an acid, such as wine, vinegar, or lemon juice

Market
Group of people (customers) with specific, similar needs or wants

Market demand
Number of potential customers who have the desire and the money to purchase a product or service

Market research
Information collected for a specific reason or project

Market segmentation
Breaking down potential consumers into smaller groups of similar individuals

Market trends
Changing attitudes, tastes in food, and political issues that cause changes in the market

Marketing
Communication and plan for taking a product or service to market

Marketing director
Responsible for generating new business, organizing special events, and conducting market research; also reviews the needs of existing markets, keeps an eye on the competition, and works with other departments to create in-house promotions

Marketing mix
Mix of product, place, promotion, and price

Marketing plan
List of important steps to sell a product or service to customers

Marketing strategy
Specific plan to achieve the organization's objectives for doing business

Media
Newspaper, television, radio, magazine, and other outlets that provide news and information to the public

Meeting and convention hotel
Lodging property constructed specifically to accommodate conferences and conventions

Menu analysis
Procedure that helps managers make decisions about keeping, cutting, or adding menu items

Menu analysis worksheet
Form managers use to evaluate menus that shows how each menu item contributes to profitability

Menu content
Selection of food items in each menu category

Menu contribution margin
Sum of all menu items' contribution margins and menu mixes

Menu mix
Number of a menu item sold during a specific time period

Menu mix percentage
Menu mix divided by total number of items sold

Mid-priced facility
Lodging property that falls between full-service and economy lodging in terms of price, service, and amenities—also known as tourist-class facility

Milling process
Process a grain to remove the germ, bran, and hull

Minestrone
Italian tomato-based soup

Mirepoix (meer-PWAH)
Combination of chopped aromatic vegetables, usually two parts onion, one part carrot, and one part celery; used to flavor stocks and soups

Mollusks
Shellfish with a soft, unsegmented body and no internal skeleton enclosed in a hard shell, including clams, oysters, mussels, and snails

Mousseline (moose-uh-LEEN)
Forcemeat made from veal, poultry, or fish and lightened with cream and egg whites

Multiple-stage technique
Technique in which potatoes undergo several processes before they are finished

Mutton
Sheep slaughtered over the age of one year

N

Net income
Final profit or loss of the business for a given period of time; found at the bottom of the income statement

Networking
Contacting people who can provide information about job openings

New potato
Small, immature, red potato that is usually prepared by boiling or steaming, and is often eaten with its skin

Nib
Broken bits of roasted cocoa bean; used as the basis for all cocoa products

Niche market
Group of people having similar interests, ages, or skills who have common travel objectives

Night auditor
Front office employee who works at night posting charges not recorded during earlier shifts and balancing daily transactions

Noncommercial
Operations that operate food services to support the actual purpose of the establishment

Noncommercial segment
Segment of the foodservice industry that includes businesses and industry, hospitals, nursing homes, schools, airlines, and the military; any operation for which serving and preparing food is not its primary function

Nonverbal communication
Subtle body language conveyed by the facial expressions, tone of voice, gestures, and overall posture of a speaker

No-shows
Guest with confirmed reservation who does not show up

O

Observational method
Conducting marketing research by observing how consumers behave toward a product or selling approach

Offal (OH-fel) meats
Organ meats from hogs, cattle, or sheep, such as sweetbreads, liver, tripe, kidney, calf's heart, and brains

Oignon brûlé (oy-nyon broo-LAY)
Peeled, halved, browned onion

One-stop shopping
Supplier service in which the buyer receives a volume discount by purchasing as many items as possible from one supplier

Opaque (oh-PAKE)
Cannot be seen through

Optimal price
Price that produces the best value to the buyer

Organic farming
Growing food without using chemicals or pesticides

Organic produce
Fruits and vegetables that are grown without the use of pesticides or herbicides

Orientation
Process that helps new employees learn about the operation, various procedures and policies, and introduces them to their coworkers

Oven spring
Sudden and quick rise of the baked item when placed in a hot oven as a result of the expansion of trapped gases

Overbook
To accept reservations for more rooms than are available

Overproduction
Making too much food at a foodservice operation

Owners' equity
Total assets minus total liabilities; tells the worth of the business

Packers' brand
Packing company's own personal grading system

Pan gravy
Sauce made with a roux incorporating fat from a roast

Par stock
Amount of inventory that should be on hand at all times

Passport
Document for an international traveler, bearing the person's name, photo, date and place of birth, and country citizenship

Pasteurization
Process of heating milk to remove harmful bacteria

Pastry cream
Denser than custards and frequently used as the filling for eclairs and as a soufflé base

Pastry flour
Flour used for baking cookies, pie pastry, sweet yeast dough, biscuits, and muffins

Pâté (pah-TAY)
Rich loaf made of forcemeat, and baked in a mold

Pâte à choux (paht ah SHOE)
Soft dough that produces hollow baked products with crisp exteriors

Pâté de campagne (pah-TAY de kom-PAN-yuh)
Country-style forcemeat

Pâté dough
Strong dough used to bake pâté en croûte

Pâté en croûte (pah-TAY on kroot)
Forcemeat encased in pâté dough

Paupiette (po-pee-EHT)
Fillet of fish that is rolled up around a stuffing

Periodic order method
Inventory system in which the entire stock is reviewed on a regular basis to determine new purchase orders

Perpetual inventory method
Inventory system that keeps track of the amount of food items on hand through the use of inventory cards

Personal selling
Suggestive selling; assisting guests by describing and recommending menu items

Phyllo (FEE-low) dough
Pastry dough made with very thin sheets of flour and water; often layered with butter and/or crumbs; used to make baklava

Pilaf (PEEL-ahf)
Technique for cooking grains in which the grain is sautéed briefly in butter, then simmered in stock or water with seasonings

Pilfering
Illegal taking of inventory items by employees for their personal use

Place value
Differences in price of a product due to the place where it needs to be shipped

Plowhorse
Menu item with a high menu mix percent and a low contribution margin

Poached fruit
Fruits such as apples and pears that are heated with a mixture of sugar, spices, and wine until tender

Point-of-sale (POS)
Promotional material displayed inside a restaurant to promote various products or services

Point-of-sale display
Attention-getting devices, such as table tents, posters, banners, and sign boards located at the foodservice operation

Portfolio
Collection of samples that highlight your interests, talents, contributions, and studies; important item to bring to job interviews

Positioning
Discovering a place in the market that gives a product or service a distinctive image, distinguishing it from competitors

Post
To enter a charge into a guest account

Poultry
Chicken, duck, goose, guinea, squab, turkey, or any domesticated bird raised for the sole purpose of eating

Premium
Merchandise items offered at a reduced price or free with a purchase of other services or products

Presentation mix
Combination of all the things that make an operation look unique

Primal cut
Primary divisions of meat produced by the initial butchering of animal carcasses

Primary sources
People or companies who grow, raise, or make the products that are eventually sold to customers

Primitive camping
Camping done mainly in unimproved areas that offer few amenities

Processed foods
Basic type of convenience food that does not require such close pricing scrutiny; examples include staples such as pasta, spices, and oils

Production records
Information used to help buyers effectively forecast their buying needs

Production sheet
Daily record of menu items served

Product-service mix
Combination of all products and services an organization offers to customers

Profit
Money left when expenses have been subtracted from revenue

Profiterole (pro-FEET-uh-roll)
Small, round pastry made from pâte à choux and filled with ice cream

Promotional campaign
Various methods and strategies that create customer interest and loyalty

Proof
In yeast dough production, the final rising stage that occurs after the dough is panned and just before baking

Property management system (PMS)
Computer hardware and software used to manage a lodging property

Public relations
Management of an organization's relationships with consumers, communities, and other public segments

Purchase order
Legally binding written document that details exactly what the buyer is ordering from the vendor

Purchasing
Process of selecting from many choices, making sound decisions, and developing solid relationships with vendors

Purée soup
Thick soup whose solids are puréed and mixed into the remaining liquid

Puzzle
Menu item with a low menu mix percent and a high contribution margin

Q

Quality grades
Standards given to meats based on their freshness and quality

Quenelle (kuh-NELL)
Mousseline formed into small dumpling-shaped ovals and poached in a rich stock or court bouillion

Quick bread
Bread made with chemical leaveners, which work more quickly than yeast

Quick-service
Service style in which guests help themselves to food set up in food bars or at a counter; common quick-service examples include drive-through, buffet, cafeteria, carry-out, and vending

Quotes
Verbal notice of a price that a supplier gives to a buyer during the purchasing process

R

Rack rate
Highest rate category offered by a lodging property

Raft
Meat and egg white proteins that float to the surface and trap any impurities that can cloud a consommé

Receiving
The process of inspecting, accepting, and, in some cases, rejecting deliveries of goods and services

Receiving sheet
Written record that accounts for all items that have been delivered and received by a restaurant

Reciprocal buying
Supplier service in which the buyer agrees to do business with only one supplier in exchange for the supplier's commitment to use and recommend the buyer's operation

Recreation
Activity that refreshes the body or mind

Recreational tourism
Visiting places to swim, lie in the sun, ski, play golf and tennis, see shows, or gamble

References
People who know you well and can provide information about you—your character, work ability, or academic standing; needed for job application forms

Remouillage (ray-moo-LAJ)
Stock made from bones that have already been used in another preparation; can replace water as the liquid in a stock

Reorder point (ROP)
Level of inventory at which it is necessary to order more goods

Request for credit
Written record that ensures that buyer's account will be credited for a supplier's error in a delivery

Requisition form
Written request for ordered items or services

Reservations manager
Manager who oversees the reservations function and manages a number of full-time reservationists

Resident manager
Manager who supervises front office operations and reservations and is responsible for emergencies twenty-four hours a day when the GM is not on duty; often lives in an apartment in the hotel itself

Resort (re-ZORT)
Lodging property that specializes in providing extensive entertainment and recreational activities for vacationers

Restaurant
Public eating place; from the French word *restorante,* as established by Boulanger

Resting stage
Most important stage when mixing pasta dough

Résumé (RE-zoo-may)
Written summary of past experience, skills, and achievements related to the job being sought

Retail
Sale of products directly to consumers

Retail cut
Cut of meat that is ready for sale

Retailers
People or businesses that sell their products directly to the public

Retained earnings
Profit that is put back into the business; one of the major sources of owners' equity

Revenue
Money that an operation takes in when it sells products or services

Rich dough
Made with flour, yeast, water, and the addition of shortening or tenderizing ingredients (sugars, syrups, butter, eggs, milk, cream)

Risotto (ree-SO-to) method
Method of sautéing rice in butter with onions, then combining with stock and stirring constantly to produce a creamy texture; risotto is an Italian method of cooking rice and not a variety of rice

Roll-in dough method
Butter or butter-based mixture that is placed between layers of pastry dough, then rolled and folded repeatedly to form numerous layers, producing a very flaky, rich pastry

Room attendant
Lodging employee who performs daily guest room cleaning

Room inventory
Total number of rooms a lodging property has to sell

Rooms forecast
Analysis of anticipated room inventory that is based on past room sales; allows front office manager to determine projected revenues and make decisions about rates and reservations

Roux (roo)
Equal parts of cooked flour and fat used to thicken liquids; used in Cajun cooking

Rule of 10
Theory that one dissatisfied customer tells an average of ten people about their bad experience

Russet potato
Standard white baking potato; excellent for baking and frying

Russian service
Service style in which bowls and platters of food are brought to guests and servers hold them while they serve the guests from them

S

Sabayon (sa-by-ON)
Fragile foam of egg yolks, sugar, and Marsala wine that is whipped constantly over simmering water until it becomes thick and light

Sachet d'épices (sah-SHAY day-PEESE)
Bag of spices used to flavor stocks

Sales mix record
Form that details the amount of each menu item sold over a specified period of time

Sales promotion
Direct motivating sales technique that offers consumers an extra incentive to buy a product or service

Salsa
Cold mixture of fresh herbs, spices, and fruits or vegetables

Sampling
Testing a small group of people and generalizing the results for the population as a whole; trial and usage promotion in which a free sample of a product or service is given out to increase customer awareness/sales

Scaling
Scrape scales of fish off of their skin, usually working from the head to their tail

Seafood Newburg
Cooked lobster, crab, or shrimp in a rich sauce made of butter, cream, egg yolks, sherry, and seasonings

Searing
To brown food quickly over high heat; usually done as a first step for combination cooking methods

Security chief
Head person for the security department; protects guests from crime, fire, and unsafe conditions; also protects establishment from theft and property damage

Semolina
Refined durum wheat, good for making pasta

Service
Intangible product sold or purchased in the marketplace

Service department
Department responsible for serving guests directly—by providing quick and easy check-ins; clean, safe, and well-kept facilities; and meeting guests' other needs to keep them comfortable

Service station
Location in dining area where additional cups and saucers, menus, napkins, silverware, condiments, and water glasses are kept

Service value
Different services a vendor provides to its customers

Sheet method
Method used to make bar cookies by pouring the batter into an entire baking pan and then slicing into individual squares or rectangles

Shish kebab
Middle Eastern dish of lamb and vegetables cooked on a skewer

Shop
Place, such as a mall, gift shop, or convenience store, at which people can purchase items

Shortening
Any fat, such as oil or butter; keeps the baked item moist, fresh, and adds flavor

Shucked
Mollusks removed from the shell

Sift
Force flour or confectioner's sugar through a sieve to add air, remove lumps, and filter out impurities

Signature item
Dish that is unique or well-known to a foodservice operation

Silverskin
Tough outer membrane that surrounds meat

Single-stage technique
Technique in which potatoes are taken directly from the raw state to the finished with only one cooking method

Skimmer
Flat, perforated spoon or scoop

Slurry
Mixture of cornstarch and liquid used to thicken sauce

Solanine (SOLE-ah-neen)
Harmful, bitter-tasting substance in green spots and sprouts on potatoes

Soufflé (soo-FLAY)
Custard dish lightened with whipped egg whites, causing the dish to rise when baked

Sourdough
Yeast dough leavened with a fermented starter

Spaetzle (SPAYT-z-le)
German dumpling

Special offer
Promotional method that usually requires customers to make a purchase or reservation within a certain time period

Specialty item
Promotional method in which an item that displays an operation's name, logo, or ad message is given free or sold to customers

Specifications (specs)
Detailed information about the products and services that an operation wants to buy

Spices
Bark, roots, seeds, bulbs, or berries from an aromatic plant used to flavor foods

Sponge
Starter made of yeast, liquid, and flour that has fermented

Sponge method
Making a yeast bread by mixing the sponge and the remaining fat, salt, sugar, and flour

Standing order
Supplier service in which the supplier regularly delivers a pre-determined amount of items to a foodservice operation

Star
Menu item with a high menu mix percent and a high contribution margin

Steamed pudding
Stable batter made with eggs, sugar, cream, and flavorings; used to make baked custard and crême caramel

Stock
Flavorful liquid made by gently simmering bones or vegetables to extract their flavor, aroma, color, body, and nutrients

Stockless purchasing
Supplier service in which a buyer purchases a large amount of goods at a discounted price; the supplier agrees to store these goods, delivering them to the buyer when needed

Stockout
Running out of an inventory item

Stone-ground
Grains that are ground and broken down; this method retains more nutrients than other grinding methods

Straight forcemeat
Very finely ground forcemeats seasoned with herbs and spices and cooked in a terrine

Straight mix method
All ingredients are combined at once and blended into a batter

Strengthener
Ingredient that provides stability and ensures that the baked item does not collapse once it is removed from the oven

Substitutions
Supplier service in which the buyer agrees to let the supplier fill purchase orders with appropriate substitutes if the specified item is unavailable

Suggestive selling
Cost effective way to promote an operation's products and services; personal selling; assisting guests by describing and recommending menu items

Supply and demand
Economic imbalance between buyers and sellers that determines whether the price of a good or service will go up or down

Survey method
Conducting market research by using telephone surveys or questionnaires

Sweat
Cook a food item in a covered pan in a small amount of fat until it softens and releases its moisture

Sweepstakes
Promotion method that requires entrants to submit their names and addresses; winners are then chosen randomly

Sweet potato
Popular tuber with thick skin and orange, mealy flesh that is high in sugar

Sweetbreads
Part of the thymus gland; an organ meat taken from hogs, cattle, or sheep

Sweetener
Sugar or syrups that add flavor to baked goods

T

Table d'hôte (TAH-bull DOT) menu
Menu that offers a complete meal or several items together for a single price

T-account
Chart (resembling the capital letter "T") used in double-entry accounting to record debits and credits

Tao (dow)
As believed by Taoists, the single guiding principle that orders the universe

Tempering
Heat chocolate gently and gradually so it will harden into a smooth, even shell

Terrine (ter-REEN)
Earthenware mold that lends its name to the forcemeats that are cooked in it

Theme park
Collection of exhibits, rides, and other attractions focusing on one unifying idea

Thickener
Gelatin, flour, arrowroot, cornstarch, or eggs that determine the consistency of the finished product

Time value
Price retailers pay for the convenience of selecting the time of delivery from a supplier

Time zone
Geographical area in which the same standard time is used

Tomato sauce
Grand sauce made from stock and tomatoes

Toque (toke)
Special pleated hat worn only by chefs

Torte
Elegant, rich, many-layered cake often filled with buttercream or jam

Tour guide
Professional who leads trips that often appeal to niche markets

Tourism
Combination of all of the services that people need and will pay for when they are away from home

Tourism office
Office established by state and local governments to provide information to people who are visiting or would like to visit the area

Trade promotion
Promotional strategy in which one business targets related, but non-competing businesses that cater to the same customers

Trade school application
Form for a trade school that asks basic information about background and education

Trade show
Exposition whose attendance is restricted to those involved in an industry

Transaction
When money is exchanged for business reasons; needs to be recorded in accounting records

Transient camping
Camping done in areas that have incorporated electricity and built bathroom facilities

Transportation
Any method of getting form one place to another, including cars, airlines, railways, cruise ships, and bus lines

Transportation value
Differences in prices that result from choosing a quicker but more expensive transportation for the delivery of goods

Travel agent
Professional who helps travelers with all of their travel arrangements

Travel package
Set of several travel services for one set price

Traveler's check
Check that has already been paid for at a bank and requires only the buyer's signature to be cashed

Trend
Current style or preference

Trial and usage promotion
Promotional methods such as coupons and sampling that get people to try new products or services

Trial balance
Procedure used to make sure that total debits equal total credits

Trichinosis
Disease caused by a parasite that lives in muscle tissue of pork

Trimming
Cutting away the silverskin, fat, and gristle of meat

Trussing
Tying legs and wings of a bird to the body, so the entire bird cooks evenly and stays moist

Two-stage method
Method used to prepare cakes in which the dry ingredients are combined with all of the shortening and half of the liquid until smooth, then the remaining liquid ingredients are gradually added

Tying
Method of meat fabrication that ensures even cooking and keeps the shape of the meat

U

Understays
Guests who leave before their anticipated date of departure

Unique Selling Proposition (USP)
Differentiates the organization's product-service mix from the competition's

V

Vacation camping
Camping that offers many amenities for people staying for longer periods of time

Velouté (vay-loo-TAY)
Grand sauce made from veal, chicken, or fish stock, and white or blond roux

Vendor
Person or company that sells food or supplies to retailers, such as restaurants

Vichyssoise (vee-shee-SWAH)
Cold potato and leek soup from France

Visa
Foreign government's written permission for a traveler to enter that country for a specific reason and length of time

W

Web site
Place on the Internet that advertises or informs the public about a service or product

White stock
Clear, pale liquid made by simmering poultry, beef, or fish bones

Whole grain
Grain that has not been milled

Word-of-mouth
Indirect promotional strategy that relies on positive communication between satisfied customers and their friends and family

World Health Organization
Division of the United Nations that, among other things, determines whether vaccinations are required for travel to specific countries and, if so, for which diseases

Wringing method
Method used to strain sauce using a clean cheesecloth

Yam
Tuber often confused with the sweet potato; they are less sweet than sweet potatoes, and range in color from creamy white to deep red

Y

Yeast
Organic leavener used when making breads and other baked items

Yield
Amount of food that is actually served divided by the amount of food purchased

Yield grade
Amount of usable meat after the fat has been trimmed

Yield management
Technique that calls for varying room rates as demand for rooms varies

Index
OF KEY TERMS